Barbel Rivers and Captures

Barbel Rivers and Captures

Compiled by the Barbel Catchers

Edited by Bob Singleton and Mick Wood

Illustrated by Trevor King

Additional artwork by Tony Hart

CROWOOD

First published in 2004 by
The Crowood Press Ltd
Ramsbury, Marlborough
Wiltshire SN8 2HR

www.crowood.com

British Library Cataloguing-in-Publication Data
A catalogue record for this book is available from the British Library.

ISBN 1 86126 660 X

The photographs in this book are credited to the author of the chapter in which they appear.

Frontispiece: Pete Tesch with his superb Kennet fish of 13lb 14oz

Typeset by Textype, Cambridge

Printed and bound in Great Britain by CPI, Bath

Contents

Foreword

By Mick Wood

In 1988 the Barbel Catchers Club produced their first book, *Barbel* (The Crowood Press). It was released, albeit unwittingly, at the beginning of a period of both rapid and dramatic change in barbel angling. *Barbel* was a fair representation of what fishing for our favourite species was all about in that era; but time moves on, and geographical location, tackle, tactics, baits and the size of the fish that we expect to catch change almost season by season. The BCC therefore decided that the time was right for the release of a new book that would comprehensively cover the modern barbel-fishing scene.

The river-by-river format as used in the first book has been retained, but is approached from a completely different angle. Thus each of the river chapters culminates in an account of the capture of a really special fish from that particular river; and although some chapters are the account of a single author, where the captor of the club river record is a comparatively recent visitor to the venue, the bulk of the chapter has been written by a 'river veteran'. Every chapter provides a wealth of information from anglers who are immensely successful on their chosen waters, each providing an insight into all aspects of their fishing, demonstrating how they have adapted modern practices whilst retaining the more traditional ones that are still of value.

It is important to note that this book is based upon Barbel Catchers Club activities over the past fifteen years. Whilst it can be seen from our River Records list (Appendix I) that we have caught barbel from virtually every barbel river in the country, those included in this book fulfil two specific criteria. First, they have received significant attention from our members during the time span encompassed by this book; and second, they have produced barbel to double figures. A benchmark had to be set, and whilst what can be termed a 'big' barbel is relative to the river concerned, a 10lb specimen is a big barbel regardless of the national record for that particular river.

All Barbel Catchers Club members are experienced and capable anglers, and every member of the club contributes annually to our quarterly magazine *Barbus*. With our geographical spread and our writing experience we are well placed to produce a comprehensive work of this nature covering the whole of the country. By contrast, it is pertinent to observe that most of the books available today covering barbel angling are based upon a high level of success and experience, but on a limited number of rivers.

There is no one specific chapter covering methods and tactics, as these are discussed river by river. Baits are another matter, because during the last fifteen years HNVs and pellets in their various forms have made a quite dramatic impact upon our sport. Both are covered in detail by anglers who have been at the forefront of their development and application. We have also included an update of our river records, our top fifty specimens, and a brief history of the Barbel Catchers Club.

We have pioneered new rivers, methods and baits, and BCC members have broken river records and the national record on more than one occasion. This book constitutes an account of the club's achievements during the most exciting period in barbel angling history.

1 Introduction: The Changing Scene

by Mick Wood

The changes in virtually every aspect of barbel angling during the last fifteen years have been quite amazing: the quality and availability of fishing tackle, baits, methods and tactics, baiting aids, easy access to information, the increase in popularity of barbel angling, and the size of fish we expect to catch – all these are worthy of discussion.

For those anglers who began their barbel-fishing careers during the third quarter of the last century, barbel tackle was all about improvisation and 'making do'. Rods were 'Avons' where you could find them, and beefed-up leger rods or light-actioned carp rods where you could not. In fact it is fair to say that carp angling kick-started the barbel tackle revolution, since much of the quality gear being produced for the specialist carp scene found its way into the bags of barbel fanatics. High quality, strong hooks, imported lines from Germany and Japan, Mitchell 300 reels, and the early Dacron braids, all doubled up for both species. Because of the demand for bespoke rods, rod builders branched out into the barbel market, and within a couple of decades we reached the present situation where superb rods can be built to order or bought straight off the rod rack at prices that, in comparative terms, have never been cheaper.

Reels have gone in two directions, with the modern bait-runners replacing the old 300s, and replicas of classic centrepins being available for those not fortunate enough to own one of the original collector's pieces. For all but a few diehards, the days of the old '300' chugging away as the rod flies round have now gone.

The variety and choice of hooks now available is bewildering. The Drennan Super Specialist led the way, as the handful of carp patterns available were eclipsed by every major hook producer trying to corner this ever-expanding market. Lines soon followed, with low-diameter monofil, hi-tech braids and co-polymer hooklengths. Every possible requirement of the modern barbel angler has been the subject of huge technological innovation, with comfortable lightweight chairs, thermal boots and superb all-weather clothing encouraging anglers to fish through everything the elements can throw at them. It is fair to say that in recent years a whole sub-industry has developed around barbel angling.

The tackle revolution has been matched by the bait revolution. Fifteen years ago the barbel angler who fished with maggots, casters, worms, bread, luncheon meat, cheese and sweetcorn could reasonably claim to have left no stone unturned; also hemp and occasionally tares would be used as supplements. It was simply a matter of matching these options to each angling situation. Nowadays, with the popularity of HNV 'specials' and a huge variety of pellets, we need a degree in organic chemistry to master all that is on offer.

Whilst bait droppers and swim feeders are still as popular as ever, carp angling has once again provided a multitude of feeding options based on water-dissolvable PVA, large-capacity catapults and 'spods' for huge rivers such as the Trent. With the release of the book *Quest for Barbel*, co-written by Tony Miles and Trefor West, anglers began to take a more serious look at barbel-angling tactics: the days when a barbel angler filled a swim with feed and waited for something to happen ended with the publication of this book. The range of ideas expressed encouraged us all to re-think our approach, to be pro-active, and to simply be active. Baiting and waiting, swim searching, upstreaming and swim rotation were explained to all, and even if all the advocated methods were not adopted, this book encouraged us to expand our ideas. It was a milestone in barbel publication.

Who could possibly have predicted that the focus on certain rivers would change in such a dramatic

Pellets, the bait of the new millennium, were responsible for this 11lb 6oz barbel for Jim Knight.

Steve Withers took this 13lb 14oz Dorset Stour fish on an HNV special.

fashion? At the time our last book was written, all eyes looking for a new record barbel were directed towards the Dorset Stour, the Hampshire Avon and the Wensum, and probably at less than five specific and well-known fish. 'Henry' and 'Beau' were the main targets, but then the Medway hit the scene as the Wealdon region of the Catchers delivered the rewards that their pioneering efforts deserved: 'Bertie' broke the record twice, attracting a flood of attention to this river. The way in which the Medway rose to prominence, and subsequently faded from the picture, is a prime example of just how quickly the barbel-angling scene can change. Then the Severn entered the fray with the Howard Maddocks' fish – until the Wensum added a few more ounces. But none of this could possibly have prepared us for the truly extraordinary turn of events on an insignificant-looking little river 'upstream of Bedford': what happened on the Great Ouse simply beggared belief, as the accepted parameters of barbel angling were blown to the four winds. Many have speculated as to why barbel weights have increased so dramatically, and whether they are sustainable: HNVs, global warming, reduced bio-mass of other species, XY chromosome imbalance and increased natural food due to improved water quality – all have their supporters. Perhaps the Great Ouse has a unique combination of several of these criteria?

A recent development worthy of mention is the appearance of the *Barbel Guide*. Well known, successful anglers such as John Bailey on the Wye, Chris Holley on the Royalty and Trefor West on the Bristol Avon have led many an angler to their first-ever barbel. Perhaps more importantly, they have led youngsters away from the tedium of video games and the trouble of street crime. Teach a youngster to respect the countryside, and respect for all that is important will hopefully follow.

As the quantity of information regarding barbel has increased, so has its availability. Magazines, books, videos, slide shows, conferences and the Internet have all led to a huge increase in the number of anglers specializing in catching barbel. During the era covered by this book, the Barbel Society has risen to prominence. A huge organization with well over 1,000 members, the society was the brainchild of its chairman Steve Pope, president Fred Crouch, and a handful of like-minded barbel fanatics. With such a membership the Barbel Society provides a voice with political clout, raises thousands of pounds for charity, controls prime stretches of river and through the dedication of its members runs an excellent junior section – all very much a product of the 1990s 'barbel boom'.

The fact that there has been a gradual drift of anglers away from rivers and into the more predictable sport offered by commercial stillwaters, makes the barbel success story all the more remarkable. The challenge of catching this most powerful and enigmatic of species in the diversity of conditions that the British climate can throw at us, will surely see its popularity continue to grow. Amongst us are anglers who are technocrats, bait gurus, solunar theorists, traditionalists and ever-so-slightly-mad eccentrics. The last fifteen years has been a period of extraordinary change and development: could it be possible that this will continue for the next fifteen years?

Barbel Society junior member Rhiannon Wood. The smile says it all.

2 The Barbel Catchers Club History

by Mick Wood

On Sunday 27 March 1977, approximately forty like-minded anglers gathered in the lodge at Packington trout reservoir near Coventry. Their collective aim was the formation of a national barbel group, to be known as the Barbel Catchers. The club was the brainchild of two keen barbel men, Stuart Hamilton and Dave Thompson; though as their plans came to fruition that afternoon they could never have foreseen that twenty-six years later the BCC would still be going strong. Nor could they have predicted the club's ongoing success as pioneers in the barbel-angling world: since the club's formation the BCC has been at the forefront of virtually every breakthrough that barbel angling has witnessed.

The club was originally formed as five regions, based in the cities of Birmingham, Bristol, London, Nottingham and York. Over the years the regions have been continually reconstructed in line with the geographical requirements of the membership, so that at the time of writing the club is based in the following seven regions: Chilterns, Midlands/Cotswolds, Northwest, Southdown, Southern, Wessex and Yorkshire. Of those who attended that initial meeting, five are still members, the 'Old Contemptibles' being Stuart Hamilton, Tony Hart, Roger Middlecote, Pete Tillotson and Alan Slater.

Each region has regular meetings and fish-ins, and these form the social basis for the club – also providing a boost in income for pub landlords up and down the country! On a national level the highlights are the club's AGM each spring, and a national fish-in each autumn. The club thrives upon the involvement of its members, and an apt motto would be 'the more you put in, the more you get out'.

At the end of the first season of the club's activity (1977–78) the biggest barbel award was won with the only double-figure barbel caught that season, a fish of exactly 10lb taken by Alan Hayes from the Royalty. This one statistic alone demonstrates how much barbel fishing has changed since those early years, because the club now accounts for well over 100 doubles each season, and this figure is increasing rapidly.

The BCC was formed to provide a framework for developing and discussing new ideas, and for debating key issues. Much of this information has been passed on to the general angling public by a variety of writers through the weekly press, monthly magazines, books and the Internet. In 1999 Andy Humphries developed the club's own website, www.barbelcatchersclub.co.uk, where information is provided regarding club activities, along with a selection of articles from the club magazine *Barbus*. All members write at least one article each year for the magazine, which also provides a medium for news and views: it is truly the lifeblood of the club, and its cover has often been graced by some superb artwork by the likes of Tony Hart and Mike Nicholls. This year (2003) will see the production of issue number 100 of this magazine. As already mentioned, in 1988 the club produced its first book, *Barbel*, which at the time provided a definitive guide to the country's barbel rivers – though it became rapidly outdated as a result of the amazing expansion of barbel throughout English rivers.

The Barbel Catchers have been at the forefront of virtually every breakthrough over the last quarter of a century, in both innovative techniques and fish captures. That 10lb Royalty fish now seems such a long time ago, as through the late 1970s and into the 1980s the collective knowledge and pioneering spirit began to pay dividends. When in the 1979–80 season Roger Baker set the Great Ouse record at 12lb 2oz, none of us could have predicted the present scene on that river, culminating in a near-20lb fish. Even when Stan Sear set a new river record at 13lb 0oz in 1989, many of us thought that

Dave Oakes with the club's first Trent double – 10lb 15oz.

this was the Great Ouse at its zenith. It now seems ridiculous that people refused to believe Ray Woods' unclaimed record of 16lb 5oz. In fact at that time, with Howard Maddocks having taken his 16lb 3oz fish from the Lower Severn, BCC members had accounted for the two biggest barbel in the country.

During the 1982–83 season, Andy Orme's immense fish of 13lb 7oz set Wessex barbel angling alight. Nowadays this would be viewed as just another wonderful fish. How important it is to keep our perspective of these historical captures. The following season Dave Plummer put the Wensum into the big league when he banked 'Beau' at her top weight of 13lb 6oz, a fish that became one of the country's most famous barbel. Beau appeared again, and became a player in one of angling's greatest stories, taken by the rod of Trefor West as he fished through the great storm of 1987. Who but Trefor would have fished through Hurricane Henry?

Even in Yorkshire where the top weights for barbel would be several pounds below those of their southern brethren, Barbel Catchers has made an impact. Dave Mason recorded the club's first Derwent double at 10lb exactly, but it was Jon

Wolfe who set the Broad Acres buzzing with a stunning Swale fish of 11lb 4oz, the culmination of a determined campaign. Meanwhile from somewhere in Kent came another historic capture, and one that led the way to a national record – something which no one in their wildest dreams ever envisaged would happen. Dave Magson, Guy Welfare, Steve Carden, Richard Storer and Ian Beadle had been quietly discovering the hidden secrets of the Medway, and it was Ian who recorded the first Medway double at 10lb 6oz. During the early 1990s the BCC dominated on this river, pioneering the use of HNV specials and producing a run of huge fish topped by one of 14lb 6oz to Dave Williams, and a then record barbel of 14lb 13oz to Dave Taylor.

The second half of the 1980s also saw another famous barbel in the nets of our members: Pete Reading and Greg Buxton both recorded the Dorset Stour fish 'Henry' during her days as a fourteen-pounder; but new venues were soon stealing the headlines. Mike Stevens demonstrated the shape of things to come in the form of a 12lb 8oz Bristol Avon fish, a river subsequently 'taken apart' by Trefor West and eventually producing a 13lb 6oz

Ian Beadle with possibly the first ever Medway double.

fish for Tony Hart. Tony Miles caught a first Cherwell double at 10lb 3oz, and in this period Tony made his way to some superb barbel as he took the river from 'interesting prospect' to 'major player' with a top fish of 12lb 5oz.

In 1989 Jon Wolfe pushed back the parameters of Yorkshire barbel fishing with a truly extraordinary fish of 12lb 6oz from the Yorkshire Derwent. The following season Mike Nicholls caught the mighty River Severn's first real monster at 13lb 14oz. Into the 1990s and Mike Burdon, a veteran of the lower Severn, took his dedicated approach across to the rivers Wye and Lugg, recording a string of doubles from both rivers. The London lads used their quiet, understated charm to tempt barbel to 12lb 5oz from the Lea; and Dave Williams used his HNV specials to take a string of huge fish to 14lb 6oz from the Hampshire Avon, another unclaimed record-equalling barbel at the time.

Often it was not the size of the fish that mattered; catching a barbel at all was a fine achievement. The Sussex Ouse and Rother, the Somerset Frome, the Churnet, Dearne, Don, Tern, Vyrnwy and Holybrook all succumbed to the spirit of adventure. When our first book was published our members had recorded barbel from twenty-eight rivers, with twelve of those having produced doubles. Fifteen years on we have caught from forty-eight rivers, with thirty of them giving us fish of 10lb plus.

It is without doubt during the last five years that the barbel scene has experienced its most dramatic period of change. BCC members have recorded the club's first doubles from many more rivers: Dave Oakes on the Trent, Steve Chell on the Warwickshire Avon, Paul Starkey on the Mole, Iain Wood on the Wharfe, John McNulty on the Yorkshire Ouse and Alan Towers on the Ribble. The list goes on. Such captures, as well as the innovative techniques used, dominate the tales recounted within these pages, and it can be seen that there is not one single barbel river within the country that has not seen the Catchers make an impact. For a small specialist group with a membership that freewheels around the fifty mark, we happen to think that we have done rather well. In fact, it is not unreasonable to suggest that our success is unparalleled!

3 Modern Baits: Pellets

by Jim Knight

Having been fairly static for many years, with only occasional small changes in tackle, techniques, baits, and even in the population dynamics of target species, barbel fishing has experienced something of a revolution in the last decade. This revolution has covered tackle, techniques, bait and even the species itself. Techniques have in many instances followed those of the carp angler, although some of these are, in my view, detrimental to barbel fishing. These are covered elsewhere in the book.

Apart from population dynamics, the major changes have been in the baits now used. Prior to 1994 most barbel anglers tended to use a few long-standing 'standard' baits: maggots, caster and worms, and others that tended to be based on human foods, including cheese paste, bread, sausage and luncheon meat. These baits probably accounted for most barbel caught between 1950 and 1990. Since the early 1990s the whole approach to barbel fishing has changed in many ways; for instance, it is no longer unusual to see a barbel angler with a bivvy sitting behind two rods and bite alarms.

On the bait side, one of the innovations is the 'trout pellet' and its many derivatives, developed to provide a high nutritional feed containing a balance of nutrients for captive-bred trout. The term 'trout pellet' or 'pellets' is now used to describe the vast array of pellets developed for trout, salmon, halibut, marine and betaine fish, and a special one for coarse fish. Over the last few years there has been a

significant amount of concern and some actual evidence that trout pellets can have an adverse effect on the health of coarse fish. Specifically, it appears that the immune systems of coarse fish can be damaged if their diet includes large quantities of trout pellets that are rich in protein and oil. Research suggests that trout and coarse fish have significant differences in their dietary requirements, and pellets specifically designed for trout are not suitable for coarse fish if used in large quantities. A further point to note is that the high quantities of oil in trout pellets can also cause harm to coarse fish if stored for too long before use; it is suggested that the maximum storage period is about twelve months. As a result of these discoveries, trout pellets have been banned on many stillwater coarse fisheries, and pellets specifically for coarse fish have been developed.

A large variety of pellets is available from tackle shops and bait companies, and many suppliers have their own versions. I first began using trout pellets in 1996 on the Lower Severn, namely the 'Elips' variety of 8mm pellets. I decided on these because they were particularly rich in oil, which appeared to

This 10lb 2oz lower Severn barbel fell to a hair-rigged 8mm Elips pellet.

A 14mm Elips attached by bait band proved to be the downfall of this 11lb 6oz Kennet fish.

be a good idea at the time, and also because they had a strong smell; moreover they were instantly recognized as food by the barbel on the Lower Severn, which is not always the case with new bait. Interestingly it took much longer before I caught barbel with them on the Kennet.

In the last few years the pellet has undoubtedly become one of the most popular forms of bait used for barbel. It is dense and sinks quite quickly, and is simple and convenient to use. The main varieties of pellet currently available are shown in the table below.

Other varieties of pellet are available, however mostly they are variations on a theme, with minor differences from the above.

The harder marine and halibut pellets will last for around eighteen hours before they start to break down in the water, but it may take up to twenty minutes before they start to go soft and give off

Type of Pellet	Description
Trout pellets in sizes from 2mm to 10mm	Designed to be a high nutrition feed for trout, with protein contents typically above 40% and an oil content of above 20%.
Elips pellets in sizes from 4mm to 14mm	High oil content. Originally for feeding reared salmon.
Marine/halibut pellets in sizes from 3mm to 22mm	A rich feed designed for commercial halibut rearing. They have exceptionally high protein contents of up to 60% and oil contents up to 25%, and also include different fishmeals. Most types usually contain the fish attractor betaine.
Betaine pellets in sizes from 3mm to 22mm	Usually contain a number of different fishmeals plus the fish attractor betaine.
Pro-biotic trout pellets in sizes from 3mm to 5mm	Developed for carp, to aid fish in times of stress. They contain hydrocarbons and micro nutrients. Although called a trout pellet, it is strictly just a more generic pellet.
Hinders Hi-Betaine in sizes from 3mm to 21 mm	Contain betaine and other attractors.
Quality breakdown pellets in sizes from 4mm to 16mm	A hybrid between a pellet and a boilie. Contains white fish, robin red, haemoglobin, seaweed, yeast and betaine.
CSL pellets in 4mm and 8mm sizes	Contains corn steep liquor (CSL), a by-product of glucose manufacture. CSL has been one of the most successful fish attractants developed over the last few years. It has a rich, Bovril-like smell. CSL pellets begin to break down after only a few minutes and are designed to get the fish feeding quickly.
Carp pellets in sizes from 2mm to 11mm	Designed specifically for carp and therefore suitable for barbel as they have a low oil content. They are usually buoyant and therefore sink slowly; they require a short hook link when used for barbel. They have a slightly fishy smell, and some makes contain betaine.
Hemp pellets in 2mm to 6mm sizes	Designed as an alternative to hemp. The main advantage is that they can be catapulted further than hemp, and they do not look like hemp.
Soft pellets in 6mm size	These are soft enough to be put on the hook. Purchased in small containers.

flavours. The softer Elips pellets and trout pellets will start to go soft after only a few minutes, and will take up to six hours to break down.

How to Use Pellets

There are a number of ways in which pellets can be presented as a hook bait: on a bait band; by using a hair rig; and directly on the hook.

To my mind a bait band is the simplest method of attaching a pellet to the hook, especially if using one of the larger size pellets, from 14mm to 22mm. Bait bands come in three sizes – micro, 8mm to 14mm, and 9mm to 21mm – and are usually made of silicone or latex. They stretch around the pellet to hold it next to the hook. Some bands have a small protrusion attached, through which the hook point may be pushed, thus keeping the bait tight to the hook shank or bend; otherwise the hook is pushed inside the band. I put mine on the shank.

Hook Bend just
proud of pellet

Pellet mounted on bait-band.

I occasionally put an 8mm or 9mm pellet on a bait band, but first score a groove with a penknife around the outside of the pellet so that the band sits in the groove and has a better grip on the pellet. The bait band does not require any changes to the rest of the terminal tackle.

Whether using a bait band or a hair rig, I normally use a size 8 Terry Eustace super-strong carp hook for pellets; this hook is based on the old Au Lion d'Or 1534 pattern, but with a thicker wire. I use mine with the barb flattened, and I do this for all my fishing except when (rarely) using worms or maggots. Sometimes the bait bands stretch a little and work loose, hence the groove round the pellet for a better grip. It is a good idea to change to a new bait band for every cast: it would be a shame to wait for hours for a bite, only for the pellet to fall out of the bait band as soon as the barbel touched it. This is where the different size bait bands come in useful, as you can match the size of the band to the size of the pellet being used. Moreover, when fishing during the hours of darkness, bait bands provide yet another advantage in that they are much less fiddly than a hair rig and stop.

I used hair rigs regularly before bait bands became available. For barbel the hair should be as short as possible, with the drilled pellet as close to the shank or bend of the hook as you can get it. Most people have the hair as an extension of the hook trail. In the early days I frequently found that the 8mm Elips pellets, being quite light, would tend to fall off the hair as I reeled in: they did not appear to have sufficient weight to maintain pressure on the hair stop, which became loose and allowed the pellet to fall off. I tried putting two pellets on the hair and using very short hairs to overcome this problem, but I am sure must have spent periods fishing with no

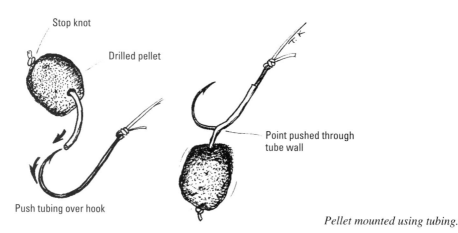

Stop knot

Drilled pellet

Push tubing over hook

Point pushed through
tube wall

Pellet mounted using tubing.

The 'method feeder' and 14mm Elips combination produced this lower Severn double.

bait. Years earlier Tony Hart had invented a method that overcame this problem by using a hair made of light fuse wire; this could be passed through the drilled pellet and curled round the outside to ensure it did not fall off. However, I was concerned that using wire could result in damage to the fish's mouth, and so did not try this method.

Later, Tony came up with an alternative that uses .07mm supple silicone tubing for the hair. A hole is first drilled through the pellet, the end of the silicone tube is pushed through the hole, and a knot is tied in the end of the tube. The tube is then cut, leaving sufficient length to insert the hook point into the centre of the tube. The tube is slid around the bend of the hook until the pellet is tight to the hook, and pushed round to the shank; the surplus tubing is cut off. For ease of use in the dark Tony pre-drills his pellets and threads a number of them on to a long piece of tube before taking up his pitch on the river bank. He uses a knot on the end of the tube to stop the pellets from falling off. Each time a pellet bait is put on the hook a new knot is tied on the new end of the tube to stop the remainder falling off.

Soft pellets have recently become available, and can be used as hook bait straight from the container. Unfortunately they tend to be quite small (about 4mm to 6mm) and do not make much of a mouthful for a hungry barbel, although more than one may be used on the hook. Hard pellets can be made

hookable by placing them in a saucepan and pouring boiling water over them; allow them to remain in the water for about forty seconds, then put them in a bait box and allow them to breathe until they go rubbery. This process can take up to six hours, and is therefore best carried out the day before you intend to use the pellets.

Feeding

There are a number of ways that the barbel angler can feed a swim with pellets. The aim is obviously to have the loose feed as close to the hook bait as possible, unless you are intending to carpet the riverbed with bait, which is not a good idea with the larger pellets. So many anglers do exactly that, and then don't get a bite. But why should the fish select your one hook bait in amongst possibly hundreds of loose pellet baits? Besides, by the time the barbel have fed on the loose baits, they may well have eaten sufficient to satisfy them for many hours or even days. That is defeating the objectives of loose feeding, which are, first, to attract barbel to your hook bait, and then to induce them to take it.

The most popular methods of feeding when using pellets are with a method feeder; with PVA net/funnel bags; with a cage feeder; and with a bait dropper. It is not always the plain pellets that are used as feed: I generally grind down the pellets in a food mixer to make a powder, and then use this to make a 'method' mixture, as I want to use the same mix as the pellets on the hook and it is not always possible to buy the exact powder to match the pellets. The mixture I use consists of 60 per cent pellet powder, 20 per cent from a standard method mix (to help bind the mix together), and 20 per cent plain white crumb groundbait to bulk out the mix. It holds together well and is not too heavy, the intention being to attract the fish without over-feeding them.

This method has given me some good catches on difficult waters, including a 10lb 9oz fish from the Kennet, and an 11lb 6oz fish from the lower Severn. In an eight-day period in February 2000 I had fish of 10lb 3oz, 9lb 0oz, 11lb 2oz and 12lb 6oz from one stretch of the Kennet.

To use this mix I wet the powder mixture at the riverside and mould it into a stiff paste. I then use a modified method feeder as my weight and feeding method. I have modified this feeder by removing some of the outer vertical spars, cutting off the elastic for connecting through the centre, adding a swivel and line clip at the top for connection, and adding more weight around the central core and at the base. I press the first layer of feed mix tight to the inside of the method feeder, then the second layer is pressed slightly less tightly on top of the first, and the third and outside layer just a little less tightly again. This allows the feed to be released at different

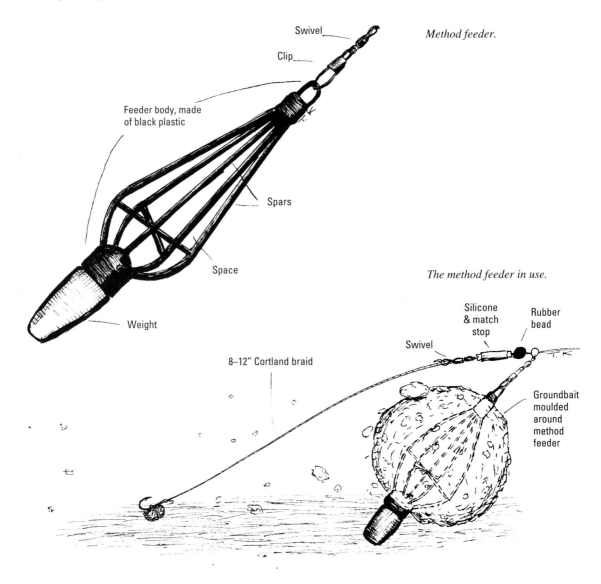

Method feeder.

The method feeder in use.

rates by the water flow, rather than falling out in one big lump and getting washed away quickly. The benefit this gives is to prolong the length of time that the mix comes away from the feeder, giving off an attracting cloud and smell, and making it more likely to attract fish to the bait. Many times when using this method I have reeled in after only ten minutes to find the inner layer of mix still attached to the method feeder, proving that it works well. It is possible to cast a fully loaded method feeder with an underarm swing without frightening the fish, allowing for accurate baiting in a small, confined area. Sometimes I lace the outer layer with hemp as an additional attractant; however, if too much hemp is added to the mix it tends to break up too easily. This method of feeding comes into its own when fishing in an area with a high population of barbel such as the lower Severn, and in the slow, deeper areas of rivers such as the Kennet.

On occasions when I know that not many fish are present, and often during the winter months, I want to restrict the amount of feed I introduce to my swim, but want it to be accurately placed by my hook bait. To achieve these objectives I use a PVA net bag, or continuous net (sometimes called funnel web), which even in winter tends to melt within seconds. These are small net bags made from water-soluble PVA that are sold either as rolls of fixed-size bags, or on a continuous reel of five or six yards in length, which may be cut to the desired size. When using the former I cut the next bag off the roll just above the closure of the bag above, bait up my hook with a pellet, fill the net bag with the chosen bait (usually 3mm pellets), and tie off the end with PVA string. Nowadays, however, I prefer the continuous net, as this means I can make the bag as small or as large as I wish. To do this I knot the end of the roll of continuous net, and then cut off between four and seven inches of net. The length is dependent upon how much feed I want to introduce, and I have found that, particularly in the winter, the smaller amounts – about golf-ball size – appear to work best. I push the hook in one side of the mesh and out through the other side, and by doing this I know that my feed will be close to my hook bait. I usually use the bags with a mixture of 3mm or 4mm Elips, Marine and CSL pellets, one of them being the same as the hook bait. I sometimes use pieces of cut-up 8mm Elips pellets the same as the hook bait. These bags may be used for many types of feed provided the feed is dry. If it is not dry then the bag will begin to melt the instant the feed touches the mesh. Towards the end of a cold spell of six days in February 2003 I used this method in conjunction with a banded 8mm Elips pellet

to catch a beautiful Kennet fish of 11lb 12oz. This fish had a girth of 18¼in, but was only 28¼in long.

During a three-week period in February and March 2003 this method proved extremely successful for me on both the Kennet and Teme, enabling me to catch barbel when most other anglers blanked. During this spell I twice caught four barbel in a session from a hard stretch of the Kennet, where the norm is to catch one fish in every six visits. In the course of one session, after three hard frosts and air temperatures of 26°F, I caught a fish of 7lb 12oz in the middle of the day. That period produced twenty-two barbel, including seven doubles, and with a best fish of 11lb 12oz.

Occasionally in the summer instead of the method feeder I will use a metal cage feeder. The one drawback with this method is that it releases all the feed together, rather than in the slow trickle that I prefer. Many anglers would not consider this to be a problem, especially on a big river, and I know that John Costello uses this method regularly with great success on the Severn. Although it is possible to squeeze the feed in the middle of the feeder harder than the rest, the mesh of the cage feeder allows the flow of the river to work away and loosen the feed throughout the feeder from the instant it goes into the river. The cage feeder does have the benefit of being simpler to use than the method feeder, and it is less prone to tangles. The feed on the inside of the method feeder is, however, protected by the two separate layers of feed on the outside, and the second layer is protected by the outside layer, guaranteeing three separate lots of feed for the swim. When I do not want any loose feed, but just an initial attractor, I will use a small ball of my method mix pressed round the outside of my leger weight. This will then give off a small trail of cloud and flavour.

The mix could also be loose fed by throwing in loose balls; however, this is rather a hit-and-miss affair unless the swim is close in with little flow. This mix may be made as above with powder, or an alternative is to scald the pellets in boiling water and then mash them down to a pulp; this can then be used as a method mix or as loose feed. A standard bait dropper may also be used to feed loose pellets of any size, including a mixture of a few of hook-bait size and the majority of 3mm attractant size.

Fishing with Pellets

When fishing with pellets I tend to leave my bait in the water for longer periods than I would when using traditional bait such as sausage or meatball. This is because, dependent upon the brand of pellet being

A PVA bag filled with 3mm Elips, halibut and CSL pellets and a banded 8mm Elips hook bait fooled this 10lb 9oz Kennet barbel.

used and its hardness, it may take some five to twenty-five minutes before it begins to give off any aroma to enable the fish to locate it. If using a hard halibut or Hi-Betaine pellet I may well have to wait up to an hour for a bite. When using a softer Elips pellet, however, I can sometimes get almost instant bites in the same way as when using traditional baits.

It is not always necessary to sit in one swim all day if using pellets, especially if many other anglers are also using them on the chosen stretch of river. When fishing the River Kennet I usually use a mobile approach, though instead of staying between ten and twenty minutes in one swim, I will stay between forty-five and sixty minutes, depending upon the hardness of the pellets I am using. To speed up the release of the pellet's attractor I may scrape the surface off each end, though without scraping too hard lest the pellet disintegrates.

I began using pellets on the lower Severn in 1997 on hair rigs, and they were instantly successful. My first fish was a barbel of 9lb 7oz, part of a six-fish haul in three sessions in February. The next time I used pellets on the Lower Severn I had three barbel of 7lb 10oz, 7lb 14oz and 10lb 2oz.

Most of the time I tend to keep my basic tackle as straightforward as possible. I use either Berkeley extra tough or extra limp main line of 10lb bs with a running link leger, using either an Arlsey bomb as small as I can get away with, or a heavy flat weight in flood situations. I use a short hook trail of about eight or nine inches of Cortland braid attached to a swivel, with a rubber bead stop and silicone tube and length of matchstick leger stop. The latter is very

soft and does not damage the line. If fishing a snag swim I will step up to 12lb bs line. One potential problem with pellets in floodwater fishing is that the bait is quite light, and if the hook trail is too long the bait may come up off the river bed and spin round in the fast flow, often becoming tangled. A shot 1in from the hook will solve this problem, but may weaken the hook link. When using a PVA net bag for feed I will use a much heavier weight than necessary to ensure that my tackle does not move away from the feed. I tend to use flat weights in sizes between 1½oz and 3oz.

In conclusion, pellets are undoubtedly one of the most popular barbel baits at present, and Barbel Catchers Club members are currently having great success with them on rivers throughout the country. In many cases success is instant, without any need for pre-baiting programmes. Pellets are a bait that works equally well in daylight and after dark. The combination of a small soft pellet and a PVA net bag is superb for winter barbel fishing.

This season I have noticed that on the more heavily fished stretches of the Kennet, the bites have become much more finicky, especially with the newer, harder and larger pellets. The barbel seem to be taking longer to decide to take the bait, spending a considerable length of time mouthing it. I have therefore stopped using the hard 21mm pellets. I have not yet noticed this on the lower Severn, but of course the rivers have little in common, including the numbers of fish and anglers present. I expect pellets in their current forms to have a longer life as baits on a river such as the lower Severn than on the heavily fished stretches of the Kennet.

4 Modern Baits: HNV Specials

by Steve Withers

If you delved into the bait box of the average barbel angler back in the 1980s it is likely you would find traditional barbel baits: meat in its various forms, sweetcorn, maggots, casters and so on. 'Fast forward' to today's barbel angler, and in many cases there won't be any of these baits – you are far more likely to see boilies, pastes or pellets in their various guises. Nevertheless, let's be clear from the start that there is nothing wrong with traditional baits, and they still deliver the goods with the right application and in the right circumstances. However, it has to be said that the baits as typically used by the modern generation have made such an impact that any angler who chooses to ignore them is likely to be at a distinct disadvantage on many of today's barbel rivers.

I first became involved with using these baits in the early 1990s as a direct result of some of the pioneering work that was being undertaken at the time by the Wealden Region of the BCC. As a group, the region had researched and experimented with baits which at that time were primarily considered to be carp baits, and some of their catches were outstanding; for example, results on the Medway and Hants Avon from anglers such as Dave Williams stand out as part of barbel-fishing history. At the same time as the Wealden Region was achieving such success, the fishing on many of my local rivers seemed to be becoming more difficult – although those anglers using boilies and pastes were noticeably bucking the trend.

In an attempt to tap into this potential, a number of us in the Wessex Region began the long haul of experimenting and assessing the various baits available in order to form a judgement on what would, and what wouldn't work for barbel. The difficulty at that stage was that very little information was available. Although a few people were using these baits for barbel, results were generally a closely guarded secret, and so it was really a matter of trial and error. The fact that several members of our region were involved certainly made life easier in terms of meaningful feedback on a reasonable timescale, but because we were fishing low-density rivers the process was rather slow and at times frustrating. Nevertheless, although early results proved patchy, enough fish were caught to encourage us to pursue the issue, and with every success our confidence increased, showing we were at least on the right track. Over the intervening period we have tried a wide range of baits, and have gradually built up confidence to the point where, over recent years, 90 per cent of my fishing has involved the use of pastes and boilies.

Within one short chapter it is impossible to cover modern barbel baits in detail; however, I would like to cover at least the basic principles we have followed, outline the thought process we went through, and hopefully lay the foundations for anyone wishing to use modern baits. My starting point assumes the reader has little or no experience of using such baits, and hopefully even the more experienced angler will find something of interest to stimulate the thought process. For those wishing to explore the subject in greater detail, there are several books and articles available that are dedicated solely to the subject of modern baits; together with bait manufacturers' catalogues, these will provide an ample source of reading matter. At the end of the chapter I have included details of base mixes and flavours of which I have had first-hand experience, and which I would confidently recommend. It is not meant to be a comprehensive list of baits that will work for barbel, but it does represent baits that have been used successfully. So if you aren't sure where to make a start, you could do a lot worse than to select from this list.

Why Bother?

If you are still being successful using your old favourites, then the obvious question to ask yourself is, do you really need to complicate matters by using modern baits? If you are lucky enough for this to be the case, then it's possibly not worth wasting your time and effort going down this route, although before dismissing the idea completely it *is* worth considering some of the potential advantages. Having had first-hand experience on my local rivers, I am totally convinced that once a water has been subjected to modern baits, then your results will suffer if you stick to the traditional ones. I'm sure many of us know waters where boilies have completely taken over and produced tremendous catches to those using them, and catching on anything else has become extremely difficult; it almost means that if you don't join in, you will be left behind. Logically if your waters have not seen these baits, it's worth considering getting in first and reaping the rewards, rather than trying to follow the crowd when the inevitable happens.

Many anglers considering trying boilies and pastes have the idea that the subject is extremely complex and that it's an expensive business. Probably this originates from their reading some of the technical bait articles that abound – but in reality there has never been an easier time to start, as the range of readily available, proven baits is huge, and creating complex mixes is no longer necessary. On the issue of cost, I don't believe that these baits, applied in a sensible manner, are any more expensive than many of the baits that barbel anglers would routinely use. At first glance they may appear costly, but if you do your sums you will soon realize that they are in fact quite economical. This is corroborated by the fact that members of our Yorkshire region, not renowned for spending freely, use these baits regularly.

Most of my fishing is done on stretches of river with a relatively low population, and our strategy usually involves a couple of us targeting a stretch and fishing it until we believe we have had the best from it. In a typical season we will start fishing seriously and putting bait in from late autumn, trickling it in steadily through to the end of the season, while probably fishing on average a couple of times a week. Generally 10kg (22lb) of dry base mix will be sufficient for two of us for the whole season. Our normal approach, once we have agreed on a bait, is to buy in bulk and spend a day making up bait into paste and/or boilies and splitting it into small portions for freezing. In that way we have a constant source of bait instantly ready for an impromptu session should conditions suddenly look favourable: when conditions are suddenly perfect there is nothing worse than having to go through the hassle of making up bait. Although the initial outlay for base mix and flavours can seem quite high, the actual cost when it is taken over a season is trivial compared to the amount the average angler spends on tackle, permits, travelling costs and so on. To put it into context, you wouldn't be able to buy a pint of maggots with what I spend on bait for the average session.

Finally, I find that experimenting with baits can add a new dimension to your fishing. There is nothing more satisfying than to catch a good fish on a bait that you have spent time first developing, then encouraging the fish to find acceptable.

If you're still not convinced, then read no further and skip to the next chapter!

Base Mixes

The aim of most popular base mixes on the market is to provide a well balanced food source that gives the fish the essentials for a healthy diet: carbohydrates, protein and fat, supplemented by a mixture of trace minerals and vitamins. Fred Wilton was the first to put forward the theory, now generally accepted by most anglers, that fish have a form of nutritional recognition that helps them identify a food source that is good for them, and that in the long term a fish will take such food in preference to something from which they derive no benefit. Whether the Wilton theory is true or not can never be proved conclusively, but what cannot be denied is that a lot of fish are caught on 'quality' baits. Moreover, looking at the condition and growth rates of fish on certain stretches that see large amounts of these baits going in, the fish clearly do benefit from a diet of good quality bait. I do not believe that the dramatic increase in size of fish that we have seen in recent years can be solely attributed to the quality and quantity of bait that is being introduced; however, I do believe that it is a major contributory factor.

Before finally selecting a base mix you really have to choose how you are going to proceed; whether you wish to:

- buy a bait that is already prepared and ready to fish;
- buy a base mix that you can customize by adding your own selected flavours and additives before making it into paste or boilies;

● start from scratch and buy the various basic ingredients to make up your own mix.

The decision ultimately depends upon how much effort you want to put into producing your bait, and what eventually you want to get out of it; but whichever way you go I would liken it to your own choice of food. At one extreme is the convenience of the ready-prepared microwave meal with limited choice and mediocre quality; the other involves buying all fresh produce and creating your own mouth-watering delicacies!

I would recommend choosing one of the many good base mixes available and customizing it to suit your own requirements. Once you have gained confidence you might consider developing your own unique mix from scratch; but looking at the range of good quality mixes on the market, it's so much easier to choose one as a base and to adapt it as necessary. I strongly believe you need to have 100 per cent confidence in bait, so choose something with a track record and catch a few fish on it before trying to get too adventurous.

Broadly speaking, historically base mixes have fallen into three categories: milk proteins, fishmeals and birdfoods. While these categories still hold true to a degree, many mixes these days are combinations of these ingredients, for instance fishmeals combined with milk proteins and birdfoods. If you study the offerings from the main bait suppliers, you will soon realize that most of the mixes are actually quite similar, and are based around these categories though with subtle variations. Also what these mixes

contain is usually perfectly evident, as most manufacturers list the main ingredients. Having said that, some of the more recent mixes to come onto the market are more difficult to place into one of these categories, and as baits become more complex, for obvious reasons bait companies are increasingly reluctant to reveal their exact ingredients. Many of these mixes also have much less scope for experimentation as they are designed for a very specific combination of components, usually being the dry base mix with one or two particular additives to be added in predetermined quantities. Whilst these baits have been shown to be great fish catchers, the down side is that they don't lend themselves to being customized; so if a number of you are using a particular mix, then you can be certain you are all fishing an almost identical bait.

In the last few years a number of baits have been introduced that are specifically aimed at barbel. I have not used any of these baits, but I'm sure they will catch plenty of fish. Personally I am more confident using a bait that I hope no one else is using, and hence I find more variety and scope for personalizing a bait by tapping into baits that are not specifically aimed at the barbel angler.

Before selecting a base mix that you hope will suit your individual needs, I would suggest you obtain copies of the many excellent catalogues produced by the main bait suppliers, and spend some time reading up on the subject; you should also talk to other anglers. And once you have made a choice, stick with it and give it a fair trial.

A fine Dorset Stour fish of 12lb 7oz taken on an HNV special.

Paste versus Boilies

Once you have chosen a base mix, the next question is, how do you want to fish it – as boilies or paste? The majority of my fish are caught on paste baits, and I believe that pastes have several advantages over boilies. First, paste is much more versatile, as it is very easy to change the nature of the bait. Size, shape and/or texture can be easily altered on the bank to suit the prevailing conditions, something that cannot be achieved to the same extent with boilies. Paste also has a much better 'leak-off', as the flavour hasn't been boiled out of the bait, or sealed in during the skinning process. A further advantage – which unfortunately is also one of the drawbacks – is that many pastes break down quite quickly in water, and within an hour or two the bait will have dissolved away. Whilst this breakdown adds to the attraction, creating a flavour trail for the fish to home in on, it also means that prebaiting with paste has its limitations, particularly when you want a bait to stay there for several hours until the fish find it. The answer on these occasions is to use a combination of boilies for prebaiting, and then stick to paste for hook baits. The other big advantage of paste is that it is much easier to make up as compared to boilies, which can be extremely fiddly.

Nevertheless, boilies undoubtedly have a significant part to play in the armoury of barbel anglers, and anything that can simplify their preparation must be helpful. So, rather than taking a lot of time to produce round boilies, I find it much quicker to roll a lump of paste into a 'sausage' and simply cut it into the desired shapes with a sharp knife before boiling. Another way is to roll out the paste with a rolling pin, and cut it into large blocks before boiling; once cooled, cut the blocks into the desired shape. Again, this allows you to produce a bait that is just a little different.

It should be remembered that the main reason for using boilies in carp fishing is to present a hard hook bait to deter the attentions of nuisance fish. This isn't a significant issue for the barbel angler – if only a hard hook bait would deter chub! As I'm not looking to produce a rock-hard bait I keep the boiling time to a minimum (thirty to sixty seconds, depending upon the size of the bait and the mix) to just lightly skin the bait and leave the inside soft. This short boiling period retains as much of the basic attraction of the bait as possible, but still prevents the bait breaking down over time.

Of course, if you don't want to go to the trouble of making your own, there is a reasonable selection of ready-made boilies available, ready to fish straight out of the bag. I prefer to use frozen boilies, rather than 'shelf-life' ones, as the latter are usually air-dried to bullet-like hardness, and contain preservatives to prevent their deterioration.

Flavours and Additives

If you thought the choice of base mixes was prolific, then the range of flavours, additives and supplements is altogether confusing. To my mind, the most important factor in terms of attraction is the quality of the base mix, and the addition of any flavours and additives should be kept to a minimum, purely to provide your own unique label. Generally, most good base mixes will catch by themselves, as they have an inherent attraction, and if you need to load a bait with flavours in order to catch, then it says a lot about the quality (or lack of it) of the base mix you are using.

You could easily spend a lifetime working through the many combinations of flavours and additives available. It is very easy to get carried away when reading through the bait catalogues, and find yourself constantly trying new flavours without drawing any positive conclusions. It really does take some time to form a judgement, particularly as some combinations may work well in cold water conditions but lose some of their effectiveness in the warmer water temperatures in summer, or vice versa. So don't be too quick to dismiss a particular combination without giving it a fair trial over a range of conditions.

Generally, most barbel anglers tend to focus on the spicy and meaty flavours, but don't ignore the fruity/sweet flavours, as these also work well and can be used in combination with most base mixes. A classic example is 'Scopex', one of the most successful flavours for barbel, and a favourite for years.

To add further to the choice, different carriers are used for flavours that have different characteristics – for example, those with a better leak-off in cold water – and flavours based on these carriers may be worth looking at for winter use. You will also find a wide range of other additives, such as palatants, enhancers (in both liquid and powder form), amino acids, essential oils and fish oils, all of which can be used to enhance your base mix. Some concerns were raised in the past regarding the excessive use of fish oils for carp, but they were used in large quantities, and with the baits soaked in oils. Although fish oils are an extremely effective addition to barbel baits, certainly you should be careful not to use excessive amounts; and if you *are* using oils, it is best to look for those advertised as 'winterized', as they don't thicken and congeal to the same extent as others in cold water conditions.

As stated earlier, in my experience it is important to keep the levels of flavours low, particularly for a long-term bait. I will always err on the side of caution with flavour levels, and would generally use between 25 to 50 per cent of the recommended levels for paste, increasing this to between 50 and 75 per cent for boilies. It really is all too easy to ruin a good bait by over-application of flavours. Some of these additives are highly concentrated, and only very small amounts need be added to a bait; so in the interests of accuracy and consistency it is important to use the right equipment when measuring out these ingredients – it is no good trying to measure out ½ml with a medicine spoon and expecting it to be accurate!

Application

It is always difficult to be sure how much bait need be introduced to get barbel to accept it readily. This often depends upon whether the fish have been previously exposed to such baits, and there are also the more obvious considerations such as fish population, water conditions and competition from other species/anglers and so on. I am strongly against mass baiting as I believe this approach shows no consideration to anyone else fishing the same water (and there are not many places where no one else is fishing) – and anyway I don't believe it to be necessary. There is nothing more annoying than to be on a water when someone decides they are going to pile in the bait, and so ruin everyone else's fishing in the process. Show the same consideration and courtesy that you would expect from others, and apply bait in a sensible manner. I have always found that it is much more productive to bait with small quantities over a longer period, rather than by just piling it in.

Providing circumstances allow, start by introducing bait little and often, to begin with up to a pound at a time, on a few occasions; and not necessarily just in swims you intend to fish, but spread around the general area. Follow this up by trickling in small amounts of bait, depending on the

Proof of the 'pudding': a 14lb 1oz Hampshire Avon beauty.

conditions and other factors such as angling pressure. Work for the long term, and in my experience results will always improve significantly with time.

Generally, once a bait is established it is only necessary to take a small quantity for a session; usually a ball of paste the size of a golf ball or a couple of dozen boilies is enough. Even if you decide to change the bait, once the groundwork has been done, by getting the fish to accept boilies or paste baits, they will quickly accept a bait change without having to go through the process again.

Recipe for Success

No, I am not about to reveal the ultimate barbel bait recipe, as no such thing exists; but having covered the main areas in the sections above, I thought a summary would be useful, and might help anyone who was thinking of starting to use these baits.

● To begin with, choose a bait with some history of catching barbel. You can always experiment after catching a few fish, and having built up your confidence; there is nothing worse than having doubts from the start about whether a bait will work. Spend some time selecting a bait to suit your own needs, either by reading some of the many published articles on bait, looking through manufacturers' catalogues, talking to other anglers, or picking one off the list at the end of this chapter. Choose a good quality bait, as there is no doubt that in the long term it will out-fish a poor one.

● Once you've chosen a bait, fish it exclusively and give it a fair trail. I've seen many anglers who start to fish a new bait, and if they don't catch immediately they resort to old favourites. Then at other times they will try a new bait as a change, even when they haven't been catching on their normal baits. You really do need to commit to a new bait and fish it over a reasonable period of time in order to make an honest assessment, and not hedge your bets by fishing it against, or in conjunction with, other baits. On the other side of the coin, don't just keep doing the same thing if it's clearly not working. There will come a time when you decide that a change is required: but make the choice on the right basis, having given things time to work.

Successful Base Mixes, Flavours and Additives

Base Mixes/Boilies

Premier
- Spiced Fish
- Aminos
- Supreme
- Matrix

Mainline
- Grange
- Active 8
- NRG

Nutrabaits
- Fishfood Mix
- Big Fish Mix
- Four Seasons
- High Nu Val
- Trigga

Flavours
- Megga Spice
- Ultra Spice
- Scopex
- Sweaty Feet (N-Butyric acid)
- Strawberry Jam
- Tuna and Sardine
- Salmon
- Peach Melba
- Pepperoni
- Malay Spice
- Sting
- Indian Spice
- Monster Crab
- Cinnamon

Additives
- Salmon Oil
- Caplin Oil
- Complete Food Oil
- Liver extract
- Sweet Cajouser
- Spice Cajouser
- Green-Lipped Mussel Extract
- Sense Appeal
- Corn Steep Liquor
- Spice Appetite Stimulator
- Multimino
- Nutramino
- Cinnamon Essential Oil
- Black Pepper Essential Oil
- Robin Red

- If you are mixing your own bait, keep it simple. Provided you are using a good quality base mix the inherent attraction of that base mix should itself be the key aspect of the bait, and any additives should be present just to provide a unique label. A good quality base mix with low levels of flavour and attractor will work over the long term, and it gives you scope to develop the bait later if needs be, by adding additional ingredients. If you start by using lots of different additives it's almost impossible to form a judgement on what is, or is not, making the bait work (or otherwise). For this reason if you change a bait I would only recommend changing one aspect at a time.

- Don't be tempted to constantly chop and change. Pick up the weeklies or the bait catalogues, and there is always another 'wonder' bait on the market. No doubt many of these are extremely effective, but ask yourself if you really need to change if you already have a successful bait? I don't believe that in most barbel-fishing circumstances a bait 'blows', as can often be the case in carp fishing. The need to constantly keep one step ahead of other anglers is generally not an issue in barbel fishing unless you are fishing a highly pressurized water. So don't just change for change's sake.

- Only use fresh bait. All baits, even dry mixes, have a shelf life and in time will deteriorate. Typically six months would be appropriate for a fishmeal dry mix, and even less for a milk protein mix. Aim to buy the freshest bait possible from a shop with a decent turnover, and then store it properly. Make the bait up quickly, split it into small quantities, and freeze it. Don't keep re-freezing bait after a session. Ensure you only use fresh ingredients, including eggs, and in particular don't use old oils. If in doubt, bin it: it's just not worth taking the chance of ruining a good catch.

- Keep putting in a steady stream of bait over a relatively long period of time, rather than large quantities over a short period. Application in this way has provided good long-term results on many stretches I have fished, and furthermore results improve with time, so don't necessarily expect instant success.

- Don't follow the crowd, do your own thing and try to be different. It's all too easy to see a few fish being caught and be tempted to abandon your plans in favour of the 'going' bait at the time. There is so much scope to experiment and be different. Changes to the type of bait, flavours, varying bait size, texture or colour can all give you that additional edge, particularly on hard-fished waters. If you really do want to be different, give this some thought when initially choosing your bait, as some mixes give more scope for variation than others.

- The key ingredient is confidence – lose confidence, whether it be in baits, rigs, location or tackle, and you are on the slippery slope. Use a structured approach. Analyse what you want to achieve with a bait for your own application, and change things progressively so that you can assess any improvements or otherwise.

Finally, and most important of all in my opinion, don't take your eye off the ball and become innured into thinking that bait is the one and only important factor. Whilst it can clearly make a significant difference to your catches, it is only one of the many pieces of the jigsaw. Without effective tackle, presentation and fish location you may as well be fishing with a bare hook!

5 The Bristol Avon

by Andy Humphries

The Bristol Avon rises at Grickstone Springs near Sherston and empties into the Bristol Channel at Avonmouth. As the crow flies the distance from the source to the estuary is only 17 miles (27km), but the river goes on an 88-mile (140km) journey through the Wiltshire countryside, taking in Malmesbury, Chippenham, Melksham and Bath before flowing on to Bristol. The river has a second claimant to its source, another small stream rising at Tetbury and joining up at Malmesbury. This river is known as the Tetbury Branch, or more commonly the Little Avon. The Bristol Avon is a classic small stream in its upper reaches, meandering over clear gravel that has pockets of streamer weed, a magnet for barbel, especially if overhanging trees or bushes are present. On stretches where these are absent, either naturally or more commonly due to the chainsaw of flood prevention work, the undercut bank can offer barbel a haven. If there is overhanging tall grass or rushes, so much the better.

The areas around Christian Malford, Kellaways, Peckingell, Chippenham and Lacock are renowned for barbel. Then the river starts to deepen and slow up, at Melksham the bottom becomes more silty, and it loses its appeal as a barbel river, although it probably harbours some very big fish for the probing angler. At Bradford-on-Avon it shallows again, and barbel are present in numbers. The river has widened by this point, and the weedbeds can be more extensive. It then flows through the incredibly steep

Avon Valley above Bath, taking in Avoncliff, Limpley Stoke, Claverton and Bathampton, before flowing through Bath itself. Below this it becomes far wider and deeper, and barbel become more sporadic, although the weirs at Kelston, Saltford and Keynsham are known hotspots. The Avon is tidal up to Keynsham during the spring tide period, and by the time it flows through the centre of Bristol and under Brunel's Clifton suspension bridge, it can be little more than a trickle at low tides, when its mud flats are horribly exposed.

Barbel are not native to the Bristol Avon: only those rivers that flowed eastwards into the Rhine system when mainland Britain was connected to Europe have naturally occurring stocks. In 1955, fifty-four fish were removed from the Enbourne, a tributary of the Kennet, and introduced at Stokeford Bridge near Limpley Stoke. Then during the 1960s and 1970s barbel were stocked in several locations, since when they have spread virtually throughout the river.

Early season barbel fishing can be frustrating as the fish rarely come out during daylight and the best chances of catching are to fish the hours of darkness. During high summer I rarely fish during the day, preferring to arrive a couple of hours before dusk to walk the stretch and bait likely swims with a bait dropper. It is surprising how far loose feed travels before reaching the bottom when throwing the bait in by hand: by using a bait dropper, a much smaller feeding area is established. The Avon often has an algae stain during the early season, and it is difficult to spot barbel even on the shallow upper stretches. I usually fish about six swims, only staying in each swim for about five minutes, and then moving on to the next. That is long enough for any fish in the vicinity to find the bait. If nothing happens, then either the fish aren't feeding at that time, or they have been spooked. Moving to fresh swims increases your chances, and it is surprising the number of bites that come very soon after a bait has been introduced into a swim.

For pre-baiting I use a mixture of hemp, tares and foreign finch mix that is soaked and cooked in a large nappy boiler. Recently I have begun adding

Classic barbel water on the Bristol Avon.

some mini trout pellets to the mixture just before commencing fishing, so that they start breaking down and pick up the juice of the hemp. Add them too early, however, and the pellets turn the whole lot to a mush. I frequently use up to four gallons (18ltr) of bait if I fish all night. That might sound a lot, but it is spread between the six swims, and it is amazing how quickly the fish can get through the bait; a dozen fish averaging 8lb will devour all the bait you can throw at them. I buy sacks of seeds in 20kg bags from pet superstores, and the bait will swell to at least three times its original size during cooking. This makes the method reasonably cheap – certainly a lot less expensive than a bag of boilies.

As soon as the light starts to fade I creep into position, and if at all possible, lower the bait into the swim, or feather down the cast so that the tackle enters the river as silently as possible. I use as light a lead as I can get away with (usually about ½oz in the summer) for static fishing. I have used braided line almost exclusively for the last four years, as nothing else comes close to its sensitivity for touch ledgering. I feel the lead and hook bait dropping through the swim, and I ensure that it lands on a solid bottom. If it lands on weed it is a simple matter of tweaking the end rig until it drops through. I fish one very productive swim that has a large strip of streamer weed running through it, and it can take about five or six attempts before the bait is finally on the bottom. I see other people fishing the same swim, who cast out and tighten up when the bait stops falling – great, if you want to fish a five-foot swim four feet off the bottom! After five minutes, if

nothing has happened I move, but I top up the swim with another couple of bait droppers of loose feed.

As this is a mobile method of fishing, I take only the bare essentials. I carry a medium-sized trout bag containing all my accessories, and my coat pocket holds a selection of leads. The rod is left made up from the last trip, and held together by Velcro straps, as is the landing net; so there is no need for a rod holdall. Seats are heavy to carry, and they restrict your choice of swim, therefore I never use one. Rod rests slow you down, and besides, I always touch ledger holding the rod. The amount of information obtained by holding the line and feeling for bites is amazing, and anglers who put the rod in a rest literally don't know what they are missing. Most of the bites I get are very tentative, and fish often test the bait for resistance. Once alarmed, barbel frequently do not return, so I always strike at the slightest indication of a bite.

The rod I use is a typical Avon that bends to the butt, and I use a push-in quivertip for most of my fishing, as it slows down the bite and gives less resistance to a taking fish. I use a Shimano Super X GTM4000 reel that is dependable and has a good clutch to give line if the fish goes on a powerful run. It also helps compensate for the lack of stretch of the braid. The terminal tackle consists of an American snap link and buffer bead, which make it easy to change the lead. I use a short hook link consisting of a swivel tied to 15lb Drennan Carp Dacron attached to a strong hook. The Dacron is fairly tangle free, although if it does tangle, it usually pulls free using slight pressure. Some of the other HPPE braids seem

Andy Humphries with his first double at 11lb 14oz.

to tie knots for no reason. My knots are always grinners, as they retain the line's breaking strain far better than tucked blood knots, which can cause strangulation of the line. For hooks, I highly rate Gold Label Tackle's Super Strong Penetrators or Penetrator One hooks in a size 4 for most of my fishing. The bait bucket can be heavy, so I hide it in bushes and transfer smaller amounts to a canvas bucket that makes moving around a lot easier.

Bait is usually meat in some form or other, luncheon meat still being my first choice. After transferring from the tin, I cut it into about six large sausages and coat it with some Pataks curry paste, stiffened with garlic granules. I then fry it on a low heat in a frying pan, turning regularly. When all the sides are cooked, it is allowed to cool on a plate and then transferred to polythene bags for freezing; this ensures that the flavour is sucked right into the bait. I have also had success with luncheon meat fried in lard and curry powder. Any sort of meat or sausage can be made to take a flavour by putting the meat and powder into a polythene bag and shaking it. Barbel can definitely spook at the sight of plain meat – during daylight I have seen them flee a swim in panic at the sight of it. But the curry changes the smell, and by cooking the flavour in, it also changes the colour. I am happy using any bait, so long as it is large, meaty and has the aroma of an Indian restaurant! I use a baiting needle to thread the meat onto the hook, and because meat can be very soft in

warm weather, I usually place a short stalk of thick grass under the bend of the hook. This absorbs some of the pressure of casting or retrieving the bait. Modern paste baits definitely work, and some of the best known brands have been pioneered on the Bristol Avon. Personally I haven't felt it necessary to go down that route yet, preferring to fish in a traditional manner rather than copying carp-fishing tactics.

In late summer the river can start to clear, and stalking fish can be a productive method. The swims are heavily baited with the aforementioned hemp mix, and will also include the particles I intend to use as bait; sweetcorn is the obvious choice as it is highly visible and takes a flavour well. I frequently use maple cream as a little goes a long way, and being quite thick it doesn't seem to evaporate in hot weather as much as other flavourings. After a while the fish may become wary of sweetcorn, and I have used chick peas, haricot beans, black eye beans and just about every other type of particle with success; they take them all without hesitation as long as they are fished over a bed of seeds.

Stalking is far easier if you can get above the fish, and so high banks are preferable; however, you won't often have that luxury. As long as the sun is overhead it should be possible to spot fish, but unfortunately they definitely don't feed as well as in overcast conditions. To overcome the problem I usually fish from dawn, when the fish should still be active and the sun bright enough to illuminate the bottom. It is then a race against time before the sun becomes too bright and they switch off. Stalking is a brilliant method for assessing the potential of a stretch, and also for avoiding nuisance fish, normally chub. If chub are a problem, then I switch back to fishing after dark, as they are then far less active than barbel.

The Bristol Avon is a classic lowland river and is ideally situated to take advantage of the warm south-westerly currents that sweep in from the Atlantic in the winter; these create the ideal feeding conditions for barbel. There is a definite art in predicting what the river conditions are likely to be. The upper river can be very quick to rise during a downpour, though it drops back down again reasonably quickly. The middle river is slower to rise, but tends to stay high for longer periods. By assessing the conditions, a decision can be made as to what area is likely to give the best chance of catching. The classic barbel feeding period has traditionally always been when the river has peaked and is dropping whilst retaining its colour. The periods of high water when the river is bursting its banks are also productive if the correct swim is selected. Smooth, slack water either close to the bank or on the inside of a 90-degree bend also instantly spring to mind. I had a tremendous evening's fishing one November when the river was

rising rapidly, taking fish of 9lb 12oz and 9lb 5oz by upstream ledgering about a rod length out. The amount of weed coming down eventually forced me to fish a downstream presentation, when I took further fish of 10lb 10oz, 8lb 5oz and 7lb 3oz from an area whose average size is far smaller than most other stretches. The fish in that swim were normally found under a row of overhanging bushes on the far bank, but the increased flow made the swim boil. The nearside margin was only about a foot deep during the summer, but it was flat, and the flow over it was very even and more to the barbel's liking.

During the winter I do not use loose feed if the river is up and coloured, as I'm sure that a lot of it gets washed away, creating a larger feeding area. Productive areas are similar to those in the summer. Overhanging trees and bushes are good on the upper river, although during floods the slacks behind them can be better, as the obstacle causes the river to slow slightly. The inside of bends are also well worth fishing, especially if the river forms a crease, the sure sign of an area of slack water next to good flow. On the middle river the overhanging trees do not seem to create such good swims as on the upper reaches, probably because the increased depth and width means that the fish have more areas to find sanctuary.

A Bristol Avon beauty of 12lb 4oz.

The fish are still found in similar haunts as in the summer, and that normally means the weedbeds or gravel slopes. Roving tactics using meat hook baits can be deadly during the winter, and it's also one of the simplest ways to fish. The bait can be cast into an area of smooth water and fished in a downstream fashion using only the amount of lead that is necessary to hold bottom. If no bites are forthcoming, strike off the bait and cast further downstream, repeating if necessary. If bites still do not materialize, move to another area and come back later to take advantage of the loose feed in the swim. Alternatively, cover a whole stretch during an evening by having just one cast in every likely swim. The better you know the stretch, and especially the features, the more likely you are to be successful.

One of the most deadly methods is the upstreaming technique. The bait is cast upstream with just enough lead to hold bottom, whilst the rod tip, or preferably the quivertip, is bent towards it. When the fish moves the bait, the lead drops back and the tip springs back. The beauty is that the fish does not feel any resistance, as the line has gone slack. With a downstream presentation the fish feels more resistance the further it moves. It may reject the bait, although it can also give rod-bending bites as it pricks itself and bolts off. Moving the upstreaming technique a stage further is the searching technique, where the lead is deliberately pulled out of position and allowed to bounce down a swim until it settles once again. This can be a superb way to find weedbeds, and as the fish use these for shelter and food, you have located potential hotspots. Bites are usually forthcoming relatively quickly if fish are present. If not, move the bait again to find the next snag.

The upstreaming method can be taken to its ultimate conclusion by trundling. Here the bait is constantly moving over the gravel. During the summer I have seen barbel inspect baits for a long time on gravel shallows: they hang in the flow just inches from the bait, wanting to take it but suspicious having been caught before. With the trundling technique they have no time to inspect the bait: they must either take it instantly or leave it. They have to pounce on the bait, literally pinning it to the gravel, and it is rare to miss these bites. The method works on the darkest night and most coloured water, so do not think that it will only work in clear water.

Barbel are masters of their environment and are equipped with keen eyesight and tremendous sense of taste and smell, enabling them to take advantage of any opportunity that comes their way. The upstreaming method is difficult in high water, especially if a lot of weed is coming down, when downstreaming static baits will work better. The method also works best in reasonably shallow water, and if the bottom contains too much weed; then probably a better bet is downstreaming using a light lead and allowing the current to sweep the bait next to the weed.

During the late 1980s I was starting to get to grips with the changing mood of the river, and was desperate to catch my first double; I had caught nine different nine-pounders, though a double still seemed like a dream. During February 1990 the country took a battering from severe storms and the river burst its banks. After being flooded off once, I returned a few days later, during which time the weather had cleared and we had had no further rain. I went to the upper river and was surprised to find the level right down. I had brought some hemp and sweetcorn just in case, and started pre-baiting some swims. As the river was still coloured it was not necessary to wait until dark, and I started fishing in the mid-afternoon. I caught a couple of chub on meat under an overhanging bush, and I wasn't too surprised to see hemp and corn in their mouths. Just as the light was starting to fade, I felt a slight pluck on the line. The fish came in reasonably easily, and it wasn't until I went to lift the net that I realized that I had caught something exceptional. My first double was duly weighed in at 11lb 14oz. A few weeks later I caught three more doubles from the same stretch over three unforgettable nights, one from under the same bush at 10lb, and two more at 10lb 10oz and 11lb 1oz.

A few years later I caught my first double from the middle river, and this also weighed in at 11lb 14oz. I was baiting a high bank swim late in the evening, and saw a huge flash of ivory belly as a good fish fanned its tail over the hemp on the gravel. I resisted the temptation to fish for it straightaway, and instead baited the swim with loose feed for a few hours until the light faded. I lowered the meat into the swim where I had seen the flash, and within twenty seconds had a solid thump as the fish took the bait in a confident fashion. I'm sure that if I had fished the swim too early, especially as the evening was bright, the fish would have detected the line and been spooked.

The current record for the Bristol Avon is a 15lb 9oz 8dr fish caught by Stuart Morgan in 1998. This fish looks certain to retain its status for a while, as fish in the 13lb plus category are few and far between. Nevertheless, the average size of barbel in the river is reasonably high, and my own average has

Andy shows off a fine specimen of 12lb 5oz.

been around 8lb for a few seasons. This is almost certainly higher than the true average for the river, but I believe that a combination of using big baits after dark and fishing when conditions are favourable for barbel, as well as fishing areas that have lower populations, tips the scales in my favour. Recently I have done some research into the effects that the phases of the moon have on rivers and hence the tidal pull, using Solunar Tables. Although they certainly don't work all the time, I have twice caught two doubles in a single session, once on the day of the last quarter, and the other time on the day after the last quarter. My two best fish have also come around the last quarter phase. The worst times on the Bristol Avon are the days before the new moon. Most of the analysis was done retrospectively and so it is difficult to explain exactly why this should be so.

The upper river has a slightly higher head of fish, and they tend to be more concentrated. However, they certainly tend to keep under cover for most of the season. The middle river has the greater potential to produce bigger fish, though large bags of fish are not as common. As with most rivers, the fish tend to be at their optimum weight at the back end of the season, and a warm winter flood offers the best chance of rewriting the history books.

Barbel from the Bristol Avon by Tony Hart

This is a story that goes back to a day in July 1993, on a blisteringly hot, sunny afternoon along the banks of the Bristol Avon. Thankfully for me it was one of those days when common sense prevailed,

and I realized that fishing would be both silly and pointless; much more sensible to lean back in the chair and soak up the sunshine.

The rod had been assembled earlier, but any thoughts of immediate fishing had been put aside until later, when the air was cooler. I was occasionally interrupted by the hostile buzzing of wasps and mozzies, made active by the heat and drawn upwind either by the oily smell of my sun lotion, or much more likely, by my salmon pâté sandwiches. Trying to ignore the interruptions, I leaned back further in the chair, closed my eyes, and began to doze.

So there I was, fast asleep under my hat – that was, until my son Shane appeared; and I could immediately tell by the urgency in his voice that I wasn't going to get any further sleep. A group of very large barbel had moved into his swim, fish he could see quite clearly in the shallow water against the rushes of the far bank. In an instant I spilled out of my seat and made haste to where he was intending to fish. The high bank above the swim was the perfect vantage point: following Shane's finger pointing to the far side, we could make out five fish, all doubles, and two that were special. The barbel were moving across a small clearing, seeming almost politely to take it in turns to swim up to, and under, a smaller bed of streamer weed above them, before dropping back again. Their upstream progress was blocked by a solid bank-to-bank wall of reed stems set in shallow water. Fascinated, we watched them for a good quarter of an hour, always expecting at some stage that they would slip anchor and drop back through the thick streamer weed, twenty yards or more, into deeper water and off the fishery. But no, to our surprise they seemed content to stay. It was plainly obvious, however, that if any attempt was made to fish at that stage, they would undoubtedly spook. With that in mind Shane made the sensible decision to rest the swim until later, just hoping that the barbel would stay.

As the last rays of sun disappeared over the skyline, Shane quietly moved down the bank and into the swim. Two rod lengths out, the middle channel between the thick tresses of weed were lightly baited. Now the serious stuff could begin. Small pieces of hot dog were flicked out to cover the baited area, and hopefully he would soon know whether the fish had moved. Strangely, even I felt tense sitting some hundred yards above him, expecting to hear at any minute a shout from his direction. But a full hour passed, then two, and still no activity. Then as the witching hour arrived, he began to get bites: solid, unmissable pulls, or so they seemed!

Half-a-dozen bites came over the next hour – and then a shout: a fish was on! Unfortunately it requires the dexterity of a mountain goat to extract oneself from some swims on the Bristol Avon, and mine, of course, was one of them. My antique legs were no match for the steep bank, and in the time it took me to cover the hundred yards of bank that separated us, Shane had landed, unhooked and weighed an immaculate barbel of 10lb 1oz – immaculate, that is, apart from a curious crimson tint down the whole of its left flank. If this was indeed one of the shoal of five, it was one of the smaller fish. It was also our first encounter with the 'red' fish. As the next few months passed I did get back for the occasional visit and caught a few barbel, although nothing of any size. Shane and Lee (my other son) did far better, with several barbel including six 'nines'. No signs of any double-figure fish though, or of the big five. Unfortunately all too soon the fishing was brought to a halt by early frosts, which badly affected what was a comparatively shallow area. The twenty-yard bank would have to wait until next season.

I did manage a few visits later that season, to the wider, deeper, featureless water downstream. On one of these occasions I landed a portly barbel of 10lb 7oz, and on another I hooked what was doubt-less a very big barbel, on a size 6 barbless hook. It's a fish we saw quite plainly in the torchlight, before it made its last dive for freedom, pinging the line against a marginal twig and slipping the hook.

With the onset of the new season curiosity took me to other waters; but the Bristol Avon 'big five' were still in my mind. Lee telephoned me one evening in late August to tell of an 11lb 6oz barbel

Measuring the 'red' barbel.

he had caught the previous night from the twenty-yard bank. He told me of the bites he couldn't hit that came after midnight, and of his fish, with an enormous tail and a huge paddle. Then he spoke of the unusual crimson blaze down the whole of one of its sides. Could it have been one of the big five? Possibly, but things were certainly getting inter-esting. I was keen to get back, but with the first frosts just weeks away and only limited fishing time, I decided it made more sense to stay away and be fully prepared for the start of the 1995–96 season.

I always view the close season as a beginning rather than an end. It's the period of nature's mending, and a good time to be walking the bank and learning for the coming season, where it's permitted of course. As April arrives, river flows are probably receding from their winter levels, revealing swims and areas of bank long since forgotten. Flow patterns change, and all-important shallows that will probably become barbel spawning sites begin to appear; for example, I often make notes of any near bank areas where the current flows beneath overhanging trees or thickets, how it is affected by the sunken roots – is it undercut, or does it back eddy? All such observations are much easier if undertaken before the leaves begin to cover the area. Time spent on the bank during the close season is never wasted.

I made a few visits to the Bristol Avon that spring, looking at other stretches as well as the twenty-yard bank, which in itself was a disappointment. I had hoped that whilst the thick growth of reed stems above were temporarily absent and the river level lower, I might find evidence of a channel moving upstream, to give a passage for downstream fish; but no such luck, unfortunately. The big five were obviously travellers, moving to the downstream deep stretch during the day, and upstream onto the twenty-yard bank after darkness.

We were to be disappointed just as the season began. The bank had become popular, and we made a seventy-five mile drive to find it occupied. But in spite of this it was worth persevering, and just fishing when we could.

Shane was the first to strike lucky, in mid-July taking a 10lb 5oz barbel, another red fish. Then in early September it was my turn, with a fish at 10lb 2oz, almost certainly Shane's fish from earlier in the season. The real breakthrough, however, was to come a week later, when Shane and Lee arrived together late one evening to fish through until the early hours. The river conditions couldn't have been better, with recent heavy rain just beginning to colour the river, which was rising. Much has been

A fine brace for Tony at 10lb and 11lb 4oz.

written in recent years about the effect a rising river has in inducing barbel to feed, and that in itself is true; but the trigger that starts the feeding frenzy is the introduction of colour into the water, and the optimum time to arrive is just as the river is beginning to rise. Once feeding, the barbel will continue until they are sated, usually for a period of a few hours. After that feeding spell, although the river might look perfect, the fish are replete and you've probably missed the party. The trick is catching it right by knowing your river.

Predictably at just around midnight, the bites began to Shane's rod. Lee was slightly downstream and couldn't get a bite, a stand-off that went on for an hour or so, much to his frustration. Half wanting to sort out the bites he was getting, and half wanting to involve Lee, Shane invited him to fish on his upstream shoulder. You guessed it: on Lee's first cast he hooked and landed a barbel of 13lb 1oz – needless to say, another red fish.

It would be a month before I could get to the Avon, and I couldn't wait. On this occasion the boys could not make it, and there were no other cars in the car park: I had the place to myself. 'An unexpected and pleasant surprise' I rather uncharitably thought as I began to walk across the open fields to the swim.

The soft earth and wet grass from the heavy rain over the last twenty-four hours was tugging at my boots and slowing me down. By now it was well into darkness, but I saw no point in arriving earlier, as the bites would almost certainly come after midnight. In another fifteen minutes I was walking the top of the bank, and could see that the river had already started to rise. Half climbing, half slipping, I arrived at the bottom of the eight-foot slope to find myself standing in two inches of water. The level must have risen by a foot, and the water was beginning to turn a lovely milky tea colour. 'That will do nicely', I thought.

With the rod set up I fastened a brass pan-type bait dropper to the size 6 hook, and gently introduced bait samples into the gap between the streamer weed in front of me, estimating the current would spread the pieces of flavoured hot dog in a line downstream. I always prefer to use smelly meat as bait in coloured water conditions. All that remained to be done was to clip a ½ oz bomb onto the line above the 12in braid trace, and gently swing the baited tackle into the head of the run, before sitting back in the chair to await proceedings.

As the next couple of hours passed I remember watching first my feet, then my ankles disappear under the rising water. The pressure on the 2ft of 8lb line being held off the reel by my left hand continued to shift with the constant sway of the streamer weed, but nothing indicated a bite. Another gentle up-hand cast took the bait even further down the swim, to perhaps three rod lengths now, and about where I estimated the bait samples to be.

I stiffened in the chair as the time passed midnight. The conditions were right, the time was right – and I remember thinking with the new day that it was my wedding anniversary, and that I shouldn't stay too late. Suddenly the spare line was pulled from the grasp of my fingers and the rod pulled over. How on earth did I miss that?! Surprised by the ferocity of the bite I just hoped I would get another chance as I re-cast to the same spot. Not only did I get another chance, I had another three over the next hour or so; but no matter how I changed the tackle, I managed to expertly miss them all. The group of five were certainly on my mind now. It had become frustrating, but what options did I have? There was the lower part of the swim just a couple of yards downstream: I could move there, but would it make any difference? I would still be above the fish, albeit closer. With time running short, that's what I decided to do, taking the gamble to cast slightly upstream in the hope that the fish would move up to the bait. An underhand cast and I felt the weight hit the bottom, bounce once, and settle. The rod went into the rest, and only then did I gingerly tighten to the weight and put tension on the rod top, crooking my index finger over the line above the reel. It worked a treat.

Within minutes the line slackened for a perfect drop-back bite, and this time I was connected to a very surprised barbel. Almost immediately my line slackened as the fish swam back past me before briefly pausing. I tightened to it and off it went downstream for the deeper water. Side pressure soon made the difference, bringing it reluctantly back to sulk doggedly in front of me. The to-ing and fro-ing between us lasted another couple of minutes before I managed to draw the fish over the rim of the net and it lay at my feet in what was now nine inches of water. The space was so confined I barely had room to move, or for that matter stay upright on the slippery, submerged clay bank. Up until now it was true to say the size of the fish in the net had not occurred to me, but I was soon to be amazed: a

barbel of 13lb 6oz, 32in (80cm) long, with a girth of just 17¾in (45cm); and yes, with deep crimson down the whole of its left flank.

At 2.30am I made a couple of calls to Basingstoke, desperate for photographs. What a relief when Shane and Lee agreed to get out of bed and make the 150-mile (240km) round trip. True to their word, an hour and a half later they turned up with a couple of cameras. Lee instantly recognized the fish as the same barbel he had caught less than a month earlier. To round off the story, Shane had to wait another year, but eventually caught the fish he richly deserved from the swim: at 12lb 2oz, this was a barbel of which we had no previous record, although it did have the characteristic red stain. Incidentally that was our last fish from the stretch before we moved on.

I often think about the enigma of the 'Big Five' and the 'Red Fish'. Quite why the affliction only affected one group of big barbel and no others is a mystery to me, and perhaps it is better that way.

Tony Hart with his BCC record of 13lb 6oz.

6 The Hampshire Avon

by Chris Thomson

A patient wait.

The Hampshire Avon rises on the Wiltshire chalk downs to the east of Devizes, bisecting Salisbury Plain as it flows south to Christchurch. Before entering Christchurch harbour the river takes in the famous Royalty Fishery, a mecca for both local and holidaying anglers for the best part of a century. The list of those who have graced its banks reads like a *Who's Who* of angling greats, and includes F. W. K. Wallis, the Warren brothers, Dick Walker and his contemporaries, and the Chiltern and Coventry Specimen Groups; the list is endless. In recent years the Royalty has once again begun to produce numbers of double-figure barbel – but it is upstream on the beautiful and often secluded middle reaches that the locals go in search of monsters. This is hard fishing, but the rewards are there to be had.

I will always look back on the 2002–03 season with great satisfaction. I have the photographs and the diary, but they only show the results. What they do *not* show is the slog, the driving, the mud, the tackle-laden 'yomping' or the mind games that go hand-in-hand with trying to capture a big Hampshire Avon barbel.

Middle Avon barbeling is the ultimate chess game, with you holding only pawns and the barbel holding all the major pieces. Location, timing, weather, water conditions, bait and baiting, plus rigs, all come into play, sometimes one at a time, and at others all at once. The three major factors are location, location and location: crack that nut, and you are 90 per cent there; foul it up, and the rest are irrelevant.

The Hampshire Avon around Ringwood contains pockets of nomadic barbel, some of which are of a size that makes me want to go through the pain and mental barrier and forsake everything, just to try and get one into my net. Most stretches in this area are either club or day-ticket waters. If you fancy the challenge, buy the map, walk the walks, keep your eyes and ears open, and it's not that difficult. The challenge starts once you have targeted a stretch.

My mate Steve Withers and I had targeted a couple of areas in previous seasons, and we had some superb fishing, with a little heartache thrown in for good measure. For the last couple of seasons we had been concentrating on a grueller of a stretch that we knew at certain times of the year could contain fish of the size we both wanted so badly. We also knew that we would have to pull out all stops if we wanted to try and capture one. Thus a Hampshire Avon 14lb barbel was on the cards if we had the commitment and the luck needed to grass the ultimate prize.

Despite the picture painted by the angling press, Avon 14s are rare, and although the average weight on many other rivers throughout the country has rocketed, the Avon has been slow in achieving that same meteoric growth explosion. Genetics? Baits? Exaggerated weights? Agricultural wash-off? Global warming? It's hard to draw a firm conclusion, but whatever the cause, the Avon barbel seem to live in the shadow of those of the Great Ouse or the Dorset Stour. As far as Steve and I are concerned, however, long may it continue! Despite all that is known, written or spoken about the Avon, there are still many stretches that are under-fished and overlooked – and we are as happy as Larry with that. A fourteen-pounder is a massive fish to us, and if nature decides that this will be the ultimate size of the big barbel that inhabit the Avon, then so be it; I'll never complain.

The stretch we were fishing had the potential pedigree and the atmosphere that made it a bit special, so we settled in ready for the long haul. All the criteria were spot on for a major result if we planned things correctly, fished it till our noses bled, and didn't walk under any ladders!

My personal best barbel previous to fishing this particular stretch had been 13lb 3oz, and then last season I bettered it with one of 13lb 4oz. I knew that if I played my cards right and with a little luck I could improve it further. The 2001–02 season had been really gruelling, but in addition to my personal best I had also landed three barbel in excess of 11lb, and one of 12lb 3oz in a total of sixteen fish; this meant that I was on the right track. I just needed to be in the right place at the right time when the big Avon 'gypsies' decided to drop in and have a munch. The major problem on the Middle Avon was that the fish we were targeting got itchy pectorals and covered huge distances. Over two complete summers, apart from odd fish and some 'nuisance' carp to 26lb, they had not seemed to inhabit the stretch during the warmer months.

Once into October and we started to pick up the occasional better fish. Steve had a brilliant night when he caught two twelve-pounders in a few hours – and on the Middle Avon that is one hell of a session. We stood there that night in the driving rain, the only two silly fools around for miles, and laughed about how *easy* it was at times, and how at others it can have you kicking your rods into the river.

Once Steve and I agree on a stretch to target, we then decide on a bait. Next to location I believe bait to be the biggest piece of the jigsaw. I am a firm believer in giving the barbel a 'food source' rather than just bait. A highly nutritious food source that is freely available to them is far more effective and consistent than just lobbing out a chunk of meat and hoping for the best; we had seen how devastating these types of bait had been in the carp world, and were quick to utilize these baits and use them on the Avon.

We had used fishmeal baits in the past and had proved how devastating they can be. Highly nutritious and attractive in all water conditions, we had both banked personal best fish by using them earlier on other stretches. I am 100 per cent convinced that we would not have been as successful had we been using (to us) inferior baits. We had not

The business end of an Avon monster.

Dusk on the Hampshire Avon.

found it necessary to bait excessively. Baiting was carried out after each session, and was dependent on the weather and water conditions. An upward trend on the barometer coupled with falling water temperature equates to just a few freebies in each swim. Conversely, if the barometer is falling and the water temperature rising, then up to a pound of bait may be scattered around half a dozen swims.

For this season we had decided to go for the ultimate food source and use a milk-protein HNV with low-level attractors, and an added enzyme to assist in the digestion process. This would help the barbel utilize the protein in the bait, and hopefully encourage them to actively seek out this easily available food source. We would start baiting from October when we hoped a few barbel would start to inhabit the area. An initial baiting cut back to a steady trickle throughout the rest of the season would, we hoped, deliver the goods. HNVs had worked for me before, giving me six different 12lb fish in a season, and I knew they would be effective here.

Rigs can be another piece of the jigsaw, and many factors can influence the correct rig to use; for example, pressure from other anglers, type of water

(regarding weed or snags), and size of barbel. I have always regarded rigs to be very important, and not just a means of tying a hook on with little or no thought as to what exactly is happening on the riverbed. I target low-density stretches with nomadic fish. If I am lucky enough to be in a swim where a big barbel moves through and decides to inspect the hook bait, then I need a rig that:

(a) won't arouse too much suspicion;
(b) cannot be easily ejected if picked up;
(c) is up to the job of landing the fish.

Nothing is left to chance with my rigs: they are changed after every session, line is tested before spooling up, knots are checked under a magnifier, and manufacturers' breaking strains and tolerances are tested and never taken as read.

I have used most of the rig-making items that are available, including braided hook lengths, Snakebite and Mantis stiff rigs; and I have finally narrowed the choice down to the following, which I consider to be the best anti-eject, anti-tangle rig I could use.

The hook has never let me down, and is strong enough to cope with big barbel in thick weed and

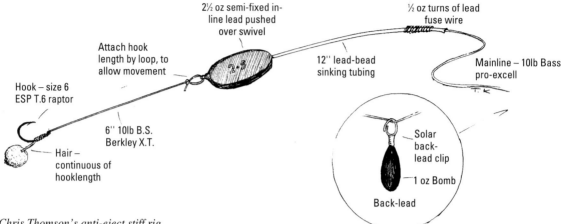

Chris Thomson's anti-eject stiff rig.

flood conditions. The short nylon hook link is stiff enough to cause the barbel problems if it tries to eject the bait. The heavy lead will hold bottom in increased flows, and will not roll out of the small holes and tangle in the weed amongst which I am usually fishing. Finally it will provide a bolt effect once the barbel moves off. The lead-based tubing is an anti-tangle aid, and also pins down the main line, which is essential when using short hook links. The back lead keeps the line out of sight and prevents drifting weed from building up and dragging the rig out of position. Main line is 10lb bs which, combined with a 1¾lb test curve rod, means that I can hopefully extract any barbel comfortably from the weediest of swims or the heaviest of floods.

So the scene was set. We had found a stretch that hopefully would give us the fish we really desired, and it did not suffer from over-fishing. The bait was designed to create some degree of 'I must eat that *now*' mentality, and rigs and tackle were designed to hopefully give us a 100 per cent ratio of hooking and landing. So how did we get on? Let me tell you about our 2002–03 season, and how it surpassed everything I had hoped for.

Almost all our fishing is done after dark, particularly from autumn onwards when the days get shorter, so it was important that the stretch we had selected allowed us to have a few hours' fishing after dark. Work and family commitments decree that we hardly ever get to fish day stints. It is a hard slog finishing work, grabbing the tackle, a pasty and a flask, racing forty-odd miles down the motorway in rush-hour traffic, trudging through the fields in the fading light, fishing till late, trudging back, driving back up the motorway and crashing into bed in the small hours. It really is about capitalizing on the times when the river is 'hot', yet still maintaining a

presence when it is 'cold'. We mostly fished two nights a week, sometimes three. My long-suffering wife was getting used to my absence, my work mates getting bored with asking 'Did you catch last night, Tommo?' and getting the moody reply 'Nah'. My two-year-old daughter could only identify me through old photos! Don't talk to me about fishing being a relaxing pastime.

The Magnificent Fourteen-Pounder

After a summer of low barbel activity with just a few carp to show for my efforts, it was not until the beginning of September that I landed my first barbel. This was prior to our using the HNV bait, and it was caught on a Mainline NRG boilie. At 12lb 10oz it was a cracking fish with which to open the score. Following that fish I didn't hook anything until midway through October. At this stage we started to fish HNV, and a fish of 9lb 1oz at least proved that any barbel around would actually eat the stuff. A couple of days later a 10lb 2oz fish graced the net, and confidence was growing. Both fish fell to hook-bait-only tactics, a method in which I have great confidence. I could write an article on this subject alone, but my basic question is, how many free offerings do you really believe are necessary in your swim before a barbel is tempted to pick up the one attached to a hook? I knew the bait was one the barbel would find attractive and which gave out the signal '*food*' – so why complicate the issue with hemp, pellets and other boilies? Single hook-bait tactics require 100 per cent confidence in your choice of bait and swim, and are highly effective; enough said!

I was fishing a swim we called the 'Motorway', an area of water roughly seventy-five yards long and which looked perfect at certain times of the year, especially if the rain had pushed up the river levels. The whole stretch had depth right under the rod tip, shelving away towards mid-river, and the pace was steady and smooth. It was an area where I could imagine a lone barbel residing for a period during its travels, and it was unfished by any of the locals. I'd caught my 13lb 4oz personal best from here the previous season, and although it couldn't be called the most prolific area on the stretch, it could throw up a big lump: it didn't let me down!

On 22 October I banked a 12lb 1oz specimen, and my confidence was growing stronger with each session. Then a couple of weeks later from the same swim a massive 13lb 10oz fish came my way again on the single hook-bait tactic, and I was starting to believe that this was going to be my season. The bait was working, I'd broken my personal best, and it was still only November.

I skipped across the fields that night elated and brimming with confidence. I prayed that the weather would be kind, and that Lady Luck would smile on us. I worked hard to convince the wife that I needed to be down there, and that I would have to neglect my marital and fatherly duties. Bless her, she left me! – No! only joking. She understands my passion and addiction – though she did warn me 'Don't push it, Tommo.'

In the period up to Christmas I struggled, despite fishing hard and as effectively as possible. The weather was poor, and despite our best efforts we concluded that the barbel had disappeared again. Furthermore Christmas was approaching, and working in London, preparing a two-year-old's Christmas, and wrestling with trees, baubles and tinsel, meant my time was being pulled this way and that. When I was fishing I was exhausted, and the dark cold nights were getting me down. Even so, I was still convinced that if the barbel showed, I'd be in with a shout – and then a window of opportunity opened for me. Three days before Christmas I managed to fish a session during which there was a warm flush of rain and a rapid rise in temperature. Surprisingly I found myself alone on the river.

The water looked perfect, and it was still light as I lowered my rig just off the edge of the bank. I put the rod down, turned round to find my flask – and out of the corner of my eye noticed my reel handle spinning. I grabbed the rod, and suddenly I was attached to a large, powerful barbel. I drew the fish into the net and laid it on the grass. Steve came walking down, and we weighed her at 13lb 10oz. An equal personal best, and caught within seconds of the bait hitting the bottom: as easy as that! An hour later I had a 12lb 6oz fish, a fantastic brace, and I don't really remember driving home that night. Christmas was going to be good.

I had a few days off at Christmas, but my fishing was going to be limited. The only opportunity I was going to have would be the day before New Year's

Chris with an awesome Avon barbel of 12lb 6oz.

This 13lb 10oz fish was half of a brace that included another huge barbel of 12lb 6oz.

Eve, and not much of that. The 30 December found me down on the river doing an early morning stint. I recorded the water temperature at 50°F, and at 7am took a 9lb 12oz barbel. I had a hunch that another good fish could be banked, so when I went home later in the morning I pleaded my case to the wife for a pass out later in the day. That evening found me again trudging through the mud and the descending gloom down to the river. I jumped in the swim from which I'd had the big brace, and quickly had an eight-pounder, followed an hour and a half later by another of 13lb 3oz. The bait was certainly selecting the bigger fish for me, and I drove home tired, but grinning from ear to ear. I celebrated New Year's Eve big style that night, convinced Lady Luck was riding with me, and hoping that perhaps I could winkle out another lump or two before the end of the season.

The weather decided against that, and a period of cold weather, high pressure and little or no rain meant that everyone seemed to be struggling. Were the fish still there, and were we good enough? All was quiet until the middle of January, when a session produced a 10lb 0oz barbel, and then later a 6lb 10oz chub – big fish, wrong species. I then struggled until the week before the end of the season. A Saturday night (fishing) session was offered to me by the wife. I umm'd and aah'd, but decided to go up there and see what was about; and if the car park was full I'd go back home, have a beer

or three and chill out. But when I got there I couldn't believe it – a week to go to the end of the season, and not a soul about: the stretch was mine. I rang Steve and badgered him to come down, as this seemed an opportunity too good to miss. I trudged down the fields and settled into the swim in which I'd had my most successful sessions. The water temperature was 46°F, so I felt reasonably confident that something could be feeding.

I had decided to fish until 'kicking off' time, and give it a real bash. Steve eventually came down at dusk and settled downstream from me, and the wait began. A few fish had rolled mid river which encouraged us no end and yet I still hadn't had a single pluck. Out of the corner of my eye I saw a fish quietly roll just downstream of my swim, and I got it into my head that I had to move to where I saw the fish roll. This in itself was odd, as once I'm in a swim I very rarely move. I cast about two rod lengths out with a walnut-size PVA bag of pellets and a 6in nylon hook line with a 3oz lead. I was now fishing in virgin territory, out of the hotspot, and fishing the downstream end of the swim where no one ever fished. Hunch, intuition or inspired piece of genius: who knows? I sat there until ten minutes before I was planning to pack in, when the rod top ever so slowly pulled down.

I picked it up and wound into a fish. At first nothing happened, then suddenly it woke up and tore upstream – and I knew I was into another big barbel.

After a few minutes I had her in the net, and as soon as I flicked on my torch and peered into the net I knew that this was something special. There lay an absolute goliath of a barbel, and I called out to Steve to 'Get here pronto and have a look!' We carried her onto the bank and carefully weighed her on two sets of scales, with only the owls as witnesses. We whooped and hollered like a couple of lunatics: 14lb 1oz of pure Avon magic, and a magnificent fish. Steve couldn't have been more pleased if he'd caught it himself. We fish as a team, sharing ideas and geeing each other up when the going gets tough. As far as I was concerned *we* caught that fish, and not just me; the success belonged to both of us.

After much photographing and a careful inspection for identification marks, we slid her back and sipped coffee under a starry sky on the banks of a very special river. We talked about how hard it had been, and yet how easy it sometimes was. We tried to rationalize it all, and failed. Fishing is fishing: no guarantees, no dead certainties, and all we could say is that we'd given it our best shot. We'd done the groundwork, and found a stretch that contained big barbel at times. We baited and fished an effective bait, and fished it until our heads hurt – and your head *will* hurt if you get the urge to catch a Middle Avon monster. I know I pushed it to the limit at times with my home life, and all I can say is, that it was worth all the grief. You will still find me somewhere up there, putting in the hours and pushing it to the limits; there's no other way. The addiction has no known cure, thank God!

Chris with a 14lb 1oz Hampshire Avon stunner.

7 The Warwickshire Avon

by Steve Chell

Weirs, weirs, weirs! Whenever I begin a campaign on a new river, particularly one such as the Warwickshire Avon that contains somewhat localized populations of barbel, I want to be where the fish are, and for me the surest locator of *barbus barbus* is a weir. If I cannot catch in the weir pools, then the main river in that area will probably not see me at all.

The Warwickshire Avon rises from the hills of the Warwickshire/Leicestershire border near the civil war battle site of Naseby. It flows west through the towns of Warwick, Stratford-on-Avon and Evesham before entering the Severn near Tewkesbury. The river is a tributary itself (of the Severn), and also has its own tributaries: the Leam, Stour and Arrow. Basically a lowland river, it flows sedately through rich pastureland often bordered by a variety of fruit orchards for which this part of the Midlands is famous. Regularly punctuated by weirs that are by-passed by short boat channels, the river is a magnet for tourists who wish to spend their holidays afloat. The margins are lined with reedmace, bulrush and cabbages, and freshwater snails are thriving since the river's water-treatment plants have been improved to EU standards: a more perfect environment for rapid barbel growth is difficult to imagine.

Fortunately for me, the Avon possesses a whole host of weirs, and therefore starting points for my barbel exploration. From above Stratford to Strensham near Tewksbury they all hold barbel, and not tiddlers either. Once I find some fish on a weir I gradually extend my fishing area downstream in order to better assess the barbel population and size, and to locate holding and feeding areas. It would appear that on a slow-flowing lowland river such as the Avon, which for large lengths has a relatively uniform depth and pace, the barbel spawn on the gravel shallows on the run-offs to many of the weirs. Consequently they can be found close to these shallows during the early season. More importantly they can also be found there at their optimum weights towards the back end of the season prior to spawning.

All the usual barbel tactics will catch fish on the Avon, with swimfeeder maggot being one of the most consistent methods. Even in the depths of winter good fish can still be taken in low, green, cold water conditions. Lots of stretches now produce barbel in healthy numbers, but the most prolific areas appear to be on the most popular, heavily fished stretches that contain well known snag swims. Such 'peggy' areas are not for me, however, as I have no wish to join the rat race for the 'going swim'. My approach is largely a roving one, so I steer clear of summer fishing when the banks are more populous, and concentrate mainly on autumn and winter – particularly winter. My autumn fishing is primarily concerned with identifying new locations, whereas in winter I am looking to catch some bigger fish from previously identified areas.

The evening weir, sunset in Shakespeare country.

A moonlight double from the Warwickshire Avon.

A typical season would see me making a start on the river in September, simply looking to catch a barbel. Initially I would target a weir in early evening, and then extend my search downstream towards dusk. I might give the weir a couple of hours as I search the various holding spots with a single bait: this might be lobworm or pellets, but is more often meat-based, my favourite being bacon grill, especially when cut into long thin slivers or flakes, which allows the bait to lift and flap enticingly in the current. I will be touch legering at all times as I am constantly 'stop-starting' the bait as it travels around the pool. This means that I stop its progress for a minute or three against a weedbed, in a back eddy, or perhaps by some boulders before tweaking the line and starting it off on its travels once again. During this process I am often recovering line, particularly so in high water, to keep in contact with the bait as the flow dictates its movement between stops. My lead will usually be a drilled bullet, which is far easier to roll around a swim or weir pool than a conventional lead. After a couple of hours in the pool I will work my way downstream, spending about twenty to thirty minutes in each swim employing similar tactics, but switching to a plasticine weight where the flow allows. This enables a more accurate and easier balancing of the end rig.

A couple of years ago I had a session along these lines, making my first cast in the bright sunshine of a late summer evening. I had only a short time to fish before a meeting, and so had to get the presentation right very quickly. In the low, stale conditions I opted for a two SSG shot rig with a short tail, and inched the bait into a back eddy where it was drawn towards the weir sill, figuring that the fish would be lying in the most oxygenated water. It took two casts to get the presentation right. The bite when it came was a single tap, and with a wide, sweeping strike I was soon into a powerful fish. From my position it appeared to be trying to swim right underneath the weir, and furthermore to have achieved this objective by some four or five yards. It was a couple of minutes before I was able to exert a measure of control – and the result, after a mere forty minutes' fishing, was a Catchers' river record and our first double from the river at 10lb exactly. How I enjoyed our regional meeting an hour later!

At present for all my fishing I use a braided mainline, as I believe touch and feel are the most important aspects in bite detection. Due to its reduced stretch, this type of line gives me quicker feedback regarding the nature of the riverbed over which I am presenting my bait; I find this especially useful in weir pools. Is the barbel brushing the line, mouthing the bait, picking it up and swimming upstream, or eating it on the spot? Each of these actions transmits different sensations down the line, and with experience and practice one can generally differentiate between them. At this time of the year I

Dusk, and as the sun sets, anticipation rises.

am also casting into those areas that are usually unfishable for most of the winter due to the increased flow levels; these can be near-bank snags or rafts, far-bank overhanging bushes, narrowings of the river, weir sills – the list goes on.

It was from one such swim during the autumn of 2002 that I landed a new river personal best of almost 12lb. I used the minimal flow of the low water conditions to inch the bait down a narrowing. The depth increased under some overhanging branches past a near-bank snag. This swim has everything a barbel angler could wish for, except that it is unfishable in winter once the level rises more than a foot. The first session in this swim produced a nine, the second a foul-hooked lump of a fish that I pulled out of, and the third a seven before I tried a number of other spots without success. It was now dark, and I had the choice of moving to a different stretch with a prolific weir, or negotiating my way back to the swim through dense brambles and over fallen boughs.

At this point Lady Luck put in an appearance, and I chose to have another go in the swim. That evening the river was about six inches above its normal level, and casting to the far bank allowed me to swing the bait easily under the overhanging branches some eight yards below me. At first all was quiet, so I lifted the rod and let out a bit more line. Nothing; so with my nerves on edge I repeated the process. The bait, now well below the branches and down by the snag, was quickly taken – but this time it was no seven-pounder. The rod immediately took on its fighting curve and hooped right round as the fish

forced a few feet of line off the clutch. I simply had to hold her. I had the rod parallel to water in order to keep the line out of the branches as I clamped down hard. Against this pressure she thrashed the surface well below the branches, and then dived for the bottom and the snag. I tried to stand up to change the angle of pull, but the power of her efforts had me slipping on the bank, and I sat down rather than fall in. My heart was racing and my knees had gone to jelly as I attempted to pump some line back, and a mighty tail showered spray into the air as she boiled directly beneath the trailing branches. Something was going to have to give, and thankfully it was the fish, as she kited right and then left and came upstream hugging the bottom. Once she was on a short line I slackened off and lifted her to the surface where she rolled, a long and glistening prize in the moonlight. She went straight into the net, and I made her secure and left her in the water for a few minutes to give us both a rest and let my pounding heart and shaking hands regain their composure.

What a scrap and what a barbel: it is times like this that make me realize why I spend so many of my days and nights out in all weathers in search of the contact that can produce such an adrenalin rush. Since then a number of trips have been blanks as the flow of the winter months caused the fish to move and spread out into other areas of the river. Incidentally at no time while fishing this swim did I introduce any bait other than that which was on the hook – flavoured bacon grill – and this is the case on the majority of my sessions. My philosophy is that I'm not going to give any barbel the chance to

Winter action.

compare my hook bait with a number of free offerings. I prefer to give the fish one choice only: do you want it, yes or no?

If some swims become off limits in winter, there are still plenty from which barbel can be caught. For me, the main river comes into its own after heavy rain, especially when the level has been up to the top of the bank or beyond and is just starting to drop; there are then plenty of creases and slacks just waiting to be searched. At this time of the year I tend to give each swim up to an hour, leaving the bait out longer and not moving it as frequently, in order to let the fish home in on any flavour/attractant trail it might be emitting. I always prefer to find my fish, rather than wait for them to come to me, so I still use roving tactics. If I have not elicited a response close in after about half a dozen swims have been fished, I change tactics, and upstream leger in the middle wherever the flow is at walking pace and undisturbed by boils.

This reminds me of a day on the river some two seasons back: when I arrived at the water the level was some five feet up, coloured and falling. Fishing a slack behind a bush, my first cast with a free-lined meatball proved fruitless. My second cast only repositioned the bait by a couple of feet, but I was soon into a barbel that tore off for the middle of the river. After a good scrap a nine-pounder was duly weighed in. Fishing with my friend Dave, we then proceeded to try a number of other similar near-bank swims, but without success – and then the penny dropped: the fish were in the flow. So that's where we fished, upstreaming with balanced leads of 1oz to 1½ oz depending upon the swim, and promptly caught a number of medium-sized barbel to liven up a grey, raw winter afternoon.

Towards the end of the season it's the weirs that get most of my attention, particularly when the river

is two to three feet up, whether rising or falling. The barbel seem to lie just off the most turbulent water, and are quite tightly shoaled, so that a smelly bait can be taken at any time. Bites most often occur when the bait comes naturally to rest as one searches the pool with the lightest lead one can get away with; this is invariably a piece of plasticine, or a drilled bullet if the flows and eddies are rather strong. The line is continually tweaked to move the bait to a fresh spot, while a few turns of the reel will be needed to keep one's finger on the line in touch with the lead, to enable bites to be identified. Fish too heavily, and the bait will not move, but will stick to boulders and dead weedbeds, inhibiting a natural presentation. Fish too lightly, and you will fail to locate the possible holding areas as your bait will simply lie directly downstream of you, or run uncontrolled into a snag. Experience teaches one to get it just right, and you can search the spot in the flow that your senses have identified as being potentially the best holding area. I cannot emphasize strongly enough how critical it is to get the weight and balance just right – and a session that I had towards the end of last season illustrates this point.

The river was three feet up and dropping, and I fished a number of swims well downstream of a weir during the afternoon, believing the barbel still to be in the deeper water where they spend most of the winter. Chub, chub and more chub was all I had to show for three hours' effort when I went to see how Dave was doing on the weir. I found him heading towards me, as the deafening noise of the water was getting too overpowering for him. However, he had found some fish. It had taken him an hour of searching to locate them, but then he had taken four, with the last a cracking, fat eleven-pounder. My turn now, as Dave reckoned they were still feeding. But alas, all seemed dead, with the usual areas close in alongside the first main flow not producing. Nevertheless, bearing in mind the time it had taken Dave to succeed, I examined the flow pattern and widened my search to the eddies on the further side of the pool. I used a larger bullet, which I kept changing until I felt it was heavy enough to enable me to keep in touch with the bait, but light enough to give me control over its movement across the river bed.

The next ninety minutes produced five barbel plus one lost fish, the fourth being an immaculate ten-pounder. Whee-hah! Two days later I returned and took two more, but with the level now only a foot up, the barbel were well scattered and the fishing was a lot harder. Despite it being early February, frosty, windy and dark, those whiskered beauties were willing to give me a chance on a quiet and deserted river. What more could any barbel angler wish for? Perhaps for that next bite to produce a memory of a lifetime, always a possibility nowadays on the ever-improving Warwickshire Avon.

My Twelve-Pounder by Mick Wood

It was inevitable that the Warwickshire Avon would eventually play a major part in my barbel-fishing plans, as it was the river from which I caught my first ever barbel. The events of that August day, way back in 1978, are still ingrained in my mind. The day was hot, but the river was a foot up after a sustained spell of mid-summer rain. I had begun by trotting corn for the large numbers of chub that inhabited Offenham Ford, but the increased flow had made this hard work and so, unusually in those days, I resorted to leger tactics. I did not have to wait long before the rod thumped round and my first barbel was soon in the net, all 4lb 6oz of it. I can also recall singing all the way home on my motorbike.

Although barbel were far from unheard of in the Warwickshire Avon in those days, the capture of one in a match would often be reported as significant news in the weeklies, and this increased the sense of achievement.

For the next two decades my visits to this river were sporadic and without specific intention of targeting barbel, but in the year 2000 all that changed. A good friend of mine was on the committee of a small village syndicate near Stratford, and had offered the venue for the Barbel Catchers annual fish-in. The stretch in question was unfished

by barbel anglers, so I thought it might be prudent to have a test fish before the big day. The time had come to return.

When I lived a few miles from the Avon in the late 1970s, the upstream limit for barbel was considered to be the weir by Lucy's Mill in Stratford. Slowly, but surely, the species has spread, until the area around Warwick is now well worth the attention of the barbel specialist. Matches at Barford are often won with barbel.

Also found in abundance are bream and chub, with a fair few tench and the occasional carp. The large number of other species present dictated my initial tactics on the syndicate stretch where my campaign would begin. I decided to feed heavily in order to wade through the chub and bream in search of the barbel. It is interesting how different anglers develop different solutions to the same problem. Whereas I chose the static approach, Steve Chell, as he has previously explained, followed a different route, preferring the roving approach to static fishing. I knew from talking to Steve that he was justifiably confident in his methods, but I was not sure whether or not the chub population was quite as high on his venues. I had been forewarned, and so when in July 2000 I once again ventured forth onto the Avon, I was weighed down with as much bait as tackle.

For the first 'test fish' I was joined by fellow Catchers Steve Smith, Pete Tesch and Dave Oakes. We met for a pub lunch before heading for the river. Dave's chosen swim was an 'Avon Special' and he caught over twenty chub! Pete and I also had our share of chub, but we still found barbel, with fish of 6lb 3oz and 7lb 10oz respectively: a promising start.

Steve Chell with 11lb 14oz of 'autumn magic'.

Early success for Mick Wood on a new stretch.

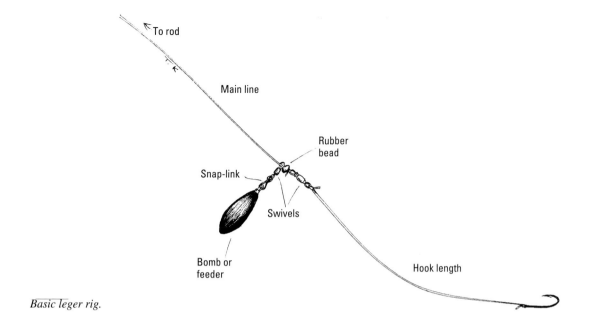

To rod

Main line

Rubber
bead

Snap-link

Swivels

Bomb or
feeder

Hook length

Basic leger rig.

Any minute now?

We had fed quite heavily with hemp, corn, chopped meat and casters, with both barbel falling to meat on basic leger rigs. When I returned to the venue in August, I thought I would try the static approach once again, but only feeding lightly, in the hope that perhaps this would attract fewer chub onto my feed. Therefore during an afternoon session I fed just two pints of the same mixed feed instead of the gallon used previously; but the result was just the same. I managed several chub, an eel, a tench and two barbel, with the best one going 7lb 13oz. I had spent the whole session being plagued by fast, snatchy chub bites, despite fishing with 8lb line straight through to a size 6 hook with the same basic leger rig. I had fed initially with a dropper, topping up at intervals when the swim went quiet. Perhaps the constant drip of loose feed would attract a different response?

The river downstream of Stratford runs at a decent pace and averages around six feet in depth away from the weirs, so loose feeding in mid-river might be difficult to judge. My thoughts were that if you don't try out new approaches, then you don't learn anything, so a catapult would travel south with me in September. This was the occasion of the BCC national fish-in, though as things turned out, the Avon was in dour mood. Over two days I managed two very small barbel, and one at 6lb. And the whole lot of us barely managed a chub between us!

The Avon was by now forever flowing through my thoughts. Next summer I would try laying-on tactics so that I could loose feed accurately by hand; but in October 2000 this turned out not to be an option. For the first time I found the Avon with extra water in it, and so resorted to feeding hemp and finely diced meat with a dropper. A basic link-leger rig was set up once again with a size 6 Drennan Super Specialist tied direct to 8lb Maxima. The rod was a 1.5lb Seer Specialist, and an ounce was required to just hold bottom.

The first cast had not been in place long when the rod took off, and a new river best of 8lb 6oz was soon admiring the autumn sunshine. A few chub put in an appearance with almost tedious inevitability, but late in the afternoon a smaller barbel of about 5lb was added to the first. It had already been a most enjoyable session. At around tea time my brother Kevin arrived for a chat, just as everything seemed to go quiet. I sat touch legering as we talked in the fading light, and I then noticed a narrow boat approaching from the distant downstream bend. The

An October fish to Mick of 9lb 7oz.

Mick with the club river record of 12lb 2oz.

A fine fish to warm up a cold February day.

lateness of the season meant that the boat traffic had been light, and as the brightly painted craft passed over my swim the shift in water pressure caused my line to go slack. I felt the faintest of plucks on the line and struck, at which point my rod tip started to follow the boat. 'Sorry, mate!' exclaimed the helmsman, but as he stopped the boat the rod tip carried on going! My new-found adversary suddenly woke up and ripped the rod around in the opposite direction as it turned downstream. In common with every barbel I have caught from the Avon, the fish seemed happy to cruise powerfully up and down the main channel making no effort to reach any kind of sanctuary, and soon she was mine.

My brother and I craned forward side by side as I parted the mesh of my landing net and beheld a quite stunning barbel. Compared to the long, lean fish resulting from the more limited feeding of my native Yorkshire rivers, the barbel before me could almost have been a different species. Its depth in relation to length seemed incredible, and I struggled to hold it across the shoulders as I quickly removed the hook. Even the boating family had stopped to watch the excitement, and had crowded onto the stern of their craft to hear the result of the weighing: 12lb 2oz, after previously catching only eleven barbel from the river. What a contrast to my barbel fishing in Yorkshire, and what a barbel!

8 The Cherwell

by Tony Miles

The River Cherwell rises in the Northamptonshire countryside close to the town of Daventry. It crosses the border into Oxfordshire close to the civil war battle site of Cropredy Bridge. The river then turns south running closely alongside the Oxford canal, from which it separates upstream of Kidlington. It then travels a singular course through Oxford before joining the Thames.

My involvement with the stretch of the Oxfordshire Cherwell in question began as long ago as 1967, when I first chub fished it in the company of Merv Wilkinson just after I had started the Coventry Specimen Group. In the summer of 1968 I was to spot a small barbel, only one fish it is true, about 2lb, but a barbel for all that. That information would not be called upon for another nineteen years. I was to take a few Cherwell barbel at a different stretch between 1984 and 1986, but this became so popular that I felt compelled to find a new area that was lightly fished, if possible. That is when the memory of that two-pounder in the 1960s came flooding back: thus was my next venue decided, and in early September 1987 I arrived on its banks for the first time since the seventies.

Much had changed. My favourite chub swim under the high clay bank had gone, swept away by the dredging in the 1970s, although enough years had passed for nature to have healed the worst of the scars. One long stretch was heavily overgrown with cabbages, and, peering over the dense bankside

foliage, I distinctly caught a flash of orange alongside a small clump of mid-river rushes. Moments later, a barbel of about 7lb drifted into view.

That was the only barbel I was to see on that preliminary excursion, but I was back the following week properly geared up with a gallon of hemp. This time there were three smaller barbel in the little clearing, and it seemed likely that there were probably enough fish to make their pursuit worthwhile, although I hadn't yet seen a big fish. That was soon to change, however.

On arrival I baited the swim with fifteen droppers of hemp, and then left the barbel to feed in peace while I investigated other swims. Several hours later, having located two other swims containing one very small barbel apiece, I was back in the prepared pitch. As I carefully peered through the head-high sedges, I caught my breath in barely contained excitement. There were now five barbel feeding with gusto over the clean gravel, the two newcomers being much bigger fish; one I estimated at about 8lb, but the other looked a definite double. I had stumbled onto a gold mine, and a neglected one at that, judging by the overgrown nature of the banks.

The rest of that day was spent in total frustration. For hour after hour the barbel completely ignored my meat hook baits, and when I left just after dark I hadn't had a sign of a bite. Success, however, came the following week. I had reached the conclusion that the large hook bait had to be the problem and baited with hemp, corn and casters on my arrival. The same five barbel were soon in evidence, but they steadfastly refused both corn and caster hook baits. And then it occurred to me that I might be missing the obvious. Perhaps I ought to use a truly natural bait for these virgin fish. Accordingly, I fetched my bucket of lobworms from the van and baited with two of the biggest.

Crouching behind the rushes, I waited patiently until the barbel had made one of their temporary excursions out of the swim, and then I silently lowered the worms to rest on the bed of hemp. That done, I settled behind the bankside foliage, my eyes glued to the quivertip. Although I couldn't see my hook bait from my sitting position, as it was obscured by a small clump of cabbages, I could see the gravel upstream of the bait, from where the barbel always entered the swim. When I caught sight of them returning I remember vividly how tensed up I was. My excitement increased to fever pitch as the leading barbel thrust its snout under the cabbages. Within seconds, the tip thumped round and that was the prelude to two hours' fishing that saw me land four of the five fish present. The first three were average fish of between 5lb and 6lb 10oz, but when I weighed the fourth I let out a whoop of joy that was probably heard in Oxford. At 10lb 3oz in weight, it was one of the most memorable fish of my career. It was also very distinctive, with a badly distorted pelvic fin in the shape of a double V. I would have no trouble recognizing that fish again.

On my arrival the following week, there were seven barbel present in the swim, all over 7lb, with two more that could have been nines. Certainly the small fish that I had caught the previous week were absent, which meant that at least four of those in front of me were new fish. As each week passed, this new stretch was becoming more exciting.

As I quietly studied those barbel, an eighth fish slowly emerged from the upstream cabbages. Before my astonished gaze, here was a true leviathan, a fish that appeared all of 13lb. Having found such an incredible barbel, the fates then played a cruel trick on me: after that day, when I couldn't raise a bite whatever I tried, the river was too coloured to find fish visually for *two years*. Only a few days later, heavy rain raised the level to that of winter, and although I still fished hard, only chub rewarded my efforts.

The following season was equally frustrating. A combination of algal blooms and heavy rains meant that not once was I able to locate barbel visually for the entire season. Once again, I had to be content with chub and one average barbel from fishing blind.

Tony Miles' Twelve-Pounder

In the summer of 1989 the river was low and clear, and I made my first visit to the barbel stretch in early September. My initial investigations were disappointing, because despite baiting several areas with hemp, I failed to tempt any barbel from under the

A long-cherished ambition fulfilled for Tony: 10lb 3oz.

The Cherwell is one of several Thames tributaries that hold barbel.

dense cabbages. And then at around midday, I was standing on a high bank adjacent to dense trees, when something moved only inches from the near bank, right under my feet, where there was a small clump of streamer. I watched carefully, and eventually was rewarded with the sight of a huge barbel tail.

For ten minutes I stood there quietly, watching the spot intently, and presently the fish very obligingly backed out slowly from the cover, did a little tour of the immediate vicinity, then resumed its station under its streamer frond. I now knew that right under my feet was the monster of two years before.

The problem was, how would I land it if I hooked it? Where I stood was a tiny gap in a dense thirty-yard length of tangled willows, alders and brambles, that hung well out from the high bank, at least four feet above water level. Dropping hemp and a hook bait where I had seen the fish would be no problem, but landing a big barbel would be difficult, if not impossible. Even with the landing net handle at full extension I could only just reach the surface of the water over the brambles. Still, the geography of the swim gave me no other choice, and so I commenced a three-hour baiting programme in which I gradually

introduced three pints of hemp and a tin of corn. In the early evening, I crept into position.

Only seconds after I had swung out my corn hook bait, I found myself attached to an average chub, and the trouble I had landing it over the brambles convinced me that it would be an impossible task with a huge barbel. Before re-casting, therefore, I stripped down to shorts, knowing that I would have to take a flying leap over those brambles if I hooked the monster.

In the event, when I did hook the barbel, about twenty minutes later, the fight was a very short-lived affair. On feeling the hook, the fish shot upstream past me at high speed, before turning abruptly back on itself and diving down into the tangle of bramble roots close to where I had hooked it. Momentarily there was an ominous grating on the line, a sudden sharp crack, and the limp line came fluttering back in the warm evening breeze.

Disappointingly, I never saw the big one in that swim the following week, and wandered upriver and prepared several other areas. In one, about ten yards upstream of the clearing where I had caught the ten-pounder two years before, I had a quick glance of a big fish as it disappeared under an overhanging bush.

In mid-afternoon, that same fish reposed in my landing net, having accepted a bunch of corn seconds after it had been introduced. Although I was pleased to get another Cherwell double, at 10lb 1oz, my pleasure was muted somewhat, because it was a recapture: as soon as it had rolled into the net I had recognized my ten-pounder of two years previously.

That fish set off an interesting chain of events. Once again, it had fought very hard and I was in mid-river, nursing the fish back to strength, when I suddenly became aware that I was being watched. After all the time I had spent with the river to myself, or so I thought, I had been found at the worst possible moment, returning a double-figure barbel. The angler recognized me, and confided that Simon Lush had taken a fish of 12lb 1½ oz a few days before. That was my first inkling that Simon was fishing the stretch. Was the 12lb fish the one I had lost? It was interesting to speculate. Also interesting was that my companion mentioned a capture he had made, of a foul-hooked, very short, fat barbel of 10lb 10oz that certainly wasn't my ten-pounder. So there was a third double which, from the description, could be one of the fish I had estimated at 9lb.

The next day saw my first visual evidence that something untoward was happening as far as sweetcorn was concerned. Although I took fish of 6lb and 8lb on corn, I did see several fish in three different swims apparently spook quite badly at the sight of the yellow grains, even though I was using it very sparingly. The next session would see casters and maggots used in place of corn. On my return home I telephoned Simon, both to congratulate him on a magnificent capture and to correct any possible false impression that I was chasing his fishing. We were able to compare notes, and agreed that in future, we would keep each other informed of developments. It was only a few days later that I was to be back on the telephone.

The following Thursday is a major highlight in my angling memories. Only minutes after my arrival in mid-morning, I spotted four big fish in the cabbages. Two looked like nine-pounders, one was my old friend with the distorted pelvic, and the other was the monster I had lost several weeks before. Was this Simon's twelve-pounder? I decided that what I had to do was resist fishing for these fish prematurely, possibly spooking them, and feed the swim with maggots, casters and hemp on and off all day, while I actually fished elsewhere. I decided not to position a hook bait in the hot spot until dusk.

At twilight, I carefully crept into position and lowered a large bunch of casters on a size 6 to rest amongst the cabbages. Perhaps five minutes passed and then the rod top bounced. My hand tightened round the reel seat in readiness and, sure enough, the rod top suddenly dipped viciously downwards. My firm strike was followed by an angry buzz of the clutch as a huge fish shot upstream. In the half light a tremendous dorsal and upper tail lobe broke

Tony displays his long-standing club river record of 12lb 5oz.

surface as the fish powered towards the rushes. I caught my breath in excitement. I must make no mistake this time. The battle was fittingly memorable for such a historic occasion, and when at last that mammoth barbel sagged into my net, with me again in the river with it, I knew that not only had I caught a personal best, I had obliterated it. I will never forget the euphoria of the moment when my scales steadied at 12lb 5oz.

The following week, Simon and I were able to confirm that his and my fish were indeed one and the same. We were both agreed that, despite its weight, it looked an old fish that was going back in condition. I don't think I was far out in my estimation of 13lb when I first found the fish in 1987.

In the weeks that followed that memorable night, both Simon and I went on to catch many more barbel, including another new double to me only seven days later, of 11lb 4oz; this one I quickly re-caught at 10lb 12oz. Apart from that fish, almost every other barbel landed for the remainder of that season was a recapture, the only exception being an immaculate 9lb 9oz winter fish. The only known big fish I hadn't caught was the short fat one, and when I had that, in June 1990 at 11lb 3oz, I realized that I would soon be moving on. I now knew every big barbel in the stretch by sight, and further fishing would simply be going over old ground. In any event, news of our catches was spreading fast, as it always will, and the intrusions of other anglers imposed irksome restrictions on my fishing.

Only a season later, my association with the Cherwell came to an end, and I moved to the new pastures of the Great Ouse. I did briefly flirt with a different stretch of the Cherwell, which I kept strictly to myself, and did manage a cracking fish of 11lb 7oz on my first serious session. But that turned out to be a false dawn, as I was not to take another barbel in over twenty visits.

I learned some valuable lessons on the Cherwell, not least the value of being able to recognize individual specimens. When in 1990 Simon and I both foul-hooked the twelve-pounder – or 'Granny' as we affectionately christened her – we both made the decision to move on. Interestingly, the big fish being caught from the river today are the same batch of fish that we were catching then. The new river record, 13lb at the time of writing, is the fish we knew as the 'short, fat one', which I had in 1990 at 11lb 3oz.

All barbel anglers would benefit from being able to spend time just observing the behaviour of fish in clear water, and those halcyon days on the banks of the Oxfordshire Cherwell in 1987 and 1989 provided a fount of knowledge that has stood me in good stead ever since. I look back on my years on the river with tremendous affection.

9 The River Dane

by Rob Stoker

The chances are that many anglers reading this chapter may not even be able to locate the River Dane on a map of Great Britain. This is not surprising, as it is probably no more than 30 miles (50km) long and does not flow through any major towns. Often described as one of the most beautiful rivers in northern England, the Dane rises at Danehead on the edge of the Peak District on the eastern borders of Cheshire. It flows from moorland through steep, wooded valleys almost due west through Congleton and Holmes Chapel, meanders across the dairy pastures of the Cheshire plain, passing Middlewich and Davenham, and joins the River Weaver in Northwich.

The River Dane offers anglers the opportunity to fish one of the smallest rivers where barbel are likely to be encountered in any numbers, and to practise a wide variety of watercraft skills on a river that is full of character. They can choose whether to catch numbers of fish, specimen fish or fish from locations where their presence may still be generally unknown to other anglers.

The Dane is a spate river: this means that levels rise and fall quickly, and the river itself enjoys an ever-changing character, season on season. It can cause minor flooding problems, bursting its banks and backing up surface-water storm drainage in Northwich town centre. Despite this, the river has been mostly spared the attentions of the old National Rivers Authority and the Environment Agency. It flows over red sandstone, gravel, sand and clay at varying depths from twelve inches or less, to about four feet. The current can be quite pacey in the shallower runs or where the flow favours one bank. At its deepest, in weir pools, there may be fourteen feet of water, but this is not the norm, even on the slowest stretches or on the insides of bends. Its banks can be steep and are dangerous at all times, especially in wet weather; the river can often be ten feet below the top of the bank, and extreme care should be taken at all times.

Because the Dane is a spate river running off the Peak District, its passage can be violent in winter, with results that are all too apparent the following season: mature trees uprooted and swept downstream, retaining walls and banks caused to collapse, and the formation of large flood rafts. In some cases the rafts are so extensive that they seriously compromise any attempts to fish. Club members form working parties to reduce them in size so that fishing can continue, while retaining sufficient of the raft as shelter to any resident fish population. At Holmes Chapel the river divides into two distinct courses, forming an island, and flows through a steep wooded valley with a cliff face more than twenty feet high. However, persistent floods and rainfall in recent seasons have systematically washed the island away from its upstream end, and caused a major collapse of the cliff face. Nevertheless, while the course of nature may destroy favourite fish-holding swims, the chances are that it will create others, and it is a challenge for the angler to identify and locate the new hotspots.

From its source down to Congleton, the Dane can best be regarded as a game fishery containing wild brown trout, supplemented with stocked brownies and rainbows that have escaped from a trout farm. Downstream from Congleton it becomes a mixed fishery. In the past it was regarded as a roach and chub river, with a 2lb roach a distinct possibility, but the chub failing to attain any size; a 4lb chub was (and still is) a very good fish indeed. The river was a well known match-fishing venue.

The roach are much less evident now, and it is more accurate to describe the middle and lower Dane as the preserve of chub and barbel. However,

The dramatic effects of a spate on the Dane.

unlike the chub, the barbel have attained significant weights. Why barbel have found the river so much to their liking remains a mystery, and while match fishing is still popular, anglers in search of specimen fish are frequently encountered on the banks.

Barbel are not native to the Dane, and were introduced into the river in the early 1970s; about 150 fish from the River Severn between 5lb and 9lb in weight were stocked in a club stretch at Swettenham, just downstream of Congleton. In 1981, rumours of large fish being caught began to circulate, and in 1982, the weekly angling column in the *Congleton Chronicle* reported the capture of three double-figure barbel. In the same year, Ian Gamblin caught a fish of 10lb 8oz, and in the following year there were two further double-figure fish caught respectively by Mick McEwan and Brian Mountfield.

In the mid 1980s there were subsequent introductions of barbel at Davenham just above

Northwich. Over 250 fish up to 10lb were stocked, supplemented by nearly 100 fish to over 8lb, and over 150 smaller fish in the 1lb–3lb category. Since then there have been further stockings at Davenham following two pollution incidents. From these initial stockings, and further introductions between Holmes Chapel and Middlewich, the fish have spread throughout the river.

Weirs on the Dane present formidable barriers, but fish movement has been greatly assisted by anglers putting barbel back upstream. In common with other rivers, the barbel population consists of a mixture of residents and migrants. Although there is little hard data on the movement and capture of specific fish, the changing profile of captures over the seasons strongly suggests large fish moving between locations, rather than an evolving population of static fish from which previously unknown large specimens are caught. As a result, coupled with the maintenance and growth of the barbel population from successful spawning soon after they were first introduced, anglers can expect to encounter barbel almost anywhere downstream of Congleton. However, the highest concentrations of fish are from Holmes Chapel downstream to Croxton just below Middlewich, and at Davenham just upstream of Northwich.

For any angler wishing to tackle the Dane, access is not difficult. Clubs in Congleton, Crewe, Davenham, Lymm, Macclesfield, Middlewich and Northwich all control stretches of the river, and they are either open to new members or have a short waiting list. Membership fees are modest, and day tickets are available on certain lengths, although they may be limited to weekdays on some fisheries. If there is a problem with access, it is because fisheries may be only a few hundred yards in length, so you need to join more than one club to ensure a sufficient variety of fishing or type of fishery. It is also rare for both banks of a fishery to be controlled by the same club, and this may lead to difficulties with other anglers fishing the opposite bank – a problem made worse by the fact that in places the Dane may be only thirty feet wide or less! Local tackle shops are an excellent source of knowledge, offering a wealth of experience to customers new to the area and the river.

Fishing the Dane for barbel generally involves snag fishing in one form or other. This means searching out fish under bank-side cover such as overhanging willows or hawthorn bushes; the roots of alders, fallen and submerged trees and flood rafts are also likely holding spots for fish. The riverbed may be strewn with sandstone boulders, the

Holmes Chapel weir in flood.

implication being that swims that appear featureless on the surface may have barbel present.

For this reason it is essential to use adequate tackle, and typically this means heavier tackle than is the norm for barbel. Specialist carbon barbel rods of 11 or 12ft in length are now widely available, and I would favour a rod at the heavier end of the range, coupled with a reliable fixed-spool reel loaded with monofilament of 8 to 12lb bs. The potential need to pull for a break in a snag means that I would never advocate the use of a braided mainline. Braided hook links can be useful in avoiding excess abrasion at the business end of tackle, and I would recommend strong forged hooks in as large a size as possible, bearing in mind the choice of bait. Even when fishing weir pools it is not necessary, in normal conditions, to use weights in excess of ¾oz. The river can be pacey, and to ensure bait is deposited on the bottom and not swept downstream, a bait dropper is a very useful accessory. Alternatively a large swimfeeder, suitably modified to permit the swift exit of bait, could be pressed into service. However, not all Dane barbel fishing requires these tactics.

I first moved to the north-west in the early 1980s, relocating from Throop. I had spent two seasons fishing the Dorset Stour exclusively by wading and long-trotting with maggots, and caught large numbers of barbel mostly between 3lb and 7lb. Adopting the same approach on the Dane, I caught more chub between 2lb and just under 4lb than I would have believed possible; sometimes thirty or more in a session of only three or four hours. I regularly hooked powerful fish, one of which ploughed past me wading in the river. I put this down to trout, but a work colleague told me it was just as likely to be barbel.

This came as quite a surprise, as I never imagined the river had a resident barbel population. With a different quarry now firmly in my sights, I concentrated on the swims at Bank Farm, Holmes Chapel, where I had hooked and lost fish in the past. I was fortunate insofar as on my next trip I was rewarded with almost instant success. I tackled up a 12ft carbon Alan Brown Avon Trotter rod with a Grice and Young Avon Royal Supreme centre-pin reel loaded with 4lb Maxima. My float was a John Dean wire-stemmed stick taking seven no. 4 shot. In those days I had great difficulty in identifying a small hook suitable for trotting for barbel. I had settled on a Mustad pattern No. 39838 called 'Chapman's Goldstrike', and I fished either two maggots on a size 14 or 16 hook or one maggot on a size 18 hook. My favourite swim was at the foot of a vertical bank over ten feet above the river level, which involved a precarious descent. Shallow water of two feet shelved down to four feet or more, with an undercut bank and tree roots on the nearside. The upper half of the swim was covered in ranunculus weed, and the lower half was shaded by overhanging branches.

I caught barbel immediately; not large, about 2½lb, but it was a joyful experience. Compared with my days on the Dorset Stour and Hampshire Avon, it was barbel fishing in miniature. I loose fed maggots, and could control the float in such way that I felt I could manoeuvre the tackle easily to wherever the fish were lying up. Identifying other similar swims, I regularly caught fish, though the biggest was only 4lb; not in the same league as fishing on the Stour, but very rewarding. I started to encounter other barbel anglers, and I heard of bigger fish being caught. Their tactics were different, mainly in that none of them float fished, but instead legered large lumps of luncheon meat to avoid the prolific population of chub, and fished weir pools 'beach-caster style'.

I left the area in early 1987, but returned to live near Northwich in mid-1989. I resumed my acquaintance with the Dane, but found the river had changed and that most of my favourite swims had disappeared through the destructive nature of winter floods. Trees providing cover for barbel had been swept away, but another major difference was that due to increased abstraction, the level of the river was probably a foot lower than before, and areas that had previously held fish were now barren. I tried my old float-fishing tactics on the Croxton fishery in Middlewich but caught no barbel, so in desperation I reverted to legered meat.

Croxton is a fishery full of features. There is a small weir, overhanging trees and bushes, and bankside vegetation. It is fishable on a day ticket on weekdays, and is regularly match fished; a popular venue by all accounts – in fact so popular that I have never been able to fish the hottest barbel swims, as they seem to be permanently occupied by other anglers. When I first fished Croxton, this wasn't surprising as the then incumbent Club record was an 11lb fish caught from the stretch in a match! Undeterred, I settled for fishing sections opposite overhanging willows or swims with tree roots. To

counter what I anticipated would be snaggy conditions, my tackle now consisted of an 11ft glass Terry Eustace custom-built fast-taper Barbel rod that I had previously used on the Stour and Hampshire Avon, and a Mitchell 300 fixed-spool reel loaded with 8lb Maxima. The end rig was simple, a ½ oz bomb buffered by a bead from a 12in Kryston Merlin hook link, to which a size 10 Drennan Boilie hook was attached by a four-turn grinner knot. I droppered in a couple of pints of hemp and chopped luncheon meat, and fished a small, single cube of luncheon meat on the hook.

Bites were so violent that there was no need to adopt any form of bite indication or hold the line: the rod simply whacked over. Extracting fish from under the bushes proved easier than I had expected, and I caught regularly, usually two or three in a session. The fish ranged from 2lb to 4lb, and so were no improvement on what I had been catching before. However, my fishing was about to take two dramatic turns for the better.

First, I was accepted as a member of the Barbel Catchers Club. This gave me an enormous fillip, and I was filled with enthusiasm to build on what I had learned, and to locate and catch some of the bigger specimens in the Dane, tales of which I had heard. At the time the Barbel Catchers Club river record for the Dane was 8lb 8oz, caught by John Winterbottom in 1984. The national river record was a fish of 12lb 4oz caught in 1990 by Mr J. Meadows – and these specimens seemed light-years away from the class of fish I was catching. I read some of the articles written by John Winterbottom and other members fishing the Dane for *Barbus*, the club magazine: they talked of fish of 8lb and bigger inhabiting impossibly snaggy swims, and of massively stepped-up tackle, 15lb mainlines and even the possible use of wire traces to counteract abrasion problems in the difficult situations. This seemed to be a different world of barbel fishing to the one I inhabited as I fished on at Croxton for another full season. I alternated meat-based baits with hemp and caster fished on size 14 Drennan Super Specialist and Starpoint hooks, but my catches failed to improve to any significant degree. However, just as my barbel fishing seemed to have stalled, I had my second piece of good fortune.

A chance conversation with a local tackle dealer resulted in my renewing acquaintance with a former fishing colleague, and being accepted into a club whose membership I thought was closed. This gave me access to some of the best barbel swims on the river, and I was to take full advantage of this facility.

I was now fishing a stretch full of snags, but with a large resident population of fish. My first trips were in December 1991 and were fruitless. Tackle losses in snags were horrendous, the river bottom being strewn with the remains of bankside retaining walls, sandstone boulders, branches of trees swept downstream in floods, and worst of all, reinforced concrete waste. I remembered from my days float fishing that I had walked the stretch and spoken to anglers who were using bolts, spark plugs and other assorted ironmongery as cheap alternatives to non-toxic leger weights.

I was now able to indulge in the luxury of fishing with two rods, and the 11ft glass Barbel rod was accompanied by an 11ft Terry Eustace Carbon Avon Plus. Each rod was coupled with a Shimano 3500 baitrunner, loaded respectively with 6lb and 8lb Berkeley XT. I later dropped the 6lb XT in favour of 10lb Berkeley Big Game. I didn't lose any fish on the 6lb line: the upgrade was to counteract abrasion caused by the state of the riverbed, that after only a few sessions turned Big Game from dark green to lime green in colour, and Maxima, when I used it, from dark brown to pink! I persisted with braided Merlin and Super Nova hook links for the same reason. Rigs were simple. On the lighter Carbon Avon Plus, fished in relatively open water, I used a ½ oz running bomb rig with a size 6 Drennan Super Specialist for meat on 8lb line. On the glass Barbel rod with 10lb line, I used a medium-sized running Thamesly feeder filled with hemp and caster, fishing three casters on a size 14 Starpoint or Super Specialist hook. This rig would be fished close to snags on the far bank, usually stumps, tree roots or reinforced concrete. I later scaled up the caster hook to a size 10 Terry Eustace Specialist Carp hook, a forged, eyed, heavy wire design that looks as if it is modelled on the Au Lion d'Or pattern no. 1534, and loaded it with as many casters as it would take – usually five or six. The Thamesly feeder was soon replaced by a less brittle polythene block-end that was cheaper and more resistant to the cracking caused by impact with the sandstone boulders and reinforced concrete on the riverbed.

My major problem, and it was a constant headache, was tackle loss in snags, which might mean losing as many as six or more end rigs, including feeders, in a session: bad for the fish, bad for the environment and bad for the pocket. I never found a solution. Some-times I could fish for weeks and lose nothing, and at others it was impossible to fish and be confident you could retrieve your tackle, let alone land a fish.

A secondary problem related to the unwanted attention of nuisance fish. If you are barbel fishing on the Dane, this can mean minnows or 2lb-plus chub! Chub were deterred by the heavy tackle, and by reducing the quantity of free hook-bait offerings mixed with hemp in the feeder. I countered the minnow problem by fishing a 'lump' bait on one rod and pre-baiting with two pints of hemp and caster before tackling up and fishing the feeder rig. To save time, pre-baiting was carried out using a 'whopper dropper' fashioned from a perforated 8oz tin: this was just sufficiently manoeuvrable when filled and attached to the barbel rod on 12lb line. By the time I was ready to fish, barbel were on the feed and small fish were not a nuisance. This tactic was not completely foolproof, but it made summer fishing tolerable and rarely failed to any material degree.

Barbel could be expected from the first cast, but the usual pattern was for line bites to signal their presence. A bite on the caster rig would be violent and unmistakable. No doubt the state of the riverbed resulted in the unwitting creation of a bolt rig, causing a hooked fish to panic. The meat rig fished in open water and upstream would either present a classic drop-back bite, or a confident take with the rod slowly arcing round. Line bites could be equally violent, and the temptation to strike had to be resisted to avoid spooking fish unnecessarily.

After the blanks before Christmas in 1991, I was rewarded in my first session of 1992 with a single fish of 7lb 12oz, at a stroke almost doubling my personal river best. Before the end of the season I had a fish of over 8lb, and was regularly catching six or more fish in a session. I couldn't wait for the following season to start, and although things began slowly, I finished the 1992–93 season with a fish of 8lb 12oz, breaking the Barbel Catchers Club river record after nine years. At the same time I learnt that the biggest fish taken from the stretch was another fish of over 12lb. So there was the possibility of at least two seriously large fish in the river.

Observing other anglers, I was surprised that my hemp-and-caster tactics, which accounted for the vast majority of my catches, were not used by anyone else. Legered meat and swimfeedered maggots seemed to be the most popular choice of methods and baits, and corn was also a favourite. The virtual absence of eels meant that worms could be used with confidence, and they proved to be an excellent bait on their day. I once saw an angler catch four moderate-sized fish in quick succession by float fishing worms into a partly submerged tree that had lodged in a swim at right angles across the current.

In 1993–94 my successes continued, and the end of the season proved to be a revelation. With high pressure dominating the weather the days were warm, and although the nights were chilly, any fall in water temperature was restored the following morning. The river was running at a summer level, and I was catching well. On the afternoon of 13 March 1994 my upstream rod, on which I was fishing a hemp-and-caster rig, pulled round in a slow, confident arc. I struck into what seemed to be a solid object, but which then decided to move! What followed was an epic tug of war. Although I had the advantage of playing the fish from a downstream location, it was so powerful that I could not persuade it to leave its sanctuary. This state of affairs seem to last for an age, with the fish gradually moving into deeper cover and me being helpless to stop it, despite my rod being bent into an arc of 180 degrees. Then suddenly the tension relaxed, and I thought I had lost the fish. I wound down to find it was still there, but now in open water. I kept up the pressure, and the fish surfaced in mid-river. My lasting impression will always be the size of its mouth as it rolled: it seemed to be big enough to suck in a cricket ball. I eased the fish towards me, mindful that a near-bank shelf often caused fish to panic just out of netting range. This fish, however, had expended all its energy and was not difficult to net. It tipped the scales at 10lb 1oz. My first Dane double! It was to be almost five seasons before I was to better that capture.

My Ten-Pounder: a New Dane Record

Throughout those five seasons I continued to catch fish of 7lb, 8lb and 9lb, and I never saw or spoke to an angler who admitted to catching or knowing of the capture of any large fish. The use of boilies became commonplace. I experimented with a paste bait developed by Steve Withers and Chris Thomson and which had proved its worth on the Hampshire Avon. Without any pre-baiting, I caught a 4lb fish within two hours of first using it, and on my next trip I landed eight fish in less than two hours, with the biggest just over 7lb. The following day I repeated the experience, and the bait continues to take fish without the need for any pre-baiting campaign.

In the late 1990s there seemed to be an explosion of fish in the 3lb to 4lb category, and my catches of bigger fish declined dramatically. The fashion in bait had turned full circle, and the bigger fish were now falling to maggots. The very back end of the season had always proved to be the best time for my fishing on the Dane, but on 27 February 1999 I was struggling. I had been fishing since 8 o'clock that

Rob Stoker with his first Dane double.

morning with only two fish of 6lb and 4lb for my trouble. I had tried a number of likely spots without any success. The river looked right and was in good trim, and the days were warm for the time of year. Everything pointed to catching, but the fish were just not willing to oblige. More out of desperation than hope I decided to try a swim from which I had previously caught only chub, and small ones at that! It was a popular place to fish from the opposite bank, and I had seen several good barbel caught from that swim where an underarm cast parallel to the bank could place a bait hard against the bank-side cover. From my side of the river I had a long cast with the risk of either burying my tackle in the cover, or dropping short and failing to tempt any resident fish.

I was casting a maggot-filled feeder on 8lb line to the same spot with a bunch of maggots on a size 10 Terry Eustace Specialist Carp hook. After about forty-five minutes and four or five casts, the rod suddenly slammed over, and I could tell I had hooked a good fish. Obligingly, it swam away from the cover into the middle of the river; it hugged the bottom, and I began to realize it might be a much better specimen than I had at first thought. But despite my efforts I could not persuade it to come up in the water. After several minutes, having played the fish across the river and done all the hard work, I was unable to bring it within netting range. The barbel was now patrolling the area of deeper water at the foot of a shelf, and I was concerned that bringing the fish into the much shallower water at the top of the shelf might provoke a panic-induced run, resulting in the hook pulling out. I eased the fish up in the water and it rolled about twenty feet from the bank, much further out than I had thought it was. It was then that I realized just how big the fish was. It rolled onto its back, and I managed to ease it over the shelf towards me and netted it without further trouble. It pulled the scales down to 10lb 4oz, a personal river best, and a new Dane river record for the Barbel Catchers Club.

10 The Yorkshire Derwent

by Jon Wolfe

The Yorkshire Derwent rises on Wykeham high moor, on the North Yorkshire moors, 900ft (270m) above sea level. It flows in a southerly direction for about 70 miles (110km) before joining the River Ouse at Barmby. The only town on the river of any size is Malton. It is above Malton that the river is joined by its main tributary the River Rye, hence from this point downstream the river increases in size very little, the lower river being almost as narrow as the middle reaches. The Derwent is classified as a lowland river, unlike the other Ouse tributaries, which are spate rivers. Quite what the river looked like before the eighteenth century we can only guess, but at that time a series of locks and weirs was constructed to facilitate the shipment of grain from Malton. Since then the locks have fallen into disrepair, but the weirs remain. It is below these weirs, on the middle river at Kirkham, Howsham, Buttercrambe and Stamford that the vast majority of the Derwent's barbel spawn. Barbel are indigenous to the river, but they are far from prolific.

When I joined the Barbel Catchers Club in 1983 I hadn't even thought about fishing the Derwent. It had a reputation that belied its appearance. The gravel runs and lush ranunculus growth at Howsham and Stamford, for instance, absolutely screamed barbel, but the reality was that a hard slog was in store for anyone setting out in the hope of landing an elusive Derwent double. Most of the Catchers members at that time were fishing the river, and most of this fishing was concentrated on a short

stretch at one time quite prolific, but which had failed to produce the double-figure fish we were seeking, just like the rest of the Ouse system.

Despite its reputation I was intrigued by the river and the prospect of fishing it. This was probably the start of my ongoing fascination with low population fisheries. We are all inspired by different things, and bagging up never did anything for me. Forget Ireland and its bulging nets, or the middle Severn where the barbel were so prolific you could cross the river without getting your feet wet. I was much more inspired after reading about the middle Avon and its sparse population of huge barbel, or by Roger Baker's campaign on the Great Ouse in the late 1970s, where barbel were thin on the ground. I was similarly inspired by John Bailey's roaching exploits on the Wensum, especially in the latter years when the population had plummeted.

This type of fishing was much more to my liking. The fact that the Derwent was so little fished and there were so many miles of it, made it even more appealing. 1985 was a milestone year for the Yorkshire region of the Barbel Catchers. In August, Dave Mason landed the region's first double from the Derwent, a truly memorable fish and a fitting reward for a fine angler. Two months later I had one from the Swale: at 11lb plus I knew the odds were against me catching a bigger specimen from this river. It was time for a change.

Yorkshire's 'wrong-way-round' river, the Derwent.

My first season on the Derwent got off to a slow start. By August I had fished twelve long sessions and caught nothing, not even a chub. I fished into dark on most days, and on two or three occasions I fished all night. I began by fishing the same swim all day. When that didn't work, I baited two or three different swims and then fished them in rotation. I tried different baits and different methods, all to no avail. This was turning out to be a struggle, but it was not unexpected. Phil Duston, another BCC member, once fished the river all season for just three medium-sized barbel. But then, after such an uneventful start, a small piece of good fortune turned my season round completely.

I was already contemplating a change of venue when I heard of a big barbel that had been caught in a match. Three hours into my first session on the new stretch I caught a barbel, and it quickly became apparent that I had stumbled onto some exceptional fishing – by Derwent standards, that is. Between the middle of August and the end of October when the first frosts put a damper on things, I caught fourteen barbel in the same number of sessions. This was a very high catch ratio, and I put it down to a couple of

factors: first, there was evidently a greater head of fish on this stretch of river than the previous one; and second, the conditions required for catching them couldn't have been better. Heavy rain saturated the catchment area throughout this period, and the barbel were undoubtedly stirred into feeding by the rising levels and coloured water. These are conditions that Dave Mason, in the first Barbel Catchers book, stated as being ideal for fishing this river.

Among my fourteen fish was one double, and at 10lb 15oz it was a new Catchers river record. Better still, after comparing photographs with the double that was caught in the match, it was obviously a different fish; all the more reason to persevere on the same piece of water for the time being.

I never expected to do as well the following season, and sure enough, my catch rate dropped to ten fish from thirty sessions; this averaged out at thirty-five hours' fishing per barbel. Little did I know that things could, and would, get much worse. Only five fish came to my net in 1989, four the following year and two in 1991: not much to show for hundreds of hours fishing. Why, then, is the

Jon Wolfe on the banks of Yorkshire's most beautiful river.

fishing so slow and unproductive on the Derwent, as compared to other barbel rivers? The main reason has undoubtedly got to be the extremely low population of fish. My own observations of the barbel spawning on the shallows on one stretch, indicate a population of no more than thirty mature fish, and even smaller numbers than this on other sections of the river. This evidence is based on observations of spawning sites, environment agency surveys, and lastly, recaptures of known fish. This small number of fish disperses after spawning into what is, after all, a very slow-flowing, deep and heavily tree-lined river: locating them again seems at times to be an almost impossible task, and there are numerous obstacles in the way of the angler.

A major weapon in any barbel fisherman's armoury is his eyesight. Walking the bank looking for barbel is an art in itself, and some anglers are better at this than others; I have fished with a few who are exceptional at locating fish in this manner. However, as there are no shallows on the Derwent other than the run-off from the weir pool, spotting fish from the bank is a non-starter.

Barbel rolling at dusk is, again, a common occurrence on some rivers and a vital clue as to their whereabouts; but it is an unknown event on the Derwent. I have seen the odd fish roll, but it does not happen with enough frequency for it to be used as a reliable aid to location. The factors discussed so far regarding location are not unique to the Derwent. What might be unique, however (and I have certainly never come across this on any other river

that I have fished), is the number of swims that produce one barbel and then, despite repeated attempts, fail to produce another fish. On one stretch that I have fished for many years I have caught barbel from nine different swims, seven of which have yet to give me a second fish in spite of concerted efforts. Does this compare with anywhere you fish? Why this should be so I have no idea. Most of the barbel seem to travel a considerable distance during the year, and they also appear to be mainly solitary. The river at first glance appears to lack certain features associated with typical barbel habitat. As I mentioned earlier, the Derwent is deep and slow-flowing, with few shallow areas. Careful plumbing can reveal certain variations in depth, as well as some considerable snags such as submerged trees; these can be completely hidden from view by the depth of water. Most of the river is at least eight feet deep, and a large percentage of it is considerably deeper. Swims that contain such features should be fished, but instant results shouldn't be expected.

There are some fantastic-looking swims on the river from which I have yet to catch a barbel. There are some swims that have given me a fish relatively quickly but have yet to give me another. There are some that have eventually given me a fish, but only after numerous blank sessions spread over a number of years. What this boils down to is that there is probably no such thing as a barbel swim on the Derwent – at least not in the way we think of a barbel swim on a conventional river. During my time spent fishing the Derwent I have come across only two

Jon with one of his Derwent doubles; this one registered 10lb 13oz.

swims that could be loosely described as barbel swims. The first one I discovered myself whilst plumbing: this is a method I have used extensively on the Derwent, not necessarily to locate swims, but more as a means of isolating featureless sections of river, that is, snag free and of uniform depth.

This swim turned out to be very consistent by Derwent standards, for a considerable period of time. During that period I never saw anyone else fishing the swim; it was on a very quiet stretch of river and mid-way between access points. And despite it being the most productive swim that I have found on the river, it was still possible to notch up a long run of blank sessions between fish. However, over those five seasons I caught about thirty barbel from this area. I know that's only six fish per season, which is a very small return for this swim to be labelled a barbel swim, let alone a hotspot; but even so, compared to any other swims on the river, that is what it was. As the saying goes: 'In the land of the blind, the one-eyed man is king.' The swim itself remains more or less the same to this day – a slight depression in an area that is considerably shallow compared to above and below. The riverbed still consists of fine gravel, again different to the silty bottom found both above and below.

The fact that the physical nature of the swim has not changed, and that my catch rate from here was a gradual decline rather than a sudden one, leads me to believe that this wasn't really a barbel swim – meaning one frequented by resident fish. It should be thought of more as an ideal spot from which to ambush passing barbel. I probably fished this swim at least twice a week through the summer and autumn in the hope that by continually baiting the area I could hold some of the passing fish long enough to catch them. But eventually they became altogether wary of feeding here; I had, after all, caught a large percentage of the total population of that section of river, even taking into account recaptures.

The second 'barbel swim' was again more of an ambush point, rather than a true barbel swim. The main difference between the two was that in this swim it was possible to catch passing fish on a more regular basis than in the first one. Let me explain.

It is my belief that the barbel in the Derwent gradually drop downstream from the spawning shallows. Take, for example, one recognizable fish that I observed spawning at the top of the stretch in early May. I caught this fish in late June about 1½ miles lower down, and caught it again in late July one mile further downstream. This movement is not definitive, but extra water seems to encourage travel. Thus a very low river will find the fish staying close

The Derwent, flowing south towards the Yorkshire Ouse.

to the more oxygenated shallows at the top of the stretch, right through the summer. If your chosen swim is, for example, half way between the weirs, and extra water has caused the fish to move, you may only get one chance to catch a passing fish. But if, on the other hand, the river is low and your chosen swim is close to the shallows at the top of the stretch, then your chances of catching a passing fish have got to be better, as these areas can be frequently visited during these conditions. Areas such as this can become relatively popular. The Derwent, due to its reputation, is under-fished, but most of the barbel anglers that I have bumped into are very keen and committed. Now, the presence of two or three such anglers can significantly increase the pressure on such a small number of barbel, and this increased pressure manifests itself in a number of ways, the main one that springs to my mind being the feeding spell.

During the first four or five years on the river, all my fish were caught during daylight. Night fishing, far from being productive, was actually quite the opposite. However, with the added presence of other barbel anglers, daytime fishing quickly became very unproductive, with dusk and the first hour of darkness taking over as the prime time. But even this period of the day didn't remain the prime time for long, as the barbel's preferred feeding time became later and later. My old mate Andy Dalby exploited this to the full one summer by taking a number of large fish long after most anglers had gone home.

Another subject that I hadn't had to give much thought to was bait. Initially a large percentage of my fish were caught on meat or corn. When fishing in the company of other anglers, however, a few blank sessions might cause me to question whether these baits had blown, especially when someone else caught a fish. Once paste and boilies start being introduced, it takes a very brave man or a very stubborn one to stick to traditional baits.

As with the first swim, the pressure on the second one eventually told. Despite catching a few fish on maggots and some on paste, I got the distinct impression that the barbel were now reluctant to feed here, and I think it was a relief to us all when a winter flood washed away the large overhanging willow tree.

The following season I failed to catch a barbel from this area, and it joined the ever-expanding list of swims still worth fishing, but more in hope than expectation.

Without reliable swims such as these two in which to concentrate my efforts, the Derwent really did become hard work. A typical session would see me baiting four or five swims in preparation for a night's fishing. I never kept a record of how long I would remain in a swim without hooking a fish, but my guess is not very long, say one hour. If nothing had happened in that time, I would move on to the next swim, maybe baiting up before I left if I intended returning. I have caught a few fish on my second visit to a swim. Once all the baited swims had been fished I would either start again or pack in, depending on the time. A typical session would end three or four hours into dark, and occasionally a lot

later. Some of these swims might be a mile or more apart, so I very rarely fished more than one rod; you are far less likely to move swims when carrying mountains of gear.

Trying to keep track of the barbel as they move downstream is obviously very unreliable. The previously mentioned fish that I caught twice in one season ended up two and a half miles below the spawning shallows by late July that year. A few seasons later I caught the same fish on the shallows in September. Had it been downstream and come back, or had it never moved in the first place? Just another piece of the jigsaw that's still missing.

What then of the future? Finding a swim similar to the two I have already described – that is, a suitable ambush point – doesn't sound too difficult a task, but I'm afraid to say that it is. My last few years on the river have been very unproductive: only one fish last season, none from the previous year, and two from the one before – a total of three barbel from over seventy sessions. Is it still worth the effort? Probably not. Furthermore, over twenty otters have been released on the river, and this controversial stocking has further reduced the already worryingly

Another Derwent double for Jon; this one weighed 10lb 1oz.

small numbers of barbel. Currently there are about the same number of barbel anglers on the Derwent as when I began fishing the river nearly twenty years ago, namely only a handful.

The river itself has changed very little: it is still extremely picturesque yet equally mysterious, and ultimately success depends on whether you have been lucky in your choice of swim. I have caught about eighty barbel from this river, including eleven doubles comprising seven different fish. This is barely an average season's tally on some rivers, and it only goes to show just how slow the fishing is. Success, however, has to be measured against the effort applied, and the capture of any Derwent barbel is cause for great celebration, especially if it's a big one. Undoubtedly the highlight of my time spent on the river must be the evening I caught my biggest fish.

My Twelve-Pounder, a New Derwent Record

After finishing work at 6 o'clock I set off for another session, my fourteenth trip of the season. So far I'd caught one barbel, and I had no reason to believe my luck was about to change. Eight droppers of hemp mixed with tiny pieces of bacon grill fried in curry paste were lowered into the near-bank swim. The trap had been set. An hour later I gently lowered my baited hook into position. This was a small cube of curried bacon grill, hair-rigged to a size 6 Au Lion d'Or hook with a PVA stringer of free offerings fished on a braided hook length tied to 8lb Maxima.

I can't remember how long I'd been fishing before the rod pulled round, but it must have been about an hour. Due to the long periods between fish, I had adopted a more relaxed style of fishing as opposed to my preferred method of holding the rod and touch legering. My first indication of a bite was the clutch screaming away on the Abu Cardinal 54 as something moved off at a fair old pace. Immediately I knew I'd hooked my second barbel of the season, and its long and powerful runs convinced me it was

Jon with his Derwent record at 12lb 6oz.

another big one. After what seemed like an eternity the fish surfaced in mid-river, and it looked huge. It dived again, but failed to reach the bottom, eventually tiring and coming to the net. I let it rest in the margins for a few moments to recover whilst I took in the importance of the occasion. Although it was still in the net, my view from above convinced me that this was a special fish, and the scales and tape measure confirmed this fact. She was 29½in long, with a girth of 17in and a weight of 12lb 6oz; a new Derwent record, beating the previous best caught in the 1930s by over ½lb.

A 12lb barbel was a big fish in 1989, especially from a Yorkshire river, and I duly had my five minutes of fame: a weekly Drennan cup win, a half-page front cover shot in the *Angling Times* with accompanying story, and at the end-of-season Barbel Catchers AGM, the outstanding fish of the season award.

Fifteen years later and my enthusiasm for fishing the Yorkshire Derwent is still as strong as ever. The river may not be as productive as it once was, but it is still a great place to settle down for the day with a good book, watch a few otters, and all the while going through the motions of barbel fishing. That next fish might just be the one that surprises a few people.

11 The River Dove

by Steve Chell

Everyone knows about the 'Teme Tigers' and how hard they fight for the sanctuary of their lairs amongst the roots of the tree-lined river – but what about the Dove Demons? Having caught barbel from some fourteen rivers from Yorkshire to Wessex I have yet to make contact with a more tenacious scrapper than the Demon barbel of Derbyshire's River Dove. Time and again I have felt I was connected to a monster, a jet-propelled leviathan that took me here, there, and wherever it wished in the river, only to land a fish of a shade above or below 7lb. They leave me in awe. How can a fish of such size fight for so long and pull so strongly? I can hardly bend the rod as much as they do. If you are one of those who always think biggest is best, then think again: come and have a try for the Dove barbel, and have your horizons rearranged!

The Dove is a spate river that rises on the peat moorland watershed known as Axe Edge, at a height of 1,650ft (500m). It flows eastwards along the Staffordshire/Derbyshire border for much of its length before entering the Trent a couple of miles north of Burton-on-Trent. The only settlement of any size that the river passes through in its upper reaches is Ashbourne, so the water quality is consistently very good or excellent, with many uncommon species found amongst the fauna of the river. In recent years, however, not all has been good news, and despite being a chemically very clean river now suitable for stocking with salmon, there has been a drop in the fish biomass. Trout are disappearing from the upper beats, and coarse fish catches are decreasing on the middle river, to the consternation of some of the controlling clubs. As far as the barbel is concerned, we all know that lower numbers mean bigger fish. Let's hope that this does not occur to the detriment of the river as a whole.

One of the most important features of the Dove to me as a barbel angler is its speed of flow. This factor governs how and when the river fishes, especially after heavy rain and in the higher levels of the winter. It is one of the fastest flowing rivers along its length in the whole country, and as such it only has to rise about a foot before most swims become unfishable. On occasions it is impossible to hold a bait in position, even by upstreaming with 4oz of lead. 'Well, fish the inside line, then' I hear you shout – but this is easier said than done. Due to the speed of the adjacent current, areas on the inside of bends or behind bushes have a tendency to boil and swirl rather than giving the more traditional slacks and steady flows of other rivers. Consequently floodwater and winter fishing can be hard and rather unreliable until you build up a picture of the few swims on your beat that *do* produce, and the range of water levels within which action is possible.

One of my typical floodwater swims is on the outside of a wide open bend, below a group of willow and alder bushes that start midway down a short stony shallow. The barbel live under the

The 'lower bushes' on the Dove.

willows in summer, but as the river rises, the flow and turbulence off the shallow become too much, and they drop back onto the bend. This is where they can be caught until the river reaches about three feet above summer norm, when the bend becomes full of boils and the barbel vacate the entire area, to where I know not. Another favourite spot is in the lee of a road bridge. During the summer the area close-in can be completely high and dry, with clumps of reeds growing in the mud and sand. The flow comes through the middle arch and hits the near bank part way along a group of hawthorn bushes, beneath which lies a shoal of chub and small barbel. Larger barbel move in during the winter, and once the river is carrying three feet or so of floodwater, a lovely slack forms above the bushes. The barbel lie either at the tail of the slack, above the boils by the bushes, or in the deepest hole, a drop-off behind the dead reeds, or on the edge of the main flow as it comes under the bridge. To date this swim has produced fish to 8lb plus, and my best catch in terms of numbers is ten barbel in an evening. Unfortunately all good things come to an end, and on a quickly rising spate river, that end can come very quickly. Once the level

approaches seven feet above normal, the swim starts to resemble a washing machine, and barbel are no more to be tempted. On my five-mile beat of the middle Dove I have only one other winter swim and that yields fish but singly, which explains why the bulk of my captures on this river come in the summer and autumn.

My first ventures onto the Dove were in pursuit of chub in the 1970s. At that time barbel were being caught from the lower reaches of the river where it joins the Trent, and eventually as high up as Tutbury with the occasional fish just scraping into double figures. During the intervening years the fish have extended their range as far as the weir by the A50 at Uttoxeter. A few fish are caught higher up, but the A50 is where the main barbel population now begins. As with all other barbel rivers, the average size of the Dove fish has steadily increased in recent years, and continues to rise – although for me, a seven-pounder is still a cracking fish and will often give you the best scrap of the day. Doubles, although not regular occurrences, are caught quite frequently from the areas around and below Tutbury, with fish to 13lb and more having been taken in recent

The 'bridge slack', with the Dove brim full.

A winter '8' from the bridge.

seasons. There have also been a few doubles landed from higher up the river close to their upstream limit. Although relatively rare, they are not the impossibility of a few years ago, and include a summer 12lb 2oz specimen and a floodwater autumn fish of 13lb 6oz, the current river record.

I turned my attention to barbel on the middle reaches over ten years ago, with an initial target of capturing just one. I earmarked areas below shallows during the early part of the season, baiting with hemp an hour before dusk, and then fishing into the dark. This strategy produced gold dust on the first evening in the form of a never-to-be-forgotten first Dove barbel of 4lb 13oz. How often do anglers race for the supposed 'heights' and go straight for the swims or areas that contain the monsters, rather than taking the scenic road and savouring all the delights to be found on their own voyage of learning and discovery. What pleasures I would have missed, had my first Dove fish been 10lb 13oz instead! I've since caught hundreds of Dove demons, 90 per cent of them bigger, but not one meant more to me than that first fish.

By pursuing the same policy, and changing swims after two consecutive blanks, I soon achieved my next target of a seven-pounder. As the season wore on I found myself having to fish deeper, steadier water further below the shallows and nearer to features such as snags, overhanging bushes and depressions. I also found that I needed to change swims more regularly, due to a fairly low barbel population: the fish did not allow more than a few

captures before they became jittery. Progress by results would on paper have appeared slow, but for me every step of the way was enjoyable. Every new swim that produced a barbel was an achievement; every new month, or occasion when I had to catch in new conditions, were important steps on my learning curve, and still are.

After two and a half seasons I moved upstream to a new area, and by baiting cover at dusk caught my first nine, a Catchers' river record at the time. The big difference on this new stretch was the higher average weight of the barbel – approaching 7½lb. This would do for me, or so I thought. But the following season showed how dangerous it is to make assumptions in fishing, because the barbel population had changed! The bigger fish had moved out, and all areas were inhabited by a large number of 3–4lb scrappers. Twelve months on and the situation reversed, and I was back to catching a high average size, but from only a few fish. Strange creatures, barbel!

Over this period I gradually investigated more of the river, and my tactics changed slightly from fishing one, or at most two swims in an evening, to baiting and rotating five or six areas. I also began to wonder whether baiting was really necessary, as my catch rate seemed to be stagnating or even slowing down. Could I use only single baits, as on the Severn, particularly as most of the time I was fishing next to or beneath some type of cover? Were the beds of seeds starting to spook the barbel, as on the Bristol Avon? I decided to abandon my hemp and

A Dove crease swim in the summer.

other seed mix in favour of my preferred method of roving, covering whatever areas I fancied at the time. I did target certain swims more than others, these being ones where I had found some different features when chest wading during the close season

My usual approach to a swim is to cast upstream of where I expect the fish to lie, using just enough weight to hold bottom. This might be plasticine, a drilled bullet or, in the strong summer flows on the Dove, a bomb with added plasticine to balance. I hold the line feeling for bites at all times. If I just sit and watch the rod top bounce, twitch and bend, I struggle to decipher the messages, but once the line is over my finger, the code becomes clear. Thus a slight tap and a gentle increase in tension, then a steady shift, a bounce or two, and a resettling, usually means a build-up of weed. If I fish a slightly heavier lead with a longer tail I can often catch in these conditions, which are very prevalent on the Dove from early September. A sharp, hard rap and then nothing indicates a line bite or a fish hitting the bait but not taking it, as it is lodged in the stones. Waiting a minute and then releasing the bait to move it a couple of feet further down the swim often induces a take. A

slight tap and then no other sensation but the feeling that the bait is moving should be struck, as a fish has taken the offering. A tap and then repeated taps and a settling of the bomb could be a fish, but the odds are that water pressure is causing the bait to shift. If it *was* a barbel, it could have another go. And so it goes on: a code that is only cracked by the experience of being out there fishing at all times of the year, in all conditions, in all sorts of different swims on your river. I could, of course, sit behind a buzzer fishing a bolt rig, but for me the greatest 'buzz' when barbeling is making contact with a wild creature, and feeling that first electric sensation of the bite.

If I get no signs of life I lift the rod and let the bait move a few feet before allowing it to resettle, and then I repeat this process down the near side of the run. I then try casting towards the middle of the run, and then the far side, after which time – forty minutes or so – I usually move, unless something has given me the feeling that I should have another cast, perhaps to a different spot within the swim, or to a particular spot with a different bait, or to present a static bait for a while. Then again, it could be that luck plays a part and stays my hand!

One particular run along some far-bank willows had been the subject of my interest more than anywhere else, as towards the top end there was a depression some six to nine inches deeper than the surrounding three and a half feet depth. Fifty yards further down there was a tree-trunk snag under the willows where the water shallowed to nearer two feet deep. I had been fishing the depression in this swim for nearly an hour one night without an enquiry. It was time to move, other swims were calling – and then the heavens opened. Up went the brolly, and I stayed put as the sharp storm blew through. I recast with a stationary bait, and eased it to the tail of the depression. Twenty minutes later the rod went round and I was into a powerful fish: a new river best at 9lb 12oz – and all down to the rain, and the fact that I was out there in the first place.

The tree-trunk snag in this swim does not have such a happy story to tell. One night in October I was fishing there in the heavy weed and fast flow that borders the willows. It is a tricky cast in the dark to drop the bait right off the branches, but one I solved by using the right rig. I used a plasticine weight that pulled off easily if it became snagged, and a braided mainline that allowed me to cast into the branches and then with a quick tug, pull the bait free and drop it directly into the run with a minimal splash. Bait was a softish paste, which meant there was no need

for the hook to be proud. On first looking at the swim I thought that there would be no way that I could get away with using paste bait. By adopting an upstream presentation, however, it was amazing how strongly I could pull the braid to release the rig from a weedbed, and yet still keep the paste on the hook. Everything worked perfectly until I hooked the fish. There is no doubt in my mind that this was the biggest barbel I had ever connected with on the Dove, and it was into the snag before the rod had taken up its full bend. To cut a long story short, I got the fish clear of the snag, but feeling as if it were covered in weed. As it started to come free it gave one last thrust for sanctuary, and the hook-hold gave. I was gutted. I returned on a number of occasions and took some nice fish using the approach outlined above, but alas, never had a further encounter with the 'biggie'.

For the next few years my single baits were mainly meat-based, such as my favourite bacon grill. I also used lobworms, which seemed most effective at dawn, and HNV pastes. The latter, although successful after pre-baiting for a couple of weeks with a few lumps in each swim at the end of a session, did not give a significant edge over the meat. Perhaps they would have taken off in boilie form and with heavier baiting, but I never like to bait heavily for fear of the surplus being left to rot on the

A fine Dove barbel of 9lb 8oz.

riverbed; and I have no desire to programme the fish onto a particular bait to the detriment of anyone else's fishing. There is no doubt that on the Dove at the moment you can catch barbel on a variety of methods and baits. Fishing maggots with a feeder, or long trotting, offers a good chance throughout the season in normal levels, and most particularly when the river is low and cold in the winter. At this time you do not get plagued by the almost ever-present minnows, and after taking a mixed bag, one can often entice a barbel to grab the bait late in the day.

I have remained faithful to my five-mile stretch, despite the lure of larger barbel the closer one gets to the Trent. I do not know one single swim that holds a double (though I do have two 'possibles'), but I have had the occasional season elsewhere on the river. Moving downstream towards Tutbury I have encountered a far higher number of fish, and some known swims that contained doubles. Nevertheless, even though I am yet to capture a Dove double (and I am usually on the water at a time when most other anglers are in bed), I cannot bring myself to try such swims for these fish. If and when it happens, I want my Dove double to be a fish that I have located.

Over the past two seasons I have concentrated my efforts on a different part of the stretch where access is difficult, and where I have found a single shoal of barbel on a three-quarter mile length of river. For the first time on the Dove I was able to watch the fish over a period of weeks, so I abandoned my usual approach and went for a number of daylight sessions. Initially I baited some 12yd (10m) above two bushes under which the barbel live during low or normal water levels. I was baiting with a few handfuls of mixed mini pellets, a pellet/seed mix or a mix of different seeds. The greatest difficulty I had to overcome was in getting the bigger fish to become preoccupied and at the front of the queue for feed, ready for when I slipped a hook bait into the swim. These fish hadn't read the textbooks. A first baiting had them rooting around in the gravel within minutes. However, following subsequent rebaiting during a quiet spell, they invariably failed to put in a further appearance at any time throughout the rest of the day, whether I left the swim alone or periodically rebaited. They did, however, appear to feed more earnestly, and stay around for longer, if I fed mixed pellets on their own.

During the initial feeding spell the biggest fish I saw in the swim was always dominant, staying in view longest and monopolizing the spot with the greatest concentration of bait: I decided that this would have to be her downfall. I baited lightly over an area of a few square yards, with a larger pile of bait at the top end. After about thirty minutes there were some eight barbel moving confidently in and out of the swim. The biggest fish, easily distinguished by a lighter marking on the left pectoral, was at the forefront of affairs. As soon as she moved, I introduced a banded double pellet and waited. Ten more minutes and a steady confident pull produced the required result and a cracking fish of 9lb 5oz. It fought its heart out, making at least three terrific runs out in the flow against a tightly set clutch. Subsequent visits saw the capture of a number of eights and sevens, with only two recaptures, all the fish falling to the same bait. When I tried meatball for a change after some rain I got indications on the line of the presence of fish, but no takes; so I quickly reverted to pellets.

Fishing in daylight and bright sunshine for a change not only gave me the chance of watching the fish, but also the opportunity to experiment with various Fluorocarbon mainlines and hook links. However, despite repeated attempts I could determine no advantage over my standard approach of using braid straight through. This section of river is one of the areas that could produce a double, especially in winter, but I am yet to crack that puzzle. As soon as the river rises, the fish vacate the bushes and do not seem to return until the back end of the season, when I have only caught further sevens. They appear to spend the winter months amongst the far-side willows, unfishable at this time of the year without a beach caster and limpet leads. Such is fishing!

Unfortunately for the visiting angler, there are to my knowledge no day tickets available anywhere on the Dove. There are, however, a lot of open membership clubs whose books offer good value fishing if you are serious about sampling the delights of a battle with a Dove demon. These include Leek Moorlands, Fenton, Isaac Walton, Stoke AS, and a number of others, most of which can be purchased from local tackle shops in Stoke-on-Trent. Similarly, many club books can be purchased in Burton-on-Trent and Derby, all at the time of writing for around £25.

To close, I have a wish: long may the demons of the Dove be a prize to be revered in terms of their fighting qualities, rather than just their size. This, to me, is the essence of barbel fishing, and one of my early sessions on the river sums this up perfectly. At the time I was concentrating on two groups of willow bushes: the top group, towards the bottom of which I had cut a small gap, ran alongside and just below some shallows; the second cluster was some twenty yards lower down over slightly deeper water.

A stunning 'Dove demon' of 9lb 8oz.

That evening I put a pint of hemp into each swim by hand an hour before fishing, adding a further handful after each subsequent visit; I commenced fishing shortly after 8 o'clock.

I began in the bottom swim using corn, but got no response so swapped over to meat, whereon the rod whanged round and a two-pounder was soon netted. Two chub from the top swim followed before I had my second cast in the bottom swim, and the rod bent round again. This type of savage take was rapidly becoming the norm in here, so I was perhaps starting to pressurize the fish too much; tonight's session would be my last for a while. The barbel tore off under the bushes, taking line. I stopped her and regained a few yards, but off she went again, repeating the run. This time as I pulled her clear I got her upstream in front of me; but she just didn't want to come to the net. Every time I got her to the surface she would steam off again. Finally, I had to put both head and chest torches on before I could see where she was and get her into the net. As I weighed her I was amazed and a bit disappointed to see her only go

6lb 11oz, when I was sure she must have been at least 2lb heavier.

The top swim then produced a four-pounder, after which I had a repeat performance and fight in the lower swim. This time I tried to assume command – the experienced barbel angler! – but the fight was dictated by the fish. After an initial run she was determined to go upstream to the top bushes, and even after four attempts had to be dragged thrashing into the net. 6lb 14oz: how can they fight so hard and only be this big, I wondered for the umpteenth time. Back to the top swim, but nothing happened until I manoeuvred the bait next to the branches to my left – and I was immediately in once more. This fish tried to dive for the bushes, but I clamped down hard and stopped her, whereupon she promptly turned upstream and dived under the bushes to the right of my tiny gap. With me clamping down hard, hand over the reel, she really hooped the 1½lb test hard over, and would she give? Not on your life! Too and fro went fish and rod, under and out of the bush for what seemed a couple of minutes as my arm started to ache. Then she surfaced, and was up and down and round in the water below me before the net finally won. It was a really amazing scrap from a 7lb 6oz fish that felt at least 10lb. That was the last action from the top swim, but the lower bushes continued to fish and produced barbel of 5lb 8oz, 6lb, and – as I was packing up at 1.30am, having used six pints of hemp – 4lb 12oz. 'Brilliant barbeling' was my summary of the evening in my diary. No southern double has as yet given me a better fight than the Dove demons managed that summer night. Here's to many more nights of the same.

My Ten-Pounder: A New BCC River Record by Geoff Dace

Although the Dove flows less than thirty miles from where I live, I had never set eyes on it until August 2000. At the start of the season I had joined a club that had a stretch of that river, and I spent half a day walking the banks. Although the river was low and fairly clear, I only managed to spot barbel in one swim – though I did note a few tasty-looking areas that I was confident would hold fish. What I especially liked was that I never saw any anglers. I intended to fish the Dove the following Friday, but having spent two hours on the M6 in holiday traffic trying to get home from work, I decided against the rest of the journey. With too many other places to fish, I never got round to the Dove that season.

My friend Roy joined the club at the start of the next season, and we agreed to fish the Dove together whenever possible. Our first visit was in late July, when we fished two swims in one of the areas I had noted. It was during this session that we discovered maggot fishing was a waste of time, as the river was full of minnows; six maggots on the hook disappeared in seconds. We also fished meat and meatballs, but had no bites. During the evening, I wandered downstream to look at another area I had noted. This section of river was lined with far-bank willows that screamed barbel. An angler was already fishing, and while we chatted he had a barbel of 9lb 14oz. This was definitely an area to try, but it was almost a month before our next visit. We tried flavoured meat, meatballs, garlic sausage and Meaty Fish Bites, but never had a rap.

Our third session was at the end of August. Having had no success on single baits, I opted for a change of approach. I baited a swim with hemp, seeds and corn, and fished two grains of corn on a no. 12 to 8lb fluorocarbon hook length. After about an hour, the rod was almost pulled in by my first Dove barbel, weighing 5lb 9oz. The seed mixture I

use is Buckton's Pigeon Conditioner, and I buy this and the hemp by the sack from a wholesale seed merchant.

The next day we were back again. I began by trundling a piece of flavoured meat in a swim I had not fished before, and caught a barbel of 8lb 6oz after fifteen minutes. With no more bites forthcoming, I baited the swim with my hemp and seed mixture and fished corn. This produced a barbel of 8lb 9oz after half an hour. Once again fishing larger baits into darkness proved unsuccessful.

The next two sessions in early September both resulted in blanks, although Roy did lose a fish on a boilie after dark. On 15 September, with the river a few inches up and carrying a slight tinge of colour, I caught the first double from the Dove by a BCC member. I baited a swim with my usual hemp and seed mix together with a few grains of corn, and took the fish on corn within a few minutes of casting. Although I thought the fish looked bigger, it weighed exactly 10lb.

Our efforts were then concentrated on the lower Severn, and we made only two more trips to the Dove, one in September and one in October, both resulting in blanks. On the first of these sessions I had trouble with minnows taking my corn hook baits, and I had to resort to using artificial rubber corn. Roy had also visited the river three times on his own, and, having had no success, decided not to rejoin the club; I was therefore on my own for the new season.

My first three sessions of the 2002–03 season were on a different stretch. I lost one barbel on artificial casters when the hook pulled out, and I caught one of 6lb on flavoured meat. For my next visit in mid-August, I decided to return to the stretch we had fished the previous season; I thought it was time to try trout pellets. There were no other anglers present, so I put four droppers of 8mm pellets into two swims. I fished a feeder filled with 8mm pellets, and super-glued a 14mm pellet on a no. 8 Super Specialist to 8lb fluorocarbon hook length. A fluorocarbon hook length of about 2ft 6in (75cm) was used because of the clear conditions. For pellet or corn fishing, I cut off the bottom of a Drennan feeder and lightly plug it with groundbait. To avoid tangles, I push a few inches of 1mm soft silicone tubing onto the swivel on the hook length. This method is virtually foolproof. Within a couple of minutes of casting, the rod slammed over and I was into a barbel of 8lb 4oz.

After a couple of hours, I moved to the other baited area and hooked a good fish after half an hour. I put on full pressure, but the fish made it to the far-

Geoff Dace and his club best of 10lb 14oz.

bank willows and the hook length broke. I had two more fish of 7lb 1 oz and 8lb 7oz from this swim: I had found the right bait at last.

The technique for playing these hard-fighting Dove barbel is to keep the rod low, apply side strain, and hang on until the fish moves away from the snags. This is no place for leaving the Baitrunner engaged! For the first time I felt that my trusty old Terry Eustace 'Barbel Leger' rod, that I had used for over fifteen years, was not quite up to the task. I had bought a 10ft Harrison 'Stalker' from Dove expert Steve Stayner before the start of the season; this rod has a test curve of 1½lb, and Steve told me the rod has tremendous power and is ideal for the Dove. On my next visit the following week, I reluctantly left the old favourite at home and put the new rod to the test. I also upped my 8lb Progold mainline to 10lb. I took five barbel to 8lb 15oz on my next three trips, and the rod coped extremely well. After losing one fish, I stepped up my fluorocarbon hook length to 10lb. I now felt I had the right tools for the job.

In early September the river was a foot up and coloured. This was the first time I had fished the Dove under these conditions, and I caught two barbel on pellets, including a nine-pounder. The barbel I was catching were averaging around 8lb, and I felt it was only a matter of time before I landed a double.

On 18 September the river was back at its normal level, and clear. I put in four droppers of pellets, and began fishing at 1.15pm. After twenty minutes I hooked a barbel that I eventually landed following a terrific fight, a bull of a fish in immaculate condition and weighing 10lb 14oz. This was a new BCC river record. With no one else around, I was grateful for the self-timer on my camera. I rested the barbel in the landing net, got everything ready, and fired off a number of shots. I carried on fishing until 8.30pm, but without any more bites – but I didn't really care. After a special fish like that, it would have been an anticlimax to have caught anything else.

12 The River Frome

by Mike Stevens

Twice in my angling career I have found barbel that I am sure no one else knew existed. Once on the Bristol Avon I found a shoal of fish that included at least six doubles, and one looking as if it might break the national record (which in 1986 was 13lb something). Then on the Somerset Frome in 1988 I found a shoal of fish to 9lb plus. In both situations the excitement I felt was incredible. No one else was even fishing the venues. They were 'my fish', their size an irrelevance . . . well, almost! Neither of these shoals is now 'mine'. The Frome fish have been lost to a fly-fishing club, of all things, and those on the Avon have achieved fame of their own as the stars of photographs in the company of anglers such as Trefor West, Stuart Morgan, Ray Walton, John Baker and Martin Bowler. Do I miss those? Not for a second. I had my share of them on the Avon for two full summers. They gave me three river records, and put our part of the world on the barbel map. Furthermore I caught them on my terms, on corn, in daylight, watching the fish I wanted pick up the bait – though never the big one, which was a shame, as I estimated its length to be around 32in (80cm). What price a 2003 boilie-fed winter fish of 32in in length?

The Frome swim gave me my second river record, and it also gave Andy Cowley the fish that is still the one to beat. Although no one famous will ever search it out, I probably have fonder memories of it, if only because, unlike the 'Mike Stevens' tree swim on the Avon, it isn't opposite sewage works! Believe me, after two summers it was time to move on! In contrast, the Frome swim was in paradise, nestling in a deep wooded valley miles from roads or buildings, the only company being the small family of roe deer that came down to drink at dusk. The Somerset Frome is a river that I don't think will appeal to many barbel anglers, simply because the river probably doesn't have the potential to produce fish over 13lb. For instance, my river record was 7lb 14oz, the Cowley monster was 10lb 15oz, and our back-up fish are now 9lb 8oz (me!) and 9lb 7oz (him!). No doubt you are still reading, because all barbel anglers grow out of the 'mine is bigger than yours' syndrome. Nevertheless, the Frome will only ever be a minor river for the species in a national context, and even in the local arena it will never threaten the mighty Bristol Avon. For me, however, it does have its own attractions: truly unspoiled countryside, relatively unpressurized fish and opportunities for stalking barbel at close range in the crystal-clear pools and riffles. It is extremely varied in character, with deep water one minute, and barely inches of fast water the next.

In his river record articles in the angling press, Brian Dowling has guessed that the Frome fish could be travellers from the Bristol Avon. I'm sure that some are, but the river has also been stocked in its own right. Indeed, Freshford Weir on the lower river was one of the original Bristol Avon catchment sites, and was stocked with Kennet fish in the 1960s. Unfortunately it is thought that this population died out as a result of a pollution incident caused by a fire in a local rubber factory. Thankfully this area does have a population now that has almost certainly resulted from migration from the Avon, since the weir is less than a mile from the Frome mouth.

A little further upriver at Iford there is a healthy barbel population. Fish at this site have migrated themselves or been helped up over the weir and are now successfully colonizing the stretch up to Farleigh Hungerford weir. Though numbers here are still low, the average size is greater. Above Farleigh Hungerford, upstream to the weir at Stowford, there is a small population of fish, including the 1lb babies that indicate spawning successes. This must mean that the Frome has a bright future as a barbel river.

The Frome in February.

Further upstream at Tellisford, twenty fish to around 6lb in weight were introduced in the mid-1980s. These were Bristol Avon fish taken from a minor tributary at spawning time by the then NRA. To the best of my knowledge, these are the only stockings that the river has ever received, and at present the weir at Tellisford represents the upstream limit of the species. There is therefore a healthy breeding population as far upstream as five weirs from the confluence with the Avon.

Upstream of Tellisford, as far as Oldford on the outskirts of the town of Frome, there are plenty of localized sites suitable for stocking with small populations of barbel. That this hasn't happened may be due to the fact that the fishing clubs controlling the upper river are not as proactive in their contacts with the Environment Agency as are some other clubs. It may also be due to a decision by the EA that the water quality in the upper river is not suitable, and in this respect the River Frome is atypical. Its source is in the limestone of the East Mendip hills, and its short length drains mainly dairy farming countryside. Near the town of Frome, however, it is under serious threat of pollution, in

that a major tributary, the Mells Stream, drains an area that is intensively quarried and often carries a heavy suspension of limestone dust. The town itself is growing fast, and I suspect that the nutrient levels in the river are artificially high as a result of inadequate treatment capacity in the town's sewage works. Certainly the river immediately below the town rarely runs clear, and the gravel shallows are often clogged with grey/green blanket algae, suggesting over-enrichment. The town also has several industries including a varnishing factory, print works and a creamery. There have been no serious pollution incidents since the 1980s, but perhaps the risks make the investment a less attractive proposition.

Nevertheless, the Frome is definitely one of the few rivers where water quality seems to improve with distance downstream. I imagine this is because the many weirs trap sediment and oxygenate the water, thus allowing bacteria to use up the nutrients. Whatever the case, once the river has travelled eight weirs downstream of the town we at last find the clear water and clean gravel that the barbel inhabit. The fish average 6lb or so, with 10lb-plus fish in at

Seven-year-old Bethamy Cowley caught this 7lb 3oz barbel on John Baker paste.

the cost of running their own trout-rearing facility. It is expensive, but you can river fly fish, and most of the time you will have the barbel to yourself. You can pre-bait and rove between swims, even on 16 June, find 'your own' swims, and even develop new swims. Personally, I think that to have such exclusive access in an era of more and more barbel fishermen is worth paying for.

So what does the future hold for barbel in the Somerset Frome? The lower river populations are well established, and I have hopes that in the long term the Tellisford stretch will return to the control of a coarse angling club. Fish will slowly colonize upstream stretches. The real hope, however, is that with the older industries in Frome declining, and those still present becoming more environmentally aware, all that is needed is some upgrading of sewage works capacity, and the upper river may run clear at last. Is a future with a clear river supporting healthy populations of barbel in open access waters, 2 miles from my home, too much to wish for? Probably!

A Memorable Ten-Pounder by Andy Cowley

My introduction to the Somerset Frome came many years ago, when I was about fourteen. The father of a friend of mine happened to be cleaning windows in the vicinity, and kindly dropped us off for a day's fishing on the river near Rode. I clearly remember three things about that summer's day in rural Somerset: the excitement of fishing a totally new venue for the first time, the monstrous minnows and gigantic gudgeon we caught, and the mole that emerged from the cut-out bank where I sat. To this day it remains the only living mole I have ever set eyes upon. It scuttled around in my groundbait bucket for a minute or two, whilst two young pairs of wide eyes looked on in fascination. Upon liberation it departed as quickly as it had appeared, leaving nothing behind but a small pile of earth and a lasting memory of an intriguing, velvet-clad oddity.

least two areas, and an increasing number of small fish that indicate successful spawning. In only a few areas could the species numbers be described as prolific, but in these lower reaches they are widely enough dispersed to be considered well established.

When it comes to the practicalities of getting access to the river, both locals and visitors have problems to overcome. On the lower river there is now very little open club membership or day ticket water. The Bradford-on-Avon Angling Association used to control one bank of the Tellisford weir stretch, but they are very much a match-orientated club, and because the venue is anything but match friendly, they gave up the lease. This is now controlled by the West Wiltshire Fly Fishers Club, which has a limited membership but does offer an October-to-March coarse-fishing-only ticket. The other bank is controlled by Avon and Somerset Police: poach it at your peril! From Stowford weir downstream there is a short stretch covered by day tickets from Stowford Farm caravan site and Airsprung AC; tickets are obtainable from local tackle shops. From Farleigh Hungerford weir downstream to the Frome mouth, the whole river is controlled by the Avon and Tributaries Angling Association, a limited access, small membership, trout-fishing club. Their Frome waters are coarse fishing only, but the high membership fee reflects

It was twenty years before I was to fish the Frome again. My good friend Mike Stevens took me along to a small, club-run stretch where for a few years he had been catching barbel up to nearly 8lb in weight. I was immediately taken with this pretty, if rather diminutive piece of river bordered by lush vegetation, which tantalizingly did not reveal its secrets easily.

A myriad of small chub seemingly resided in every swim, together with a number of very obvious bream of 5lb or so. Pike plus occasional carp, roach

Eight-year-old Amy Cowley with a 6lb 14oz barbel caught on a meatball.

and perch were all spotted in the clear, shallow water; but the barbel proved to be rather shy on that visit in August of 1992. I was living in Bristol at that time, about twenty-five miles from the Frome, and so was not to sample its delights again for a couple of years or so.

Following a house move in 1994 the Frome became my local venue, as well as my beloved Bristol Avon. Both of these rivers now flow only half a mile from my doorstep, and not surprisingly much of my angling time is spent on their banks.

In the summer of 1995 I decided it was time to target the Frome barbel. Mike's interest in these fish had waned and he rarely fished for them any more, and he was therefore quite happy for me to have a go at beating his Barbel Catchers' river record, which stood at 7lb 14oz. He actually accompanied me on my first attempt in early July, when we had difficulty spotting anything due to coloured water. We took consolation in the form of several chub and bream, which were happy to accept our crudely presented baits without question. I remember that we both caught bream of 5lb 2oz, at that time the largest that either of us had actually weighed. Those

obliging fish saved many a blank session on subsequent trips, even on one occasion taking hook baits directly to 11lb line, with no suggestion of being tackle shy. It was unfortunately not so simple with the barbel, which provided considerably more of a challenge.

My return to the river one month later on a hot, sunny morning was greeted by much improved water clarity. I gradually worked my way downstream whilst baiting up likely looking swims on the way, hoping to entice any barbel out from their cover and onto my hempseed and sweetcorn, where I could see them. Upon approaching the old barbel stronghold, I was faced with a number of fish happily feeding over gravel behind a tree in Mike's favourite swim. They seemed unaware of my presence and continued foraging in relatively open water, preoccupied with natural food items of some sort.

I decided to introduce a small quantity of particles above the tree to see if the barbel would move up onto them. Even though it was not a practical place to present a hook bait, I wanted them to abandon their present position long enough for me to prepare a banquet of hemp and sweetcorn there. This area provided a better vantage point for both observing the fish in the morning light and actually trying to catch one.

The plan began to come together nicely as the barbel disappeared upstream, but a lone bream of 4½lb moved onto my loose feed almost as soon as it hit bottom. I quickly caught it and encouraged it to seek out pastures new by moving it to another swim whilst the barbel continued rooting around higher up. The last thing I needed was to hook a 'splashy' bream amongst the barbel later on. I then wandered back to the top of the stretch for an hour or two to check on the other swims, and occupied myself by teasing a few more bream, letting the barbel settle down to lunch.

Despite some lovely looking barbel swims, the barbel themselves were obviously less than impressed with my baited areas as only chub, bream and roach were found in residence. I concluded this could be because most, if not all, the resident barbel were concentrated in the one shoal in 'Mike's swim', a phenomenon I have encountered elsewhere. I returned to find them grateful for my offerings below the tree, and feeding confidently again.

Although fish constantly moved in and out of the baited patch of gravel, I estimated there to be at least fifteen barbel from a little over 1lb upwards in weight. I eventually classified half a dozen or so as worthy of capture, estimating them at between 7lb and 9lb. There was, however, one occasional visitor that was of greater proportions than the others, and which was my ultimate goal. Plan A was to catch any of the better fish initially, and learn a bit more about them in the process by seeing how they reacted to my tackle and how they fed together.

The swim was never devoid of barbel at any time, so a tentative cast was made while they were fewer in numbers. Momentarily startled, they soon forgot the intrusion into their world but remained obviously aware of my 9lb bs Sylcast main line. Indeed, it resembled a length of towrope from my bankside perch. I considered it justified, however, for the security it provided in the event of a running barbel seeking the sanctuary of the nearby tangle of branches and tree roots.

The bunch of sweetcorn grains on the hook was continually being attacked by minnows and tiny chub. Occasionally it would vanish behind a rock,

The Somerset Frome in winter at Ilford bridge, guarded by Britannia at Ilford Manor.

and then miraculously reappear a foot away attached to the nose end of a 4in (10cm) chub with his friends bringing up the rear; a bit like an underwater game of rugby. The strike, though, was reserved for the first good barbel that proved unable to contain itself any longer. The sweetcorn disappeared, the rod hooped over, and after a short but spirited fight, my first Frome barbel lay within the folds of my landing net. A beautiful, unmarked fish of 7lb 9oz, not a river record, but very close to it, and very welcome. I quickly returned the fish fifty yards downstream to enable it to rejoin the shoal later without agitating them further. I was back at home in time for lunch, and the afternoon's parental and domestic duties.

Keen to improve on my debut performance, I was back the next morning. As I made my way gradually downstream, I was sidetracked by a very modest chub which demanded that I attempt to catch it. As I landed and unhooked it, a rather unsociable character hurried past me without a word, the first angler I had seen in the area other than Mike and a few children. That chub proved to have been a tactical error, as my new 'friend' promptly installed himself in the only swim on the stretch I didn't want him to be in. I forced conversation upon him, and learned that he had caught a number of barbel from here up to 12½lb. When questioned, he clearly confirmed that the fish had not been weighed, so I was rather perturbed when he subsequently backtracked and claimed it *had* been weighed. The true size or even existence of this fish therefore became clouded in doubt. Certainly neither Mike nor I ever saw a fish even approaching that size in all our visits to the Frome.

A third consecutive morning found me on the river bank yet again. My fishing diary for the day begins 'Obsessed with big barbel in Frome'. With clear intent I marched straight down, thankful that the swim was vacant this time, and was pleased to see a few barbel out on the gravel again. I flicked in some grains of corn to see how they would react, and was surprised to see the largest fish emerge from the cover of the tree and immediately start feeding. I wanted to get the barbel actively searching for food and hopefully less concerned about my tackle, so I introduced small amounts of hempseed and corn over the next hour or so, spread over a fairly wide area. This worked well, as it did not spook the fish and got them feeding confidently.

Using just two SSG shot on the line, I could easily cast the short distance to the far bank from where I could carefully tweak the bait back across the flow and into position. The barbel were again disturbed by the sight of my line in the water, and would swim up to it, then suddenly veer away or turn back downstream. My answer was to pin the line to the bottom using more SSG shot a few feet up the line, and this improved the situation substantially. Bite indication was not a problem as I was actually watching the bait. I used two grains of sweetcorn balanced with a piece of yellow rig foam roughly shaped to a similar appearance, to counter the weight of the size 6 hook and thus allow more natural movement of the hook bait. This was attached to a short braided hook length to both enhance the movement of the bait and provide a material that the barbel's delicate mouth would find less detectable than monofilament.

It was another sunny morning, and observing both the fish and my bait wasn't a great problem in the shallow water. What became obvious was that the largest barbel in the shoal had a distinct preference for feeding in a particular spot towards the end of the swim. Despite its less frequent visits to the bait, it spent more time picking up food from this same area than elsewhere. The other barbel appeared less discerning. My efforts were therefore focused on keeping my hook bait in this small area as I felt it would improve my chances of hooking the fish selectively.

Success looked imminent when the big fish approached my bait with a companion by its side. I watched its mouth pause directly over the balanced corn – but at that moment my vision was obscured by the other barbel moving alongside. I saw the big one's gills flare as if it had taken my hook bait, so I took a chance and struck – and my end tackle flew from the water and past my left ear into the adjacent bush. To add insult to injury, shortly afterwards about ten canoes came through the swim, an intrusion I just could not believe on such a small river. The fibreglass bottoms scraped over gravel where it shallowed up to almost nothing at the end of the swim, some even getting stuck here! Although annoyed, I reasoned that this whole incident had probably upset *me* more than it had the barbel, so I decided to stay put.

Only fifteen minutes after the armada had left, the barbel gradually started to feed again. The problem I now faced was muddied water due to the canoes ploughing through such a shallow and overgrown river. It was about half an hour before the situation had improved sufficiently to start fishing again, and even then I couldn't keep track of the hook bait easily as I struggled to see it. I tried to deal with this by placing a small, white polystyrene ball on the hook-length swivel, which was quite easily located against the gravel; my bait could then be identified a foot below it. I could also double check a pick-up by looking back at the polyball to see if it moved when the light or visibility became less favourable. Despite a barbel actually trying to eat the polyball at one point, the technique worked when a good fish in a mixed-size group appeared to pick up the bait. My strike met with little resistance, however, and a small barbel of just 1½lb came to the net. I wasn't quite sure how it happened, but I imagine the little fish had been at the far side of the other one where I couldn't see it, and the coloured water prevented me from seeing a second nose over the bait. But my time was up and I had to get back home so any more opportunities would have to wait.

The next evening was our Barbel Catchers' meeting, and I was unusually enthusiastic about my barbel fishing due to my recent encounters with the Frome fish. These were the topic of conversation for much of the evening, and I was pressed to estimate the weight of my target fish. I reluctantly said that it may be ten and a half to eleven pounds with two or three others possibly around nine pounds in weight.

The following day I managed to finish work early and I got to the Frome at 4.15pm. The position of the sun at this time made it far more difficult to see into the river, as the light reflected back at me off the surface despite my polarized sunglasses. Fortunately the place with the best visibility happened to be where the big barbel preferred to feed towards the end of the swim. Since the big one came out in response to feeding a little corn on my last session, I first tried doing the same again, but with my hook bait already in place where I could see it. Suicidal chub dashed this method on the rocks within minutes, spooking the barbel into the process, so it was aborted.

I baited the tail end of the swim with a little hemp

and corn in the small area previously visited by the biggest barbel, but also introduced other small beds of bait just a little further upstream. I was attempting to split the feeding barbel into small groups, and hoped the large one would prefer the same spot as before. I couldn't see the fish properly unless they moved to the downstream bait where I could manage to pick out individuals quite well. The big one, although unsettled today, appeared a couple of times. My patience was finally rewarded when a large head emerged from the gloom, worked its way up to my bait and liked what it saw. The corn was sucked into those whiskered lips and suddenly it was on. My trusty old Tricast rod dealt with the initial rushes like a professional, and in no time she was mine.

The barbel had a couple of well-healed scars, but was otherwise in excellent condition, and a typical clear-water fish with vivid coloration. She measured 29½in long, with a girth of 16½in, and she pulled the Avon's round to 10lb 15oz. I was overjoyed with the capture, which was the end result of a combination of very basic fishing methods, watercraft, much determination and a bit of luck. She recovered quickly after being immortalized on film, and swam off none the worse for the experience.

I sat and pondered my success for a while, and after twenty minutes the other barbel were back out and feeding once more. My job was done, though, and I didn't cast again, but just sat watching them for a while.

Since these events I have caught many more barbel from the Frome, but none bigger. That 10lb 15oz fish remains one of my most memorable barbel, for many reasons, and my thanks go to Mike Stevens for introducing me to the Frome barbel and providing me with the opportunity in the first place.

13 The Great Ouse

by Roy Bates

The River Great Ouse rises between the villages of Whitfield and Brackley, which lie close to the borders of Northamptonshire. From here, the river flows in an easterly direction through Bedford and the Cambridgeshire fens before finally emptying into the Wash just above King's Lynn.

Whether or not the species *Barbus barbus* is indigenous to the river remains something of a mystery. When land mass displacement occurred at the end of the Ice Age, barbel were found only to inhabit easterly flowing rivers. The Yorkshire Ouse, Trent and Thames catchment areas have a long, documented history of producing barbel; however, this is not the case with the Great Ouse.

As recently as 1806 there was no mention of barbel by the early recorders of local natural history. During that year the Reverend Lyson writes: 'The fish of the Ouse to be pike, perch, bream, chub, eels, dace, roach and gudgeon.' Similarly, in the *History of Bedford 1837*; the Reverend Blyth mentions the same species with the single addition of the crayfish. American signal crayfish were not introduced until the mid-1970s, and it is therefore safe to assume that the crayfish mentioned were native species.

The earliest documented record of barbel in the Ouse was in the *Victorian History of the Counties of England 1904* by A. Thompson. In this book he writes that barbel were introduced by the Bedford Angling Club in 1876. Thirty-one fish from the Thames, ranging from 1lb to 5lb, were donated by

the Maidenhead Angling Association, and were released into the river at Kempston. In 1888 an additional thirty-eight barbel from the Thames, weighing between 3lb and 10lb, were released at Clapham and Renhold. The lack of river obstructions in the form of weirs and locks enabled the fish to breed and colonize new stretches both above and below Bedford.

A 12lb fish was caught at Sharnbrook in 1898, and a large fish was apparently killed by an otter at St Neots in 1901. These are just two of many documented recordings showing the successful spread of the species. However, throughout the next fifty years there was little documented evidence of the presence of barbel, until in the 1960s local myth and rumours began to suggest that fish were again being caught from the river.

Mr Eric Rogers, a Birmingham AA Fisheries Officer, is believed to have stocked fifty-one mature fish from the Severn, ranging between 2lb and 5lb, into the Ouse during the 1970s. These fish were released into waters controlled by the Vauxhall Angling Club at Radwell, Sharnbrook and Milton Ernest. During the same period, further barbel were introduced downstream of Haversham Weir on the Great Linford Lakes complex, though the exact number released was not recorded. A further rumoured stocking of thirty fish up to a foot in length took place in 1976, upstream of Harrold Bridge; and during the same year a further 500 fish, up to 5lb in weight, from the Severn were also released. These reports were all based upon local knowledge and hearsay, as no recorded evidence exists to support their authenticity.

In more recent times the environment agency has attempted to increase the distribution of barbel in the Great Ouse at several suitable locations. One such venue is the New Cut, a gravel channel that runs off the Ouse and through Bedford's Priory County Park. Following habitat enhancement by the introduction of boulder groynes and tree management in 1994, a re-stocking programme of juvenile barbel took place between 1994 and 1997. This stocking consisted of:

1994:	4,000 fish of approximately	12cm in length
1995:	1,500 "	16cm "
1996:	1,000 "	16cm "
1997:	1,000 "	16cm "

These barbel appear to be thriving, with a fish of 8lb 8oz being reported by an angler in 2002. Natural recruitment of barbel in the cut is highly probable, as a fish of 2lb 6oz was also caught in December 2002. Similar stockings have been undertaken during this period in areas of suitable habitat where barbel populations were either low or non-existent; these areas include the river at Offord, Godmanchester and Harrold. The fish were largely sourced from Calverton fish farm.

The barbel population in the Great Ouse is now widespread and at an all-time high; the fish are growing well, and natural recruitment is on the increase. Environment Agency surveys have recorded juvenile barbel at several sites, which are not associated with stocked fish. Historically the highest densities of barbel have been recorded at Adam's Mill, Newport Pagnell, Turvey, Radwell and Sharnbrook. The record barbel (at the time of writing) is a fish of 19lb 6oz, caught from Adam's Mill, a syndicate stretch of the river leased by the Milton Keynes Angling Club.

Although barbel can now be caught from most areas above Bedford and a few areas below, the following clubs control some of the better stretches: Milton Keynes Angling Club, Vauxhall Angling Club, Northampton and Nene Angling Club, Bedford Angling Club and Shefford Angling Club. All of these club waters contain large barbel in excess of 16lb, and many are only lightly fished so there is a genuine possibility of a new record barbel from these waters.

Despite the fact that barbel are found in most areas upstream of Bedford, the Ouse cannot be classed as providing easy barbel fishing. Barbel location, especially during the winter months, can be extremely difficult. As with many rivers, however, the larger fish are often caught during flood conditions, and because recent weather patterns suggest that floods will become the norm during winter, it is important that the barbel angler makes the most of these conditions. With a little effort, and concentrating on two different types of venue, the rewards can justify the inevitable blank sessions.

A fine summer barbel for Roy of 12lb 6oz.

In many areas the riverbanks are very low and flood easily. In such areas, swims that produce in normal summer conditions will be totally unfishable in flood conditions. There are two methods that can be employed to identify winter barbel swims, one of which may appear obvious, the other less so. The first is to walk your chosen fishery when the river is in flood. The slacker areas often look inviting, and of course can, and do, hold fish; however, the angler will have little awareness of the nature of the riverbed and/or any snags present. The second method, and also the most satisfying, is to walk the banks during the close season in order to study the riverbed (when water clarity will allow). This approach can also be followed during the late summer months. Remember that the objective is to identify potentially productive swims for flood conditions. Features to look for are a high bank, above normal summer level, with the main flow running along the far bank. If such an area is enhanced by trees and bushes upstream of the swim, so much the better, as in flood conditions these will break up the flow. During the summer these areas can be totally unfishable, as reeds and/or rushes would have to be cleared to allow access.

The swim could be covered with a mass of streamer weed or the yellow 'brandy glass'-type lily and its accompanying sub-surface cabbage leaves. These should not be a cause for concern as they will die back during the winter months, and the remaining root stalks will then provide shelter for the fish against the strong winter flow. Do, however, look for large obstructions such as fallen branches, and remove them as required. Remember to cut a hole in bank-side vegetation such as nettles or loosestrife, because during floods submerged vegetation can constitute unseen snags. If possible prepare several such swims in the same area to give yourself more options (bearing in mind local club rules).

Last, but by no means least, mark your swims in some way, as they may not be instantly recognizable in winter flood conditions. Ways of achieving this is could be either to take a snapshot of the opposite bank, or to create your own identifiable feature (but don't make it too obvious).

Catching a barbel from your own virgin swim is one of the most rewarding experiences in angling. Who knows? It could be a previously uncaught monster.

For winter fishing on the Ouse a tip to middle-action rod of 1½lb test curve is about right. My personal preference is for a Richard Walker Mk IV-built cane carp rod, coupled with either a 'Trudex' or 'Rapidex' centrepin reel. In my opinion this is the ultimate combination for close-in barbel fishing. I fish with 8lb 'Maxima' as mainline and hook length, as I feel this is capable of landing any barbel I may encounter. Importantly the rod and the line are in balance. Of equal importance is the welfare of the barbel, because should a fish become snagged it must be possible to 'break off' without damaging the fish. Try pulling for a break with 15lb line, and you will appreciate the point being made. The hooks I use are Drennan Super Specialist, size 8 and barbless.

The mainline and hook length (usually about 18in) are joined by a 'Drennan' ring that also acts as a leger stop. Whether using a feeder or a lead weight, the rig is a basic free-running type used in conjunction with a 'John Roberts' quick-change ledger ring. My choice of swimfeeder is a 40g 'Kamasan' block-end, with a red power-gum link attachment. Whilst there are exceptions to every rule, I find that if a 40g feeder will hold the bottom, then the conditions will be suitable for 'Old Whiskers'. The hinged top of the feeder is cut off, and the feeder is filled with 3mm or 5mm trout pellets that are plugged with a piece of bread. Hook bait is usually trout-pellet paste. Upon casting out, once the feeder has hit the bottom the rod is given a quick jerk to displace the bread and allow the feeder to empty. This concentrates the feed around the hook bait. During the winter it is important not to overfeed, and often if fish are present in the swim,

Roy shows off a winter barbel of 14lb 6oz.

this method will produce a fish on the first cast. If bites are not forthcoming I re-bait every hour, or occasionally I will move to a different swim.

I have been using trout-pellet paste as my main hook bait since 1995, and I find it equally effective in both summer and winter. It appears to be a bait that works instantly, and will often catch fish immediately on waters that have never seen the bait before. Furthermore it appears irresistible to fish, and does not seem to lose its effectiveness (or 'blow') over a period of time. I recall that in the 1950s and 1960s Richard Walker caught many large chub on trout-pellet paste from the upper Great Ouse. What's good enough for 'RW' is certainly good enough for 'RB'!

A 1kg bag of trout-pellet powder is cheap and will probably last a full season. It can be made into a soft paste by mixing the powder with eggs, a drop of cooking oil and perhaps a binder such as breadcrumb until the desired consistency is achieved. When using a hair rig and/or requiring a harder bait, mix a packet of gelatine in boiling water, stirring well until all the crystals have dissolved; add the powder, and mix until a strong, workable paste is formed. Shapes and sizes can then be moulded to suit. Note that when using the gelatine mix it is important to keep it warm; if it is allowed to cool, the crystals will tend to break up when moulded together. If the mix does cool, simply re-heat in a microwave before re-mixing with a sturdy fork. Either mix can be stored and re-stored for several weeks in a freezer.

During the close season of 2000 I began to look for winter flood swims along several stretches of the Ouse. We eventually marked up six potential swims that, judging by the bank-side vegetation, had never been previously fished. We were extremely fortunate with our selections in that all six have provided us with barbel, although only two of these swims are fishable under extreme flood conditions. Success came at last on the morning of 14 November, the last day of a three-day fishing trip. I had previously suffered fourteen blank sessions, and during the preceding two days the river had been into the fields. On this murky wet morning the river was still over its banks and I was restricted to the two fishable swims.

At the start of that third day I sat in 'Barbel Bay' in perfect winter conditions, the water temperature

The 'Hawthorn' swim in the flood conditions that produced Roy's 13lb 9oz specimen.

being 9.8°C. The first four hours failed to produce a bite, and I decided that no barbel had moved into this particular swim during this latest flood; I therefore decided to rest the swim and moved fifty yards upstream to a swim we call 'The Hawthorns'. I had to stand in eighteen inches of cold floodwater, and although this was uncomfortable, the swim looked promising. The simple fact that the rain had now stopped increased my sense of anticipation as I cast out. Looking at my watch, the hands read exactly 1pm. I decided to give it until 2pm and then return to my original swim for lunch and a coffee. Time passed, and a glance at the watch indicated 1.55pm; time to return to base. As I stooped to pick up the rod, the centrepin clicked, turning a quarter of a turn and giving a quick 'zzzz'. My hand hovered over the rod expectantly. 'Probably a chub mouthing the bait,' I thought. Then the reel screamed into life with that magical sound only a centrepin can make: 'zzzzzzzzzzzzzzzzz'. A gentle strike set the hook, and the cane arched over into what was obviously a very good fish – and certainly no chub!

All hell broke loose as the first run all but emptied the fifty yards of 8lb 'Maxima' from the reel. Incredulous as to the power of the fish, I wondered if it could be foul-hooked; but at last it slowed. I regained line slowly: for every two yards I managed to gain, the fish took one yard back. Then the line suddenly went slack, and for a fleeting moment I thought I had lost her. But I soon realized that the fish had actually turned towards me, and I managed to reestablish contact. Again the fish took line, and I was concerned that she would win her freedom. But at last she tired, and slowly slid over the waiting net.

Fish and angler were equally exhausted. I glanced at my watch, which read 2.17pm, so the fight had lasted an incredible seventeen minutes. I rested the fish in the landing net, and enjoyed a well-earned cup of coffee whilst reflecting on her fight and her sheer power. I relived each moment, recalling her long runs and her reluctance to leave the riverbed even for a few seconds. Even after breaking the surface she had still had the strength to dive again more than fifteen minutes after being hooked. I wondered if she set a new personal best. She looked enormous as I placed her in the weigh-sling, and on the scales she registered a pleasing 13lb 9oz. Although not my largest barbel, she was a magnificent winter fish and one I would always remember.

By the end of July, the Great Ouse usually becomes gin clear, allowing for easy fish observation and consequently the stalking of barbel. Stalking a fish and then catching it as close to the bank as possible is, for me, the ultimate barbel angling experience, and certainly gets the adrenalin going. Although tackle is basically the same as for winter fishing, I dispense with the swimfeeder, preferring instead either a small bomb or a link leger with just enough SSG shot to hold bottom. The link-leger method is ideal for fishing weedy swims where a feeder or bomb would snag up too often. A link leger is easily made: simply take a 6in length of monofilament (I prefer 4lb or 5lb) and fold it in half. Press on the required number of SSG shot, leaving a loop by which to attach it to a John Roberts quick-change leger ring. In the event of a snag the SSG shot will simply slide off, hopefully recovering the situation.

Bait is again invariably trout-pellet paste, either moulded directly around the hook if fishing a weedy swim, or hair-rigged if fishing a heavily fished area for shy-biting fish. When using a hair rig I prefer the hair coming from the top of the hook shank, just below the eye. I use a hair long enough to leave approximately ⅜in between the bend of the hook and the top of the bait. When baiting up a swim in the summer months I use a different approach to the one I adopt during the winter months. In winter it is important to introduce feed tightly in one small area, as the fish will not be moving around significantly and will feed sporadically. In the summer, however, they will (hopefully) be feeding much more enthusiastically, and if the type of swim permits I will scatter my loose feed liberally around the whole area surrounding my hook bait. I want the fish to move around the whole swim hunting for food. If I'm fishing a popular swim I will try to place my hook bait in an area of the swim where most anglers would not put theirs. In order to catch a fish you often have to move it from its 'home' or from its usual feeding area. If, for example, the fish inhabits the roots of an over-hanging willow, to cast there could be fatal as the fish would almost certainly spook – and even if they didn't spook, you risk being smashed up or snagged in the event of hooking a fish, something I try to avoid at all costs.

Often it is possible on the Ouse to feed hemp and pellets by hand or by catapult, and the noise of bait falling on the water will attract fish from many yards away; thus a previously barren swim can soon be swarming with fish, including the barbel that you are stalking. I prefer to see other species feeding in the swim, as this will make the barbel feed more aggressively and confidently. Large hook baits are required in these circumstances, to avoid catching the smaller non-target species. It is important at this stage to emphasize two points: first, ensure that you

The 'Aquarium' swim in winter.

cast accurately first time: this is the most important cast, as the noise of the bait hitting the water could attract fish into the swim. A second cast, if necessitated, could then frighten the fish away. And second, position the hook bait correctly prior to introducing any loose feed. Casting into an area where fish are already feeding can often be the kiss of death.

As mentioned previously, I prefer to catch my fish close to the bank, as this has several advantages. The bait can be lowered into position with little disturbance, whilst the bank itself will shield the angler from the fish's natural vision. This latter point is of vital importance, as I catch most of my fish during daylight hours. Fishing in this manner is extremely exciting and often produces a fish within minutes of the bait being introduced into the swim. Give it a try!

In late July 2002, Jim Collins and myself were walking the banks of the Ouse fish spotting, and came across a swim that the club members call the 'Aquarium'. This swim is perfect for stalking tactics, having a high bank from which one can look down onto the barbel; this bank has been gouged out during frequent floods to form a pool twenty yards in length. In flood conditions the water moves in a washing-machine motion, turning back on itself after hitting the bank at the base of a willow. During

the summer months this back flow is quite gentle, so loose feed can be introduced by hand to the top of the swim; it will then gently fall into a six-feet deep hole directly beneath your feet. Some will get caught in the current and be carried down to the willow where the barbel and chub lie.

Carefully we looked down into the water, and at first no fish were visible. But as our eyes adjusted to the polaroids, the shapes of three barbel became clear. All three were large fish; the smallest we estimated at 10lb, and the largest perhaps 12lb. Mesmerized, we watched them feeding on small particles drifting down with the current, their golden flanks flashing as they turned to intercept food. At this stage we noticed that the swim had not been fished since last season and, looking up to the top of the pool, the reason for this became apparent: a small tree had collapsed into the swim during the floods, and now lay partially submerged, held by its roots, rendering the swim unfishable. To remove it would not be a problem, however, and within the hour I had returned equipped with chest waders, a bow-saw and a rope. We attached the rope to the tree, and Jim held the rope while I sawed through the tree roots; and within ten minutes we had removed the obstruction, and the swim could be fished.

Ever the gentleman, Jim invited me to fish the swim, but I declined as I thought that the disturbance had probably ruined the chances of a fish for the rest of the day. Jim therefore decided that he would give it a go, but although the barbel did return to the swim, unfortunately no bites materialized. Two days later I returned to the swim: would the barbel still be in residence? I carefully crept up and peered into the water. At first the swim appeared barren, but then from out of the depths three barbel emerged. For a full half hour I watched their behaviour, admiring the ease with which they manoeuvred as they fed in the fast current. It was time to try and catch one. I quickly tackled up my beloved Richard Walker Mark IV cane rod with a Trudex centrepin loaded with 8lb Maxima line. The end rig consisted of a simple 1oz running lead stopped by a small ring, with a size 8 Drennan Super Specialist hook. Hook bait was hair-rigged trout-pellet paste.

I gently lowered the hook bait into the water, watching as it came to rest on the golden gravel two feet from the bank. Standing well back, I began loose-feeding hemp and trout pellets by hand, observing their passage as they drifted down through the water. The majority of the particles settled around the hook bait, but some were swept down towards the waiting barbel. Through my polaroids I watched the barbel react to this new supply of food. Snaking along the bottom, they worked their way to my hook bait. And then as if from nowhere, the barbel were joined by a dozen chub. Although good fish, with some possibly as large as 5lb plus, they were not my intended quarry.

For the next hour my rod never stopped moving – hardly surprising, as I had almost twenty fish feeding ravenously around my hook bait and constantly making contact with my line. Each time a fish hit the line it immediately spooked, causing the others to fly in all directions before reforming as another handful of loose feed was introduced. I quickly realized that whilst this behaviour continued I had little chance of success, and therefore a change of approach was required. I needed to get the line out of the way, but how? The bank at my feet sloped away at an angle of about sixty degrees, and I realized that if I lengthened my hook length to about six feet by using two SSG placed two feet apart, I could 'pin' my line to this slope. Lying on my stomach to avoid being seen, I positioned my bomb against the bank, just below the surface. Then I watched with a satisfying grin as the bait settled with the six-feet hook length lying tight on the gravel. I did not have long to wait, as a couple of handfuls of hemp had the barbel, closely followed by the chub, back on the feed.

The reel screeched into life. Gently striking, the reel arched over as the barbel sped back from whence she came, heading directly for the willow roots. Only by applying maximum pressure did I manage to turn her away. Suddenly the pressure went from the rod, and my heart missed a beat as the cane straightened. She had, however, simply changed direction, and was now moving upstream heading towards me. Winding madly for what seemed an eternity I regained contact, and the rod arched over once more. I counted my blessings, realizing that I had been fortunate; but the barbel knew exactly where she was going: she headed up a narrow stretch of water only six feet wide between my bank and the rushes opposite, and had she achieved her goal and reached the upstream weir pool, then I would have lost her. I piled on the pressure, and the cane creaked in protest.

Stalemate ensued as she flared out her pectoral fins, which, aided by the current, kept her stationary as if snagged on some unseen object. So there I was, looking down onto the fish in gin-clear water, a powerful Mark IV unable to move her. The stalemate lasted almost five minutes, and I actually phoned Jim telling him that he ought to be with me to witness what was happening. At last the fish moved and attempted another run downstream; but now she was tiring. After a couple of half-hearted bursts, she came to the net. After resting her, I placed her in the dampened weigh sling and watched the needle on the scales settle at 10lb 9oz.

I knew this to be the smaller of the three fish; then on 17 September that same year I caught a beautiful barbel of 11lb 10oz from the same swim, and finally on 24 September a third fish at 11lb 5oz. This completed a fine hat-trick from the 'Aquarium' swim.

My Fifteen-Pounder: a Personal Best by Stan Sear

There can be no doubt that the angler who fishes for barbel on the Great Ouse is targeting fish that are beyond the wildest dreams of those of us who started barbel angling anything over a decade ago. During the river season barely a week goes by without a Great Ouse monster gracing the pages of the angling press, and whilst a 'double' remains the target on the majority of our barbel rivers, it is a fish of 15lb plus that really turns the head on this tiny little river. A 'double and a half' is a realistic target for anyone who is prepared to put in the effort, although press reports do give a false impression of the numbers of huge barbel present. The time put in by the lucky captors who appear in the papers constitutes but a tiny proportion of the overall effort being applied to this river.

Parts of the Great Ouse are under a lot of angling pressure, which is understandable when you consider the unprecedented record of the river, particularly around Adams Mill and Kickles Farm. The pressure on these may, however, have been eased recently by their syndication. The area is far from being the only one worth fishing, but it is certainly the most talked about and written about. I personally try to avoid such venues, so I can fish for barbel on my own terms, away from the crowds and in comparative peace. It was in search of this relative isolation that I settled on a stretch that, after a great deal of hard work, was to produce my own personal best, my 'double and a half'.

I hope this account will give the angler some idea of the degree of difficulty involved in such a venture, and of the ups and downs experienced over seven seasons on a particular venue. I first ventured forth onto my chosen stretch in June 1996, and after a couple of blanks, recorded my first two barbel, one of which weighed 10lb 5oz. This capture provided all the encouragement I needed, and during that first season I caught a total of ten barbel. The quality of the fish was superb, three being doubles; and although I suffered fifteen blanks, I considered this an excellent start to my campaign.

The following season I had been made redundant and my commitment was not very high, but I still managed four fish to 10lb 15oz, alongside sixteen blanks. The 1998–99 season saw me back on form, although the fourteen barbel I caught were again accompanied by those inevitable blanks, twenty-six in total. By now you should be getting a fair picture of what fishing this river entails: a low population means that anything other than single capture sessions are rare, but the fish, although sparse in numbers, are good quality, and a high proportion of doubles makes all the effort worthwhile. October 1999 proved a real highlight when my friend Dave recorded a new best of 13lb 14oz, an exciting capture that gave me renewed hope for the future.

As regards methods, my preference is for a basic link-ledger arrangement with monofilament mainline and a braided hook length. Baits are mounted on a hair-rig, and in the early days were flavoured meat; more recently I have switched to boilies surrounded by paste. My feed of hemp, pellets and hook-bait samples would always be deposited by means of a bait dropper.

The 2001 season turned out to be very hard indeed, but it also proved to be a watershed in my Great Ouse barbel campaign. Twenty-seven blanks and just seven barbel by the end of October speaks for itself – but early in November I was to turn my season on its head. I arrived on the river to find it over the banks, full of rubbish and pulling hard. I struggled away until about 5pm, when suddenly the rod slammed round hard and I found myself attached to an extremely large barbel. After a protracted battle in the raging torrent, the fish of my dreams was enfolded in the landing net, a perfectly conditioned barbel of 15lb exactly; a 'double and a half'. That fish turned out to be my last of the season, as it was followed by another eleven blanks! However, I must record that I did not mind in the least.

The following season I returned once more to the fray, unaware as I gradually worked my way up to a total of forty-eight fishless sessions, that the season would turn out to be my best ever. Following a couple of barbel early in the season, I then hit a run of fifteen consecutive blanks; but on 5 November there would be fireworks at the end of a real up-and-down session, one that I would remember for a very long time.

Arriving at the river at about 3pm in the company of a few friends, we found our chosen venue deserted and so walked the banks before selecting our swims. I settled for a shallow run with a good flow between beds of streamer weed that separated a couple of deeper holes. Depositing some feed onto

Stan Sear with his first 'double and a half'.

the clean gravel of the riverbed by means of a bait dropper, I then wandered off for a chat, after a little while returning and topping up the free offerings before making my first cast. I then settled back, hoping that this would be the evening when my extended run of blanks would come to an end with an elusive Ouse monster gracing my net. For four hours nothing disturbed the tranquillity – and then wham! A barbel at last! Following a very spirited fight I had my quarry on the surface and it looked huge: a definite double. A local angler who had arrived on the scene rushed to help. Seizing my landing net, he then slipped and hurled himself down the bank. Although he avoided a ducking, this was all too much for the barbel, which promptly shot off once more, shedding the hook in the process.

Every angler reading this will know how I felt: the sense of overwhelming disappointment is a common denominator in every branch of our sport. This feeling was compounded by the fact that I felt my chance had gone for the night. But little did I know! Amazingly I was actually on the point of packing up when once again I found myself doing battle with a big Ouse barbel.

The rod was wrenched down in a violent lunge as the fish tore away, then swam along hugging the bottom, plodding slowly but irresistibly around the swim – always a good sign. After what seemed like an age it surfaced a third of the way out, still stubbornly refusing to concede the struggle. At this point my erstwhile assistant arrived yet again; however, this time I quickly beat him to the landing net, sparing myself of his well meant help. He watched as I carefully played and landed a very large barbel indeed.

Stan displays his 15lb 1oz specimen.

After resting the fish in the margins and gathering my thoughts, my friends arrived to witness the weighing. To my amazement I discovered that I had caught a new personal best, at 15lb 1oz. Photographs were taken, and then the magnificent fish was carefully released, hopefully to fight another day.

The Great Ouse has undoubtedly provided me with the hardest and most challenging fishing of my angling life, but such results, when they do arrive, make all the effort worthwhile and keep you going through the lean times. Which is just as well, really, as I followed that capture with just one more barbel of 10lb 8oz – and then twenty-eight blank sessions!

14 The Holybrook

by John Sheldon

The fascination of fishing small rivers, often not much more than streams in proportion, seems to be a common stimulus amongst the anglers with whom I meet and talk. Small rivers have always had a romantic attraction that is difficult to describe, particularly to hard-bitten barbel enthusiasts. Perhaps it rekindles our enthusiasm by reminding us of our younger days when we made our first attempts to catch the elusive small roach, or the more willing perch. More likely, however, is that small rivers never fail to rekindle the competitive instinct in anglers. They are a real challenge to the rivercraft built up over many years by the specialist and generalist angler alike.

The pressures of modern life have dramatically changed the availability of leisure time and the way we spend it. Importantly we have less opportunity to spend many day-long sessions on the riverbank, as other responsibilities dominate our lives. In common with many modern anglers, my own angling time became limited to short sessions of just two to three hours at the most, and in such circumstances the chosen venue must be reasonably accessible or the trip is just not worthwhile. Moreover, the opportunity for the short-session roving angler has also become severely limited on some of the more popular rivers: the overcrowding and the long-stay anglers are real disincentives. For all these reasons I began to search out smaller rivers, often under-fished and which leant themselves to the short stay, roving approach.

In the Thames/Kennet catchment area there are many small rivers that are ideal for roving tactics. One of the major benefits of the continuing nationwide barbel explosion is the availability of small river angling for those interested in stalking barbel.

The fascination of small rivers is the very real challenge they offer the angler, their one common feature being that they are difficult to master; though this characteristic can frustrate even the mildest, most even-tempered individual. On the other hand, many small rivers are often under-fished, they are usually set in pleasant surroundings, and enjoy abundant wildlife. For three years I fished the Holybrook, a tributary of the Kennet, searching, experimenting and trying new tactics.

The description of the Holybrook as a Thames tributary is not wholly accurate, because in reality this small river is a breakaway from the Kennet. It leaves the Kennet south of Reading near the village of Theale, and rejoins the main river in Reading town centre, a distance of not much more than four miles. Throughout its length it flows largely parallel to the Kennet, forming part of the extensive floodplain as the rivers meet the Thames just east of the Reading conurbation. A local historian (who just happens to be a member of the BCC) asserts that the name Holybrook has a direct link to the now disused Reading Abbey, and that this small waterway was an important medieval commercial route for the monks of the abbey.

The Holybrook has two completely different aspects and characteristics. For half of its length, the river is in its natural state; it runs through agricultural land, and resembles a mini Hampshire Avon or the Kennet in its upper reaches. Reading AA controls a good stretch of this water from the point where the Brook leaves its parent river. A variety of local clubs control shorter stretches before the Brook changes its character as it hits urban Reading. The presence of housing development, garden fences, retail outlets and footpaths has not affected the reputation of this stretch for producing larger fish. Location, in theory, should be less of a problem, as the swims are more obvious because of angling attention. Again in theory, the fish should be less susceptible to bank-side disturbance. However, this stretch has a proven reputation for being particularly hard, although it produces the occasional double. It has been suggested, and not always tongue in cheek, that the dumping of edible waste by local residents may have had a positive effect on the quality of the fish in the area. Rumours abound of huge barbel caught on chicken skins, turkey remains and bacon rind, and similar catches have been reported from the lower stretches of the Kennet, where once again it flows past the end of suburban gardens.

The upper stretches are a completely different proposition, presenting the angler with a different set of problems. The fishing is very hard, but in a slightly more hospitable environment. The railway system that follows the line of the Brook forms a defence against urban encroachment, although housing development can be seen and heard on all the stretches. The irritating hum of the motorway traffic may worry some anglers, but it cannot be avoided.

The river is never more than two rod-lengths wide, and is often significantly narrower; the depth is surprisingly uniform, say three to five feet in summer conditions. The constant twisting and turning, followed by short thirty- to forty-yard straights, gives variety, and also helps swim selection. Weed growth remains strong throughout the river, which I believe aids fish retention and the maintenance of a stable population. This factor is significant, as the parent river has recently suffered major weed loss. Theories abound regarding this phenomenon, but so far the Holybrook remains unaffected, and in the summer months the weed growth and water clarity are significantly better than in the parent river.

The criteria regarding choice of swim do not differ from those we use generally on larger rivers, though one missing factor is the evidence of regular fishing, often a useful pointer to a swim's potential. On this venue the bends are very pronounced, often becoming real horseshoe shapes, and in this small river the barbel have a preference for the slightly deeper water at the commencement of these bends. They also seem to favour the area where the water begins to shallow up just after the bend. Naturally the far side is the favourite holding area, particularly if weedbeds are present. In the summer, however, just trundling a bait around the deeper far-bank area can bring results as the barbel seek out the heavier current.

Trees and snags are the mainstay of the barbel fisherman on most rivers. The Holybrook remains virtually unspoilt at present, and appears to have escaped the worst excesses of the Environment Agency – though how long this situation will last is a matter for real concern. Cutting back the overhanging bushes and trees, and the inevitable removal of the accumulated mid-water snags, would damage this type of venue irreparably. The trees and snags are invaluable to the process of location, and a gravel bottom with streamer weed and tree cover describes a barbel swim to die for. The barbel need the cover of a weedbed, the deeper water or the far side of a bend or an overhanging tree or bush to feel comfortable and to feed. On this water, however, the slightest hint of heavy footfalls or clumsy approach work will completely ruin the chances of a fish, irrespective of the classic nature of the swim.

On the forty- to fifty-yard straights there are a number of long glides with plenty of weed, a gravel bottom and a steady current; certainly the barbel seek out this steady current when there is cover nearby. The chances of success improve if a subtle change in depth can be detected, such changes often being the result of an underwater obstruction. The criteria that dictate swim selection are often exactly the same as those used by the all-rounder seeking other species. There is a good head of bream, chub and roach in the Brook, but it is seldom fished by the silver-fish anglers – though this may simply be a reflection of the general decline in the numbers of anglers fishing our rivers.

The choice of baits really does depend on individual preference. Experimentation and perseverance (taking into account that the Brook is generally under-fished) will eventually bring success. My recommendation is to identify a couple of swims where a more concentrated static approach could be successful, and on every visit drop in a pint or so of hemp or the attractor of your choice. It's useful to return to these swims for the final few minutes of each session. For the rest of the session, test your watercraft by adopting a roving approach.

The use of particle baits was an experiment I soon abandoned. This approach will work if you have the time to adopt the traditional method of feeding out the small fry. Smaller rivers generally have more than their fair share of minnow and gudgeon, and these will play havoc with particles so it is just not worth the hassle on a short visit. Luncheon meat and its variants such as bacon grill and meatballs have proved successful: three smallish pieces threaded on a no. 4 barbless gives plenty of leakage and seems to do the trick. This method is ideal for roving and upstreaming, although a decent paste or pellet can

Barbeling at close quarters on the Holybrook.

also be successful. The introduction of half-a-dozen meat pieces into each prospective swim is enough. Each swim can be revisited two or three times during a session. If barbel are present, the action is often instantaneous.

For a successful short session, the old sporting adage of 'keep it simple' certainly applies. In summer, two or three SSG shots on a straight-through rig are all that is necessary to trundle the bait near weed or obstructions. Keep the tail short, never more than twelve inches. The bait has to be natural, without flapping uncontrollably on two or three feet of line below the shot. The addition of more shot enables the bait to be held on a far-side crease or to lodge comfortably at the end of a weedbed if a static bait or downstream touch legering are necessary. My preference is for an 11ft, 1½lb T.C. Avon, with a minimum of 8lb line, on the reel of your choice. The key is to use a set-up that is easily handled, and which can withstand the sudden violent surge of a hooked fish.

A quick analysis of two years on the Brook gives a reasonable picture of the fun and frustration of small river barbel fishing. During the 1997–98 season I made four visits of average duration 2hr 40min; these visits yielded five fish, their average weight 6lb 9oz, with the two best fish weighing 8lb 10oz and 10lb 6oz. Season 1998–99 saw twenty-five visits, with an average duration of just under three hours, in which I caught twenty fish with an average weight of 6lb 2oz; the best fish weighed 9lb 10oz, 10lb 2oz and 10lb 10oz (they were not recaptures).

Until the capture of the 10lb 10oz fish on 11 December 1998, I had not managed to extract more than one fish from any swim during a session.

During the late 1990s and up to the 2003 season, a couple of other BCC members have fished the Holybrook reasonably regularly and taken fish of over 10lb. We have worked on the basis that the more information you share, the better it is for everyone concerned, and the sharing of our accumulated knowledge and experience has cemented our friendship. We have been able to discuss tactics and strategy, baits, methods, weather and river conditions to our mutual advantage. Following these discussions with Bob Turner and Trevor King, we have drawn up some detailed points – we hesitate to call them conclusions – which we believe are relevant to the pursuit of barbel in smaller rivers such as the Brook.

The fishing is hard, sometimes verging on the impossible. The barbel are easily spooked. In spite of plenty of weed cover, overhangs and the occasional deeper hole, a clumsy footfall will ruin everything. There are, of course, some clear contradictions, that in certain conditions the use of an attractor is essential, and getting that attractor in exactly the correct position is of paramount importance. Generally, neither Bob nor Trevor use a bait dropper and prefer, in spite of the lack of precision, to feed by hand. On small rivers it is often impossible to get into position to use a dropper without creating a huge commotion on the bank, and a mighty crash as a dropper hits the water can often ensure that fish won't revisit the area for hours. We agree that in certain swims an attractor is essential, as it clearly creates a situation where the larger fish feed with a degree of confidence. Droppers and stringers can be used, but with the clear limitation that the swim has to be less than a rod length from the bank so that the attractor can be dropped gently vertically from the rod tip; though Trevor points out that even droppers, with care and practice, can be cast with barely a ripple if the rod-point is dropped at the correct moment.

It is our experience that baiting and waiting for the bigger fish at dusk or during the first couple of hours of darkness is a successful method. Recognizing that this is the generally accepted position on most rivers, the difference is that night fishing on smaller waters is extremely difficult. The prerequisite for success is to know the swim well and to make it as easy as possible to avoid all the snags, weed and overhangs. An additional factor, and one that gives us cause for concern, is the potential damage to the fish. Hit-and-hold tactics are difficult enough in the daylight on larger rivers, but it is a completely different scenario in a small, snaggy, weedy river in the dark. Our concern is that the lack of control and the real possibility of damage to the barbel should make the caring angler think twice before settling down to an after-dark session.

We've had hours of discussion about baits and pre-baiting, and it's no surprise that the jury is still out on what is generally most effective. We have had no problems with the traditional meat baits, probably because of the relatively low angling pressure on the Brook. The added confidence of garlic flavouring has proved useful, and we've found that garlic salt or oil as a simple additive has made a difference. Lately Trevor has had success with home-made HNV-type bait, taking a best fish of 10lb 7oz. Experimenting is satisfying in its own right, and small rivers provide a terrific opportunity to change bait and tactics to suit the very varied conditions.

In summer conditions with clearer water, more weed and less flow, we are inclined to fish four or five swims on a rotating basis. In winter flood conditions we cover as many swims as possible. Still using an element of pre-baiting known areas, the successful short session is often achieved with the classic tactic of rolling meat in the nearside creases and slacker areas round snags and bends.

Returning to some anecdotal thoughts on fishing after dark, and bearing in mind that the primary concern is the welfare of the fish, our personal welfare must also be a consideration. The Holybrook has a spooky reputation, especially as it flows nearer to the centre of Reading. It is well known locally that there have been several accidents and deaths associated with the water over the years. I'll spare the reader the gory details, and I know that most will totally disregard such stories as just hearsay and exaggerations; but what is *not* in doubt is that many anglers will not venture near the place after dark. Trevor, who has spent many sessions in the urban environment, has not personally experienced anything supernatural, but has reported that both he and some of his mates have been particularly uneasy when fishing the river after dark. Trevor and Bob are big fellows and not easily put off, but syringes and the rescue of an attempted suicide would be enough to put off those of us who are less capable of looking after ourselves in exceptional circumstances.

Discussing these and other issues affecting the river and the surrounding area is part of the pleasure of angling. As far as the actual stalking and landing of fish are concerned, our experience suggests that multiple catches of barbel from one swim are definitely the exception rather than the rule. This fact applies even when the conditions are theoretically perfect. The roving approach has a proven track record of success. An element of pre-baiting may help, and the choice of bait depends upon the angler's preference. It is extremely unlikely that any of the conventional bits will be 'blown' due to angling pressure.

A Fish of a Lifetime

A number of significant factors could have influenced this capture. The swim in question happened to be one of those I had chosen to occasionally feed with a couple of pints of hemp. Prior to the capture of the '10lb 10oz' the swim had produced only an occasional fish, but it was a swim I almost always tried when visiting the venue.

The weather in the fortnight leading up to the capture had been exceptionally cold. The south-westerlies and low pressure with plenty of rain returned on 8 December, and when I arrived at the venue on 11 December, the river was that lovely brown colour that we dream about, and dropping slightly after overnight rain. The temperature was surprisingly high at 7°C. The session began at 2.15pm, and on this occasion I dropped in a few lumps of meat and began fishing immediately. I targeted a crease I knew was adjacent to the roots of an extensive but dying summer weedbed. I landed a nice fish of 5lb 9oz, re-cast, and ten minutes later banked an even better fish at 7lb 2oz. Following those successes I decided to move and do some

John's club river record fish, in immaculate condition.

trundling in other favoured swims. Before moving I dropped in two pints of loose-fed hemp and just half-a-dozen pieces of meat, as I intended to return later and finish off the session in that swim. I returned after an hour or so of unsuccessful exploring. The very first cast produced a scale-perfect 10lb 10oz fish that I am certain was not a re-capture. My diary records 'great bite, great fight, terrific fish'. It was also my first multi-fish catch from any swim on the Brook.

The Holybrook, and other small streams like it, are generally under-fished and offer an exciting challenge to the dedicated barbel angler. To tempt a fish from an area only a few yards long and a couple of feet wide is a real achievement. Small river fishing is an attractive proposition if you fancy a change of scene and a good walk on an uncrowded river. The fishing is hard, but the chance of the very occasional double is enticing. If the dream becomes a reality, the catch is bound to be recorded as a fish of a lifetime.

15 The River Ivel

by Phil Dunn

The River Ivel is a small but intimate river that starts in North Hertfordshire at Radwell (near Baldock) and wends its way to the River Ouse at Tempsford in Bedfordshire. It runs for approximately seventeen miles from source to end over mainly shallow, gravel-bottomed, weed-ridden runs. It has seen many changes over the years; it was once renowned for the quality roach and dace that could be found twisting and darting in the crystal-clear waters, but more recently has been the scene of some superb chub fishing, the average size being well above 3lb. Carp have always been present, whilst pike are the main predators to be found.

The river averages three to four feet (about a metre) in depth, with shallower areas and some considerably deeper. It has always been a favourite venue for match anglers, and the old Ivel Open has seen entries into three figures on many occasions. In recent years the river has undergone yet another change, and the results of this are still unclear. The major change has been in the general state and quality of the water due to abstraction, and it is only this last season (2002–03) that the water level has returned to its original levels.

The other serious issue the river had to contend with was the introduction of barbel back in 1992, when three thousand fish were introduced at an average size of six to twelve inches. Just days after this stocking was carried out over the middle reaches of the river, it suffered a major flood, actually leaving the confines of its banks for three consecutive days. The fish were immediately distributed all over the length and breadth of the river.

Although this did not cause any problems for the barbel angler, it did in fact compromise the natural spawning sites for the indigenous species, and this resulted in reduced roach and chub recruitment, and in a general decline of the normal silver fish stocks. The upside of this is that the barbel have less competition for food and suitable spawning sites, and as such the numbers have now started to increase, with the fish breeding on a regular basis. It is now possible to catch barbel in most areas of the Ivel from Clifton to Tempsford, and several areas are now producing double-figure fish on a regular basis.

The main areas targeted by barbel anglers are often closely guarded secrets, with some stretches privately syndicated. However, there are many areas open to anyone who possesses a club book for one of the affiliated Ivel Protection Association fishing clubs such as Vauxhall and Letchworth, to name but two. There are even stretches that cover common land, and where free access is allowed, one of the best being Biggleswade Back Meadows, above the weir.

The river itself generally features raised banks that are man-made, allowing access to public footpaths and the Ivel Way, a nature walk taking in areas such as Clifton, Langford, Broom and Biggleswade. It pushes on to Sandy and Girton Bridge, and then to Blunham; and it ends at Tempsford by the old lock. In general terms the river is quite exposed and often suffers the ravages of any winds that blow; in many areas it is also quite featureless. However, all this belies a river that is fast returning to form: this time around it has the potential to give anyone of a pioneering instinct the chance of a real surprise or two.

I caught my first barbel from the Ivel at Biggleswade Common in 1995; it weighed in at 4lb. Three further fish followed, though all below that weight – but nonetheless they were barbel. Feeling pleased with my efforts, I began to consider the possibilities for the river in the years to come, and

Dick Walker's river, the Ivel.

decided I would follow with interest the reports of any further fish caught.

Some two years later reports began to appear of barbel being repeatedly seen and caught from several areas not actually around the original stocking points. It also became obvious that some of these fish were not part of the 1992 stocking. In 1997 I heard through a reliable source (a keen angler and well known local gunsmith) that fish of 10lb were being caught from an area below Clifton; here the river is narrow and often referred to as 'The Canal'. It was generally neglected, but some anglers had obviously done their homework and were reaping the benefits. Eventually another report filtered through of two fish spotted downstream of Biggleswade in an area renowned for the quality of the chub fishing. The situation was becoming interesting, and plans were made to cash in.

Why is it that the best-laid plans always seem to go pear-shaped when you least want them to? When the days are right, the river is spot on and the fish are clearly feeding, why do we struggle to even get a sniff? I tried everything I could think of, including worms, free-lined and rolled meat, corn, casters, hemp and tares, but nothing seemed to make any difference. Work, family and all the usual outside influences combined to hijack my detailed plans, and the season drifted by without any further ado.

My focus then switched to a private stretch of the Ouse that I had managed to secure on a lease, and my fishing on the Ivel fell away, save for the traditional winter chubbing and the odd session when time constraints meant that a trip to the Ouse

was impractical. I still visited the Ivel, but only as and when circumstances allowed, and such visits didn't always coincide with the best conditions the river had to offer. One day in the summer of 1998 the chance of an afternoon's fishing arose and I managed to catch a few small barbel. The first of those fish went 5lb plus, and then later that summer a 7lb fish graced my net. At around the end of October/early November the papers were showing pictures of a fish that really turned up the heat. It weighed 10lb, and it couldn't have come from a more suitable area.

Many years previously Dick Walker had moved to Biggleswade and had the good fortune to have the River Ivel running past the end of his garden. He spent many long hours watching the fish darting around in the clear, fast currents over the gravel-bottomed riverbed, then flashing back under cover whenever a rambler passed by on the opposite bank. Eventually he decided to take matters into his own hands and plant willow trees. These grew and grew, eventually creating a canopy of cover from the trailing branches, the roots diverting the flow and creating a slightly deeper channel. The river narrowed at this point and the changes eventually led to the formation of a small pool below the willows where the chub and eventually the barbel settled, feeling safe and secure.

The swim obviously became a magnet for the local angling fraternity, and many a good chub was lost under those branches. Many people tried various ways to combat the flow and the changing currents in this area, and eventually they started to hook fish

Early season on the Ivel.

that they simply could not hold. Then along came the Environment Agency and down came the trees. From an angling point of view the area was totally destroyed, and all that remained was a bare stump where once stood a great willow tree.

With this tree gone, the barbel and chub had to move, and this they did by pushing out to other areas of cover above and below the pool. It was from the upstream end of one of these areas that the 10lb fish had been taken. Whether or not it was from the 1992 stocking is open for debate, but I would suspect that this fish probably came from one of the many illegal stockings that had taken place, with fish coming from the Ouse at Radwell roadside and other such places. Once news of this capture spread the banks were inundated with anglers chasing the same fish. Then another capture hit the papers, one involving a reputed catch of four fish ranging from 10lb down to 6lb. It suddenly became impossible to fish the area, when previously most anglers had passed by with little more than a glance.

As this type of catch became more frequent, people began to look to other stretches above and below Biggleswade for other pockets of fish. They soon began to find that the fish in actual fact had spread very well, and that they were prospering in the good conditions the river offered. Areas such as Biggleswade Common, Sandy New Road and the final reaches of the river at Tempsford all began to produce good fish on a regular basis, if you were prepared to work at your fishing. Above the Biggleswade section, areas such as Langford, Broom and Clifton all began to give up their hidden treasures. The Ivel had now become a barbel river.

The river is now seeing a steady flow of good fish captures from most areas. The fishing is getting better and better all the time, and it is good to see the fish really thriving. There have been many fish reported over the 10lb mark, and the current record now stands (April 2003) at 12lb 11oz, caught by local Hitchin angler Alan Rumble. The best guess for potential weights is around the mid to upper 14lb

*Phil with a 10lb 10oz
specimen.*

over the next couple of seasons, even eclipsing this if the river receives regular attention and bait. With the number of anglers from the local area who fish for barbel on the Great Ouse, and the possible loss of the Sharnbrook Pits section on the Vauxhall Club ticket, the attention the river gets could increase significantly.

A friend of mine recently described the capture of a barbel from the Biggleswade Common section of the river, and this story really shows how things have changed, and highlights the potential for a real surprise package at any time. An angler decided to fish an area of the river from a section of private bank. He had heard tales of barbel captures from this area, and had in fact seen barbel during the previous close season. He started his fishing with a standard method for attacking the chub population on the river, using mashed bread and flake and the occasional ball of cheese paste. Having the section to himself, he decided to bait several areas before setting up his tackle and enjoying the fresh air and early morning late summer sun. He also marked out three swims into which he deposited approximately half a pint of hempseed.

After about thirty minutes he decided to fish his first chosen swim, introducing a small walnut-sized ball of mashed bread, then swinging out his hook baited with a large piece of flake. It landed in mid-river, just at the head of the bend below him to his left, and then the bait rolled round to land alongside a small bed of streamer weed. Watching the river in front of him, he caught the faintest flash from a fish that turned and dropped below the weedbed. He

fished the swim for approximately forty minutes before moving on, but not until he had introduced some further mashed bread. As is often the case with the Ivel, the morning gave way to the early afternoon without too much action, although the capture of a couple of 3lb chub maintained interest. On the second visit to the swim in which he had begun to fish, he again saw a flash, and this time made out the shape of a barbel twisting about under the trailing weeds just on the crease line of the bend.

More hemp and mashed bread entered the river, along with several balls of cheese paste. This swim would be rested until the early evening. Over the course of the afternoon other visits to the swim were made, but horror struck on the fifth visit, as another angler had arrived unseen and dropped into the bend swim. Not only had he arrived unseen by coming in from the bottom of the stretch, but yet another angler had walked up the opposite bank from the Biggleswade Common car park and settled into the second area that had been marked out for attention in the evening.

With the two prime spots now taken, our intrepid angler settled into the third swim that had received hemp earlier in the day. It was approximately forty yards along from the bend swim on a straight and fairly steady stretch, but one that had a land drain entering from the right, creating a crease line close to his own bank. He fed several more balls of cheese paste and sat back to open his flask when he heard the splash of a fish from the bend. Standing up he saw the rod of the angler thud over and pull down very suddenly and he decided to see if he could lend a hand. Arriving at the swim the angler seemed to have the fish beaten and slipped the net under a fish of around 7lb. It would have been the first barbel for our friend, but circumstances had conspired against him. Eventually he returned to his own swim, though he had already made up his mind that today was not his day.

Arriving back at his chair he decided to swing out a bait while he finished his flask before going home early. Out went the cheese paste, and he held the line and felt the lead and bait bounce back into the near-side crease. He put his rod in the rest and reached round for the flask. Within seconds the rod top pulled over violently. Grabbing the butt of the rod and sending hot coffee all over his jeans he was pulled to his feet by the effects of a 'three-feet twitch' as the fish left the scene. The clutch on the reel was set fairly loosely, as the suspected chub had no real snags to make for, and the 5lb line would be easily up to the task of holding the fish if necessary. But this was unlike any chub that he had ever latched into.

Standing up and realizing that the fish he had hooked was bigger than expected, he began to move down the bank to follow the fish's initial run. Grabbing the net, he set off through the nettles and reeds, trying to keep in contact. Ten yards down the bank another swim had been cut, and he managed to get there and stop. Dropping his net he adjusted his clutch as much as he dared, but the fish kept on going. He was in trouble, and thought that a carp had picked up his bait. He decided that the best option would be to try and play the fish out, but it had other ideas and took off again downstream. He stood up and followed. It carried on going, and he then realized that he had forgotten the net.

Options being very limited now, he called to the angler on the bend, who eventually heard and came to his assistance. The fish made several more lunges downstream but the fight had begun to take its toll, and he was now able to contain the runs. Managing to turn the fish, it rose up in the water and turned on the surface, flashing full golden flanks as it did so, and revealing a brilliant white underbelly. This carp had suddenly become a barbel, and a big one at that. After several more minutes it was netted some 30 yards downstream from where it was first hooked. Once he had composed himself and made his way back to his swim, the scales and weigh sling were produced.

On the scales the dial swung round and quivered before settling at 11lb 2oz. This particular capture was our friend's first barbel, and what a way to start. Photographs taken, the fish was returned and held in

A 7lb 8oz Ivel fish.

the current to recover before sliding away as the light failed. Goodbyes were said, and one happy angler left the river elated with the capture of a fantastic fish.

For the next six weeks he visited the area twice weekly, and caught one single fish in all this time. He only ever saw one fish in the area in this same period. He moved to another stretch eventually in the October, and still awaits his next Ivel barbel.

Phil Dunn's 11½lb BCC Record

I have had the pleasure of catching barbel from the Ivel and Ouse for many years, both from popular areas, and from areas not renowned for barbel. It was in fact one of these less renowned areas that gave me my personal best, a fish of 11lb 8oz. This particular stretch of river is quite narrow and fast-flowing, and the swim that produced my fish is at a point where the river bends very slightly just downstream of a reedbed. The current is brisk on the inside line, and the weed sways in channels about eighteen inches from the edge of the reeds. The ideal place to put your bait was always the inside of this first weedbed, and if possible the best tactic was to hold the rod at all times and keep the tip pointed at the bait. It was common for bites to take the form of a sawing sensation on the line, and having experienced this several times I knew to wait and let the bite develop, rather than striking early. On this particular occasion, I actually missed two bites before connecting with the third, another rod-wrenching lunge that came after a period of indications and twitches that were frustrating but un-hittable. As the tip flew round I was almost dragged to my feet as the fish turned and went downstream towards the bend. Applying maximum pressure and side strain I managed to stop the fish, and thought that the fight was under my control; but the fish had other ideas. I had managed to gain back some line when suddenly it turned and made another run. This time it was able to reach its target, although I tried everything I could to stop it. I always barbel fish with a tight clutch, and the 10lb Shimano Technum line and Fox barbel rod were both being tested to maximum. At this point a stalemate was reached, whereby the fish was just on the inside of the bend, the rod was at maximum curve, the line bow-string was taught and the fish was holding station. With maximum side strain I had no choice but to simply hold on.

Things looked bad, but then suddenly the tackle began to take effect and the tip gradually began to straighten once more. The fish had been held from going any further, and was turning back. I quickly wound down to gain more line and started to draw the fish back towards me. It lunged into the flow and attempted to get under the weed, but it had probably taken too much out of itself and the tackle was now doing its job perfectly. I moved down to the edge of the water and got the wet foot treatment, but I needed to get a better angle on the fish. At this point the net was needed, and I was fortunate to have help on hand. Dave slid down the bank onto the edge by my side and held the net steady. I lifted the rod high and started to guide the fish upstream so that once above our position I could then use the current to guide it into the net; but the fish lunged again.

Fortunately, Dave had reacted quickly and duly swiped the net upwards and engulfed the fish in the mesh. Not a long fight, but definitely an aggressive one. The rod and line combination was perfectly matched, and the fish had no answer to the constant pressure. I was a relieved and happy angler as I finally saw the scales pull round to read 11lb 8oz, a new personal best.

I would like to close with a final piece of advice. I would recommend that anyone wanting to fish the Ivel or Ouse obtains a Vauxhall, Shefford or Hitchin

11lb 8oz: Phil with the BCC river record for the Ivel.

and Biggleswade club book, grabs some Polaroid glasses and goes a wandering. There are many miles of river available to anyone with a club book affiliated to the IPA, and the final stretches of the Ivel where it joins the Ouse at Tempsford would be one of the best places to start.

It may be a small river, but the fish are spreading and thriving very well. Don't be fooled however, it's not easy. It can sometimes be the most frustrating of rivers, and it can also seem devoid of fish. The fish are there, however; they can be caught, and they are growing. Anyone who wants to fish a river that holds its secrets well, and who is prepared to pioneer, could end up with a very special prize.

16 The River Kennet

by Pete Tesch

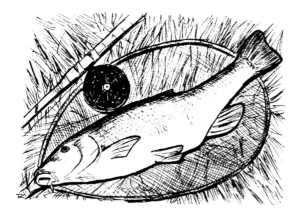

Over the last ten years or so, barbel anglers all over the country have been aware of the changes in the rivers that they fish, one of which is the Trent, currently undergoing a dramatic revival. The Great Ouse is also responsible for producing some incredible fish, and currently holds the British barbel record. What we must not forget are the smaller, less populated rivers such as the Medway or the Ure in Yorkshire, for these are also producing fish of a size that a few years ago were only dreamt of.

I had begun to think that the Kennet was a late starter; however, in recent years double-figure barbel have been reported increasingly throughout its length. The Kennet rises west of Marlborough in Wiltshire, flowing through chalk downland as it traverses the picturesque county of Berkshire. It dissects Hungerford and Newbury on its way to Reading, often merging into canal, and back into river before finally spilling into the River Thames.

From an ecological point of view the Kennet has seen considerable change over the last ten or fifteen years, and in many respects is a different river to what it was in the late eighties. Some of these changes are by no means unique to the Kennet; however, the ones that are, I feel have had a profound effect on its habitat. There is no doubt that the scourge of the Kennet appeared in about the mid-eighties, first around Aldermaston, then spreading like a bush fire up and down the river: the American signal crayfish. Whether the introduction of the

crayfish was by accident or by intent I do not know, but in my opinion this invader has had a devastating effect on the fish population. Most anglers will vouch for the fact that these little aliens will devour anything and everything – and barbel eggs deposited on the gravel at spawning time are a great favourite. Even the eggs of other species clinging to weed fare little better. What was a prolific barbel river has seen fish stocks drastically reduced, in part because of this pest.

Climate changes that have affected weather patterns are another reason for a changing Kennet. No longer do we see light, gentle rainfall over several days, especially in autumn and winter: now we have heavy deluges that cause the river to flood, scouring the riverbed and ripping out the ranunculus weedbeds. These floods are also responsible for bank erosion, with the loss of trees and foliage. The increased boat traffic on the canalized stretches of the river may be just one of the reasons why the water always seems to carry a tinge of colour, and this coloration inhibits the sun's rays from penetrating and regenerating weed growth, even in the shallower water, let alone in depths of six to eight feet. The sight of streamer weed rising from these depths and waving over clean gravel runs is but a distant memory.

There is also the question of changes in farming techniques and chemical usage. The high level of pesticides, for example, used in previous years would run off into the river, and the situation was made worse by low water levels caused by over-abstraction, which increased the concentration of these chemicals in the river. In more recent years I believe that the use of these chemicals is less widespread, but the water abstraction problem is still with us. The Kennet is no longer a river with water that sparkles.

The picture is not all doom and gloom, however. On the contrary, from a barbel angler's point of view, some of the above points have worked in our favour. We all know that barbel and anglers alike love a river with extra water and warm, south-westerly winds. These conditions, coupled with higher-than-average temperatures, mean that barbel will feed almost throughout the year, which in turn will have a dramatic effect upon their growth rates. The crayfish may have played a large part in reducing the once-prolific barbel numbers, but it may have helped to increase the average weight of individual fish. What also cannot be overlooked is the part that anglers have played in this process. The numbers of anglers pursuing barbel has increased considerably in recent years, thus providing the fish with a much greater larder than ever before.

The use of 'high nutritional value' (HNV) baits, pellets and particles has had a great effect on barbel growth rates – though I must include a word of caution here: all seeds and nuts must be prepared as recommended by the supplier; if they are not, they can be fatal to fish. Common sense must also be exercised regarding the quantities of seeds and nuts being introduced, in order to avoid saturation. In spite of this trend, all the old, tried and tested baits such as maggots, casters, worms, bread and corn, still work on the Kennet. Even luncheon meat straight from the tin or with added flavours will still catch barbel, and will often out-fish the more modern baits.

To locate fish and then set about their capture is what angling is all about. The use of polarizing lenses to cut the sun's glare from the water enables us to peer into the depths and recognize the pinkish hues of barbel fins, then see their shapes materializing over the gravel; this is a sight not to be missed. Once fish are located, we can use a variety of methods, such as trotting with the float, or legering with either the straight bomb or the open-ended or block-end feeder. All these methods will catch Kennet barbel under the right conditions. Another method that works well on the Kennet, and one that I find most rewarding, is 'trundling'. To trundle (or roll) meat is one of the most natural ways to present a bait, but more importantly it is one of the most productive ways to catch barbel, especially from rivers with a high level of angling pressure. It is quite common these days to find anglers fishing for barbel all year round, and it is no surprise that catch rates begin to tail off as the season progresses. The fish have seen all manner of baits and end tackle, making them very wary, particularly when static techniques are employed. Moving from swim to swim when trundling enables the angler to gain a great deal of knowledge and information about the particular features of each swim, or how the fish react to the changing conditions throughout the year, in the low, clear water in the summer or the high, coloured floodwater in winter.

When I first began trundling for barbel, I used shot 'pinched' onto the line (as do most anglers). However, I found that the shot was causing considerable damage to the line, and in order to eliminate this problem, I tried first threading pole float tube onto the line, and attaching the shot to this. But although this minimized line damage, I felt that it was unsafe to continue using shot in this way. Furthermore, there was not enough flexibility when changing swims. Across any area of river, from one bank to the other, there could well be varying

Pete Tesch with a Kennet fish of 13lb.

strengths of flow, either due to a natural bend, snags, weedbeds, or anything that could obstruct or divert the current. Fish in any of these varying flows require baits presented at different speeds, sometimes very slowly, and sometimes at the same speed as the current, plus anything in between. It is therefore vital to be able to change weights quickly and easily to suit any given situation.

After a great deal of experimentation I found two items of terminal tackle that enabled me to minimize line damage whilst trundling, yet which also achieved the standard of presentation that I was looking for. The first were the Fox Kwik Change Pop-Up Weights. These are produced in various sizes, but the ones I use are AAA, SA and SSG. They can be changed in seconds, and are locked in place by a piece of rubber. The second were John Roberts' Feeder

Booms, with the tube cut to approximately half of the original length and coupled with flattened bombs of different weights. This allows a much greater control over the speed of the bait through the swim, and the snap links enable leads to be changed very quickly.

I have tried most of the modern hook-length materials, from the very supple examples of the Kryston range, through to the stiffer braids, and of course monofilament. All of these materials have a time and place according to conditions throughout the year, but it is the slightly stiffer materials that proved to be the better option. These helped to prevent tangles that sometimes occurred when using very supple hook lengths, as with the latter the bait could easily overrun the lead.

There is no doubt that the most suitable mainline for trundling is a sinking braid. The sensitivity it

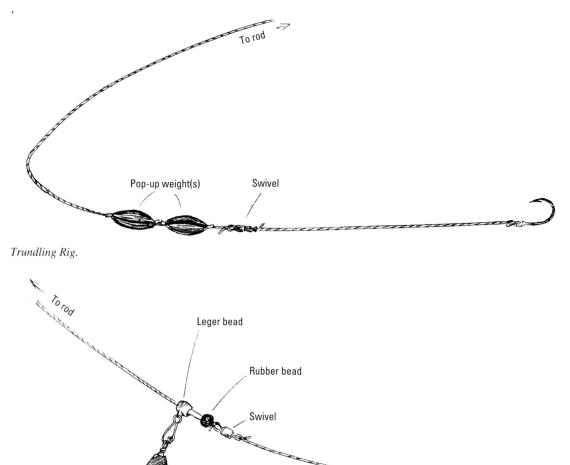

Trundling Rig.

Basic leger rig.

The middle Kennet early season.

affords for bite detection, either a very delicate pick-up or the classic drop-back bite, is second to none. When trundling it is very important to strike at anything that appears to feel different, no matter how slight. The most you could lose is a piece of meat, but conversely you could hook a fish. Another good reason for using a braided mainline is that it can help you identify the type of area through which your bait is travelling, such as gravel, silt or weed. This information is invaluable in building up a picture of each swim that is fished.

I am aware that a lot of anglers have experienced difficulties when using braided mainlines. I, too, had problems initially, but by analysing these problems, and often with a slight change of technique, I feel they can be overcome very easily. There are, of course, alternatives, and one that I have used on occasion is Shimano Technium. This line has only 12 per cent stretch, which is mid-way between a braid and a mono; although it is not quite as sensitive as a braided line, it is well worth a try.

The rigs and tackle for trundling that I have described in the previous paragraphs will cover most situations and conditions throughout the season. Now, with the boring theoretical bits out of the way, we can take our tackle onto the riverbank for the more pleasurable part: putting theory into practice.

'A Bar of Pure Gold': my Thirteen-Pounder

A short evening session early in the previous week had resulted in the capture of several barbel, the largest weighing in at 8lb – a satisfying evening's work that kept confidence levels sky high. The river's condition and air temperature seemed quite favourable as I walked downstream to the first of the swims that I had targeted for this evening.

Unfortunately there were quite a few anglers on the water, some static in swims and one or two moving around; I just hoped that the swims I wished to fish were vacant as I worked my way back upstream. The water level was up even higher, about ten inches above what I would call normal for this time of year, and three or four inches up from my last visit, the water itself with a little more colour, and a little more of a defined current. From experience, extra water, even when it is only a few inches, is enough to move the fish to different locations where they will feel a little more comfortable.

The first swim I wanted to fish was at the bottom of a straight, which fortunately still had a reasonable amount of weed present across the width of the river. This area always seemed to hold a few fish all year round; in the low water conditions of summer it affords them shelter over their heads, but in the winter floods what remains of the weedbed interrupts the flow. This gives the barbel a more comfortable area in which they can hold station, just waiting for a large lump of meat to approach them from upstream – mine, I hope!

Casting upstream, I felt the weights hit gravel, releasing two or three metres of line into the current; the bait began moving downstream, only to be held up momentarily by the weed. After several seconds I lifted the rod top, and the bait resumed its journey downstream. Searching the width of the river produced two medium-sized barbel, then nothing for a short while. It was now time for a move.

The second swim was completely different, as it contained no weed. The current just upstream from my fishing position was along the nearside bank, but

Pete shows off a 12lb 11oz Kennet barbel.

in front of me it diverted to the offside bank, and in so doing it created an area with a much less powerful flow just downstream from where I was standing. Swims where the main current changes from one bank side to the other I find the most challenging to fish, as the bait has to follow the direction of the current. Baits that swing across the flow are unnatural, and will be totally ignored. No takes were forthcoming from here, but one take from the third swim, a classic drop-back bite, resulted in a spirited 5lb barbel.

With approximately an hour-and-a-half of daylight remaining, I noticed that the next targeted swim had become vacant. This was a very different area that possessed several features worth exploring with a bait, some of which I will try to describe. The current flows from right to left, most of it on the near side under the rod top. To the right is a tree, and the only place from which to fish this swim is from under the overhanging branches. To the left are a few small trees, one of which had fallen into the river some years previously, creating an area with underwater branches that have collected quite an assortment of debris. The majority of anglers I have seen in this swim have their baits within this area,

but on all the occasions I have placed baits there, the only taker has been one suicidal chub. A quarter of the way out from the near bank is a weedbed, on the other side of which there is a clear gravel run a metre or so from the opposite bank. At the downstream end of the gravel run, which is only visible in the summer, there are a few strands of bulrush where the bottom begins to fall away; in higher water conditions I have taken one or two sizable fish here.

Removing one of the pop-up weights, I ran the bait down under the rod to the snag area several times. This produced nothing. Replacing the weight, I cast upstream and landed mid-river onto gravel. To enable the bait to work its way through the weedbed, I released a small loop of line into the current. The weed was still quite dense, so the bait would not run through very easily on it own and would require a bit of help. I covered all the weeded area without result, which left just one more area to try: the gravel run. I elected not to change the end rig, and a pinpoint cast landed the bait in the perfect spot. I again released four or five metres of braid into the current, and the bait moved downstream in a straight line following the direction of the flow. Five or six casts varying the speed of the bait down the run produced nothing,

This winter double was caught despite a hard frost.

yet I knew there must be at least one or two fish in the area, especially in these conditions.

Removing the weights I put on a John Roberts anti-tangle boom with a ¾oz flattened bomb attached. My idea was to run the bait downstream and then try to stop it upon reaching the rushes where the depth began to increase. The flattened bomb would then drag, rather than roll, and would be easier to control. It worked: by lifting the rod top and removing a fair amount of line from the current, the bait slowed and eventually stopped. It was a little frustrating at times, as due to the finely balanced tackle it only required a small amount of weed, or a leaf, to come into contact with the line and the bait would commence to trundle downstream. Although it was still quite a natural presentation I wanted the bait to remain stationary for a little longer next to the rushes, or even just up close behind them.

The gentlest pressure change from the braid over the finger signalled a pick-up, the rod lifted quickly, and the hook was set. The fish was as surprised as I was – the strike must have pulled it off balance. It rolled just under the surface, its tail out, and with a large swirl it forcefully made its way downstream. Line was being stripped from the centrepin, and added pressure was having no effect. With the fish well downstream, it was now in danger of kiting to the near side and the underwater branches. I dropped the rod top and the line fell limp onto the water. The fish turned and faced upstream, at which point very gentle pressure allowed me to persuade it to move gradually upstream and away from the danger area.

The practice of dropping the rod top and releasing all pressure from the fish I feel requires an explanation at this point. Have you heard of the saying, 'The more you pull, the harder the fish pulls back'? The truth of this saying really came home to me on one occasion while trotting a lovely smooth glide on the Kennet. I had landed a few barbel up to 8lb, but then lost a couple of fish in an obstruction at the downstream end of the swim. On hooking the next fish, which had the same idea of reaching the obstruction, I dropped the rod top, letting the line fall slack. It worked: the fish stopped its run and turned. Its head was now upstream, and with very gentle pressure it was led upstream until under the rod tip,

A fine view of the upper Kennet.

and played until ready for the net. Admittedly, trying this procedure for the first time takes a lot of nerve; it is far more natural to pile on the pressure and risk breaking off, which is something none of us anglers enjoy. Perhaps the next time you are out float fishing and have hooked a small fish such as a roach or perch, try releasing all the pressure on the line and just see what happens.

Returning to the fight, the rest of the proceedings were quite uneventful. It wasn't until the fish was netted and on the bank that I saw I had realized an ambition (one of many): 31in from the nose to the fork of the tail, and with an 18in girth, the scales registered at 13lb 14oz. A bar of pure gold and the highlight of 278 barbel caught trundling in one season from a pressurized section of the Kennet.

Despite the highs and lows over the years, the Kennet has been good to anglers, and is still a beautiful river to fish. There are times when she will give up her inhabitants readily, whilst at others only extremely hard work will achieve any kind of result. For the novice angler, match angler or specimen hunter, the Kennet is a river that has a great deal to offer, and deserves the respect of all who seek pleasure upon her banks.

17 The River Loddon

by Nick Tigwell

My passion for the River Loddon has now developed to the extent where I feel I can truly say 'the Loddon is in me'. We all have our own personal reasons for pursuing the majestic barbel across the length and breadth of this sceptred isle. Recently the real motivating factor in my own barbel fishing has been to access and fish waters that I feel still hold some real barbel mysteries. That is, of course, not to say that all rivers do not have their mysteries (no matter who is fishing them, or how often they are fished); but it is that mysterious feeling I get from underfished or less popular barbel venues that gives me that extra buzz and heightened sense of anticipation. In these respects the Loddon fits my requirements supremely well, being within easy road access of several major areas of population.

I am still amazed how lightly fished this glorious Thames tributary actually is, and particularly for barbel. Internet sites will tell you that many anglers have whole stretches completely to themselves on many occasions, and certainly this has been my own experience and that of my small group of Loddon regulars. Great, long may it continue! I am not sure how long this situation will persist, however, with larger clubs now starting to obtain Loddon water. Guided days are becoming available, and recently there has been a marked increase in publicity concerning Loddon barbel captures in the weeklies and monthlies. This is one of the reasons why I took some time to decide whether I really wanted to put

this piece together; but ultimately I have never been a secretive angler, and to me, angling delights are there to be shared. If I did not share my experiences I feel I would almost be doing the river a disservice. So let's do some sharing. . .

For those of you who are not familiar with the Loddon and its tributaries, just what do we have on offer? Pick up any OS map of the Berkshire/Hampshire area, and you will quickly be able to trace the water's course from upper to lower river. The Loddon actually rises as a spring-fed source at West Ham farm near Basingstoke. It then flows in a north-easterly direction for some 30 miles (45km) until its ultimate confluence with Old Father Thames (the longest barbel swim in the country) at Wargrave, just downstream of the lower end of St Patrick's Stream. It is not hard to see over the years how the river has been affected by man, through dredging, gravel extraction, residential building and road-building in and around Reading. The long, straight, deep dark sections with the characteristic 'humped banks' are immediate evidence of this fact, and this gives certain ticket sections a real Jekyll and Hyde character. You can be walking one minute along the banks of a typical, small, intimate Thames tributary with bends, riffles, gravel glides, narrows and jungle swims – and then suddenly the river disappears in front of you in a long straight run with more sedate flows and almost still water in places. Rarely are you far from these character changes, which certainly keeps the angler 'on his toes', and gives some really good variance in types of possible hunting grounds for *Barbus barbus*.

It should also be noted that the river used to have several working mills along its banks, all of which are now in decay or have been redeveloped as upmarket residences. However, where fishing is still permitted near these old mill sites, the small feeder streams and mill backstreams provide even more variety. Being very narrow and low in the summer, the onset of rains makes these small streams potential little gems. I know of one that has thrown up doubles from places you would not think twice about if you have been fishing the main river course for a while.

The main tributaries of the Loddon are the rivers Blackwater, Whitewater, Emmbrook and Bowbrook. Indeed, the current acknowledged record for Blackwater is quoted on the internet. When you consider for a while *where* some of our double-figure barbel are now being caught, who knows the future potential of these streams? Truly the stuff of a pioneer's dreams. I have heard of barbel as far up as Sherfield-on-Loddon, and from the Duke of Wellington's country estate park. However, Stanford End, which has had regular feature coverage in our sports weeklies, is the first real point where consistent barbel angling possibilities begin. In fact I believe that the fish weighing out at the accepted river record of 14lb 4oz lives in, and was landed from, this stretch.

Much of the Loddon's course flows over London clay beds, although chalk sub-strata does characterize its upper and lower reaches to some degree. Add this London clay to the fact that the river is underlain by almost totally impervious rock types, and it is easy to see how the Loddon exhibits many of the features of more widely acknowledged 'spate' rivers. Sustained precipitation causes it to rise at a rapid rate, but then it also drops at an alarming rate. I have lost count of the number of times when a really succulent-looking, coloured, high river has dropped almost unbelievably back to near normal levels literally overnight. Lack of weirs, and the keen desire of the local authority to get floodwater downstream to the Thames and beyond, are key background reasons here.

I have commented on many occasions to other BCC Southern Region members that the Loddon in summer could be compared with the River Kennet of a decade or so ago. It has a good flow rate, reasonable water levels and prolific weed growth. Walk the Loddon pre-season and you will see exactly what I mean. The unmolested stretches bubble and gurgle along at a refreshingly swift pace, and the colonization of weed and water plants is prolific. Solid beds of reed mace, dense beds of bulrush, uninterrupted trails of ranunculus, and even two varieties unique to the river, the Loddon lily and Loddon pondweed, give the river a really 'alive' feeling. It provides a great experience and keeps me walking on and on.

The average depth in summer is three to five feet, as a rule of thumb. Width can vary between sections: three to four rod lengths on natural sections, and sometimes twice that or more on dredged ones. Water quality has improved steadily on the Loddon since the early 1990s, helped by the fact that there are only two treated effluent sewage plants along its whole length. Water abstraction over the years has lowered levels quite substantially, as is evidenced by many 'high and dry' tree roots at the start of the season. In terms of fish populations, in my opinion the Loddon, for whatever reasons, is a long way behind the Kennet. Recent changes in the nature of match returns on the latter, however, maybe indicate that the two rivers are now a little closer in this respect. Why the Loddon lags behind in terms of numbers is probably open to debate, but cormorant predation, poor water quality for many decades and possibly fewer planned stockings on the river could all be contributory factors. A differing pH value: who knows? I would certainly like to know more about this aspect of Loddon barbel fishing.

Angling access on the Loddon is a combination of controlled and free stretches. There are several clubs holding varied and interesting barbel waters, and all can be joined with suitable research and some personal 'selling'. The main ones are Farnham AS, Farnborough and District AS, Wyvoles Court, Arborleigh Angling Club (formerly NIRD), Dinton Country Pastures (Wokingham District Council), Twyford and District, Reading and District AA, The 21 Club, RMC, BBONT, Swallowfield and Gerrard's Cross Angling Club. In addition, Cove AS and the Royal Aircraft Establishment Farnborough have some rights on the Blackwater tributary. Access is quite easy via the M4, M329, M3, A33 and A4 routes. There is generally adequate parking on most venues, but many are out-of-the-way places, and security must always be a consideration in respect of being able to drive yourself home!

After Stanford End, the next stretch with barbel form is Wyvoles Court, flowing under the A33 south of Reading and on to Riseley Mill. We then follow the river down through Swallowfield until we arrive on the banks of the Aborleigh Angling Club stretch. From the downstream boundary of Aborleigh we have Carter's Hill on the Farnham ticket, running under the M4 between junctions 10 and 11, and meeting up with the Sindlesham Mill complex on the Farnborough ticket. Next is a free stretch, skirting the edge of previously the largest urban estate development in Europe, the Lower Earley housing estate.

We then come to the Dinton Pastures Country Park, through which the Loddon (and Embrook) flow. Adjoining the bottom end of Dinton is the first of the Twyford stretches, Sandford Mill. This then flows into what is basically free fishing until we reach Whistley Bridge. I say free fishing, as some of the bank on this part of the river is within the Dinton park boundaries, but certainly beyond the gravel conveyor there appear to be no controlling clubs on most of both banks. RDAA have recently taken over the Whistley area from the Barnets Angling Club, although I understand there is still some kind of shared rights continuing for the next couple of seasons.

Twyford and Charvil now begin to loom in the distance, from whence the remainder of the above listed clubs take their fishing. Below Twyford the river flows under the Reading/Maidenhead A4 before passing the downstream end of St Patrick's Stream and on into the Thames. I have been in several of these clubs over the years, and if you are seeking the same type of barbel angling that I look for, then most of the clubs can offer what you require.

In common with most of the contributors to this book, I prefer to keep my tackle and methods as simple and uncomplicated as possible. My presentations are generally variations of the running link leger, with either hair-rigged or hook-mounted single hook baits. Feedered pellets or the method feeder also work, although I have as yet to really investigate these methods on the Loddon.

I must confess to being a keen tackle enthusiast. The two rods upon which 99 per cent of my Loddon barbel have had cause to fight angrily are a second-hand Seer Rover and a Sharpes' Scottie Barbel Supreme. I tend to use the latter rod primarily in the summer, and the former when the water begins to clear later in the season (although in really high

water I will go back to the Scottie). The Seer appears a fragile piece of kit, but it possesses a lovely action and is as strong as an ox. However, it is a bit under-gunned for distance 'Wallis' casting with a centrepin reel and heavy weights. The Scottie is one of the few barbel rods that I have owned that really has 'the feel' when you are holding it. The tip is nice and supple, and the bottom end has plenty of necessary power. Casting heavy leads presents little or no problem on the Loddon for me.

Most of the time I have coupled these rods with centrepin reels (again, second-hand buys). My favourite is a Fred Crouch 1960s wide drum, match aerial copy, although a wide drum deluxe Speedia is also excellent for off-the-reel Wallis casting. This technique enables me to get my bait to nearly all the spots I wish to fish. Line is usually monofilament of 8lb to 10lb bs. I have reservations on the use of braided main lines as I am concerned regarding potential fish damage. I do, however, use braid hook lengths, though usually weighted down with a putty substitute. Weight is normally plasticine, an SSG shot link or a running weight, usually a flattened Arlsey or Dinsmore round flat lead. Hooks and other essentials are all from major manufacturers.

As I like to travel light I rarely take a chair, preferring to sit on an unhooking mat or directly on the bank. Umbrellas are also out for me: I prefer to spend a little more on a really good waterproof, breathable outer layer. I possess a range of stalking waistcoats, lighter versions for summer outings and

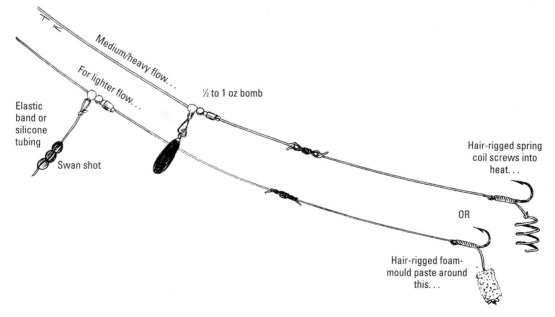

Nick Tigwell's choice of rig.

padded versions for later in the year. I rarely use a rod rest, so I have to either hold the rod, or lay it down and point the tip at the bait; I think the latter is preferable to a rest-held rod, as the line angles are so much more natural.

Loose feed is normally introduced by hand or via PVA netting bags. Although I make my own bait droppers, I have never really considered them necessary on the Loddon; I have not found a need to concentrate feed bait too tightly, preferring to bait a wider area and let the fish do the finding. I am increasingly considering using balls of groundbait (with stones for added weight where needed) when the river is up and pushing through, and using brown crumb, Vitalin, garlic, mini pellets or pulses to get a good scent trail going in.

Despite having fished numerous stretches (both controlled and free), I still find the Loddon a really tough proposition in the summer months, particularly before the vegetation begins to die back. On first inspection a majority of swims look really promising, literally breathing barbel at you, but five years on from my first Loddon double, and I still regard the river as 'peggy'. Groundwork is so important to the Loddon angler. Many sections are heavily choked from bank to bank with plant life, which can and does make fish spotting and bait presentation difficult. Add to this heavy, boggy bankside growth, and even landing fish can be a problem. In addition, the volume of natural food means that a summer campaign can take some willpower. You really do need to study your chosen

water closely, and if this means getting in, then do so. Careful consideration of feed and hook-bait placement will be essential, as many swims will produce nothing at all in summer conditions.

Whilst it may sound as though a light, mobile approach would be the one to adopt, sitting it out in a swim and really building up the feed and the scent trail is also a good option. Carp anglers who fish one particular stretch have used this tactic by way of a change during long overnight sessions on an adjacent pit, and have taken some nice double-figure specimens over the seasons. An added bonus of this static approach is that if you really get the barbel (and the carp) rooting around for your feed, clear areas are made on the bed of the river as the fish thrash around hoovering up the feed.

When adopting a mobile approach, two methods seem to score well. Lightly legered, oily baits that find their own holding spot, and heavily legered static baits at the tail of bulrush beds, are both worth trying when the opportunities present themselves. Rolling baits is a tactic that I always like to use, but to date it has been one of the least productive methods for me. I now only consider using a rolling bait in summer when I am tackling a wier pool, a run-off from such pools, or where there is a sudden decrease in river width on the approach to a bridge or bankside pilings. I have also landed fish on the maggot feeder approach, but this was generally when I just fancied doing something different to my normal favoured methods. Recently with the refinements in the 'method' approach, Loddon fish

A superb winter fish for Nick of 10lb 14oz.

have been targeted right on the inside line, where it is generally easier to find clearer holes for bait presentation. You need to sit well back from the bank, sit on your hands, and certainly be using a baitrunner or centrepin reel.

I have yet to really go down this particular tactical road, but I am thinking about the possibilities more and more. The majority of my Loddon fish have been caught from no more than half distance across the river, but another tactic that I am considering involves the sustained targeting of far bank swims. Many of the stretches on the Loddon are single-bank-only venues, and even where they are not, one bank always seems to curry favour with the angler. This, I am certain, results in far-bank hotspots during the summer, many of which I know have never seen a bait. I have not really worked out yet how to approach these situations. Fishing the far-bank swims is usually a logistical nightmare due to heavy undergrowth and overhanging trees; but it is just another brain-teaser for the Loddon angler.

There is no doubt that late autumn and winter – and particularly on a rising river – are the periods to really maximize your chances whether you are going for numbers of fish banked, or looking for a really fat, well fed Loddon specimen. The abundant weed of summer literally disappears, more swims become fishable, and you can now cover more water yardage, potentially more fruitfully; though once again, this is dependent upon your goals and personal barbel-fishing aims.

During my time as a member of the Dinton Pastures Syndicate I was able to introduce some consistency into my Loddon barbel angling. My time in the group really sums up what I have said previously about the change in season and river conditions on the Loddon. For the seasons 1998–99 and 1999–2000 I was accepted into Dinton. Prior to these seasons I had had tickets for Twyford, Farnborough and Aborleigh, and whilst I had landed fish, my results were disappointing, even by my own average standards. Now the Loddon bug had me and I had to keep going. Improved success had to come my way sometime.

After fifteen trips to the venue in my first season with only one resulting in fish (three fish as alike as

When the Loddon floods it takes no prisoners.

peas in a pod, taken by rolling meat under a wooden footbridge) I really was beginning to wonder if the Loddon was just unlucky for me. I know now from other sources that other anglers were having equally dire early seasons, but when you are largely fishing on your own, the doubt sets in and I found myself really chopping and changing methods and baits at an alarming rate to try and get more fish. However as I have found throughout most of my working life, the more you put in, the more you get in return. And so it proved for me in my quest for the barbel of the Loddon at Dinton Country Pastures.

Throughout the month of October 1999 the river was carrying some nice colour and extra water on a consistent basis. I now believe that generally, colour levels are a more dominant factor in barbel catching than water temperature. Selecting five swims that had really caught my eye back in the summer, and using an *Angling Times*-inspired bait recipe (popular commercial liquid flavour on meat with gravy granules) on my first trip, I had two fish in the first two casts. Both were caught by lightly dragging a link-legered, hook-mounted bait back towards me, just beyond where the first near-bank summer weedbed had grown so prolifically only a couple of months previously. The largest weighed 8lb 15oz, a Loddon best for me. I continued to use this method for more fish, as well as static fishing with the same hook bait but with a stringer of baits attached to the swivel link. In the last two weeks of the season I landed two doubles, one at 10lb 4oz and a second at 10lb 15oz, a new BCC record for the river. Thank you, Dinton, for that unique experience in any barbel angler's diary: my first double from a river.

I had been playing around with paste recipes during the summer months and had certainly seen carp anglers using the mass boilie approach to get the fish going further downstream. Whilst I had no desire to use these methods exclusively or with the same intensity, I kept in mind what I had seen for the following season.

And so to the 2000–01 season: hello again, Dinton; same old early summer Tigwell blanking again. By now I had become used to it, and knew that this 'hard learning' time would be rewarded. At about this juncture I decided to get into the river itself and begin some swim clearing in a few chosen places – not too drastic, more of a thinning out of the 'under rod tip' areas. I remember how large and coarse the gravel was in my hands as I pulled up the weed, and how sore my hands were at the end of these sessions due to the roughness of the gravel. Over my next few visits I used the special paste to pre-bait, but not fish, the two swims I had previously cleared. I finally decided to try my paste on the hook one evening in the first of the two swims, and on my very first cast I got a real screamer of a take, from a fish of 9lb 13oz.

This capture, plus a conversation with the fishery manager during which a 12lb fish was mentioned, really got me focused. I continued to catch for the remainder of that season, having now introduced back-leading, the 'knotless' hair and a punctured oil capsule inserted into my paste hookbait presentations. My most memorable day was a catch of five fish, the best going to 11lb exactly, a new BCC record. The method continued to work, although I still had my blanks, even in what appeared outwardly to be very favourable conditions. I had my fourth Dinton double in December 2000. For personal reasons I did not fish Dinton as often during January to December as I had done the previous season, but I had succeeded well beyond my expectations, and was a contented angler.

Due to redundancy and a move to Wiltshire I did not apply for another Dinton place, knowing that day

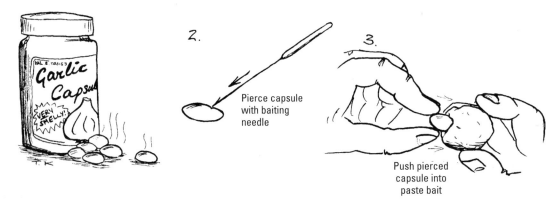

High water paste dodge.

2.

Pierce capsule with baiting needle

3.

Push pierced capsule into paste bait

tickets could be purchased from a car park dispensing machine if one was required. The question now was, could I take my Loddon barbel fishing to another level?

My Record Fish

After my experiences on the Dinton fishery I tried to interest some of my angling acquaintances in fishing the river on a small group basis. This did not materialize, but closer collaboration did, and the following season saw me fishing less as a solo angler. Again due to work circumstances I took a half-year ticket on a stretch near the M4, along with two other keen barbel fishers. By now all the 'Tall Trees' advertising was having an effect upon me, and I purchased some well known barbel ingredients for the coming campaign's paste approach. During my first session on the half-year ticket stretch I had a fish on my first cast. Having been criticized in previous seasons for making paste mixes too complicated, my associates now began to use my mix with my blessing. This regular (but not overdone) freebie introduction served us all well, and every week the phone would ring with news of new and interesting captures. My current BCC river record of 11lb 4oz came on 14 January 2002 at 20.30 hours. It was a really windy, squally, but mild evening, with the river running quite fast but still with a touch of colour. A good barbel angler and personal confidant, 'Friss', was also on the venue. The combined fishing efforts of the small group had by now identified three or four hotspots, and more importantly we felt we had probably identified areas that, for various reasons, were potential heart-breakers.

On this particular occasion I was fishing a favourite type of swim feature, just downstream of the remains of an old rush bed. The rod tip was pointed directly at the bait and only a few inches above the water surface; the rod was lying on the bank. The bite caused the rod to lurch quickly a couple of times, and then the tip to be pulled under the surface. I picked the rod up and the fish was on. It was netted first time after a short fight, and, after pulling myself and the net up the slippery bank, I

A 15lb 14oz Loddon barbel, more than enough to keep the angler coming back.

Nick celebrates the capture of his BCC Loddon record, a fish of 11lb 4oz.

knew that this was my new Loddon personal best and a club river record. Again, all the lessons of the hair-rigged, back-leaded paste approach seemed to have worked. Friss did the camera honours.

The remainder of that season saw a range of eights and nines plus further doubles fall to my rod, and to those of my mates. Some of these fish were undoubtedly recaptures, but the publishing of information regarding a 15lb fish, apparently taken from the Loddon, has really kept us going.

Subsequent research has proved the fifteen-pounder came from the 'half-year' ticket stretch. Due to personal reasons I did not fish the Loddon during the 2002–03 season as often as I would have liked, but one of my associates has subsequently gone on to break the river record (now at 16lb plus).

Fish like this and the effort I have put in, and more importantly the rewards I have gained from this river, really do mean that 'The Loddon is in me'.

18 The River Medway

by Mark Daley

In the late 1980s it was probably fair to say that a barbel of 10lb or more was considered to be a specimen, although some rivers, particularly in the south of England, produced fish in the 12lb to 13lb range at times. In the period from 1990 to 1995 the Medway fish grew to match the weights attained in the country's major barbel rivers, and then overtook them in dramatic style, at least for a time. These fish that caused such a stir in the 1990s were perhaps modest when compared with the current record of 19lb. However, when records were being broken with great regularity it was new and exciting, and for me it was a privilege to play a small part in all the dramas that were taking place.

At the time we were fairly sure from photographic evidence that there were two fish that weighed over 15lb by the middle of the 1990s, and these of course attracted much of the publicity. A good number of fish in the 10lb to 13lb range were also caught, but as the focus was on the record, these fish were comparatively ignored. This is a pity, as they were also exceptional by contemporary standards. We lesser mortals watched as the size of some of the bigger Medway fish that were caught grew from 10lb through 12lb to 14lb. The national record was equalled in 1992 by Dave Williams at 14lb 6oz, and subsequently by Dave Taylor and then by Bob Morris, before culminating in a 16lb 2oz for Peter Woodhouse in June 1994 (I hope I have not missed anyone out!).

The dramatic weight gain was due to a large extent to the impact of new high-protein baits that were increasingly being used by more and more anglers; furthermore, these were mature fish with the frames to pack on weight. Also the increase in angling activity, and the resultant increase in bait entering the river, coincided with much warmer winters – all of which factors combined to make the growth spurt possible.

Much of what follows recounts how we fished at the time, including some successes and failures. Above all I hope it conveys some of the flavour of this special river, which was demanding, often slow, but always exciting to fish.

The River Medway rises out of the High Weald near Turner's Hill in West Sussex, and flows roughly eastwards through Weirwood Reservoir, the pretty town of Forest Row and onwards to Hartfield. The river is joined by a series of small tributaries such as the Kent Water and the Grom, before then flowing north to Ashurst and entering Kent close to Fordcombe. At Penshurst it is joined by the Eden, and then flows onwards to Tonbridge and Maidstone; it becomes tidal just downstream of Maidstone at Allington, then cuts through the chalk of the North Downs and eventually joins the Thames estuary at Gillingham. This comprises a total distance of approximately 70 miles (110km).

Generally speaking, from Ashurst to Penshurst the river is fast flowing, with occasional deep slow pools and glides. In many parts the banks are steep and deeply incised, with the river effectively running through a narrow clay canyon, a bit like the River Severn in miniature. In summer the upper reaches normally run clear with reasonable weed growth on gravel shallows, although certain areas on bends can be up to eight or ten feet deep. In the runs the depths are perhaps between two and three feet, interspersed with shallower riffles.

During the winter the river floods very easily, although most of the time the flow is held within the banks in the upper reaches. Further downstream the increased frequency of flooding has been a major news story in recent years, the low-lying ground around Yalding taking much of the water. In its upper reaches and particularly above Ashurst, the Medway is a small stream, holding wild and stocked

The lower Medway near Yalding.

trout, grayling and coarse fish. Barbel angling becomes a viable proposition at Ashurst, with the areas around Fordcombe and Penshurst historically offering the best chance of a fish or two. From Ashurst to Penshurst and below the river holds chub, barbel and carp, as well as bream, roach, pike and perch, with some dace and the occasional trout.

The river becomes navigable for small craft at Tonbridge. It has now changed in character, becoming deep and slow flowing, noted for quality roach and bream fishing, with carp increasingly prominent. Below Penshurst, barbel are caught from time to time, and the various faster stretches and areas below weirpools are an obvious choice. In recent years barbel have shown up in various spots between Tonbridge and Maidstone, although it is difficult to find evidence of any consistent areas.

The Medway does not naturally hold barbel; they were stocked in the 1950s and 1960s in the upper river, although it is perhaps fair to say that they have never become a dominant species, as they have in some other rivers. Maybe the number of fish present never reached the critical mass needed to become self-sustaining, or perhaps the level of predation of

ova and fry was too high. Equally there are relatively few spawning sites, and those that are available are frequented by chub and dace in the spring spawning season, both of which will consider barbel spawn as another source of food.

In 1986, as part of a joint project to increase numbers, twenty barbel were loaned to the Southern Water Authority by the Thames National Rivers Authority (I am grateful to Mike Huxley, formerly of the fisheries department of Southern Water, for this information). These fish, which came from the River Lea catchment, were held in the outflow of Bewl Water in a simulated river environment. In June 1987 they were stripped of spawn and milt, after the application of induced spawning techniques. A significant number of fry were produced, some of which were placed in the Upper Medway as three- to five-inch fish in 1988. In later years I understand that further stockings of fish in the twelve-inch range were made, which augers well for the future. In the 1990s it therefore might have appeared that we were fishing for barbel that had been stocked in the river some thirty or more years before. Obviously not all the fish caught were of specimen size, so were the 4lb to 7lb fish just old males, rather than the progeny of the stocked fish, as I would have preferred to believe?

Unfortunately the Upper Medway received a bad press in the 1990s. Myths developed that the big fish were somehow captive and easy to catch, although these statements did not stand up to scrutiny. The reality was that the head of barbel was low, and the fish were both highly mobile and easily scared in this small river; indeed the prospects of catching a barbel on any given day were lower than on more prolific rivers. In dour spells a typical remark might be 'I saw a barbel roll there a few weeks ago, so it may be worth a try' – which perhaps indicates the extent of the problem.

If you talk to Medway barbel anglers you will probably leave with the impression that they catch 'some', but never a lot. If you are used to a 100 fish or more a season on the more prolific rivers, then be prepared for some quiet times if you decide to fish the Medway. However, you may well be phoning your friends at midnight to tell them excitedly about your first fish, caught after many unproductive sessions.

After the first fish, confidence kicks in and it becomes relatively easier – though it is still hard. Medway barbel are extra special because they are comparatively rare, so be prepared for some long waits – but above all, enjoy the challenge and your time in this scenic part of the country.

In 1990 the then Wealden Region of the Barbel Catchers Club decided that since this was our local river we should fish it instead of charging down to the Kennet, Avon or Lea. We also decided to fish as a group, which meant that we pooled ideas and experiences. The group included Dave Magson, Steve Carden, Dave Williams, Richard Storer, Andy Hunt and myself; and our efforts would follow in the wake of early pioneering work by, amongst others, Ian Beadle.

In the past we had used conventional baits for our barbel fishing, but after guidance from those with experience of high protein baits, we decided to change our direction. This was new to those of us who had not had a grounding in carp fishing, and it was perhaps fair to say that the ideas were treated with some scepticism. Having selected an appropriate bait we did some pre-baiting for a few weeks, and started fishing.

The first few weeks produced a number of big barbel. On the second weekend of the season in 1990 Dave Williams caught two double-figure fish, of 10lb 8oz and 10lb 14oz. Richard Storer followed this in the next few days with an 11lb 6oz fish, and he also had several in the 4lb to 5lb range. A general slowdown in activity was then noted until August; but by the latter part of that month the best fish had been landed, a specimen of 12lb 14oz (thought to be the Medway record at the time) by Richard Storer. This fish was caught just a few hours after Dave Williams had lost it in a snag: his hook was still in its mouth.

A few weeks later Dave Williams caught the same fish at 13lb 7oz. This all sounds very exciting, but it does not paint the true picture. In between the captures there were many blanks, and at times it was

The Medway at Chafford weir.

A 12lb 6oz Medway barbel caught by Mark in September 1995.

easily possible to believe that with the river in one of its dour moods, all the fish had perhaps taken an extended holiday. Most of us agreed that we always saw more barbel than we caught. Occasionally, on hot days prior to the start of the season, small groups of spawning barbel could be watched in the fast runs with opportunist chub swirling behind them clearing up the eggs. When the season began they would be gone, taking refuge in the deeper pools or glides or behind the many snags, only venturing onto the shallows at night.

I am sure that we made life hard for ourselves by making too much noise, and perhaps being too conservative in our choice of swims. Indeed, the nature of the upper river is such that one's chances always depend upon the amount of angling pressure and bankside activity. We were fairly certain that the fish lived either a solitary life or in small groups. If a fish was caught, the individual or group might well move, or cease feeding, or both; though how far they moved would depend upon various factors, including water levels. Suffice it to say that there were many areas in the upper Medway that were not heavily fished – and who knows how different the results would have been had we adopted a more adventurous attitude. Nevertheless, the need for a careful approach to the river cannot be overstated. This is a small river, in some places less than fifteen feet wide, and sessions can be effectively ruined by a clumsy footfall echoing off the high clay banks, or perhaps by a garrulous white-shirted hiker passing the time of day.

The best conditions on the Medway hold good for most barbel rivers, rainfall freshening the river in summer, and floodwater and mild temperatures creating good opportunities in winter. There is nothing really to add here to the many excellent books and articles on the subject. However, it became clear that there was a pattern to the fishing, and early season was a good time to be about.

The fishing also changed in nature through the year. In the early season there was always a good chance of finding a fish in the shallow runs between the big pools, as well as in the pools themselves. As the season progressed the water would clear and warm up; and in the high summer, as the surrounding farmland became dry and dusty, the river would become lethargic. Sport could pick up in the late summer and into early autumn, but the timing would depend primarily upon the first rains.

The first flush through in the autumn would often trigger activity in terms of both feeding and movement between areas of the river. Whilst it was never possible to establish a clear pattern of fish movement, floodwater could allow fish to pass over the shallows and move into new areas. The ideal winter profile from November onwards was colour, water at 46°F or over and settled muggy conditions. The end of the season seemed to be capable of producing a fish or two provided it was relatively mild. So there was nothing intrinsically different in the way the Medway behaved when compared to other rivers; the key factors were the low fish density and their considerable mobility.

Even if barbel were not around, the chub were often obliging; at times they could be either a nuisance or a welcome bonus in a quiet spell. Picture the scenario in which you creep up to a shallow, weedy run, and then gently lower your bait into place, maybe with some hemp, and wait as dusk settles. The bats flit around searching out the last of the late mayfly spinners or a night moth, periodically sounding off audible bite alarms as they touch the line of an angler. You soon get a nod on the rod top, followed by a 'wrap-round'. A 3lb or 4lb chub cavorts across the river, sending up a huge wake, and comes quickly to the net after trying to bury itself in the bank under your feet. You now have a decision to make. The commotion would most probably have killed any chance of barbel for hours, it's 11pm, you have to work in the morning. Maybe some more chub could come later or you could move just down the run and try again. It was easier sometimes in one's weaker moments to go home and accept with good grace that it was not to be your night, and make plans for next time.

Whilst the Medway could be very moody and dour, there were days when the river had what can only be described as an electric atmosphere. Everywhere fish would be rolling or topping and the rod top would flicker; it would seem that everything in the river was trying to eat your bait. In several years of fishing the river, two short sessions really stand out.

The first was in September 1995, when I had baited a stretch of river that had had a little less pressure than other areas. It was three or four feet deep, and a little snaggy. Arriving earlier than usual at 3pm, I found the river was quiet; only one other angler was present, there was thunder in the air, and the water was warm and coloured. A barbel rolled, then another, which meant I had a chance. After the ritual of some hemp and some free samples, I made a short upstream cast into the run over the area where the fish rolled. At 5pm a light tap on the rod top was followed a few seconds later by a slow pull round: the result, a 12lb 6oz barbel, but no witness. One hour later I had a faster bite, but after a brief fight the fish shed the hook; then it rained hard and the river came up – and being of weak constitution, I went home.

Dave Williams with an astounding 28lb brace.

Dave Williams, who in 1992 had equalled the then national barbel record at 14lb 6oz, was made of sterner stuff. He sat through a whole night in November 1994 in a thunderstorm and a raging flood, to take barbel of 13lb plus and 15lb plus. The fish were caught many hours apart, so maybe I should have stayed as well – I have found out subsequently that it is quite hard to catch fish whilst at home!

The really successful anglers on the Medway were prepared to do the time and endure the long quiet periods, knowing that the low numbers of fish demanded a dedicated approach. This was no place for 'gentleman's hours'. Whilst I can only speak of the experiences of our group, it is probably fair to say that to catch with anything approaching consistency, say ten fish a season, you had to put in the hours. To ensure that you were there both when conditions were right and also when fish were responsive, you needed to spend a lot of time on the bank. This doesn't mean to say that others before, during or since may not have done better; it is just how we saw it at the time. On speaking to colleagues, we regret perhaps not spending more time fishing new areas and generally doing more pioneering. It was the case that large tracts of the upper Medway seldom saw an angler, and even today who knows what could be there for the more enterprising individual. Maybe our results could have been different.

Tackle was strong, with 1½lb test curve rods, 10lb mainline and braid hook links. We did not spend too much time worrying about rigs since the effectiveness of the bait was the key in those early days. The amount of lead did, however, seem to matter. The least possible weight was used, normally on a running paternoster, with the rod top for indication. A bowed line would also show the bites. In the summer, the amount of weight needed could be just a few SSG shot, but in the winter the lead count would obviously increase, to 2oz or more in a torrent. Sometimes bobbins were used in slack water areas. Other anglers used audible bite indicators, a new approach on rivers in those days, but maybe for long sessions they were advantageous; I found the noise irritating, but each to his own.

How did we fish the Upper Medway? The easiest way was to divide it into the three main types of swim that were available: the shallow riffles, the deep pools, and the glides or deeper runs. The pools were always the most popular because they looked easy to fish and were deep, and of course anglers like fishing holes – they looked as if they should hold fish, and invariably from time to time they did. The pools formed on the tight meanders, of which there are several on the upper river, were all capable of producing barbel over the years. These pools were characterized by a fast run into the deeper water, which then slowed the current, with the main flow following one bank and then on to a run-off as the pools shallowed into the next run.

It was hard to locate fish in the big pools, even if they had betrayed their presence. The fish could be anywhere in a pool, but even in flood conditions it

A typical Medway pool above a narrow run.

did not necessarily follow that the fish were in the slack water. Bites were to be had in areas of flow, provided the flow was even and without boils. In high water it was tempting to drop a bait into a nice slack, but very often the barbel were in the flow; the twitches on the rod top in the slacks were often caused by bream or chub. Both the entry and exit points of pools were also a worth a try, since they were obvious ambush points as fish moved to the pools from the shallows or vice versa.

In summer it seemed that the fish responded best in the pools by feeding hemp in a tight area with a dropper. In the winter (if conditions allowed) it was best to hand feed over a wider area in smaller quantities to get the fish moving. I always liked to use hemp as well as loose bait offerings; others just loose-fed hook-bait samples and caught just the same.

I preferred to fish the runs or glides between pools. Fishing these areas could be difficult due to the level of disturbance from 'nuisance' fish: these could seriously reduce your chances. You could move about and try various areas, but after dark this could be problematic: you could disturb others simply by approaching an area, and the steep clay banks could be slippery and make a quiet or even safe approach a challenge. With coloured water the runs could be easier to fish since the fish would not be as shy, although in a big flood, fishing such areas was generally out of the question. There were safety issues in winter, and some anglers even had a rope handy just in case they slipped.

In the shallower runs or riffles it was sometimes possible to roll a bait or free-line into areas between weeds or depressions in the riverbed, near to snags or overhanging bushes. Historically these were the most productive areas. After dark barbel would travel through these areas in between, and if they were not scared off, a trap could be laid.

The glides or deeper runs were potentially productive and often provided moving water of a greater depth than the riffles or shallower runs between the pools. These areas often came alive after a flush through, and whether this was due to fish moving in, or purely being invigorated by, higher oxygen levels, is open to debate. Again it was tempting to fish the deeper, slacker areas of the glides, but all too often the fish would show themselves in the shallower, faster-flowing areas.

Barbel-feeding periods were often short and unpredictable, and those who could stick it out all night had the chance of capitalizing on these short spells. We all had differing views on what was the best time of day; for some it was late at night, for others the small hours just before dawn. In the early season the timing did not seem to be so important. Richard Storer had most of his fish at tea time, whilst others seemed to do best in the first two hours after dark. There was no real pattern, and probably no best time.

My Biggest Barbel

The great advantage of fishing with others is that you accumulate pooled information over a period. In

Mark Daley and the fifteen-pounder.

February 1995 it was mild and damp, conditions that have recurred regularly in recent winters. I had fished five out of the last six evenings during these conditions and had caught some good chub. On 7 February the river was fining down and was nicely coloured, and the evening still and muggy; the water temperature was 48°F.

This evening was different from the previous few: there were lots of swirls and rolls, and fish seemed to be on the move as the water fined down. There was an air of expectancy that success was possible that evening. At 7pm I had a flicker on the rod and then a solid pull round, and found myself connected to a fish that moved slowly around in circles before making the odd half-hearted run towards deeper water. After a very short time it had turned on the surface, and was soon netted. It was clearly a huge fish, but elation was short-lived as we discovered that the hook was embedded just behind the mouth. The fish weighed 15lb 3oz and was – and still is – my biggest barbel. Whilst not foul-hooked in the classical sense, the nature of the capture created some doubt in my mind as to whether or not it was entirely legitimate. In the end, whilst it may not have been a clean capture, the chances are that the fish took the bait into its mouth at some stage during the proceedings. Being of a philosophical nature, I can now see the funny side: after so many years of trying for a big Medway fish, I had found the right combination of conditions, at a time when one of the big fish was feeding in front of me – and then this happens! Some photos were taken by a friend, and the fish was carefully returned. I arrived home in time for the 9 o'clock news.

Whilst these events occurred some time ago, the general principles still hold good, and the tactics for a small river will not change much, even if the technology has moved on a bit. Most of my friends still use much the same tactics on other rivers. There are now more baits to choose from – but never overlook conventionals: meat, maggots and worms all caught barbel during this period.

The Upper Medway is a wonderful place and a real challenge. Even if the barbel are a struggle at times you can experience excellent chub fishing, maybe come across the odd carp, but above all enjoy fishing one of the toughest but most rewarding of rivers. Whatever else can be, and has been said about the Medway, it was a truly exciting place to fish, and I hope that in the future many more anglers will get the same pleasure from the river as we did.

One of Yorkshire barbelling's greatest captures. Iain Wood with his 11lb 4oz Wharfe fish.

Warwickshire Avon fan Steve Chell with a cracker from the 'Bard's River'.

Jim Knight displays a 12lb 6oz Kennet barbel, which fell to a 14mm Elips pellet.

A big barbel is safely returned to the Bristol Avon by Andy Humphries.

Tony Miles with a Cherwell double of 10lb 12oz.

Tony in action on the Cherwell.

At 9lb, this was a BCC
Dove record when caught.

BELOW:
Rob Stoker with his BCC
river best of 10lb 4oz,
from the Dane.

Andy Cowley with his 10lb 15oz Somerset Frome record, caught on sweetcorn.

Roy Bates with an 11lb 10oz barbel from the Great Ouse's 'Aquarium'.

The ultimate achievement for a 'Swaley': Rob Newton with a middle Swale fish of 10lb 3oz.

Phil Dunn with a typical Ivel barbel.

*Mick Wood with a Wharfe
barbel illuminated by the
setting sun.*

BELOW:
November dawn on the Trent.

Face to face with a Ribble barbel.

BELOW:
The 'meatball kid' strikes again. Howard Maddocks with his Wye 12-pounder.

19 The River Mole

by Paul Starkey

The River Mole is by no means a prolific barbel river; it is more of a classic chub river with the odd smattering of barbel found along its length. From its source in North Sussex near Gatwick it is generally quite a narrow river. It twists and turns its way through the countryside as it gently meanders northwards across Surrey through the North Downs to join the River Thames below Molesey weir near Hampton Court. Although limited, free fishing is available, the majority of the fishing on the river is controlled by local angling clubs and is operated on a season ticket basis only.

The upper Mole runs from Gatwick to Betchworth and is mainly clay based, and as such the river reacts quickly to rainfall. The majority of the river's tributary streams are in this area, although water quality is largely affected by discharge from sewage treatment works, Gatwick Airport and the surrounding towns. The upper reaches support the usual populations of small to medium-sized coarse fish, and chub, dace, gudgeon, pike, perch and roach may all be caught, along with the occasional surprise brown trout. The roach tend to dominate this stretch of river. Rumour has it that in recent years a small stocking of barbel has been carried out on the upper Mole in the Gatwick and Sidlow Bridge areas, although I have heard of no significant catches.

It is on the middle stretches of the Mole, as the river runs downstream from Betchworth to Hersham, that the barbel start to appear, and the quality of fishing significantly improves all the way down to the Thames. Whereas small- to medium-sized fish dominate in the upper Mole, barbel, bream, carp and pike, along with quality chub and perch, are now resident. The barbel, carp and pike all run into double figures, and chub and perch to 4lb can be caught.

The barbel have grown on from a small number of juveniles that were stocked downstream of Cobham weir and around the Leatherhead and Dorking areas a few years ago. From this original stocking the quality of barbel in the river has improved in recent years due to increasing water quality and flow rates. Many parts of the middle Mole are regularly match fished, and as a result of this increased pressure the barbel can be quite difficult to catch. Barbel have filtered throughout much of the river, although populations are very localized and can be hard to locate. The numbers are possibly reduced in some areas due to a lack of suitable spawning habitat. A number of weirs also restrict fish movement throughout the river.

From Betchworth to Dorking the river runs with a reasonable depth, and the barbel show strongly in this area. Below Dorking the river passes over a band of chalk and the overall water quality improves. Cracks in the riverbed allow the water to pass into underground channels, and as a result of this the flow of the river decreases. Many people believe that this is how the river gained the name Mole, due to its burrowing underground. Others claim that the name originated from Molesey where the river joins the Thames. As a result of this subterranean activity it is not unusual in summer for the river to run extremely shallow, except for a few deeper holes between the lower reaches of Norbury Park to Leatherhead. Below Leatherhead the river level is again topped up by a series of springs, and by the time the river reaches Cobham the bed becomes mainly clay based again, and fish to double figures can be found.

The lower part of the river runs from Hersham to where the river joins the Thames at Molesey. Below Hersham the characteristics of the river change radically, in part due to flood alleviation schemes for

The River Mole.

the rivers Mole and Ember. The Mole Ember Flood Relief Channel was dug during the early 1970s to protect the surrounding areas from severe flooding. This channel runs much wider and deeper with a reduced flow when compared to the rest of the river, and although this has destroyed much of the natural river, large barbel, bream, carp and pike can be found in attendance. Excellent free fishing can be had on these parts of the Mole and Ember, with the barbel reportedly reaching 13lb plus.

The river joins the Thames a few miles above Teddington Lock, and this maintains the river in its freshwater state without any contamination from the tidal stretch. A noted hotspot is at the mouth of the Mole opposite Hampton Court, where the local carp anglers complain of being pestered by barbel when fishing with boilies over beds of groundbait and trout pellets.

Although actual numbers of fish are unknown, the density of barbel within the river is not particularly high; at the time of writing, the average stamp of fish appears to be around 6lb 8oz. Generally a season's results will include a few fish of 3lb or so, and this fact indicates that at least some of the barbel are spawning, as these fish are too young to be part of the original stocking. Currently the majority of barbel are in the 5lb to 7lb class, and this has been the case for the last few years.

There are a few fish of 9lb and over within the river, with fish rumoured to have been caught to 15lb. As with other rivers, there seems to be the usual game of Chinese whispers going on, and one does have to filter out the truths from the rumours. Personally I only believe what I see or what comes from trusted sources, otherwise I would end up believing that the Mole was very prolific and absolutely full of doubles, which is definitely not the case. Although a handful of double-figure fish are caught each season, a number of these are recaptures.

Over the last decade a few double-figure fish have been reported in the various angling magazines. The River Mole barbel record has increased over the years from a fish of 10lb 11oz caught in September of 1996, to one of 13lb 4oz caught in February 2002. October 2002 saw another Mole record set, with a surprise fish of 14lb 9oz being reported. This fish was previously unknown to those anglers fishing the Mole, and is definitely not the 13lb 4oz fish mentioned earlier.

With the current increasing popularity of barbel fishing there has been a significant increase in pressure on the Mole's limited barbel stocks, and some of the stretches are now fished quite heavily. The most pressurized stretches of the river are popular because of the number of people fishing for the barbel, and not necessarily because they are the best stretches. The majority of anglers are unfortunately lazy and are influenced by other people's success, tackle-shop talk, information gained through the angling press and more recently the Internet. Equally a lot of these stretches tend to coincide with easy access and parking.

This increase in angling pressure has had an interesting impact on the location of the barbel within the river. The popular stretches still contain good barbel holding spots, and barbel can still be caught in the known swims; but generally they are now more spread throughout the river, and most stretches hold a few fish. Away from the popular areas the barbel can be very hard to locate. There are some very good fish to be had, along with a few doubles, although they are not easy to catch.

A number of weirs along the length of the river restrict fish movement. Barbel are able to (and some do) travel a few miles within each section, which enables anyone seriously fishing the river to target specific areas before moving on, knowing that barbel are at least contained within each section. The less pressured stretches of the river will not contain many, if any, barbel anglers, and you will be very much on your own to locate the fish. Once the fish have been located on these stretches, then they will be less wary and should as a result be easier to catch. Visual location of barbel is somewhat problematic apart from a few shallower areas. Fish spotting is generally out of the question, even in the summer, as the Mole usually carries some colour. If you are lucky, however, it is possible in a few areas to spot the occasional fish spawning on the shallows during the close season.

As with most small rivers, the Mole has a good diversity of swims available, and is ever-changing throughout its course. All the usual barbel-holding features are worth trying, although multiple catches of barbel are quite rare, and one or two fish a session can be considered a good day's fishing. For the specimen barbel angler, fishing short sessions for one bite can be the norm unless the river conditions are exactly right.

Good watercraft and hours spent on the bank are the key to successful location, and any swim that has a change of depth or holds weed or snags is a good starting point. Swims that hold bream seem to be worth a try, as more often than not they also hold

barbel. It can be a benefit to travel light, and to bait up and rove a few swims, although this is not so easy on some of the more popular stretches. Roving enables new swims to be tried out whilst dropping in on some of the known favourites, and this can improve your odds.

Generally the Mole is not a particularly fast-flowing river, and the average level is such that most swims can hold barbel throughout the year. During the summer after long periods without rainfall the flow of the river can be a bit slow and the water can have a greenish tint. At these times it can be especially worth searching out some of the swims with an increased level of flow caused by the river narrowing, or where the flow is diverted by gravel beds and nearside bushes. Often in summer the river needs a good flush through to get the fish really back on the feed.

The quality of barbel fishing during autumn is generally more predictable, with the river running in a better condition. It is after periods of rainfall that the Mole can really switch on. The river can easily rise or fall a couple of feet overnight, and if you catch it right this is when your chances of a few barbel are improved. The river seems to fish best when rising, and most swims are worth trying.

Time spent fishing any of the deeper holes usually produces a fish. If using roving tactics in times of increased river levels, those swims that are normally too shallow to hold fish are definitely worth a try. Whether it is because the barbel do not normally graze over these areas I do not know, but spots that normally carry only a foot or so of water seem to be especially productive during any rise in river level. The Mole colours up extremely quickly, and will often run a muddy brown colour. This does not appear to affect the quality of fishing in any way, however, and the barbel will find any smelly bait that is presented.

Winter barbel fishing on the Mole is usually quite slow going. However, over the last few years we have had quite mild winters, and it can be worth spending a few hours on the bank. Any barbel that is caught is likely to be in prime condition and of a good average weight, and any angler has a chance of catching one of the larger specimens.

Most of my fishing is what I would call 'short session fishing', usually around four hours on the bank, so I try to travel as light a possible – although no matter how hard I try, I always end up carrying far more bait and tackle than I ever need. As it is a small river I only ever carry one rod when fishing the Mole, usually a 1½lb TC Harrison Triptych matched to a 3000 series Shimano reel for summer, and a 5010 GTM Baitrunner for flood conditions. When I began fishing the Mole I used a 1¼lb TC through-action Avon rod, which was ideal for normal conditions, though I was frequently caught out by flood conditions, when I found this rod to be a bit underpowered. The Triptych is quite heavy for catching chub, but it is more than capable of dealing with any barbel and is a good compromise for the variety of river conditions that may be encountered. The rod performs well during times of extra water, and without being over-powerful, reduces the time spent on long-drawn-out battles with barbel that do the fish no favours. Equally, being a three-piece rod, it tends to live in the boot of my car fully made up, just waiting for when any opportunity arises.

I recently acquired a 1000 series reel that I have dabbled with for rolling baits. This reel is extremely light and reduces arm ache when holding the rod for a long session. Unfortunately it has double handles, which are a serious nuisance when trundling – I am frequently unwrapping the line from the handles.

I normally fish with 8lb bs mainline, which meets the majority of my requirements, although if I know I am fishing an area of heavy snags or the river is carrying a lot of debris, I tend to increase this to 10lb. A few SSG shot and a selection of leads up to 3oz cater for most situations, enabling me either to trundle a bait or to fish it hard on the bottom. The lead is usually attached to the mainline via a sliding run ring and snap swivel, enabling a change of lead to suit swim conditions.

For baiting up swims at the start of a session I carry a large baitdropper. Once fishing, any further baiting up is done with a large swimfeeder or via PVA stringers or mesh depending on the bait I am using.

Hook lengths are generally made up on the bank to suit river conditions, and a good starting point is about twelve inches long. When the river is running low and clear I tend to use fluorocarbon hook lengths, and have found these can give a definite edge. During normal river conditions I find braid tends to work better.

As I generally fish short sessions I never bother with a rod holdall, and I only take a chair when the mood takes me, or when I know I am planning to fish just the one swim, as I find you are less likely to move if you have too much to carry.

For those who fancy giving float fishing a go, Mole barbel can be caught on a maggot and caster approach; but it is mainly bags of chub that are caught on this method.

Most barbel bites on the Mole tend to be absolute slammers that can come totally out of the blue, especially if you are not holding the rod. Over the years I have been slowly converted to touch legering and now hold the rod, whether it is in the rest or not, with the line looped around my finger. The amount of feedback you get from the swim by holding the line can give confidence as to whether fish are nearby, or whether it is time to move on. I feel this method makes my fishing more interesting than simply gazing at the rod top. With time you start to identify all the little knocks and pulls that may be caused by fish or weed, and any movement of the lead is easily identifiable. This method, quite apart from being more enjoyable, has definitely increased my bite-to-hook ratio, and the days of watching the rod tip fly round only to strike at nothing are now hopefully in the past. Strangely, when touch legering I never actually have time to notice a bite, usually finding that I have already struck and that the rod is bent into a fish.

A few years ago now, after spending too much time sitting around stillwaters chasing carp and pretending to be a garden gnome, I realized I was just going through the motions. I enjoyed fishing, but what I was doing at that time was becoming a bit repetitive. I had not spent a lot of time river fishing and had never caught a barbel, and at this time there were many rumours of barbel on the Mole, although finding anyone who had actually caught one was a different matter. Those anglers who were in the know tried to keep things as quiet as they could. One summer's evening I decided to ignore the lake and go to the river for a change. The results of that evening were to change my preferred venue type, and I now rarely fish lakes at all, much preferring the river and its more natural surroundings.

That particular evening I was legering with meat, and although not being totally sure of what I was doing, being an inexperienced river angler, I was thoroughly enjoying the challenge. An angler fishing above me was using floating crust for the summer chub, and after a while a regular stream of crusts started drifting past me. At the end of my swim a few large swirls were appearing from a good fish taking the drifting crusts off the surface. Meanwhile nothing was occurring with my legered meat, and after a while I was distracted enough to decide to have a cast for the fish. I swiftly modified my rig to enable me to flick a piece of crust downstream, and amazingly, the fish took it immediately. It was a good carp, and I was stunned by the power the fish had, as opposed to its stillwater counterpart. After a good fight, the fish was on the bank; it weighed in at about 12lb.

I switched back to legered meat, re-cast, and had a bite almost immediately. Again the fish stormed off downstream, and its power led me to believe I had hooked another carp. Upon netting the fish I was surprised and extremely pleased to be looking at my first ever barbel, duly weighed at 4lb. From that evening onwards I rarely visited the lakes, much preferring to spend my time on the river. Results were slow, however, and I realized I was at the start of a long learning curve in getting to know the river.

It was during the next season on the river that I renewed my acquaintance with Chris Dodge, another gnome from the lake who had decided to move on to fresh pastures. Chris and I had spent many a year having a good laugh at each other, and it turned out we were both keen to discover the mysteries of the Mole and its barbel. That season, through fishing together and swapping notes and ideas, we both managed to catch a few barbel and to learn a bit about the river.

During the early seasons spent on the Mole, luncheon meat was the bait par excellence, and a good day's fishing could be had catching numerous chub and the odd barbel. I don't know whether it was down to increased pressure from other anglers (by now there were a lot more anglers fishing for the Mole barbel), but slowly over the years meat became less productive. Smaller pieces of meat fished particle-style over a bed of hemp still managed to catch the odd fish, but the barbel seemed to be becoming wary of meat, and even the numbers of chub being caught were reducing.

Generally, the average weight of barbel being caught around this time was 5lb to 6lb, and a seven-pounder was considered a good fish. One Christmas during flooded conditions Chris managed a barbel of 9lb 14oz (no matter how hard he tried he couldn't make it 10lb – how's that for honesty!); this fish was easily identifiable by the fact that it had a split in its left pectoral fin, and even though I hate naming fish, inevitably it became known as Split Fin.

A few fish could still be caught on the ever-reliable lobworm when roving about, or if you were prepared to fish an obvious feature and fill the swim with maggot, then you might have good results. However, the fishing was definitely becoming harder.

The following season Chris and I met Richard Donnelly, another Barbel Catchers member, and his results were much the same as ours when fishing meat. In an unusually productive session during an autumn flood I managed an amazing bumper catch of six barbel, all on meat. Split Fin was part of this catch, and again weighed in at 9lb 14oz. That season Split Fin was also caught by Richard at the same weight, and there were rumours of another

nine-pounder, plus a fish of 10lb 7oz being caught by other anglers.

It seemed that unless the barbel were on the feed, we were all struggling to catch on meat, and the number of blanks endured by us all far outweighed the number of captures. It was decided that the following season the three of us would try something different, and fish as a team using a fishmeal-based boilie mix. We decided to name our bait CPR after Chris, Paul and Richard – as good a name as any. During the close season, pre-baiting was carried out in earnest using soft chopped baits of CPR. This was done on an 'every-other-day' basis, and a small amount of bait was liberally distributed throughout the river, with a preference being given to favourite swims. The general idea was to try to get the fish used to eating the bait in unpressurized conditions. The carp obviously took a liking to the bait, and many a pleasant evening was spent watching carp grazing over a few baited areas, before we headed off to the pub to discuss our findings. We never did see a barbel on the feed, though this is not particularly unusual for the Mole.

Paul 'Ringo' Starkey with a Mole double at 10lb 4oz.

Came 16 June 2000, and the three of us started our campaign on the Mole full of renewed enthusiasm. However, it quickly became apparent that our observations of the close season were to be confirmed: we all caught carp. It was quickly obvious that the carp were definitely switched on to the bait, and this was confirmed in the following incident: Richard lost a good fish when his hook length snapped; then just ten minutes later I stalked a carp in two feet of water. A good mirror carp of 14lb 4oz confidently took the bait – and upon netting the fish, Richard's hook length was seen hanging from the fish's mouth: amazing. By the end of the session the three of us had all managed a barbel, an absolute mountain of carp and a few chub. The most successful tactic seemed to be baiting up with a couple of pints of partiblend and hemp, and fishing a few freebies over the top.

That summer the weather was extremely hot, and the river was running very low and clear. I had managed another barbel of about 6lb and suffered a couple of blanks. Then on 2 July, Chris and I popped down to the river for a short evening session. Upon arrival I baited up a swim with twelve catapults full of partiblend and hemp, added about fifteen freebies of CPR and then went off to fish elsewhere. A while later, having frustratingly lost a couple of carp, I dropped back into the pre-baited swim and cast in a light lead with a hair-rigged piece of CPR, bouncing the bait down to hold under a nearby bush. Hair-rigged baits for barbel work a treat, the barbel usually being cleanly hooked just inside the lip. I instantly had loads of line bites, and fish were obviously in the swim. Vibration of the line could constantly be felt through my fingertips, and after a minute or so I felt a good strong pull: I struck, the rod hooped over, and I was into a good fish. The fish dived further under the bush, and it was very much a case of hit and hold. By this time I was convinced it was yet another carp. Once the fish was clear of the bush Chris, who was fishing in the next swim, came to give me a hand. On getting the fish to the bank, it became apparent that it was a good barbel – and once netted, it became apparent just how good. It was a totally immaculate barbel of 10lb 4oz, a new personal best and (at that time) a Barbel Catchers Club river record.

That season Richard had a couple of nine-pounders, one of them being Split Fin again, and the remainder of the fish we caught were all in the 5lb to 7lb bracket. Sadly the outbreak of foot and mouth disease finished our season prematurely; however, our results for that season were a lot more consistent than when we were using meat, and we each averaged a fish every other visit. The only time meat outperformed CPR was during flooded conditions, although even then we were catching on CPR. The CPR seemed to fish more effectively in paste form, which allowed a greater leakage, although during summer this was somewhat problematic, with small fish nibbling the paste away.

The following season the fishing was even better, with an increase in both the number of barbel caught and their average weight. However, results when fished over beds of hemp and partiblend seemed to reduce, and I switched to fishing CPR over a bed of mini pellets introduced via a feeder. Strangely, despite the increased catch rate, we didn't encounter any of the bigger barbel that season. The last day of the season I did manage one of 9lb 5oz; but other than that it was mainly barbel in the 6lb to 7lb bracket.

The season of 2002–03 was a strange one, to say the least. Due to work pressures and the hassle of making up paste mixes, the team baiting campaign sadly came to an end. Time spent on the banks of the Mole was considerably less than in previous years as I had started to target a couple of other venues. Equally the number of anglers targeting the Mole for barbel significantly increased. The majority were fishing with pellet, and the similarity of this to CPR seemed to affect its results; the bait still worked, but sadly not as well as it had done in previous seasons. An interesting result of this increased pressure was that meat now seemed to be as productive as any other bait, and you could say what goes around comes around over the seasons. An assumption may be made that with the amount of pellet generally going into the river, and there being only a relatively small head of barbel, the fish were either becoming wary of pellet, or they were getting their fill very quickly with the amount of freebies that were being introduced.

That season my sessions on the Mole were mainly short opportunistic visits, only fishing when I couldn't face the long drive to alternative venues or when I felt conditions would be favourable. If the river was carrying any colour, then I fished meat; otherwise I used worm. It is fortunate that the Mole does not hold many eels, so worms can be used with more confidence than on many other rivers. They are ideally suited to a roving approach, with two or three mounted on a size 6. That season I managed three nine-pounders, including a brace, all in very short two- to three-hour sessions. Interestingly, one of these fish was caught by Chris a couple of days earlier, about half a mile downstream. Upon casting, if I began to get chub pulls then I would move immediately. If I didn't get a touch for five minutes from any smaller fish, then it seemed to be worth sitting it out for a while in the hope of a barbel.

A Record Fish

Towards the end of January 2003 we were in the middle of an unusually mild spell, and Chris and I made a spur-of-the-moment decision to spend a couple of hours on the Mole. Being an unplanned visit, I got caught out, and upon opening my bait cupboard for a tin of luncheon meat found that the cupboard was bare. A rather old tin of hot dogs, well past their sell-by date, was all that was available, so they would have to do. We had had some rain in previous days, and the river had a nice steady flow and was a couple of feet up. This was to be a social session as much as anything, although conditions were perfect for barbel, and we duly set up in adjacent swims in an area we knew to be productive under these conditions.

I tackled up with a 1oz lead fished on a run ring with a one-inch length of hot dog mounted on a size 6 hook on my standard braid hook length of about a foot long. After casting, a handful of freebies were introduced upstream. I missed a small bite after about half an hour or so. Another half hour passed, and I was considering trying out another swim when I felt a couple of pulls on the line. Upon striking, the fish was hooked and it proceeded to swim upstream in a slow, heavy manner. It was obviously a good fish, and held its position deep in the middle of the river for a short while. Meanwhile Chris, seeing that I was into a fish, came over to offer his usual support. Slowly I managed to bring the fish into the near bank. I still had not seen it, but when it rolled in the edge it was obviously a big barbel. After another couple of runs it was finally netted and withdrawn from the river to be admired. Chris and I looked at each other and grinned; this was a big fish! It was lightly hooked, just in the corner of its mouth. When we unhooked it we allowed it to rest in the landing net in the river for a while, and then carried out the weighing duties.

The barbel weighed 13lb 5oz, a new personal best for me, and a new Barbel Catchers Club river record. Upon inspection the fish was in good condition, apart from a slight nick in its tail fin. It was instantly recognizable as a fish I had weighed for another angler the previous summer at a weight of 12lb. Photographs were taken, and the barbel was then rested in the landing net before being allowed to swim off when good and ready. Next cast I had a barbel of 6lb. All in all, for a spur of the moment

Ringo and his Mole monster of 13lb 5oz.

decision to go fishing, it was an unbelievable session.

Upon having the photographs developed and comparing scale patterns and general fish shape, I believe that the 13lb 5oz barbel was indeed the fish I had caught two and a half years earlier at 10lb 4oz. It was nice to be reacquainted with an old friend, even though I didn't know it at the time. The fish must have picked up its split tail fin sometime between July 2000 and February 2002, as it is can easily be identified as the same fish that appeared in the barbel river records published in *Coarse Angling Today* at a weight of 13lb 4oz. I guess this is its optimum winter weight or thereabouts. In recent years the growth rates of barbel within all rivers seem to have increased, and the Mole is up there with the rest of them. Personally I believe this is due to a number of contributory factors, these being milder seasons, cleaner rivers and an increase in both the quantity and quality of bait available to the fish. Another reason could be the populations of crayfish that seem to have appeared in some areas.

Looking at some of the photographs of 9lb barbel caught in recent years they are generally quite long and thin. Hopefully over the forthcoming seasons these fish will fatten up to provide us with future double-figure fish. So you never know what future seasons may hold.

Incidentally, Split Fin has not been seen for a couple of seasons, and one can only assume that this fish has now either died or has taken up residence in a different stretch of the river. Let's hope it is the latter.

20 The Yorkshire Ouse

by Iain Wood

Unlike all other major barbel rivers in Yorkshire, which have their sources high in the Pennines (or, in the case of the Derwent, the North York Moors) the Yorkshire Ouse comes into existence on the Plain of York. Around one and a quarter miles below Aldwark Bridge, at Thorpe Underwood, the Ouse Gill Beck joins the main river, and the lower Ure becomes the Ouse. A signpost on the flood bank marks the point of change. It is already a significant watercourse at this point, over thirty metres wide in places and with depths running to well over twenty feet.

From its source down to the weir and locks at Linton-on-Ouse, the river is best known as a winter roach and chub fishery. Barbel are present but scarce, and captures are infrequent and usually accidental, taken by anglers fishing for other species. It is from the weir downstream that the most prolific barbel areas are to be found, taking in the fisheries of Linton-on-Ouse, Newton-on-Ouse, Beningbrough and Red House. Barbel are present throughout these stretches, and down as far perhaps as Nether Poppleton, but are not by any means evenly spread, and location is the major hurdle to success. Below Nether Poppleton, running through the City of York down to Naburn Locks, barbel are rare. Personally I have not heard of a capture from these reaches for many years, though others may of course know better. Below Naburn Locks in the tidal river, the Environment Agency has in recent seasons found encouraging numbers of small barbel during their sampling surveys.

Fish populations are never constant in any fishery, and it is clear that the Yorkshire Ouse, whilst still holding a significant head of barbel, is not as prolific as it was during the 1960s and 1970s. A major factor here may be the building in 1978 of a gauging weir on the River Nidd, a delightful tributary of the Ouse that enters the main river at Nun Monkton. Generations of Ouse barbel have used the lower reaches of the Nidd for spawning, particularly around Kirk Hammerton, but their annual upstream migration was severely hampered by the installation of this man-made obstacle. Angling bodies campaigned against this structure for many years, but it was not until the results of a radio-tagging survey by Dr Martyn Lucas of the University of Durham were published in 1995 that anglers' concerns were taken seriously. The study proved that the weir did indeed restrict barbel migration, and it was finally removed in the spring of 2000, twenty-two years after its construction. Hopefully in seasons to come we will see the benefits of the barbel having unrestricted access to their spawning grounds.

The Yorkshire Ouse has always been regarded as one of the county's better specimen waters, and it has produced big barbel in the past. In July 1951 a 10lb 8oz barbel was captured at Linton-on-Ouse by a Mr J. Thornton, a fish that was set up and displayed for many years in a glass case in York AAs headquarters. In 1958 a 12lb 6oz fish was reported to the angling press by G. Dean, also from the same venue. These were very big fish both regionally and nationally at the time of capture. Clearly these fish are now history, but in recent times the river has produced barbel of comparable size, including a 10lb 10oz fish taken by former Barbel Catchers member John McNulty, and the 10lb 6oz barbel taken by Jon Wolfe and featured in this chapter. Fish of 8lb and 9lb, whilst not common, are a realistic target at the present time. Considering the increase in size of barbel in most of Yorkshire's rivers in recent years, it may not be unrealistic to think that the river may again be capable of producing a fish around the 12lb mark. It may, however, be

The stately depths of the River Ouse upstream of York.

Iain Wood with a fine 9lb specimen.

appropriate at this point to remind any angler hunting big barbel in Yorkshire of the need to keep a sense of realism and perspective when setting targets and assessing success. Although the average size of Yorkshire barbel has increased in recent times, it still lags well behind that of almost any other area in the country. Anyone judging his results with those of anglers from these other areas is likely to become very disillusioned. In Yorkshire, 8lb and 9lb barbel are still big fish, and many very competent and dedicated barbel anglers still await their first 'double' from the county's rivers.

Any barbel angler tackling the Ouse for the first time, particularly one who has fished other feature-packed Yorkshire rivers such as the Swale or Nidd, is likely to find this large, deep and relatively featureless river a somewhat daunting prospect. Indeed it can be so, but with a little thought and effort progress can soon be made. As stated earlier, location is the key to success. Baits and methods for fishing the Ouse are relatively straightforward. My first approach on a new stretch would be to walk the river on a warm evening around dusk. Barbel on the Ouse are often active at this time and give

*Mick Wood with a
good Yorkshire Ouse
fish.*

themselves away by rolling on the surface. Once located, these areas can be investigated further by careful plumbing to look for sub-surface features that might prove to be significant. A large sliding float carrying a bulk of several SSG shot or a large olivette (without a hook length) can be trotted down a swim to reveal useful information about the riverbed, for example channels, shallow spots and snags.

Although they are not as immediately obvious as on some of the other Yorkshire barbel rivers, similar features to those that attract barbel on, say, the Swale, are also found on the Ouse. The outside of bends, places where the river narrows and speeds up, sudden changes of depth, depressions in the river bed, are all worthy of investigation. Sub-surface snags are reliable fish producers and can often be spotted by surface disturbance, or of course by the well known method of getting 'hung up' whilst fishing! Some areas of the river contain wooden piles, originally placed along the bankside to prevent erosion. Many of these remain visible, but others have been eroded over the years and have disappeared beneath the surface. These can be difficult swims to fish, but they often prove attractive to barbel.

On many of the shallower Ouse tributaries, willow bushes are often a feature of productive swims, providing safe haven for both barbel and chub. Few Nidd fish, for example, are found far from such overhead cover. On the Ouse, however, I feel that they only occasionally come into play as a

significant feature of a good barbel swim. Many of the willows barely reach beyond the shallow marginal shelf, and whilst it is aesthetically pleasing to see them, that is the limit of their value in the majority of swims. In my opinion, features within the river channel are the key to the location of Ouse barbel. In this respect the river can be deceptive, as beneath its often featureless surface it can be full of surprises. A couple of years ago Jon Wolfe and I surveyed one or two stretches of the Ouse from Jon's boat, using an echo sounder. The results were remarkable, with numerous clay lumps, snags and dramatic changes of depth present.

In past years the river was heavily match fished, and match results were a very useful source of information. More recently, since commercial stillwater fisheries became so popular with the match men, this is much less the case. However, the Ouse still hosts a limited number of matches, and snippets of information regarding barbel catches, or anglers being broken by big fish, can lead the barbel angler to a previously untapped swim. It is then down to him to exploit this knowledge.

Traditionally the Ouse is not regarded as a good early season water, and it is usually well into July before barbel begin to show in any numbers. It is likely that following spawning, significant numbers of fish are still in the Nidd and around Linton weir at the start of the season, taking several weeks to drop back into their normal haunts. The best of the fishing is usually from August through to the end of October, and the Ouse Championship (held at the end of October) is usually the last match in which barbel figure in any numbers. Barbel can be, and often are caught during the winter months, but the barbel specialist is very much at the mercy of the conditions. The Ouse is very prone to flooding following heavy rain, draining as it does the Ure, Swale and Nidd catchments. The mild conditions usually necessary for successful winter barbel fishing tend to coincide with moist, westerly air streams and heavy rain on the Pennines. A dirty, rubbish-filled Ouse, several metres above normal, is neither a safe nor productive place to fish.

During the course of an average summer and autumn on the Ouse, the barbel angler will encounter varying river conditions. These in turn will affect the mood of the barbel, and the angler will need to respond accordingly. Whilst nothing in angling is written in tablets of stone, as a general rule under normal conditions and particularly in daylight, a particle approach is usually the most effective. Caster, maggot or corn fished in conjunction with hempseed, take some beating. Hempseed works well as an attractor, but should not be used too liberally as it is easy to overdo it and have your quarry totally preoccupied with the seed. After dark and in flood conditions, larger, smellier types of bait such as flavoured meat, sausage-meat paste, Meaty Fishbites and lobworms are preferred, although particles can still take fish. At the end of the day, bait choice is down to the individual, and what works for him and gives him confidence. I am certain that some of the more modern barbel baits used around the country would also be effective on the Ouse; however, perhaps because the Ouse is not heavily fished for barbel, standard baits still prove very effective.

My ideal conditions for barbel fishing on this river would be a mild, overcast day (or night) with the river carrying a couple of feet of coloured water without too much debris. In such conditions one can expect the barbel to be actively foraging, and whilst location is still important, it is not quite as critical as at other times, as the fish cover much greater areas in their search for food. Under these conditions, daylight fishing can be very productive. A wet summer, although not favoured for the family holiday, can result in some productive conditions on the river.

In periods of low rainfall the Ouse can become painfully low, slow and clear, and these can be difficult conditions under which to barbel-fish the river. Barbel can be caught, but at these times location is crucial, as they will tend to shoal tightly, perhaps in an area of greater flow or close to a snag. If they are located, good catches of several fish can

sometimes be taken, but some areas will be quite barren. On the few stretches where it can be legally pursued, night fishing can be an advantage under these conditions, whilst daytime, especially in bright conditions, can be the kiss of death.

Whilst float fishing has taken many barbel from the river over the years, without doubt the most efficient method of fishing this deep waterway is legering. Feeder fishing is favoured, except in more extreme conditions. The use of a feeder, perhaps in conjunction with a bait dropper, ensures that loose feed is placed accurately on the riverbed.

On a normal river in daytime, there is little, in my opinion, to beat caster fished in conjunction with hemp. One method is to use a block-end feeder (a Kamasan Black Cap is a good choice) with the holes opened up slightly, enabling the bait to be fed neat, without any groundbait. The hemp and caster, although inert, will almost all spill from the feeder during its descent, and the residue at the start of the retrieve. Due to the slow flow, the particles will not spread far, and the method tends to lay a trail of bait a couple of metres long below the point of entry. When using maggots (with or without hemp) the feeder holes are not adapted.

An alternative approach, and a better option in my view when the river is flowing more strongly, is to use an open-ended feeder and feed the mix of hemp and caster trapped between plugs of crushed grilled hemp and crumb. If the groundbait is mixed on the dry side and pressed firmly into the feeder, the

Night time is prime time on the Yorkshire Ouse – an 8lb 13oz barbel for Mick Wood.

feeder hits bottom with its load intact. Within a very short period, water causes the plugs to swell and the bait is pushed out of the feeder. This would also be my preferred choice when using corn or meat as a particle feed.

Once conditions become more challenging and the river is carrying significant extra water, say over three feet, I personally prefer to use a straight leger set-up. In these circumstances I would be using larger, smelly baits, and any free offerings I felt were necessary would be introduced via a heavy bait dropper set up on a second rod, or by means of a PVA stringer. Others, however, prefer to continue employing a feeder with the appropriate amount of extra lead attached. Although the Ouse can appear intimidating at such times, providing the water-borne debris is not too severe, it is quite fishable. Barbel can be caught, although leads up to the 4oz mark may be needed.

One piece of advice I can offer regarding fishing in these conditions is not to be frightened to fish out in the flow. It is my experience that barbel do not move far from their normal haunts, and are easily able to hold station in the fiercest flows. Most of the barbel that roll in these conditions do so right in the main flow. If that is where they are, then that is where one must fish. One tip for fishing under these conditions is to cast above your seating position. As the lead hits bottom, feed out several yards of line before closing the bale arm and placing your rod in the rest with the tip well up in the air. It is surprising how often the lead will hold out like this when a lead of the same weight cast down and across will be bounced across towards the near bank.

At the time of writing the Ouse is probably the least exploited for barbel of any of Yorkshire's rivers. Some stretches hardly see a barbel angler from one month to the next. There is much potential for the angler who wants to do his own thing, rather than follow the crowd. It can be dour fishing at times, but I find the river rather mysterious and exciting. Due to its depth and size you never know what may be in front of you. When the light begins to fade and the bats emerge, a rolling barbel or a line bite heightens expectations – and the bite, if and when it comes, may just be from the big one.

An Exciting Ten-Pounder by John Wolfe

The River Ouse has always attracted an interest from the Yorkshire-based members of the Barbel Catchers Club. In 1978, after the formation of the club, it was a widely held belief that this would be the river that would finally give us a fish that would break the magical 10lb barrier. With the possible exception of the Derwent, the average size of the Ouse barbel was bigger than that of any of the other Yorkshire rivers. The club river record of 9lb 14oz jointly held by Brian Pinning and Dave Mason, showed just how close these two anglers had come to achieving this aim. Alas, that fish was to remain the club's river record for a long time. Possibly due to the fickle nature of the river it remained more of an occasional venue for club members rather than the target of a sustained campaign.

As already mentioned by Iain, John McNulty finally realized the potential of the river in 1998 with the capture of a magnificent barbel of 10lb 10oz. This was the culmination of a serious amount of time and effort expended by John in exploring what is, after all, a very large river. I am not sure that John set out with the sole intention of catching such a fish, but full credit to him. We all thought that the river had the potential to produce such a fish, but it was John who actually set about proving it. During my time as a Catchers member I, too, had only flirted with the river on an occasional basis, but it had always remained in the back of my mind as a potential venue whenever my interest in the Derwent began to fade.

Each year, sometime in September, the region has an evening 'fish-in' on a local river, and in 2002 it was on the Ouse. A good choice, I thought, for such a get-together – and so it proved. We met in the pub in time for last orders, and although only one fish had been landed, no fewer than six of us had each hooked a barbel in the period either side of dusk – only for the fish to come adrift shortly afterwards. To experience so many losses was a very strange occurrence in itself, although on the plus side it was a good indication of a reasonable head of barbel. As I was having such a struggle on the Derwent at that time, with only one fish from nearly thirty sessions, I decided to concentrate all my efforts on the Ouse, for the next two months at least.

I did not know a great deal about the Ouse from a barbel-fishing perspective, but I had fished the river for many years whilst winter chubbing, and, as previously mentioned by Iain, the two of us had mapped out the barbel-holding regions of the river using my boat complete with sonar. This provided an unbelievable amount of information, showing drop-offs, snags, and some quite major variations in depth. This information, in conjunction with the barbel's habit of rolling at dusk, can make location significantly easier than might first be thought. However, as Dave Mason pointed out in the first Barbel Catchers' book, a rolling barbel does not necessarily mean a feeding one. My first couple of sessions on the river proved this theory to be correct, with barbel crashing and rolling in both my baited swims. At times like this it can be very frustrating sitting there waiting for the rod to pull round, especially if a blank is recorded. This surface activity does not seem to happen every night, so when it does occur it is really important to pinpoint where; these swims can then be fished at a later date. Although the sonar does provide an instant picture of the riverbed and its contours, it is not really a short cut to catching fish; it merely fills in the detail of why the fish are there. Having said that, I will also add that although some barbel are indeed holed up close to snags or in a deeper gully or depression, plenty more are seen rolling over an area that is snag free and of totally uniform depth.

Two of my favourite areas for chub fishing on this river have absolutely nothing in common. One has an average depth of over twenty feet, very little flow at normal river level, and is littered with various submerged pilings and sunken trees. The second area has a maximum depth of seven feet, plenty of flow and is totally snag free. This can be very confusing when trying to define the features of a good swim, especially so when trying to tell someone else what they should be looking for. What these two areas do have in common is that historically they have always been good areas from which to catch chub. I know for certain the same scenario applies as far as barbel are concerned. Why some areas are, and always have been, better than others, I don't know; even the fish finder can't explain it.

My next session on the river started just like the previous ones. I baited two swims about half a mile apart with hemp and corn using a dropper. My intention was to fish the first swim for about an hour into dark, and then move upstream into the second one should nothing materialize. Although the swim was reasonably deep, I continued to bait through the evening with a catapult on a little-and-often basis. The danger with this method in deep water is obvious, but the river was very low with little flow, so I was confident of hitting the right spot.

Just as the sun was setting, the rod top banged over and then sprang back as the lead was dislodged; I was in! I had previously lost a few leads and a bait dropper in this swim, so it was imperative to get the fish off the bottom – and after a lively fight, a nice barbel was soon in the net; it weighed 8lb 11oz. After sacking it, setting up the camera and firing off half-a-dozen shots, darkness had fallen. Another fish

Yorkshire Ouse doubles are extremely rare: Jon Wolfe with a superb fish of 10lb 6oz.

had rolled in mid-river whilst I was photographing the eight-pounder, so I decided to stay in this swim. I put the dropper out just to top up the swim, then cast in slightly upstream of where I was sitting. The beta-light glowed against the dark sky, and with the occasional fish still rolling I felt confident of catching a second fish. The sky had clouded over and it felt quite muggy.

An hour later a carbon copy of the first bite signalled that another barbel had picked up my bait. This fish initially stayed close to the riverbed, but the powerful rod soon had it away from danger. Match anglers on the Ouse frequently lose numerous barbel through fishing too fine, though to be fair to them, most are hooked unexpectedly. By using 8lb line as a minimum in conjunction with a suitable rod, very few fish are lost. Within a few minutes the second barbel of the evening was resting in the net. I let the fish recover in the margins whilst I readied the scales and weigh sling. The camera was still set up, and although it didn't look like a massive fish, it was similar in size to the first one, and big enough to warrant a photograph.

It wasn't until I lifted the net complete with barbel out of the water that I realized it might weigh more than I first thought. The scales recorded a weight of 10lb 6oz. At only 26½in long it was 1½in shorter than any of my Derwent doubles, and a good sign in terms of the potential of the river. I am a lot more optimistic of catching a really big fish when the barbel are of this build. Let's hope that in the years to come the River Ouse can fulfil its potential as one of Yorkshire's best bets for a huge barbel.

21 The River Ribble

by Alan Towers

The River Ribble is approximately sixty-five miles long. It rises in Yorkshire on Cam Fell eight miles north of Settle, where two small becks, the Cam and the Gayle, join forces to form the fledgling river. From here it flows south, passing Horton-in-Ribblesdale and then Stainforth, enters Lancashire and turns west, eventually to join the Irish Sea at Preston.

From the headwaters down to Mitton, at the confluence of the rivers Hodder and Calder, is the preserve of the game angler, although the occasional chub is present, and grayling are certainly taken on the fly. It is from this point downstream to where the river joins the sea at Preston that coarse fishing predominates, and certainly barbel are known to be present throughout this length. The majority of coarse fishing takes place from Ribchester to Preston town centre, a distance by road of twelve miles. A number of different clubs control the fishing rights on the lower reaches of the river, including Preston, Bolton and Wigan Anglers, Preston Centre Federated Anglers, Northern Anglers AA, Warrington AA and Prince Albert AA.

Barbel are present throughout the lower reaches of the river, and are becoming increasingly evident. I believe they were 'introduced' to the Ribble in the 1970s, having been transported from Yorkshire rivers. Some fish were also introduced at the stretch to the rear of the Tickled Trout Hotel adjacent to the M6 motorway, having made the journey north from the River Severn. The last legal stocking of barbel of which I can find any record, was carried out by the

then National Rivers Authority in the early 1990s; it consisted of around a thousand small barbel, again introduced at the stretch to the rear of the Tickled Trout Hotel.

I first started fishing the River Ribble for barbel in the early nineties on a stretch about two miles upriver from the Tickled Trout Hotel at Balderstone. Access to the river here was at Balderstone Farm and at Lower House Farm, and the stretch did not appear to be as featureless as the one at the Tickled Trout Hotel. The water was actually controlled by Northern Anglers Association, with day tickets available on the bank. The bailiff was a great character called Ray, who used to cop me for a ticket every time I went; in my first season it cost me more in day tickets than it would have done to have bought a season permit. Ray used to fish the river regularly for salmon, and like all bailiffs he was a mine of information; he certainly helped me a lot during my first year on the water. Invariably his opening greeting was something like: 'You should have been here yesterday, So-and-so had an eight-pounder!'; or 'So-and-so fished here yesterday, and never had a bite all day!' Such remarks did not exactly fill an aspiring barbel angler with confidence; however, I did persist with the fishing, and over the next three or four seasons caught quite a lot of barbel from both stretches, mostly in the months of September to November. The early season fishing was blighted by eels: they were everywhere and would eat anything! My personal best fish from the stretch was 8lb 2oz, caught at Balderstone Farm in September 1996.

In early 1997 I joined Prince Albert Angling Association to fish for barbel in the rivers Severn, Teme, Dove and Dane. My fishing on the Ribble took a back seat for the next three seasons as I fished all the above waters, catching plenty of barbel but only the occasional one bigger than my previous best from the Ribble. Prince Albert Angling Association did in fact also have several stretches of prime barbel fishing water on the River Ribble, including the stretches immediately above and below Balderstone. I had fished the occasional session on one of these stretches at Salmesbury, just upriver from the

The Ribble, Lancashire's major barbel river.

Tickled Trout, catching a few barbel to just under 8lb. At the start of the 2000 season I decided to concentrate more on the Ribble in search of the elusive double-figure fish; I had heard that the PAA stretch at Salmesbury, where I had dabbled the previous season, had turned up some larger fish, and I decided to target that particular area.

The stretch consists of approximately 1½ miles of single-bank fishing from opposite the Tickled Trout Hotel up to a point called Red Scar Wood. The river here is non-tidal, the tidal stretch ending about half a mile below the lower limit. The river is wide (forty to forty-five yards), and has varying depths, with no obvious fish-holding features along its length: there are no trees, bushes or anything else that could be considered as a likely holding area. There are no matches fished here, so there are no permanent pegs or spots that look as if they are fished on a regular basis. I quickly realized that location, as always, was going to be the key to success; however, in this case it would undoubtedly be more of a challenge than usual. I decided to concentrate my efforts on the area from the weir below Red Scar Wood to Salmesbury Church on the opposite bank, a distance of about three-quarters of a mile.

I can recall one visit in the close season when the weather had been particularly hot with little or no rainfall for a few weeks. It was possible to walk across over half of the river from below the weir; vast areas of riverbed were exposed, and lower down the fishery there were parts of the far bank similarly exposed, with huge slabs of bedrock stretching out across the river. The actual river itself seemed to snake its way between the areas of exposed rock. I found these trips extremely useful, as later on, I was able to form a mental picture of the river, and so eliminate areas of water that I considered would prove to be unproductive. I identified four or five areas where I felt I could fish with a reasonable level of confidence, and this analysis was further compounded on another visit to the water. In conversation with the security guard in the quarry car park that anglers are allowed to use, he kindly took me into his hut and showed me an aerial photograph of the stretch taken at very low water level, and I was amazed: the photograph, about four feet by three feet, showed the weir and the river down past the church, and from the weir it was easy to see the river flowing through a channel cutting its way through the rock. Starting on the far side at the weir, the channel gradually moved towards the centre of the river at the point of the bend, before moving back to the far bank, and then out towards the middle again opposite the church. Every so often it would widen out to form a pool, then would narrow up again as it carved its way downriver.

It came as no surprise that when the season started, the popular spots were the ones coinciding with the pools; the picture in the security guard's hut must have been well known! I could imagine the fish moving up and down the channel, congregating in one of the pools before moving off again. I decided to start fishing early in the season, despite the presence of eels. My work had necessitated a move to Preston and I would be driving past the stretch every night on my way home. I therefore decided to fish two or three sessions each week after work. I had specifically identified my first, second and third choice of swim, each coinciding with a 'pool'. In the event of these being occupied, my fall-back plan was to bait up an area in the channel and hope a passing fish would oblige.

The stretch proved to be more popular than I had imagined. Usually my first three choices were occupied, which left me little alternative but to fish the channel. This in itself created problems, as feeders and leads were continually becoming snagged on boulders and rocks, or the line would be cut off on the slabs of bedrock that overhang the channel.

In the first month I tried several different lines, including Maxima, Sylcast, and even 12lb bs Berkeley Big Game, none of which effectively solved the problem; it was a tackle nightmare. Eels would still pull meat to bits, maggots, casters and worms fared the same fate, and even corn was eaten by eels or chublets. The first couple of weeks were a steep learning curve. I settled on 12lb bs Big Game as a mainline, and 10lb bs Dacron as a hook length; hooks were usually Super Specialists in either size 8 or 6. Trout pellets appeared to be the favourite bait, and seemed to be fairly eel proof. The method was a big feeder full of mini pellets, with a larger pellet as hook bait. I very quickly decided that I would fish trout pellets, if only to reduce the attention from the eels. My groundbait consisted of mini trout pellets, hemp, and grilled hemp mixed together in a bait bucket. The water from the cooked hemp was used to dampen the pellets. I would fill a large feeder with this mix, and if fishing the channel I would cast the feeder without a hook length about ten or twelve times in order to get some bait on the bottom. I resorted to these tactics simply to avoid the loss of hook lengths during the baiting process. If I was fishing a pool where there was less chance of getting snagged, then I would cast the feeder and baited hook length every five minutes for the first hour to get a bed of bait down. My method for mounting the hook bait was to scrape a groove out along the length of the pellet and then 'Supa Glue' it to the back of the hook. With the method and bait sorted out, I did manage to catch a couple of small fish, although the larger ones continued to elude me.

A Personal Best

Saturday 27 July 2000 was the start of my annual two weeks' leave. The rest of the family had jetted out to Tenerife the day before, leaving me at home for a week; I would fly out to Tenerife to join them for their second week. I had arranged three days fishing on the River Teme in Worcester and was really looking forward to it. It was totally different to fishing the Ribble, a complete contrast.

Saturday was really hot, and I contented myself with pottering about in the garden until late afternoon. I decided to go up to the Ribble that evening and fish till about 1am or so. Upon arriving at the car park at about 8pm I was surprised to see only one other car present. This was a good sign, as it meant my first-choice swim might well be available. It was still very warm as I marched across the quarry workings from the car park to the hill on the far side: up the hill and down the other side, over a fence, and I was at the river. As there had been no rainfall for the two or three weeks before, the river was exactly as I had left it the other evening, very low with not a great deal of flow. As I had hoped, my first-choice swim was free, and I settled down to bait up the pool. Every five minutes for the first hour the feeder went out. I concentrated on one side of the pool adjacent to the channel that led off down river, hoping to intercept fish as they came up the channel into the pool.

I supplemented the initial baiting with a pouchful of hook-bait-size pellets every ten minutes; these were aimed at the mouth of the channel so they would drift down and hopefully be picked up by fish on their way up to the pool. Everything seemed to be going fine: no snags, and no mess-ups with the tackle; it was a lovely warm summer's evening at the side of the river – just perfect, all I needed now was a fish. My confidence was high, as everything was falling nicely into place that evening; I was quite content, and knew I just needed to be patient.

Summer on the Ribble.

I had the rod set up on two bank sticks; the rear one was under the butt of the rod and level with my shoulder, and the front one was extended so that the rod pointed skywards – in order to keep the line out of the water and away from the rocks. As soon as a fish was hooked I knew it would dive for the channel that was protected by the overhanging bedrock, risking line breakage. I had replaced the Berkeley Big Game with Corastrong braid at 17lb bs; hook length was as normal. Hook bait was a single 14mm trout pellet glued to a size 6 Super Specialist.

All was quiet and there was no sign of any fish topping or rolling; it was still very warm. At about 10pm I struck at a sharp tap on the rod top and managed to propel an 8oz chublet straight out of the water. Encouraged by this little bit of activity, I quickly re-baited and settled down again. Within a few minutes there was another small tap on the rod top, which this time I left alone – then almost immediately the rod pulled over in the classic 'three-feet twitch'. I bent into the fish and quickly stood up, holding the rod up high to keep the line away from the rocks. I soon subdued a lively barbel of 5lb. Quite pleased with myself, I was confident that there were more fish to be had, so quickly re-filled the feeder and re-cast, adding another pouchful of hook baits.

Half an hour or so later the previous scenario was repeated, and a smaller barbel of around 3lb was quickly landed and then returned. Again the swim was topped up with bait, including a couple of pouchfuls of hookbait. There was an increasing number of very small taps on the rod top that I put down to line bites caused by fish moving over the bait and out of the channel into the pool.

What happened next has happened to everyone who goes barbel fishing: I turned to my left to lift my flask out of my bag, when without any prior warning the rod hooped over. The butt flew up out of the rear

A Ribble barbel safely netted.

rod rest adjacent to my shoulder, and I just managed to catch hold of it as it quickly sprang back again. I reeled in, and found that the braid had frayed, obviously across one of the rocks. Was it a big fish? Impossible to say. I re-tackled and re-cast, again followed by a couple of pouchfuls of hook bait.

Sitting there in the dark I reflected on the events of the previous few minutes. No one likes losing a fish. Of course it happens to everyone at some time, but that doesn't make it any easier. I had conducted a couple of experiments with that same braid earlier in the week in my garage, when I had deliberately dragged it over all types of surfaces (including a chisel) to assess its abrasion resistance; however, I don't think any test could have prepared it for the sudden lunge of a barbel dragging it across the edges of razor-sharp bedrock.

It was about 11.30pm and still incredibly warm and muggy, when the rod top tapped slightly indicating that fish were still moving in the swim. I sat in my chair with my arm resting along the handle of my rod. I just knew I was going to get another bite, and I was determined that this time I would be ready. Another few minutes went by, and I heard the church clock strike midnight. Suddenly there was a tap on the rod top, followed by a slow pull over. I immediately stood up and bent into the fish. Holding the rod high above my head I walked out a few yards in the very shallow water. The fish lunged down to the right and was determined to get down the channel. Expecting this, I kept the pressure on, and walked out a few more feet to try and increase the angle of pull. For what seemed an age, but in reality was only seconds, there was stalemate; then the fish turned and came back towards the pool. I knew at that point that I would win the battle, and quickly played the fish out in open water; it went into the net at the first attempt.

Standing there in the pitch black, the water was up to my knees. I let the fish recover for a couple of minutes whilst I peered into the net: it looked huge. I knew it was bigger than anything I had previously taken from the river. I tethered the landing net in the water with a bank stick whilst I readied the sling and scales. The weight hovered between 10lb 6oz and 10lb 4oz. I settled for the latter, which was a new personal best and also a new river record for the Barbel Catchers. I nursed the fish for about ten minutes in the shallow water before it had recovered sufficiently to swim strongly away. I did not fish on; wholly satisfied, I packed my gear away and returned home a very happy angler.

22 The Lower Severn

by John Costello

In Pete McMurray's contribution to the first BCC book in 1988, he made the point that there was an enormous amount of water on the lower Severn, much of which was totally unfished for barbel. And despite the many changes in barbel fishing, this still holds true today. When you consider that the majority of anglers who fish the lower Severn for barbel can be found in the eight miles below Worcester, there is still a lot of river that has never seen a barbel angler. The tidal river below Tewkesbury is still untapped, and when you look at what the tidal Trent has produced, the possibilities are endless. Likewise much of the river between Worcester and Stourport-on-Severn is virtually unfished. Whilst I have my doubts about the Lower Severn ever producing a fish to challenge the 18lb and 19lb-plus fish from the Great Ouse, there are more uncaught double-figure barbel in the Severn than in any other river in the country, with the possible exception of the Trent.

To understand the river, its moods, and the barbel that live there, is what draws me back season after season, as much as the chance of hooking a big, wild, unknown barbel. Admittedly this river is not to everyone's liking, but to dismiss it as a featureless flowing drain is rather naïve.

Unlike the middle Severn, the lower Severn was never officially stocked with barbel; fish have simply migrated from either the middle Severn or the Teme. To have migrated from the middle reaches

to below Worcester requires negotiating several weirs, but as most of the weirs disappear with more than four feet of extra water in the river, they are not an obstacle throughout most of the winter. Ken Cope's *Book of the Severn*, published in 1979, mentions the 'cables' at Beauchamp Court as a good area for barbel with the chance of a better fish or two. It would seem, therefore, that there has been a viable head of barbel in the lower Severn from the late seventies onwards. Certainly by the early 1980s it was apparent that there was a huge population of barbel established all the way down to below Tewkesbury weir. Throughout the 1980s, whilst the average size was good, genuine doubles were rare, but the fish steadily gained in weight. By the early 1990s the river's reputation was established with the capture of such fish as Mick Nicholls' 13lb 14oz in 1990 and Steve Pope's 14lb 8oz in 1993. The highlight for me has to be that grey November afternoon in 1997 when Howard Maddocks landed his 16lb 3oz fish, the national record at the time. The future looks positive with a huge head of fish and a wide spectrum of sizes, from ounces to the teens of pounds. The lower Severn has never had the problems of natural recruitment that rivers such as the Thames seem to have.

I have always considered the lower Severn as beginning at Stourport, the upstream limit of navigation. There are three weirs between Stourport and Worcester, also one at Worcester and at Tewkesbury, and one on each of the two arms of the river at Gloucester, which mark the end of the river and the start of the estuary. Whilst the distance between each weir varies and there is some migration between the sections, I think it is reasonable to assume that each impounded section is a fishery within a fishery, since they all share the same general characteristic of the faster, shallower water being at the upstream sections nearest the weirs, and the deeper slower water immediately above the next weir downstream. The longest impounded stretches are between Worcester and Tewkesbury, and Tewkesbury and Gloucester, and it is in these downstream reaches that the lower Severn is most typified.

The river varies between forty and sixty yards wide. In most areas the depth drops off about a rod-length out from the marginal shelf down to anything from eight to fourteen feet. It then shelves gradually to the middle of the river, which in most areas is fourteen feet plus; indeed, there are a few areas between Worcester and Tewkesbury where I have found as much as twenty-two feet. At normal summer level it flows fairly sedately away from the immediate vicinity of the weirs. Once there is more than a foot of extra water in the river the flow picks up to what could be classed as heavy, rather than fast.

Location on the lower Severn may seem a daunting task, but the main ingredient for success is confidence. There are plenty of fish in the lower Severn. In normal summer and autumn conditions, if I haven't caught or seen fish roll in a couple of trips, I would assume there were no fish locally, and would consider moving to a different area. Note I said 'area' as opposed to 'swim', because it is important to remember the scale of things on the lower Severn. Precise location of a 'barbel swim' is not as important as finding an area holding barbel. A few feet on a smaller river may be the difference between success and failure, but a good swim on the lower Severn might be two hundred yards long, and anywhere in that area will give you a chance. The important thing to accept is that some areas of the river are attractive to barbel, and that at times, 90 per cent of the barbel in a mile of river may be confined to three adjacent swims. But they are in these areas because they want to be there: their requirements in terms of food and security are satisfied. The nice thing is that, by and large, these areas remain attractive to barbel year after year. There may not be fish there throughout the season, or the area might not fish at all one year, but the majority of lower Severn barbel are caught from swims that have been known fish producers for twenty years.

Why some areas fish well at certain times, and why in some years the river appears devoid of barbel, is one of the mysteries of the lower Severn. My feeling is that the abundance, or not, of their natural food, and also difficult spawning conditions in the spring, are partially why at times they disappear. Seasonal movements and river conditions also have an influence. I am sure there is plenty of natural food in the Severn, and I find it hard to believe that the barbel are somehow influenced in their movements by the anglers' bait: there is no way that the huge head of barbel (and other fish) in the river could thrive on the hemp, pellets and maggots thrown in by the few dozen anglers fishing the river these days. The bait that actually goes in is all but confined to the summer and autumn, and for eight months of the year the fish must exist on what the river provides. Therefore, I believe that the barbel congregate in those areas where they find the food that they require, and which later in the season provide comfortable living quarters throughout the winter months. Maybe cycles of natural food glut, or conversely crash, and this results in years when either the river fishes exceptionally well, or parts of it seem devoid of fish.

John Costello with a 12lb 3oz specimen taken on swimfeeder and trout pellet tactics.

So what do they feed on? Amongst the most interesting things I ever learnt was from Martin Cullen, who described what a friend had discovered during a scuba dive on a popular lower Severn fishery. First, beyond the clay of the marginal shelf, the riverbed was fine gravel. Second, the riverbed was virtually wall-to-wall snails. Third, Martin, who was acting as ropeman, could clearly see his mate's scuba tank on the bottom in fourteen feet of water. I am sure the river is as rich in natural food, mainly molluscs, as any of the gin-clear rivers traditionally associated with barbel.

So what do I look for when searching for these areas for the first time? Walking the bank I would initially look for areas of increased flow, or bank-side evidence of increased flow. Then I would look for places where there was a change in the direction of flow, for example where the main flow was first on one side of the river, but then switched to the other side. The principles of river location and river craft apply as much to the lower Severn as to any other river: it's simply on a larger scale. The current is on the outside of a bend, whether that bend is twenty yards, or half a mile long. Where the river narrows there will be an increase in pace, where it widens it will slow down, where it shallows or deepens again there will be a change in pace. At normal summer levels such areas aren't immediately apparent, but walk the river with a few feet of extra water on, and the subtle variations become more obvious.

Bank-side features give clues as well. Any bend, no matter how gradual, is worth looking at. A steep bank on one side of the river and a shallow sloping bank on the other would indicate which side of the river carried the main flow. Likewise, reinforced banks on one side of the river would indicate areas of increased flow. Conversely, silty margins as opposed to a firm clay margin could indicate a lack of flow. Any funnelling by either high natural or reinforced banking on both sides of the river, could cause an increase in flow. These are the types of area that consistently produce barbel on the lower Severn.

I seem to have laboured the importance of current speed, but it is the only common factor that I can find in the areas from which I catch barbel. Obviously snags and other underwater features attract barbel, but I believe that they only take up position near such features if the current speed is to their liking. Fortunately, at certain times of the season some areas seem to be one long barbel swim, but closer investigation usually reveals that whilst fish can be drawn by baiting, there are specific areas that they consistently prefer.

Lower Severn barbel have a very convenient habit of rolling during the summer and autumn, and once one recognizes a rolling barbel for what it is, it can be a very reliable form of location. Sometimes chub, carp or bream are responsible, and on the lower Seven, barbel roll in all sorts of different ways, from head and shouldering to full-blooded, salmon-like leaps. Even if you don't see the fish responsible, a lot of barbel make a double splash, as they smack their tail on the water at the completion of a roll. At times they will roll over one specific area

John with a cracking winter barbel of 12lb 5oz, taken in a big flood.

continuously, whilst at others they might be spread over an area up to one hundred yards long. Yet again, you may only hear or see the occasional fish at dusk – but any area where you see barbel rolling is worth investigating.

Over and above finding such generalized areas, one must bear in mind the potentially nomadic nature of the barbel. They have the room to move many miles, and at times there are quite large areas virtually devoid of barbel. Once you accept the nomadic nature of the fish, then some of the mysteries unravel: how, for example, one stretch can appear devoid of fish, whilst two fields away there might be numbers of barbel; how you suddenly start catching large numbers of 'shoalies'; or best of all, how numbers of big fish start coming out of relatively small areas. I believe most of this movement is confined to the warmer months. Come the late autumn, the fish settle in an area until the early spring, when they start to move in response to the changing seasons and their natural urges. Over a period of time it becomes apparent that different areas of the river fish at their best at different times of the year.

As a generalization I think that within each impounded section there is a downstream movement of fish as the season progresses. At the same time it might become clear that the fish move, within a limited area, as the river conditions change: for example, in summer and early autumn it might be found that the barbel prefer the outside of a bend. But come the winter they might have moved a few hundred yards up- or downstream to where the river widens or deepens, and where the current is just a bit more comfortable during the winter floods. Above all else, bear in mind the size of the river. If you're not catching in one swim, try another, not the next one down, but two hundred yards away, or even the next field. Lower Severn barbel are not difficult to catch once they are located. Have confidence in your chosen methods, and assume that if you are not catching, fish are not present, and be prepared to move.

The nice thing about the lower Severn is that whatever works for barbel on other rivers, works here. You can catch them in the daylight, at night, moving around, or sitting in one swim, although the

The lure of the lower Severn: John with a 15lb 7oz monster.

conditions on any particular day may dictate that one method is better than another. Most of my fishing takes place between 4pm and 11pm, so during the summer most of my time on the bank is in daylight, and in the winter mostly after dark. Until the first big autumn floods my approach is essentially a static one, and I will bait a swim in mid-afternoon and wait for the fish to move in; in the higher water temperatures, if there are any barbel in the area they will find my bait in a short time. In winter, when the fish are less active, I tend to use a more mobile approach. My feeling is, that there are plenty of times during the winter when barbel will happily take a bait that is presented on their noses, but they are reluctant to move more than a few yards. Whilst I might be in a good area, there might not be a fish within a hundred yards, and rather than chance them coming to me, I go looking for them. I also learn a lot about the river, and which areas and stretches fish best in which conditions.

Having identified an area holding barbel, or when trying a promising area for the first time, how I fish will be dictated by any features that I might find, and also by the number of anglers about. There might be a feature such as a prominent near shelf, a sudden change in depth, or a mid-river snag that might be attractive to barbel, but they can usually be drawn from such features. If fish consistently roll in one spot then I will bait close to, but not necessarily on top of, where the fish are rolling. By drawing fish a short distance away from their chosen resting place there is less chance of spooking them. If I know an area well and am confident that I know where the fish will be, then I usually bait one swim. If I am searching an area for the first time, I favour baiting a couple more swims as back-ups, should my first choice prove incorrect.

On a new stretch my preferred tactic is to bait or fish my chosen swims at least two or three times over the course of a week or so. And even if I am unable to fish, it is well worth the effort of baiting in between trips. Whilst I don't think they are dependent upon anglers' bait, lower Severn barbel respond very positively to areas that are regularly baited; thus if my first-choice swim proves unproductive, bait has already been introduced into another swim to try on the next visit. It is probable that once found, any bait is cleared very quickly, but I am sure that for a short period it will become part of the barbels' regular patrol route. The more regularly that you can introduce bait, the more consistent the swim will become. Barbel may even take up residence in such a swim in preference to their normal resting place.

Obviously this approach is not always practical on the more popular stretches, but even on these, baiting swims slightly away from the most popular areas can sometimes produce. Back in the summer of 1996, the Beauchamp Court/Pixham Ferry stretch of the river below Worcester was fishing very well. As there were plenty of other anglers fishing there, I chose to bait an area a couple of hundred yards upstream of a well known spot, using a mixture of hemp and peanuts. For a couple of weeks I held enough fish to catch quite a few, including a 12lb 11oz specimen from a place that is not normally regarded as good in summer. Eventually they moved back to their usual haunts, and rather than compete with other anglers, I moved on to another stretch of the river.

As most of my fishing in the summer and early autumn is in daylight, I tend to use particles as my first choice; but you don't have to fish this method to catch. Mike Burdon catches a lot of very big barbel fishing lumps of luncheon meat, and most of the time he catches in daylight. Mike, however – and I am sure he will forgive me if I am wrong – pays a lot of attention to being quiet, not disturbing the swim and concentrating on striking what can be very tiny bites. That is the nice thing about the lower Severn, there is no right or wrong way to catch barbel.

Virtually any particle will catch fish, and I have had multiple catches on tares, maples, peanuts and sweetcorn. These days my choice would be either pellets in their various forms, or the deadly maggot/caster combination. For all-round consistency, maggots and caster cannot be bettered, but you *do* need a reasonable amount of daylight hours to get the best from this method. I have at times started on maggots and switched over to a less 'eel-attractive' bait as darkness approaches. You can, of course, switch over to fishing paste or meat-based baits after dark, but if I am fishing into the night I tend to continue fishing particles.

For ease of baiting I usually tend to bait the swim from the near margin up to a quarter of the way across the river. However, there are swims that, because of a mid-river feature, I might bait and fish to a mid-river line. I have never been keen on putting a big bed of bait down. If the fish are not feeding hard, I am reducing my chances in the six- or seven-hour sessions I usually fish. If, on the other hand, there are a lot of fish in the swim and they are feeding well, they can easily clear a bed of bait in a relatively short period of time. I would initially put a maximum of two pints into a swim and use a feeder to top up. If fish are feeding well I would loose feed by hand as well. A bait dropper landing on top of feeding fish is a good way of spooking them.

The lower Severn, fourteen feet above normal level.

There are also exceptional days when you can't put in too much bait. In August 2000 I had a nineteen-fish catch, including four 9lb-plus fish, in a six-hour session on feeder and maggots. I was fishing a mid-river line, and because of the range it was impossible to loose feed, so I had a second rod set up with a bait dropper. It was a case of catch a couple of fish, put a couple of droppers out, catch a couple more fish, make a couple more casts with the baitdropper, and so on. Despite this apparently continual feeding, in point of fact I only used four pints of hemp and four pints of maggots. The point is that your baiting pattern should be determined by how the fish are reacting on the day.

Although I like to know where my bait is, I don't usually keep it very tight. An initial baiting with the bait dropper gives me a tight cluster, which is where I usually place my feeder. Further loose feeding creates an area downstream that is lightly baited, and where I hope the fish gain enough confidence to move up to the main area of bait. Sometimes they seem reluctant to move over a bed of bait, and I have caught fish by fishing 'off the bait', sometimes even fishing mid-river despite baiting down the inside. If I am fishing a second rod, I would invariably fish one off the bait and one on the bait. There are many occasions when the only fish of the day would be on the rod out on its own. This is particularly the case with pellets, where only a single feederful leaves a strong enough attraction to draw a fish. I can only guess why it works, but it does.

My attitude to tackle and rigs is based upon the assumption that if it isn't broken, then don't fix it. Rods are 12ft 1½lb TC Harrisons that I have criminally abused when lobbing half-pint bait droppers half-way across the river. So far they haven't snapped, and they are nice to play fish on, as well! Reels are baitrunners, just in case a fish catches me sunbathing. Mainline is 8lb bs in the summer and 10lb bs in the winter, or in snaggy swims. Hook lengths are nylon, which makes for tangle-free fishing and ease of replacement. Hooks are usually Drennan Super Specialists, sizes 8 to 12. When fishing maggots in normal summer conditions I use big block-end feeders, but for pellets and other particles I prefer open-ended feeders. I also use open-ended feeders when using maggots if there are more than a few inches of extra water in; because of the depths and the extra flow I don't want the feeder releasing its contents until it reaches the bottom – my aim is to keep a tight cluster of bait around my hook bait. Hook lengths are short, less than twelve inches. Once the bait is on the riverbed it doesn't move, and fishing a longer hook length is putting your hook bait away from the feeder and its contents. It also increases the likelihood of foul-hooking fish.

I have never noticed barbel showing any shyness of feeders: once they are confidently feeding on a bed of particles they appear to hoover up as much as possible before turning downstream. Even with such short hook lengths I have deep-hooked the occasional fish on both corn and pellets. I am creating a situation that utilizes the way barbel feed on a bed of particles, to create a trap whereby almost every fish hooks itself. I have never found hair rigs an advantage, except as a means of mounting the bait. I prefer a sliding rig because it seems to be easier to read how the fish are behaving and reacting to my bait than with a semi-fixed rig, but I have used semi-fixed rigs with single grains of corn when the fish have appeared nervous. When fishing under the rod top I use a sliding back-lead to keep the last couple of feet of mainline on the bottom, but I usually dispense with this if I am fishing mid-river. By casting parallel with my fishing position, the river puts enough of a bow in the mainline to ensure that it doesn't rise directly from the feeder. To be honest, provided the line isn't too tight and as long as I don't react to liners, I haven't found lower Severn barbel to be as spooky of mainline as other barbel can be on smaller and shallower rivers.

With the arrival of the autumn rains my tactics change, and the majority of my winter fishing is mobile, using single hook baits. I very rarely bait swims, and rarely spend more than twenty minutes in a swim relying solely on the attraction of the hook bait. The only time I would adopt a more static approach would be in clear, cold conditions. My favourite conditions are when the river is between two and six feet on, a good colour, and either steady, or slowly falling or rising. If it is rising or falling fast it doesn't fish so well. Given a good temperature and the above conditions, I usually work through an area, and then move on to the next one I fancy. Even on a big river the fish will find the bait very quickly, and by far the majority of my winter fish are caught within ten minutes of casting. After a period of time an overall picture builds, of which areas fish at different heights and states of the river, and which areas fish best at different times of the season.

What bait is used is not important, as long as you have confidence in it. I am happy using flavoured meat, but anything that stays on the hook and is attractive to barbel will work. Because I am not baiting swims I want to be sure that whatever I use is instantly attractive to barbel; these days they are pretty much aware of the dangers of meat, but they are still prepared to pick it up, albeit rather tentatively at times.

This mobile approach works on the lower Severn in most winter conditions, given reasonable water temperatures. Whilst the method is at its best when there is a decent colour in the water, it will work after dark in clear and warm conditions. It also works however high the river is – even when it is bursting its banks, there is nowhere on the lower Severn that is too fast for a barbel, so I will try and cover as much of the water as possible. I might be in a good area, but if the only fish prepared to take a bait are lying in mid-river, then I am only going to catch them by putting a bait near them. I regularly use 4oz and 5oz leads to combat the drag on the line by the sheer depth of the river. With six feet on, much of the time you are fishing in twenty-plus feet of water. When fishing baits on the hook I prefer a slightly stiffer rod and a braided mainline, simply to pick the line up and set the hook. Hair-rigging paste

The Severn has burst its banks, but John is undeterred: 13lb 4oz.

or meat works if the fish are being particularly cagey, but I haven't found the need for a stiffer rod or braid when the fish are (hopefully!) hooking themselves. Upstreaming also works with wary fish, although it is hard work with 4oz leads! The fish are learning, and one has to adapt one's methods in response to how they behave.

The advantage of covering a lot of water is that in the winter when the barbel are not so active you are presenting baits to more fish than is the case when fishing statically. You may have fish in the swim, but they might not be prepared to feed, so in winter I prefer to increase my chances by presenting baits to as many fish as possible. The other advantage of a mobile approach is that in time you find spots on the river that consistently produce fish whatever the conditions. When conditions are poor I concentrate on these spots and fish a boilie or pellet with a crumbly method-type mix either in a feeder, or moulded around the lead, in the hope that the scent trail will draw fish to the hook bait without feeding them. Even in cold conditions I would be prepared to move regularly, although I might spend an hour or so in a swim.

The beauty about the lower Severn is that anyone can catch a big barbel. There are no exclusive stretches that hold all the biggest fish, and you don't need to go to extremes in terms of tackle, bait or time. There are plenty of fish and, best of all, miles of available water. You can try a well known area, fish a couple of hair-rigged baits and catch plenty of good fish, or you can go exploring and find your own productive spot. There is no right or wrong way of fishing the river, and each angler can therefore use his preferred method with confidence.

A Record Sixteen-Pounder by Howard Maddocks

I would never have believed when I first began fishing on the middle reaches of the River Severn around Shrewsbury in the late 1970s, that I would eventually see my name in the record books for catching a 16lb 3oz barbel on 29 November 1997 from the lower reaches of the river below Worcester.

My method of fishing for barbel has changed tremendously. At first I used a swimfeeder, fishing the mid-river gravel beds; nowadays I mostly touch leger in the margins. On this particular November day I was off down the motorway with two other Barbel Catchers Club members to fish a day-ticket stretch that a fellow BCC member had suggested might be worth some effort.

We arrived mid-morning after a drive of just under two hours. I had telephoned the river line the previous night: a water temperature of 8.7°C had been recorded on a rapidly rising river (great conditions). On the day, the weather was quite cold and overcast, and we donned our thermal suits upon arrival. Sure enough, when we reached the water's edge we could see the river was rising rapidly. We all went to our preferred swims. I had a look at a slack I had never fished before and decided to try it. I pushed a bank stick in at the water's edge to keep an eye on the rising river, and then tackled up. I fished the swim for about an hour, when I noticed the river had risen about six inches above the bank stick. It was rising very fast. Having had no bites in the swim I decided to move down river ten yards; it was the best move I have ever made.

I touch-leger 95 per cent of the time, but on this occasion I found this method all but impossible in the flooded conditions, due to all the debris coming down the inside line. I hooked three halves of meatball on a size 4 Starpoint hook, and cast in a rod length out. I then decided to put the rod on the rod rest and have a cup of tea. This is usually when the rod goes over, but not on this occasion: I had enough time to drink my tea and put the flask down on the riverbank. Just five seconds later the end of the rod bent round. I struck immediately, and was into a barbel. I could tell it was a good fish as it fought so doggedly in the near-bank swim without ever careering out into mid-river. As always, I hoped it might be a double!

When the fish first came to the surface I could see she was a good size. The alarm bells immediately started to ring in case the hook came out and I lost the fish whilst playing her to my net. She rolled three times on the surface before sliding into my landing net at the first attempt. As I looked at the barbel in the net I realized that it was more than 'good': it was enormous! I secured the landing net with bank sticks, and placed the fish in the net to rest whilst I set off to find my friends downriver.

When we arrived back at my swim we took the barbel out of the landing net. We all thought that we could be looking at one of the biggest barbel we had ever seen. On close inspection we found that the fish wasn't particularly long, but it had a massive back and was very thick across the shoulders. We returned the fish to the water, allowing it to rest again in the landing net whilst we made preparations to weigh, measure and photograph it. We didn't realize how heavy the fish was, and we certainly didn't think it would go 16lb plus.

When everything was ready we all looked at each other, not saying a word, just wondering how much this massive barbel might actually weigh. I lifted the

Howard Maddocks with his one-time national record of 16lb 3oz.

fish from the river again, laid it gently in the weigh sling and attached the scales. The tension was unbearable. As I lifted the scales the needle swung round to an incredible 16lb 6oz; we couldn't believe it. We all stared at each other in disbelief as we realized that this was a record barbel. Recovering my composure, I placed the fish back in the river to rest in the landing net. We all decided to pack up fishing immediately, and proceeded to call a few friends from the barbel world to help witness a piece of angling history.

By the time the witnesses arrived, the fish had regained its strength. We checked the weight again: it was still the same, at 16lb 6oz (although when the scales were sent off to be checked they were found to weigh 3oz overweight, and so the record was later confirmed as 16lb 3oz). The fish measured 32in to fork of tail, and had a girth of 19½in. Not surprisingly, many photographs were taken. I released the barbel back to the river, and she swam away strongly, none the worse for her capture. We then all stood around discussing the happenings of this memorable day for about an hour or more.

During our long journey back to Macclesfield we were still feeling shell-shocked by the day's events.

When we arrived home I rang around my fishing mates, and they were all firmly convinced it was a wind-up. The next few days the telephone never stopped ringing; I had calls from friends, other anglers, journalists, and even a radio station! I also received some great letters, some of them from top anglers. I now have a scrapbook full of cards, photographs, newspaper cuttings and letters to remind me of that memorable day. I then had all the hassle (though enjoyable) of making a formal claim for the record. The scales had to be verified by the weights and measures authorities, and as I have already said, they were found to be recording 3oz overweight; my record was therefore confirmed at 16lb 3oz – still an incredible fish. In some ways the formalities were trickier than catching the fish! As a perfect end to the story, the capture of a record barbel won me the Shimano Cup that year, and I went to London for the day to collect my trophy.

I have achieved what might be considered the ultimate aim of a barbel angler – but nevertheless I remain determined to learn more and to strive for an even bigger fish!

23 The Middle Severn

by Stuart Wortley

In the mid-1970s the *Fisherman's Handbook* made reference to barbel fishing on the Severn, and included a photograph of the river in summer with the Ironbridge in the background. The river looked magnificent, with fast flowing, clear water and great forests of streamer weed. It was described as one of the 'premier barbel rivers', with a continuous barbel swim around Ironbridge and the perfect place to catch your first barbel. As a twelve-year-old living and growing up in barbel-barren Lincolnshire, I remember day-dreaming of one day fishing for these hard-fighting fish. When twelve years later I was offered a job in Telford, only five miles from Ironbridge, I jumped at the chance – and hence began my love affair with the river.

The Severn is Britain's longest river. It rises in North Wales within two miles of the source of the Wye, and flows for 220 miles (350km), passing through six counties before entering the sea at the head of the Bristol Channel. The river can be split into three reaches: upper, middle and lower; each has its own reasonably distinct character, though where one ends and the next begins is harder to identify, since each blends into the next. There are recognized boundaries, but those considered by the BCC to be definitive are Shrewsbury for the upper and Stourport for the lower river where it becomes navigable (although some writers have quoted Worcester's Diglis Weir as being the start of the Lower Severn).

Above Shrewsbury the river's upper reaches hold an ever-increasing barbel population. The number of fish present certainly makes barbel fishing a viable proposition (for the pioneering angler) as far upstream as Newtown, where the river is little more than a large stream. I personally know of confirmed doubles several miles upstream of Welshpool.

As the river approaches Shrewsbury it starts to mature into a large and magnificent river with the riffles and rapids of the upper river becoming fewer, and steadier glides and deeper, slower stretches becoming the norm.

Below Shrewsbury the middle river's character really begins to shine through. For approximately the next fifteen miles it runs fairly shallow over mainly gravel bottoms, averaging between four and eight feet in depth and ranging in width from approximately thirty to forty yards. The river twists and turns through some spectacular Shropshire countryside, with green fields and small riverside villages such as Atcham, Wroxeter, Cressage and Leighton all contained within a mile-wide flood-plain valley. Notable barbel hotspots are at Atcham, approximately three miles below Shrewsbury, and Buildwas, a further ten miles downstream, both available on day ticket. Atcham is one of the places where barbel were originally stocked by the Severn River Authority and *Angling Times* in 1956. Much has been written about Atcham, and seemingly every other book about barbel describes the fishery and the fishing to be had there. The most famous areas are the snag swim, which is a sunken wall just below the car park at the top end of the fishery, and the area opposite the mouth of the Tern, which runs in on the left bank between Atcham and Wroxeter. Buildwas, two miles upstream of Ironbridge, is the start of a slower section of river after the shallow S-bends of the previous three miles, and always holds a large head of barbel.

Ironbridge is the first area of significant urban population through which the river passes after leaving Shrewsbury, and it marks a significant change in the nature of the river. The wide flood valley narrows suddenly into a steep-sided gorge, and the river deepens and slows. Depths of between eight and twelve feet become the norm, interspersed with fast, narrow sections as the river is forced through passages in the gorge often less than fifte

The famous Ironbridge gorge.

yards wide. The nature of the bottom changes, the gravel frequently giving way to sandy, silty bottoms, and stretches of rocky sandstone with huge boulders. These can be treacherous places to fish, and even 8lb or 10lb line proves useless when dragged over the sharp, abrasive rock. When I first began to fish the Severn in the late eighties, some very big barbel, 15lb plus, were being reported from the Ironbridge area. However, I have fished the area reasonably regularly for the last sixteen years, and during that time I have personally witnessed only a handful of very low doubles. My conclusion therefore is that a large pinch of salt needs to be taken with the majority of these reports.

As an example, several years ago Ian Beadle and myself frequently fished a stretch opposite the power station, and almost every Saturday would see the same local pleasure angler fishing the same 'armchair' swim. The first time I encountered him I asked how he was doing, and the reply was 'a bit slow, had one about six and two eights.' Bearing in mind this was over twelve years ago, when an eight

was a decent fish, I replied, 'Nice one, that sounds like a result to me. How big were the eights?' 'Oh – exactly 8lb, both of them.' A bit of 'over-guesstimation' I thought, and moved on. Over the next couple of years we encountered the same guy perhaps a dozen times, and invariably he had the same story – a six and two eights. Yet in all that time we never saw him with a set of scales. Our experience was that there were very few anglers who carried scales, and that guesswork and over-estimation of the size of barbel was rife in this area of the river. The reports of 15lb fish were probably low doubles at best. On the positive side, twelve years on we see far more people with scales and weigh slings fishing the area, and there are genuine occasional reports of 11lb and 12lb-plus fish being caught. Somewhat significantly, since these reports we have heard no more of 15lb and 16lb fish.

After the previous meandering of the river, it runs fairly straight through the Ironbridge Gorge for approx-imately five miles before the gorge starts to widen, maintaining its predominantly rocky sandstone bottom for another five or six miles until it reaches Bridgnorth.

Bridgnorth is synonymous with barbel fishing on the Severn, and this lovely small town is a mecca for both anglers and holidaymakers during the summer. There are dozens of 'bed and breakfasts' catering for anglers, and a number of static caravan parks directly downstream of the town that are used by scores of 'Brummie' anglers for fishing holidays during the summer. The area is the most heavily fished on the river, and is not the place to head for some quiet fishing. That said, the quality of general coarse fishing is excellent even in the middle of the town, with anglers trotting for roach, chub and barbel under the backdrop of the old stone bridge.

Immediately downstream of Bridgnorth there begins almost twenty miles of some of the best all-round barbel fishing in the country. Famous stretches such as Quatford, Knowle Sands, Hampton Loade, Arley, Alveley and Ribbesford are incredibly popular match waters, and will be well known to anyone who reads the match reports in the weeklies. These stretches run through some magnificent scenery, with the picturesque Severn Valley Steam Railway running alongside the river from Bridgnorth to Bewdley.

My personal favourite, and typical of this section of the middle Severn, is Quatford, two miles downstream of Bridgnorth. This three-mile stretch run by the Birmingham Anglers Association has almost everything a barbel angler could want: fast, shallow gravel fords where fish can occasionally be observed (a rarity on the Severn); long, steady sections with masses of streamer weed; slower, fourteen-feet deep sections; and one of the highest heads of barbel per metre of riverbank of any section of river in the country. This makes the area very popular throughout the summer months, but the fact that there is only one access point at the top of the fishery means that as long as you are prepared for a good long walk you will be able to find some solitude at any time of year.

There are some notable spots on this stretch: for instance the 'Glory Hole', halfway along the first meadow, is a smooth glide immediately upstream of a 200m-long shallow section; it always holds a good head of shoal fish, and almost always an angler. It is known as the 'Glory Hole' because it is renowned for providing many novice barbel anglers with their first big bag from the river. 'The Stack' is a reasonably deep swim in the middle of a fairly anonymous section, opposite the chimneystack from the old tile works. 'Harris's Pitch' is another smooth glide above a very shallow section opposite Hay Brook, a good half-hour walk from the car park. The last pitch is where Birmingham angler Ken Henderson made possibly the biggest haul of barbel in a session, an estimated 200lb, on feeder-fished maggots back in the summer of 1975. I said it was a good walk, and please be prepared for the sharp rise just before you get back to the car – they don't call it Cardiac Hill for nothing!

I mentioned earlier that Quatford has almost everything that a barbel angler could want; however,

*The Kinver Freeliners'
stretch at Hampton Loade.*

like the majority of sections on the middle river, it does not contain a significant head of big fish. In twelve years of fishing this particular stretch I have had only one double, and witnessed only a couple of others.

From Quatford the character of the river remains unchanged for the next fifteen miles as it passes through such pretty hamlets as Hampton Loade and Arley before reaching Bewdley, yet another picturesque town, now well known to most people in the country following a series of major flood problems over the last few years. Downstream of Bewdley the river begins to slow and deepen as it approaches the large weir below Stourport. This point, at which navigation becomes possible, marks the start of the lower river.

As a rain-fed spate river with its source in upland Wales, the Severn can change its mood very quickly. Following heavy rain in North Wales it can rise ten feet in twenty-four hours, and fall back to normal level almost as quickly. As a result of these rapid changes the river can seem unpredictable, but with a little work the angler can turn this to his advantage. For example, by monitoring the weather forecast for North Wales it is possible to predict rising water levels several days in advance, and be ready for some excellent floodwater fishing. The Environment Authority has a very useful river information line (at the time of writing 0906 619 7744) that gives daily water levels and temperatures throughout the year; Severn anglers find this service invaluable. I do not often use it during the warmer months, but would never contemplate fishing the Severn in winter unless I had called the service. The information they provide will always influence my decision whether I fish the middle or lower river, whether I fish an alternative river or, if indeed, I stay at home.

Along with sudden rises in water level the river can also suffer from sudden falls in water temperature, due to cold rain in upland Wales, or during dry spells when compensation water is released from Llyn Clywedog reservoir. The effect of these releases is subject to much debate among anglers on the Severn, and is frequently blamed for those occasions when the fish suddenly stop feeding.

Although heavily fished, the river is not frequented by specialist anglers to the same extent as, say, the Hampshire Avon, Dorset Stour or Great Ouse. As a result the barbel are relatively naive when it comes to baits and methods, and all standard barbel baits are effective and will produce fish on their day. There is no real need for pastes and boilies, although they can be equally effective; personally I simply don't feel the need for the effort involved. By far the most popular method on the Severn, due to the number of match and pleasure

The middle Severn is a fine winter fishery. The river is twelve feet up, over the bank and still rising. Mick Wood shows off a fish of 8lb 15oz.

The popular Quatford stretch.

anglers, is the feeder with either maggot or a hemp/caster combination. This method is used very effectively for large bags of smaller fish, and will, on occasion, produce larger specimens. Generally speaking, however, the fact that you have to wade through all the shoal fish first tends to put off the larger fish, and it is a method I seldom use.

The most effective way of sorting out the bigger fish is to operate a 'bait and wait' regime. This method involves heavy baiting with particles such as hemp, 'Partiblend', maggots or pellets, and then leaving the swim for as long as possible before fishing. It has two major benefits: it gives the larger fish more confidence to feed and, if left long enough, they will push the smaller fish out, increasing the average size of barbel in the swim. On the down side, on some rivers that receive a lot more specialist barbel pressure, this method has been used extensively to the point of fish being wary of large beds of particles, especially hemp. I am pleased to say that I have never found this to be a problem on the middle Severn.

How long should you wait before fishing? The longer the better! Over the years I have experienced too many evenings when, having caught a fish within half an hour of baiting up, I have then had nothing else from that swim for the rest of the session. I have learnt the hard way to appreciate the need for patience. Whenever possible I will leave a swim for at least a couple of hours before fishing. In a short evening session after work when time is of

the essence, I will bait up a handful of swims to allow me to fish a couple of swims immediately, leaving the best one alone for a while. Some of the best evening sessions I remember have been when I have baited swims up at lunchtime, returned to work, and then fished the swims in the evening (. . . how I miss the days of flexitime!). Quite often I would catch fish within a couple of minutes of casting in (I have caught fish within fifteen seconds), and would continue to catch fish all evening. I remember one such session following a lunchtime baiting when I had two eights and a seven in successive casts.

In the mid-1990s a number of us took this 'bait and wait' approach to its extreme. We baited a stretch with boilies three times a week for nine months without using them on the hook. Although I am not a big fan of boilies we wanted to try something completely different as an experiment. We were fairly sure that no one had used specials on the stretch before, and we had no idea how long the fish would take to accept boilies as food. Our plan was to leave the fish alone for as long as we could in order to improve our chances of success. The theory was that the larger fish would lose their natural caution and would no longer hang back and allow the smaller fish to feed first. We hoped that they would be so confident that they would muscle in at the same time and perhaps even bully the smaller fish out. In the month after first using the baits in autumn 1995, I had two doubles, six nines and three eights in amongst twenty-seven fish. Not particularly special in isolation, but when you consider that the average size of fish over that month was almost 8lb, these really were amazing results for the middle Severn. Unfortunately they did not last. My friends moved away from the area, and I could not carry on with the mass baiting programme alone. As the bait stopped being introduced on a regular basis, the results also slowed. Boilies still produce fish, but they no longer outfish other conventional baits.

The Severn offers most of the attributes a barbel angler would want in terms of types of swim: slow, deep sections for the winter and flood fishing, fast glides for early season, lots of streamer weed, snags, overhanging trees and bends galore. There is, however, one attribute that to the 'purist' is lacking, and that is the water clarity. I have fished southern chalk stream rivers such as the Kennet and Hampshire Avon and watched fish in twelve feet of crystal clear water, but on the Severn it is rare to be able to spot fish in water over five feet deep due to an almost constant tinge of colour. On the popular stretches it is possible to locate 'hot' areas by finding the swims that have well trodden banks, but on less popular stretches, and because it is not possible to locate fish visually, swim selection almost always has to rely upon river watercraft.

My favourite areas are where there is a change in depth. Barbel love a sloping riverbed, as the change in flow is an excellent place in which to lie in wait to intercept food. Underwater obstructions producing boils at the surface, or creases are also popular holding places. Combine any of these features with bends, snags and overhanging trees, and you will not go far wrong. Good swims are not always obvious, and whilst I have discovered many productive areas by trial and error, I have been unable to pinpoint why they hold good fish. I have known these types of swim to be excellent hotspots for several years, then suddenly to switch off. One such swim at Buildwas, the one where I had two eights and a seven in successive casts, was a consistent producer for several years until suddenly in the late 1990s it produced blank after blank. It is still one of the swims that I bait up whenever I fish the stretch, and I will always have half an hour in the hope that it will come good again, but it has failed to produce a bite for the last four years. It had no obvious features, and was a swim I found by trial and error by baiting up a handful of swims and fishing each in rotation. It is not a heavily fished stretch, and the fact that it was an excellent swim for six or seven years leads me to believe it was not angling pressure that caused it to switch off. All I can presume is that during the floods whatever made it attractive was moved out.

The point I am trying to make is that you shouldn't rely on the obvious areas, and equally, don't ignore any areas.

Several points regarding the River Severn that were made in the first Barbel Catchers' book are now worthy of review. Observations were made that '. . . barbel fishing to all intents and purposes ends after the first sharp frosts', and that 'normally barbel will not be taken in temperatures below 7°C', finally '. . . fishing is seldom rewarding in anything below 9°C'. How opinions change. It is true barbel fishing does slow dramatically as the water temperature, and therefore the fish's metabolism, falls. The large bags of fish possible during higher water temperatures are rare during the winter months when feeding spells are short and sharp. Consequently there are usually periods during each winter when it is scarcely worth bothering. However, as long as you keep an eye on the changes in the water temperature by using the river information line, and fish when the temperature is either steady or, better still, rising, it is possible to be reasonably successful at water temperatures as low as 6°C or even 5°C. With this approach it is possible to fish throughout most of the winter with some consistency. We had a couple of members some years ago who religiously fished every weekend whatever the conditions, and recorded barbel captures with water temperatures as low as 2°C. I am not suggesting that fish can be caught consistently in these temperatures (a lot of blanks were also recorded); however, with the large head of fish in some stretches, if you adopt a mobile approach and fish a number of areas, you will probably end up putting a bait directly in front of a fish, and stand a chance of a take.

The second issue is the size of the fish. It is still true that the 'average' size of the barbel in the middle Severn is smaller than in many southern barbel rivers such as the Dorset Stour, Hampshire Avon and even the Kennet; but in common with virtually all other rivers over the last ten years, the average size has increased substantially. Whether this is due to global warming and/or the increased use of HNV baits, I will leave to others to speculate. When I began fishing the river in 1987, a 7lb barbel was a notable fish, and an eight was worth a photograph. Apart from my very first barbel, a 4lb fish that I excitedly photographed, I fished the river for a further four years before I caught another fish worthy of a photograph.

Twelve years later the average size has increased to the extent that doubles are present in far greater numbers, and I hate to admit it, but these days I rarely photograph fish of less than 10lb. Doubles are

Stu Wortley with a hard-won double of 10lb 4oz.

present throughout the river, with 12lb and 13lb fish being reported every year. But such fish are *not* the norm, and to put it into perspective, only a handful of barbel of this calibre are reported each year from approximately fifty miles of possibly the most heavily populated barbel river in the country. If you fish the river effectively, regularly and often and you catch enough fish, then you can expect to average a double a year, more if you are very lucky. Seeking out doubles consistently on the middle river is very hard work, and possibly luck plays a bigger part than on most other rivers. This makes the capture of fish such as Geoff Dace's even more special.

A Monster Fish by Geoff Dace

The middle Severn has always been special to me, as I caught my first barbel from Atcham about twenty-five years ago. I was a stillwater angler in those days, and that was only my second attempt at river angling. Over the next few seasons I made the odd trip to Atcham and Ironbridge, catching more small barbel. But it wasn't until I joined the Birmingham Anglers Association in the early 1980s that I started putting in more time in pursuit of barbel on the river below Bridgnorth. In those days it was possible to take up to twenty fish during an evening session in the summer months. The method was invariably a swimfeeder filled with hemp and casters, with casters as hookbait. Most of the barbel were under 5lb, and a fish of 7lb was exceptional. It wasn't until 1990 that I caught my first Severn barbel over 8lb,

and I still regard a barbel of this size from the middle reaches as a worthy capture.

During the early and mid-1990s I began catching more fish over 8lb, together with the odd nine pounder, and one fish in excess of 10lb. The most successful method at the time was a feeder filled with hemp and corn, with two grains of corn on a size 12 hook. During September 1992, a friend and myself caught around twenty barbel between us using this method, while the matchmen on the next two fields struggled to get a bite using maggots and casters.

With so many average-size barbel present, catching a big one from the middle Severn is a bit like looking for a needle in a haystack. Middle Severn barbel often crash out during the summer months, especially on warm evenings, and a bigger fish can sometimes be located by keeping your eyes open. If you are determined to set your stall out for a big fish, I believe that you can increase your chances by using huge pieces of meat. I have seen this method used successfully on a hot summer afternoon with the river low and clear, although it is not a method I have used very often as I like catching all sizes of barbel. I prefer to concentrate on the areas where fish of above-average size are present. By catching as many fish as possible, I will (hopefully) eventually land the biggest.

My lucky day finally arrived in November 1999. I was still on a high from my previous visit to the Severn earlier in the month when I had smashed my personal best with a barbel of 13lb 6oz from the lower river below Worcester. Little did I realize that lightning would strike twice. I had booked a day off work on the Thursday, and was undecided where to fish. As I already had a trip planned for the lower Severn or Teme on the Saturday, I made a last-minute decision to make the shorter trip to the middle Severn.

That season the middle Severn had been fishing poorly, and I had not fished there for two months. There had been a spell of cold weather lasting for about a week, but the two previous days had been mild with some rain on the Wednesday. The Rivercall service gave a water temperature of 7.4°C, a rise of 1.3°C on the previous day's reading. The river level was steady at around a few inches above normal. Conditions looked perfect for maggot fishing, and I called in at the local tackle shop in Bridgnorth and bought a couple of pints.

I decided to fish my favourite stretch; it had produced just fourteen fish from my seven trips earlier in the season, with the biggest fish only 6lb 4oz. Upon arrival I was pleasantly surprised to find the river carrying a nice tinge of colour from the previous day's rain, but the swim I was hoping to fish was already occupied by the only other two anglers on the stretch. I don't really know why, but something told me to fish a swim that I had tried earlier in the season without so much as a bite.

I introduced some maggots by bait dropper, and began fishing at 11.40am with feedered maggots, concentrating my feed just off a downstream bush. After an hour or so I was surprised by the arrival of Phil, a friend of mine, who dropped in a couple of swims above me. Having had no sign of a bite by 1.15pm, I changed to flavoured meat on a size 2 Super Specialist to 8lb Pro Gold hook length. I had stopped using braided hook lengths on the middle Severn some time ago; they are prone to tangling in the faster swims, and can be cut through where there are sandstone ledges.

Still biteless at 3pm, I topped up the swim with a mixture of hempseed and maggots, and went for a chat. After half an hour I returned to the swim and continued fishing with flavoured meat. I spent half an hour or so casting towards the middle of the river, but nothing was happening. Phil was also biteless.

At about 4.45pm, as the light was beginning to fade, I recast to the baited area just off the bush. After a couple of minutes, there was a slow steady pull on the tip and I struck into what was obviously a big barbel. After a determined fight, with the fish hugging the bottom, it eventually surfaced and I could see that it was a definite double. The barbel then made another plunge for freedom, and there followed another anxious couple of minutes before it was ready for netting. Panic then started to set in as the net became stuck on the wooden staging built for the match anglers, and it doubled over. I eventually got half the barbel into the doubled-up net which I then grabbed, and manhandled the rest of the fish into the mesh. When I had finally sorted things out I saw that the barbel had a tremendous girth and shouted to Phil that I had caught a monster.

Phil arrived and took a number of photographs, and we weighed the fish at 13lb 4oz. Before releasing it, we left it to recover in the water between the bank and the wooden staging. It looked absolutely enormous as it rested in the margins.

On checking through my old photographs I discovered that this was the same fish as my only other previous double from the middle Severn. I had caught the fish at 10lb 8oz from a swim about thirty yards away, in November 1994, and although I don't usually like to recapture fish, on this occasion it was a pleasure to be reacquainted with an old friend.

Geoff Dace with a superb middle Severn barbel of 13lb 4oz.

24 The Dorset Stour

by Huw James

The Dorset Stour was the first river that I really fished. I know I dabbled in the Cleddau and the Syfnwy, freelined a little worm foraged from my Dad's compost heap along the banks of the Narberth brook, but the Stour was the first river that I really fished. This to me was a true English county river, not the spate rivers of Cornwall or the Devon moors, not the rugged, rocky, fast-running salmon rivers of West Wales: this was a true coarse fisherman's dream, a river of riffles and glides, of pools and sweeping bends, of weeping willows and sturdy oaks, of historic bridges and mills, of tumbling weirs and ageless farmlands. A river of romantic and famous names carved indelibly in the history of angling; of people and places that have entwined themselves into angling folklore. This is the river of Owen Wentworth, of 4lb roach, of Longham, Canford and Throop, of Terry Lampard, of 8lb chub – and now truly one of the premier league, joining the Severn, Wensum, Great Ouse, the Kennet and the Medway as a river that has produced a 16lb barbel.

Rising at St Peter's Pump in Stourhead Gardens and gathering its waters from south Somerset and west Wiltshire, the Stour flows majestically and unhurriedly through the Blackmore Vale and down towards the coast. Its name comes from the original meaning of 'a strong and powerful one', perhaps hinting at its historic impact across the fields of southern Wessex. As it ambles along its 59-mile course from one corner of Dorset to the other, it passes through the clay Blackmore Vale that gives the river its particular character. Unlike the chalk

streams of its lower tributaries, the Crane and the Allen, and unlike its larger, more powerful neighbour, the Hampshire Avon, the Stour is greatly affected by the geology of its upper catchment area. Its total drop is 230 metres (about 748 feet), and it flows through mainly arable and dairy-herd pasture fields that are particularly responsive to rainfall, meaning that after rain the Stour can rise from a tranquil, gliding, clear water to a raging, chocolate-coloured torrent. In some respects it behaves more like a spate river than does the Avon. It rises and colours quickly, but runs off and fines down just as fast.

This state of affairs suits the angler fine, of course! Timing is everything, and by watching the conditions along its length, a well timed trip can pay dividends. I work in Blandford, and know that if the river is rising and colouring as it passes the old Georgian town, it will take up to twenty-four hours for the floodwater to hit Throop and the lower Stour. This allows time to fish a rising and colouring river, or depending upon the rain, a further thirty-six to forty-eight hours for it to run off and fine down.

The character of the river has changed over the years, and abstraction and dredging have reduced and altered its flow. It no longer gently floods as once it did, the water meadows and floodplains are now rarely called upon to do the job that nature intended, namely soothing the raging torrent and moderating its flow. Nevertheless, we can squeeze it and channel it and naively pretend that we have tamed it, yet there are still occasions when the all-powerful forces of nature conspire to 'cock a snook' at twenty-first-century engineering and planning, and the river returns to its primeval and malevolent state. Julian's Bridge and the pastures that were once water meadows around Wimborne still provide an annual testament to the river's nature, in that once or twice a year it becomes an island in an ocean as the fields between Corfe Mullen and Wimborne lose their battle with the river and succumb to its watery blanket.

For barbel anglers the Upper Stour, although picturesque and eminently 'stalkable' for trout and chub, contains very few of our prized quarry until

The Dorset Stour in winter.

downstream of Sturminster Newton. Here the river runs deep and lily-lined, favouring bream and tench, but as it starts its run into the chalk valleys of Shillingstone and Blandford, its nature and character change and it begins to stir our interest in the pursuit of *Barbus barbus*.

Reports, gossip and rumour abound regarding how far barbel have spread up the Stour. We know they were stocked at Throop in about 1877, and, depending upon whom you believe, word has it that many of the famous Royalty barbel made their way down the Stour into Christchurch Harbour, through the Clay Pool and into the Avon. This theory is perhaps not as crazy as it sounds, in that reliable sources have caught carp from Christchurch Quay at the mouth of the Stour, which have been identified as the same fish previously taken from the Royalty.

Throop has for many years been a barbel-fishing paradise, and was formative in my own slow-burning love affair with the species. One of my first experiences of this majestic fish was watching an angler winkle out six fish on a hot summer's afternoon in mid-July 1989 just below Barbel Corner. I was fascinated not only by the apparent ease with which this fellow tricked these truly magnificent creatures from their watery lair, but by the staggering beauty of their bronze flanks

glistening in the summer sun. That's where it all started for me, on that hot summer's day as I struggled on hopelessly with inadequate tackle and inept tactics. It gradually became an affair of the heart, both with the Stour and the barbel, an affair that culminated some twelve years later with a personal best and a Barbel Catchers Club river record.

As you wander upstream through Throop, the names of the swims are almost legendary, all steeped in barbel myth: Blackwater, High Banks, Nettlebeds, the Ladder Tree, the Gallery, and onwards to School Bridge, Barbel Corner, Chibbs, the Copse and the Weirs. As we venture further upstream, leaving Throop we pass the free stretch at Muscliffe, then on through Parley and towards Manor Farm. Ah yes . . . Manor Farm. This lovely beat situated between the free stretch at Longham and the upper reaches of Throop/Parley is a noted big fish venue, and produces big doubles every season. Above Manor Farm and opposite Dudsbury golf course is the noted Longham free stretch; and as you stop for a pint at the Bridge House, and then amble across the road bridge – or rather dodge the incessant traffic – you view the Waterworks and its weirs.

There is always something magical about weir pools – they exude a sense of mystery and the

Huw with the sort of barbel for which the Dorset Stour has long been famous.

The Stour at Throop; the same view as that opposite, but this time in the summer.

unknown: what lies beneath? Where do the fish gather? Longham has a bit of everything: islands, weirs, sluice gates, shallows, mid-stream weedbeds, and yards of open, easy access banks. This is the stretch where the 'barbel bug' really took hold of me. I fished it on the then Bournemouth Waterworks ticket over the summer/autumn of 1992–93. Those were indeed magical times, with mist-laden mornings and clear, starry evenings.

One of the advantages of the Waterworks was a very handy footbridge across the end of the weir pool between the two banks; this gave the angler a wonderful viewing platform, and as the sun rose behind you, with a pair of Polaroids you could view the watery inhabitants below. I had often seen people bailing in the hemp, and after a little bit of experimentation settled on introducing frozen lumps of maggot-box size hemp into the weir pool. Being heavy and frozen solid it would sink nicely where you threw it, and once settled on the bottom would break up in the water leaving a nice mound of hemp. Standing on my vantage point I would then watch as the small dace and roach pecked at it first, before being ousted by the bullying chub. Finally a brassy flash out of the corner of my eye would signal the arrival of the barbel. As anybody who has witnessed barbel rolling and flashing across a swim can testify, there is nothing quite like it for making you rush to your waiting rod and bait up.

Initially I was targeting the chub, and on one memorable morning came away having caught ten beautiful fish of up to about 5lb on waggler-fished maggots. Then one Sunday morning as the waggler dipped I was subjected to a whole new experience. This was no chub, and as the float rushed against the current towards the foaming lip of the weir sill, I realized I must have hooked one of those, until now, elusive barbel. I rushed to the footbridge maintaining the tension, and began to retrieve the line. Below me the drama revealed itself. I had firmly foul-hooked in the pectoral fin a very annoyed 7lb barbel. After a knee-trembling tussle I slipped the net under the fish and laid it gently on the bank. It wouldn't have warranted any special accolades, but it was my first barbel on the bank, and it stunned me with its mixture of power and beauty.

It was soon followed by my very first intentionally caught fish. One evening after casting a lump of meat onto the weir sill and allowing it to just trickle off the edge into the foaming water below, I connected with, and landed, a doughty 7lb fish; deep joy!

The next two seasons were spent upgrading equipment, learning new techniques, and observing the anglers around me. August and September evenings were spent with a small, friendly group of anglers gently lobbing out lumps of meat into the foaming pool and waiting for that telltale thump. I caught a few, learned a lot, and fell deeper under the spell.

But alas! all good things come to an end. The weir pool became busier, tempers frayed, swims became harder to get, and the barbel became harder to tempt. The water company erected metal railings around the pool and prevented access to the island, and the place began to lose its magic. I saw some lovely fish landed there, notably a 12lb specimen, and watched otters and lampreys in the water around me. I even landed a 5lb sea trout during the foot and mouth crisis. My most memorable fish was an 8lb 6oz barbel taken as the sun burnt through the mist on the morning of the first day of the 2000 season. I still have a ticket for the place, and now visit it once or twice a year. This year one of the regulars tempted a lovely 14lb fish – so they are still there, cruising up and down between Manor Farm and the weir pool.

Leaving the Waterworks and following the river further upstream, the next notable stretch is Canford School. Much has been written about, speculated on and achieved from this stretch, most notably by Terry Lampard. Wimborne, Christchurch clubs and the Canford syndicate have access to some of the beats on this stretch, with fish to 15lb being taken.

As we now move towards Wimborne and Julian's Bridge we arrive at the stretch that once held the famous 'Henry' that graced many an angler's net as a personal best. Barbel of around 13lb are still rumoured to inhabit this area.

Other noted holding places are the river and millstreams around Corfe Mullen Mill, and possibly a few below the bypass bridge at Blandford. There are also some fish above Blandford at Handford/ Stourpaine, which is on the Ringwood book. The last big fish holding spot is considered to be the stretch at Fiddleford Mill. Rumours abound as to how many and how big, but some notable big fish hunters have spent many hours trying to trick one out!

Although it has always been a big barbel river, the Stour has certainly come into its own this year with a number of notable captures pushing the record weight past that magical 16lb mark. There has also been a marked increase in the number of 14lb fish and even a 15lb fish or two. Even with its popularity there are still underfished and unexplored stretches between Christchurch and Sturminster. There are still pioneering stretches of the river out there that will respond to a bit of time and a lot of commitment: as ever, it won't be easy, but the rewards could well be huge!

Huw displays another Dorset Stour 'double'.

Dave Cutler with a good Stour fish.

A Special Fish

My personal odyssey along the Dorset Stour culminated in the capture of my personal best and the BCC river record. It isn't the biggest fish in that particular part of the river but it was, and still is, a very special fish for me.

They say good sportsmen make their own luck, and I believe that this certainly applies to anglers. I have pondered over this point time and time again, usually fuelling my deliberations with a pint of the landlord's finest. Is it a time thing? Is it a numbers game? Is it luck or judgement? Does the more time you put into a stretch result in a greater chance of you catching? Is it a case of becoming 'as one' with the river? Is it an almost intangible, mysterious symbiosis of angler and quarry, of crafty hunter and wary prey playing out a complex chess game on an ever-changing board, its rules governed by the weather, the seasons, the moon and the wind? Is it true that the longer you sit on the bank, the more likely you are to be there when the feeding times switch on? Or is it, perhaps more importantly, that you get to know the river and its moods, its foibles, its secrets? Perhaps the more time you spend listening and watching the river, the more you become in tune with its rhythms, its slow rise and fall, its ebb and flow.

Is it a skill thing, or is it purely chance? I strongly believe that you develop an angling 'sixth sense', a sense that can guide you to that special swim, that makes you cast to a certain spot, that makes you venture out on that particularly wet and windy night to brave the elements, leaving the snug, cosy sitting room with its crackling log fire and Sky digibox; a mysterious gut feeling that silently guides your hand and influences your thoughts. In our twenty-first century, digitally addled brains there is still a pre-historic hunter-gatherer submerged deep in our sub-conscious.

In reality it is a combination of all of the above, the knowledge of experience that can only be gained by a long, slow, laborious slog of trial and error. There are good fishermen who can instinctively pick the best time of day and state of river, who can spend a few hours and catch a fish that many anglers dream of, but few can achieve. There are others who set out their stall, lay their traps, and wait to snare their quarry.

There is another element to all of this, and that is enjoyment. Let us not forget, in this statistic-laden, performance-driven, time-pressured life we lead, that the *reason* we went fishing was for enjoyment, purely and simply. When the flag goes up and the anti-brigade start chanting, we should remember what it is all about – not size, not quantity, but pure enjoyment, the innate thrill of feeling that rod shudder, and admiring the glistening flanks of a fish, be it big or small. I for one will stand unashamedly and declare I still fish for the fun of it – and woe betide anyone who tries to take that away from me!

But as I clamber off my soapbox and think back, it was that very desire that took me out one night in October 2000 to the banks of the Stour. I wanted to catch a fish, but more importantly I wanted to be out on the river bank to enjoy the company of some friends, to wet a line, and sit and lose myself in watching a rod tip nod gently in the gathering autumn dusk. In hindsight the sixth sense was working overtime. Looking back, everything was perfect – or was it just perfect because of the outcome? How many perfect nights have we sat there and blanked, and somehow it doesn't have quite the same feel? But I digress . . .

It was a Friday. I'd finished work early and arranged to meet Steve Withers for an evening session. Incredibly I'd never fished Blackwater before, although I was aware of its reputation. It was hard, sometimes a 'ball breaker' where one bite per session would be the order of the day, but its treasure, if ever unearthed, could be bountiful.

The weather was warm and muggy. A fine, misty drizzle drifted in from the south west across the fields, shrouding the slowly shedding oaks in a fine dew. A low pressure system was filling as it passed over, and the rain it had brought during the previous few days had lifted the colour and the level of the Stour to a very inviting autumnal shade of coffee. Thus the stage was set, the players were ready, and the show was due to begin.

I started at Highbanks, absentmindedly trundling a large lump of paste through eddies and runs, across gravel and dying weedbeds, and slowly moving to the main stage. I had a couple of tentative knocks, sort of 'was it, or wasn't it?' taps. Steve was already ensconced in a neat little swim by the white fence. Pleasantries were exchanged, the world was put to rights, Everton's forthcoming relegation battle was mulled over (bearing in mind this was early October!) and it was seriously and studiously agreed that the conditions were just right. As those of you who have had this experience will understand, it even smelt of barbel, a heady mix of wet grass, fallen leaves, muddy water and a hint of gunpowder from early fireworks. It was an unmistakable autumnal aroma.

No true angling account would be complete without its detailed and sponsor-laden description of the tackle used, from the serial and code numbers of the individual hooks to the breaking strain in Newtons per square inch of the braided hook length. To those of you reading this who revel in such minutia I will indulge you; to those of you who would be happy with a long willow twig and some cotton . . . skip the next few lines!

I am not a traditionalist. I take my hat off to those of you who do battle with split-cane rods and nobly crafted creels. I, as a child of the 1960s, want – nay, crave – technology. I usually fish two rods with a slightly different set-up on each; this I feel enables me to contrast and compare lines, baits and presentations; however, this night I had just the one rod, an 11ft Avon style made by a company whose name starts with an 'Sh-' and ends with an '-imano'. It was accompanied by a reel from the same manufacturer, loaded with a thin braided mainline of 8lb bs. I enjoy the feedback from braid. It gives me the ability to feel the lead across the riverbed, and as I will explain later, suits my style of fishing. The lead is a free-running leger of between 2oz to 4oz attached by powergum to a run ring, which will allow it to break free in the event of it becoming snagged. The hook length is three to four feet of fluorocarbon or microbraid. The hook is a barbless

size 7 ESP or Fox, with a piece of cork attached hair fashion with a knotless knot. The bait is the euphemistic 'paste', which I'm happy to share is a fishmeal and milk protein base mix with plenty of Robin Red, flavoured with caviar and cranberry. The are a few on the market of similar composition, notably the Carp Company's Icelandic Red, Nutrabaits Big Fish Mix and Premier Baits Spiced Fish mix, and I have had success with all three.

As regards hooks, why barbless, I'm often asked? Well, they are a whole lot easier to get out of a fish's mouth, and that is all important to me. I haven't had one straighten out on a fish yet, and only rarely on a snag! They bite and hold deep – and yes, I have lost a few when they have become snagged up in weed, and I *have* lost the tension on the line. However, I sleep well in the knowledge that they are easily shed should I snap off, and, contrary to some opinions, I feel they do less damage to the mouth than barbed hooks.

The technique is straightforward. Find a gravel patch between the dying weedbeds by methodically casting and retrieving, 'feeling' the bottom with a heavy lead and the minimal stretch of the braid. Once a suitable patch is found, the heavy lead ensures it remains in place. I find that a lighter lead will trundle into a slacker area, or become displaced

Huw displays his Stour monster of 14lb 2oz.

by the drag against the line. Once it's on the gravel, I want it to stay there! The hook length is varied from six inches to four feet, depending upon my mood plus the water level and colour. A longer hook length will allow the bait to be wafted gently by the current under the dying weeds, rather than pinned six inches from the lead. Barbel bites on this set-up are rarely tentative affairs: a tap, a tug, a nod, and the rod arcs round and into the fish. Effective, yes; refined, maybe not!

That night everything went according to plan. I dropped into the swim above Steve, surveyed the water and picked out a spot where the surface was smooth and glassy, betraying a gravel run underneath. The bait was gently lobbed out underarm into the current, allowed to settle, and gently 'felt'. The reassuring bump, bump indicated I was where I wanted to be: on the gravel. The rod was placed in its rest and I settled back into my chair, hood pulled up against the misty drizzle. At 7pm the tip pulled round, and a quick lift of the rod confirmed a hooked fish. Its power immediately gave portent of its character. Not a screaming run across the current, no jagging runs and weaving escape attempts, just a solid, deep, powerful response to the singing braid and arching carbon. I gained some line, the drag ticked methodically back, inching out braid to the fighting leviathan. I gained line once more and brought the fish upstream. It was having none of it. It was happy to hold station mid-current and use its streamlined shape to deny me sight of its bronzed flanks.

Time stands still at these moments. The unquestioning belief I have in modern materials goes out of the window. I begin to think about the prize, its size and its power. Will the barbless hook hold, is the drag too tight, has my braid been rubbed against something, will a flick of its huge tail paddle part my high-tech line like cotton? Time passed. The line came in bit by bit, and with a last tail-slapping lunge the fish lifted its head and slipped over the rim of the net. Steve dragged the net up the bank and we slowly parted the wet mesh.

The first thing that struck us both was how broad its back was. This wasn't a particularly long fish, but it had an immense girth (something I wish I'd measured now). Steve smiled knowingly; having landed fish to 13lb, he knew it was going that way. I had never seen anything like it. Carp, yes, but a barbel? My personal best was just over 10lb, and looking at this wondrous fish lying in my net I felt the joyous numbness one experiences before finally realizing it is not a dream.

The scales read 14lb 2oz, a single ounce over Greg Buxton's previous and long-held river record; my river best, a personal best, and a new BCC river record.

That evening I could fish no longer. I sat on the bank and watched Steve fish for a while. I knew in my heart that I may never top that fish. It could well have been my 'fish of a lifetime'. If it is, I will always treasure that moment when it slipped into the net. And if it isn't, I look forward to seeing the next wonderful bronze torpedo, and wondering . . . what if?

25 The River Swale

by Duncan Mellors

Any of the Yorkshire Dales could be defined with superlatives: they are all beautiful. However, for its scenery, Swaledale is arguably the most breathtaking. Rising two and a half miles above the village of Keld, and gathering waters from Great Shunner Fell (2,344ft/714m), the River Swale travels over seventy-two miles to its confluence with the Ure below the village of Myton, a few hundred yards from the ancient site of the White battle of Myton Meadows.

The Swale is a healthy fishery throughout its length. For the barbel angler however, the story doesn't start until Richmond, which is the natural upper limit for the species nationally. Barbel are now regularly caught further north on the Tees and Wear, although they are not thought to be indigenous to these rivers, but to be there as a result of stocking. The Swale, however, has held barbel since the end of the last Ice Age.

As a barbel river the Swale can be separated into three distinct parts: the upper, middle and lower river. All three display different types of river character, and more importantly all are subject to different levels of angling pressure. The small part of the upper river of interest to barbel anglers is approximately sixteen miles long (by the meander), from Richmond downstream to where it begins to change around Morton Bridge. Here its character is typical of all freestone Dales rivers, with dramatic evidence of the effects of changes, as boulder, shingle and gravel deposits are constantly moved by

heavy spates. The middle Swale consists of the seventeen miles downstream from Morton to a point above the weir at Topcliffe, and is characterized by deeps, slower flows, and the softer banks typical of alluvial pastureland. The lower river is the final ten miles from Topcliffe to Swale nab at Myton, and is the most popular barbel fishery in Yorkshire; I believe it contains more double-figure barbel than any other stretch of river in the county.

The upper river cannot be dismissed as unworthy of attention, as it has to my knowledge provided at least two genuine doubles. The first was caught by angler Paul Chester in September 1989, taken close to the Richmond upper limit and weighing 10lb 12oz. The second, a fish of 10lb 4oz, was caught in September 2002 by Newcastle angler Steve Hoggins. He took it within five minutes of his first cast with a piece of luncheon meat into a shallow swim. He had been pre-baiting for two days with hemp. However, both of these are rare and exceptional captures. I have spent some early season sessions during 2002 on another stretch of the upper Swale trying to capture fish spotted in the close season, two of which I conservatively estimated to be over 9lb. The upper reaches receive very little pressure from serious anglers, and the potential for first-time captures of specimens such as these remains a distinct possibility.

We are all aware that many swims scream 'barbel', but don't actually hold them. On the Swale, the shallower upper river is an easier proposition to read, with riffles, runs, pools and occasional deeper glides. This makes float fishing a sensible approach. Here I feel you are not generally dealing with large shoals, so attempting to bring small numbers into competitive feeding mode is going to be more difficult than on the lower river. A less intrusive presentation is required than standard feeder tactics, and stick float fishing achieves this. This often involves compromising on line strength for the sake of presentation, which increases the risk of losing a fish. I consider this to be both unforgivable and avoidable with modern tackle, therefore I exchange the disturbance of the feeder for a light bomb and loose feed.

The result of two days pre-baiting, Steve Hoggins with a rare upper Swale double of 10lb 4oz.

Location of specimen fish in the river's middle reaches is the ultimate Swale challenge, and the capture of a double from here is a success that should not be understated. The middle Swale still presents new frontiers to be crossed, which is the quintessential spirit of barbel fishing: just imagine, it may still be possible that its waters contain monsters to rival those caught on the lower river. Such thoughts keep barbel fishing fresh, and hopefully the day will never dawn when every aspect of a river's potential is well known. Currently any kind of consistent achievement on the middle Swale will only be as a result of very determined and dedicated angling. Angling on the whole is changing, and some popular stretches receive fewer visits from those who once came from all corners of Yorkshire and beyond. At Maunby, Pickhill or Skipton on Swale it may not be too difficult to find a day's sport – but big fish location is another matter. Jim Taylor, one of the most experienced Swale anglers I know, told me of two recent 9lb 4oz fish caught in different matches. One of these he weighed himself. We also discussed his capture from the middle reaches of an unweighed barbel that a small number of us 'Swaleys' had heard whispers about, which he believed to be in excess of 11lb. I realize giving credence to an unweighed fish may be unacceptable; however, this angler's reputation is, to my knowledge, impeccable, and he has also caught doubles from the lower river.

Rob Newton also achieved what is the ultimate Swale capture, a rare middle Swale double of 10lb

3oz, in August 2000. The fish was caught on maggot at Skipton on Swale at 7am after an all-night session. This season also produced seven more fish over 9lb from the stretch.

As far as the lower Swale is concerned – the last ten miles from Topcliffe weir to Swale nab – much of what has been written in the past, particularly in the Yorkshire section of the book *Barbel*, written by Barbel Catchers Club members, still applies to this part of the river. The Barbel Catchers Club river record of 11lb 6oz, a fish taken by David Mason from the lower Swale in the 1987–88 season, still stands, although larger fish have been taken. Historically most of the great captures were taken on the lower river, and for anyone wishing to attempt a Swale monster, the Asenby stretch would be my choice. It has the feel and atmosphere of big barbel territory, and even though it receives considerable attention, there has not been a definitive capture announced for some time.

It is always difficult to speak with authority about the validity of individual captures, but there are few stretches of the lower river that have not produced fish in excess of 10lb: Topcliffe, Asenby, Cundall and Helperby have all produced double-figure fish in the last ten years – although I would not like anyone to think that these special fish come at all easily. Even so, as we travel through the lower river on mostly day-ticket and club stretches, what were massive fish for the north of England are no longer rare. I would say that once-scarce captures of 9lb-plus fish are as common as eight-pounders were ten years ago.

Regarding methods, there are two distinct ways of pursuing barbel. The first is for the angler to bring the bait to the fish by stalking, trotting or rolling a bait into likely areas without the use of pre-baiting. This involves carrying a minimum of tackle and keeping on the move. This is often a method of diminishing returns, with perhaps a maximum of three fish caught from a going swim on a good day. The barbel do not become preoccupied by bait and are therefore very easily spooked, and to capture a monster with this kind of approach on the Swale requires great skill and knowledge of each swim. The second method is to bring the fish to the bait by selecting a likely swim using watercraft and experience; the chosen swim can then be either pre-baited or fished with a feeder (or bomb if the swim is close enough for loose feed). Relentless and accurate casting and loose feeding are the key to this approach, coupled with an instinctive feel for how the swim is reacting. This would always be my preferred method on both the middle and the lower Swale, as I believe that if done properly it will feed up the chosen swim over a period without spooking what fish are hopefully in residence.

In reasonable conditions this should be a method of increasing returns, reaching a point in the session where you could be quite literally hooking and landing a barbel every cast. This period may not last very long, but usually only comes to an end as a result of angler failure – running out of bait, or losing a fish that spooks the shoal. On rare occasions you might actually have caught all the fish in front of you! It works because it relies on fishing a high-density fishery where there are enough barbel to create competitive feeding; eventually this causes the fish to become totally preoccupied, which overrides their natural caution. This approach has been responsible for most of the multiple captures of barbel on the Swale in the last fifteen to twenty years, and what may be surprising is that many of the big fish have been caught during multiple captures. The most deadly exponent of this method is David Stonehouse (see later, page 175).

Times are a-changing, however. In the last two seasons there appears to have been a reduction in barbel numbers in many of the previously high-density areas of the river; this is evident from the fewer occasions when multiple captures in excess of six fish are taken by experienced anglers. This is now a much-discussed subject amongst a number of the lower Swale regulars: theories abound, though it may be simply down to that 'old black dog' of negativity, and nothing more. Recently a number of events have had an impact on both the river and

(potentially) its barbel population. The great winter floods of 2000 were one source of concern. Most of us who fish the river regularly noticed that up to this point we had enjoyed a honeymoon period. The lower Swale seemed to be bursting at the seams, with an increasing number of specimens over 9lb, and certainly more low doubles up to 10lb. But this has not continued in the last two seasons, and multiple captures have certainly reduced.

Many theories have been extended for this reduction, including the possibility of fish becoming stranded on the landward side of flood banks, or being able to travel upstream in high spates over previously impassable weirs. Conversely fish may have been pushed great distances downstream. Perhaps the nature of the bed material was changed as a result of scouring, and natural haunts for invertebrates were destroyed. The list is quite long and may also include natural mortality of year classes. Other factors are those impacted on the river by the anglers themselves. Some fisheries have changed dramatically as they became privately owned and no longer received mass attention from day-ticket anglers, diminishing the amount of bait being put into the river. Similarly the whole face of angling itself is changing. A great many anglers have deserted river fishing in favour of modern-day, purpose-built stillwater fisheries, with the same effect. The Swale in particular is geographically close to many of these fisheries.

Fish location necessitates a word of caution. The popularity of the lower Swale over decades of barbel fishing has led to the defining of typical barbel swims. Experienced fish, particularly the older, wiser and bigger fish, feel the need to live close to, or they always travel to, the sanctuary of snags, dead trees, pilings and willow roots. This means that the more an angler learns about the location of big fish, the more often he is fishing tight up to some tackle-busting tank trap of a snag, which has the potential to ruin the day and, more importantly, inflict unnecessary suffering on our beloved barbel. In most such cases the use of 8lb monofilament mainline is irresponsible, 10lb is not enough, and even 12lb may not be the right choice. Abrasion-resistant monos, fused lines and strong braids are now available, and these lines, coupled with purpose-built rods, give confidence in one's ability to land a powerful fish quickly, and thus return it with the minimum of stress.

These heavy tactics may be difficult to accept, but they are based upon thousands of hours on the bank and many a competent angler's experiences. Think about it: the alternative means lost fish still attached

The River Swale.

to hooks and end rigs, or long-drawn-out battles which, although they may be the stuff of legends, something to relive in days to come, in reality can cause the fish immeasurable damage. During such a scrap the fish produces massive amounts of lactic acid within its muscle tissue, which means that immediately afterwards it requires large quantities of oxygen. At this point it is usually highly stressed, and what is more, is being contained in the oxygen-depleted margins – the worst possible situation. In extreme cases this has the potential to kill the barbel, something we should just not contemplate. I live and breathe barbel fishing, but truly I would rather sit without a bite than have this on my conscience.

All barbel fight hard, but I believe lower Swale fish are exceptional, being typically short, fat, powerful creatures. Many a fish landed looking all of 6½lb actually weighs over 8lb, having the length of a five-pounder but the girth of a nine-pounder. There have probably been quite a few eight-pounders that never saw the scales, as they may not have been considered worthy of weighing. Most experienced barbel anglers would once have subscribed to the view that fit fish of 4½lb to 6lb gave the hardest scrap for their weight. I believe that has changed, however, as the more powerful 7½lb to 9lb fish seem to be just as athletic, and give a passable impression of a submersible Range Rover.

Barbel fishing on the Swale may be considered easy when compared to that of other Yorkshire rivers such as the Derwent and the Ouse – the nursery slopes as compared to the north face of the Eiger. The banks are accommodating, and most swims have easy access. However, any barbel angler fishing this river to the exclusion of all others could, if he wished, find seclusion, mystery and monsters equal to any other Yorkshire challenge.

As far as tackle and baits are concerned, anglers tend to change their approach/method, quite often trying something new and innovative. This is the normal way of things, I suppose; but for my own part I rarely change from the traditional caster and feeder approach in summer, maggot feeder in winter, and meat or lobworms in highly coloured, floodwater conditions. Casters and maggots are fished 'piggy-back' style on a hair-rigged, smaller hook, and this has accounted for most of my barbel in the last fifteen seasons.

I have every faith in traditional methods, and in my case five Yorkshire doubles have succumbed to such methods, four to casters and one to maggot. But one angler's preferences are of little importance, and without any doubt the pellet and boilie revolution is here to stay – and it does seem to be having an impact on the Swale in recent seasons. As more becomes known about any changes and movements in fish populations, more Swale anglers may have to consider new baits and methods.

I have always continued to fish for Yorkshire barbel in winter, although generally speaking the number of anglers who do likewise is quite low. But there are many perfect winter swims on the lower Swale, and the fishing can be excellent. The Swale has a larger barbel population than most other Yorkshire rivers, with perhaps the exception of the Wharfe. Whilst catches will reduce during the winter months, knowledge of location, coupled with a water temperature above 40°F, will give an excellent

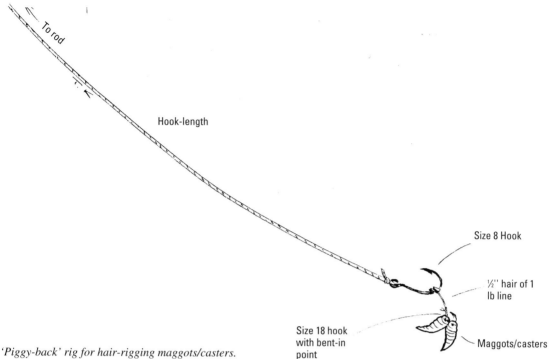

'Piggy-back' rig for hair-rigging maggots/casters.

chance of success. A winter barbel with which I was particularly pleased was an 11lb 1oz fish taken on 23 January 2000 from Topcliffe in a water temperature of 40°F using a heavy feeder and maggots.

Another approach to barbel angling that works well on the lower Swale is floodwater fishing. Given reasonable water temperature and using the right tackle, the angler can enjoy the best sport of the season in terms of multiple catches; the key is to fish out in the flow with heavy tackle, and not in the margins as you might normally fish in such conditions. Fishing a quarter to a third of the way out in the flow, in swims of a uniform depth and with heavy feeder tactics or meat, you will find barbel, although it may take a few hours to bring them to maggot, my favourite floodwater bait. It doesn't take long to identify a couple of swims to target in these situations, as much of the river will be a torrent. A rough rule of thumb is to look for a constant smooth surface; but prior knowledge from normal conditions should also influence your choice. To catch, I occasionally need to use very heavy feeders weighing up to 17oz, with, say, thirteen feet of floodwater in the river. Holding a third of the way out with 6oz to 8oz attached has also resulted in a number of multiple catches of up to fourteen fish in a session during recent winter flood conditions. Heavy tackle, rig tube, shock beads and sea-gauge links are

a must. It is unlikely that you will ever arrive to find your chosen spot taken, as most anglers still dismiss flooded rivers as unfishable, even now when so much has been written on the subject in recent years.

I know of many Swale anglers who could be classed as 'achievers'. The general level of angling commitment and ability has multiplied recently, as has also the number of anglers actually targeting barbel. Two individuals are worthy of special mention: one is David Stonehouse, whose tally of Swale doubles exceeds that of any other angler from all the Yorkshire rivers. For his secret, look no further than the feeder tactics mentioned above, and add experience, confidence and 100 per cent commitment, winter and summer. Another angler, Terry Baxter, deserves mention for the unique way in which he has addressed his fishing. Terry is one of a few northern anglers who has learned much of his trade as a barbel angler by trundling baits/rolling meat. This skill is a rare thing in the north, but something I believe we should all know how to do. Many of us have caught barbel this way, but talking to Terry, there is much to learn about the method. Some of the bites are as imperceptible as a fly settling on your finger, and he has gone through several levels of bite recognition over many seasons; but by improving his ability he has caught on days when others who knew the particular stretch very

Duncan's floodwater feeders ranging from 2.5oz to 17oz!

well have not. In the 2002–3 season his tally was ninety-seven fish landed, with seventy-two falling to rolling meat tactics.

A monster barbel of 12lb 12½oz was taken from Asenby in October 1991. This fish should give the title of Swale or even Yorkshire record holder to its captor, Halifax angler Brian Barton. The fish was witnessed by father and son Mick and Geoff Wilson, and was weighed on Avon scales. Photographs were supplied to the local papers and the angling press. The fish was almost thirty inches in length – long for a Swale fish, but unsurprising considering its colossal weight. There is a further much discussed capture of a fish of 13lb from Asenby, which may never receive the recognition it deserves. My discussions with many other anglers lead me to conclude that this was indeed a massive fish. Does the angling press have the last word on this? They have stated on a number of occasions that this was the Swale record.

The 1995–96 drought demonstrated that additional water resources were urgently required by the various Yorkshire water services. An identified source was Kielder reservoir water via river transfer; the route was down the upper Tyne to the Tees at Blackwell, and from there to the treatment works at Moor Monkton on the Yorkshire Ouse via the rivers Wiske, Swale and Ure. To facilitate this operation a pipeline was constructed between Blackwell on the Tees to Birkby on the river Wiske. Whilst construction went ahead, actual use of the pipeline required permission from the Environment Agency and the Wiske Internal Drainage Board. A campaign against its use was conducted by SOS, a local action group of which I am proud to say I am the secretary. Finally an undertaking was received by SOS from the water company not to consider its use until at least 2025. Had this undertaking not been obtained, the potential for disaster to river life was immense,

particularly for the barbel populations of the Swale below the Wiske confluence. The thermal impact alone on the river would potentially have denied barbel the ability to spawn, and may have sounded the slow death knell for Swale barbel. A matter of concern to all anglers is that we have only won a temporary reprieve.

The Ultimate Prize

On my first outing of the 2002 season on 18 June I netted two barbel, the first fish being 7lb 14oz and the second a Swale beauty of 10lb 6oz. What a boost to kick-start the new season, a double at almost the first chuck! I had planned to fish on the upper river, but on arrival I found it to be carrying extra water the colour of molasses, and the kiss of death to barbel: these conditions are not for fishing new, hard, low-density stretches. I had to revert to fishing on a length of river I knew well enough to winkle out a couple of barbel. One rod was cast tight to the far bank, the end rig five casters hair-rigged on a size 18 match hook piggy-backed to a size 8 forged hook, initially with a 3oz bomb. This was cast very tight to where there is sometimes a large shoal of barbel early in the season.

The first cast was left for thirty minutes fishing for a bite. After the wait, the cast rate was increased to every ten minutes, but now with a large weighted Drennan feeder. I rained casters across with a catapult strong enough to break a siege, and after two hours I was rewarded with a fish of 7lb 14oz, a welcome sight in a river of this colour. The second rod was fished tight up on the inside line in deep, dead water. Here there was little or no flow, in what most of us would consider to be oxygen-depleted water, and not where barbel want to be. That kind of generalization can be a mistake, however, and they are often there. Again I fished for a bite, this time for

A fine start to the season for Duncan Mellors – 10lb 6oz.

at least an hour. Then after baiting heavily with casters and hemp, I cast a large but light feeder and waited for the trap to be sprung. This time I fed casters gently, little and often by hand, but with no recasts. One and a half hours later the rod walloped over and I was playing one of the first Swale doubles of a new season. I felt the plodding power and heaviness that can mean anything from a big eight-pounder to an 11lb fish. During these rare battles it is the realization that you cannot raise the fish from the bottom that fuels your hopes that it may go over the magic number! It is this feeling, rare for Yorkshire anglers, that makes our barbel fishing unique and special.

The close proximity of some horrendous snags meant that I was unable to give much line, which was a potential disaster. But eventually, and after an unsuccessful first attempt, the fish came to the net. As it lay there I reveled in the moment, then unhooked my prize in the net, knowing it was over the magic figure, and still amazed at my good fortune – only the beginning of the season, and I had a double! I wrung out the weigh sling, zeroed the Avons and a minute later, yes! 10lb 6oz, 27in long and with a girth of 16in plus. I tucked the fish up in a pike tunnel and asked an angler from three pegs below me to come and confirm the weighing. Then I got out the camera. The season looked a lot rosier having already captured the ultimate prize in my first session with the season only two days old!

26 The River Teme

by Roger Middlecote

My introduction to the Teme occurred when I attended a Barbel Catchers Club's regional 'fish-in' hosted by my own Midcot region. From the moment I first saw the Teme from the high bank of the car park, I was immediately captivated by this most beautiful of barbel rivers. On this, my first ever day on the river, I managed to catch a small fish of about 2lb; but most of my time was spent walking around familiarizing myself with the venue. From this first trip I determined that I would make this river my main fishing venue; this was about twelve years ago, and as I write the love affair is still ongoing.

The Teme starts life quite close to the source of the Severn, but rushes into the English border counties as if keen to escape its birthplace. It runs in a roughly straight line to its meeting place with the Severn, just below Worcester, and so is very much shorter than its bigger sister. The route it travels through is largely rural landscape, and so it manages to avoid the worst pollution shed by our more extensive industrial areas; the largest area of population by far is contained in the town of Ludlow.

The river in summer is generally quite clear, with just a hint of tea-like coloration. In times of flood, however, the water will take on the colour of rich milk chocolate. Steep banks of twelve to fifteen feet are normal (a rope is an essential part of my tackle); width is typically fifteen to twenty-five yards; and depths average around five to six feet. Much of the

river has tree-lined banks, many of which end up in the river during storm conditions; as the river is non-navigable, they are left to be swept away by the next floods. These snags and areas of overhanging vegetation provide the main areas of shelter for the barbel, as there is often very little in the way of weed growth in the river. Though the general course of the river is in a straight line running southeast, there are many tight bends where gravel deposits will build up and form features. Most of the riverbed consists of gravel, although there are often stretches where the bed is made up of sheets of sedimentary rock. The river has many shallow gravel runs mixed in with deep slow pools, all overhung with alder and willow. The whole of the Teme valley is a wild-life haven, with otters now making a comeback and competing effectively with the verminous mink.

Most river species inhabit the river, from carp in the lower reaches to trout and grayling further upstream. There is a good run of salmon in some years, and recently I have seen sea lampreys spawning during early summer. Although barbel have undoubtedly been introduced illegally by anglers, the main body of fish migrated from the lower Severn, and, finding the water to their liking, have colonized the river as far upstream as Ludlow and above. Since the mid-1960s, when the first of these fish found their way into the Teme, they seem to have undergone a change, in that their fins are noticeably larger than barbel in other rivers. They certainly seem to fight much harder, possibly as a result of living in a water that can be in flood for four months of the year.

In the 1970s the barbel averaged 2lb to 3lb, and there were seemingly vast numbers of small fish in some stretches. The occasional specimen of 8lb was considered an exceptional fish. At the present time, as with the Severn, the barbel population in the Teme has reduced to what I believe to be a more natural stock density. Fish sizes are generally higher, with the average weight of fish caught being around 6½lb. A fish of 8lb, once a difficult target, is now a quite achievable goal. Most stretches are capable of producing double-figure fish in the right conditions, but they are still very rare.

Most fish are caught in, or very near to, snags or overhanging vegetation, and a lot of my fish have come from such swims. It can pay dividends, however, if you take the time to find a feeding area and introduce bait to entice the fish to feed away from their normal daylight cover. By drawing the barbel upstream there is less chance of spooking the whole shoal than if you were to hook fish from the middle of a small group sheltering under the bank-side cover. I used to believe that having caught a barbel you would be well advised to move swim to avoid spooking the rest of the shoal; as a result I used to spend a lot of time rotating swims. In the last couple of years, however, I have found that it can pay to fish on for a second, third or even fourth fish from one swim, as long as you avoid spooking the rest of the group.

Basically, I find it much more interesting to catch fish by using stalking tactics, and the Teme, with its high banks, clear water and bankside vegetation, lends itself ideally to this approach. Not only is there the thrill of the chase, but you can also attempt to be selective regarding the fish you hook. This is in the daylight hours; after dark I will still move about, but like everyone else I have 'banker' swims that I tend to choose, and I will move around far less. As a rule I will fish just two swims. I do feel that the chances of a larger fish are improved during the hours of darkness, and furthermore it can be dangerous scrabbling up and down a rope too often with handfuls of tackle.

Over the years I have experimented with most of the fashionable methods and tackle, but have always come back to what works for me. Quite often I am fishing very close to snags, so my gear tends to be on the strong side. I use a 1½lb TC rod of about 11ft in length, and 10lb Maxima line, which I like for its forgiving nature, heavy 'boilie'-pattern hooks, and a simple link-leger end rig. Sometimes I use freelined baits, sometimes a loop of line over the mainline formed with a couple of large shot stopped with a single shot, and sometimes a blob of plasticine if fishing a really snaggy swim; but most often of all I use a small link swivel so that I can change weights as each cast demands.

Each swim must be approached using the most appropriate method, and it would be a mistake to just blindly follow a set formula. As an example, on a number of swims I have found that it pays to cast in first, and then bait up by loose feeding hemp by hand. In these swims usually the first fish caught from the swim will be the largest, and the take will be almost instant. Some swims are best baited up with a dropper, and barbel can be seen coming onto the feed from all over the river, even while the dropper is still in use. In fact the fish have learnt to associate the dropper with a free meal, but they will often be quite wary of an angler's tackle, and presentation will need to be spot on to tempt them. Certain swims need to be built up with care over a period of a couple of hours, before the larger fish are freely taking bait. Several of the swims I fish need to have the line firmly nailed to the riverbed by back-leading. I will always try to freeline if the conditions are right; it just pays to ring the changes and see what works. Circumstances may often dictate a change of approach during the course of a session.

Considering that on the majority of occasions I am simply casting to the nearest snag, my back-leading method is simple. I position a second lead, slightly lighter than the main lead, which is able to run free on the line above the end rig. Upon casting, the second lead will tend to slip up the line and fall short. I then tighten up to this very carefully, and there it is. I was able to observe the importance of this method while fishing a swim I had just created, with fish easily observed close in, in four feet of water. As the fish were so close to me I had to lower the tackle in by hand, and I had a bird's eye view of the proceedings. After loose feeding some hemp, the barbel and a couple of chub were feeding enthusiastically, hoovering over the bottom, but staying well back from my bait. Lowering the rod tip until it touched the bottom, thus pinning the line down, had the fish instantly moving up to my bait.

First onto the bait was a chub of around 4lb. Had I been fishing for chub I might have been pleased to catch this fish, but as there were some decent barbel in the swim I simply raised the rod off the bottom – and the chub backed off. Next up to the bait was a barbel of about 4lb, so I repeated the process. The fish weren't spooked, they just let the current back them off out of harm's way. Next in line was the barbel I wanted, and in a moment it was hooked and putting up a terrific scrap on such a short line. It weighed just under 8lb.

The time spent finding, creating and watching the swim was about three hours; the total fishing time was about ten minutes! It was brilliant fun, and I certainly learnt something.

During the summer months and early autumn I try to have at least a couple of float-fishing sessions. There is definitely a magical feeling about hooking and playing a barbel on float tackle, and it can be very productive, though I have found that the average size of fish can be smaller. The sort of swim I would be looking for would have a good, even depth of five to six feet, and with a steady flow of about walking pace, with no boils on the surface. The longer the swim and the nearer the water I am the better for the sake of presentation, as it is easier to follow the line of the float. Ideal rod length is around 13ft, with a through action combined with a centrepin loaded with fifty yards of 6lb line. Too much reel line will tend to cause line 'bedding'. I favour an old-fashioned style crow-quill Avon float, with the bulk of shot near the bottom. But instead of just running the tackle through the swim, I will often overshot and fish over depth, to enable me to hold back hard and really slow down the progress of the bait along the bottom. This is where the centrepin is really useful, as is the ability to get right down to the waterside.

Don't assume, though, that barbel will only take a bait 'creeping' over the bottom: on many occasions I have hooked fish well off the bottom in really pacy water. A matchman's tip here is to ignore the eye often provided on the bottom of quill floats, and simply attach the float both top and bottom with float rubbers (and I will always use three); if the float becomes snagged during a fight it can often slip free, and it is surely better to lose a float than a fish. It also

means you can change floats very quickly, thus enabling you to try different methods. Using three float rubbers means that when you decide to change floats there is a chance that two of them will fit. If I am loose feeding hemp I will often use a black float rubber on the hook to simulate a grain of hemp (don't laugh, it does work!) – and if it can fool roach, it can certainly fool barbel. Ultimately it comes down to trial and error; see what works for you.

Winter flood fishing can be very productive under the right conditions. Do not be put off if the river is fifteen feet up and steaming through like the proverbial express train; if you have fished the river in more moderate conditions, you should have identified swims to fish in floodwater. I favour fishing the small open gravel areas (where you would normally be sat in the summer). I am afraid I just do not enjoy fishing with 3oz or 4oz leads in the main stream, although I do accept that this can be a very productive method. I am basically fishing clear areas with the river about two or three feet above normal summer level, spending a few minutes in each swim. If I catch from a swim I will often return to it a few times during the course of the day; the rest

The Teme is an excellent trotting river.

of the day is spent roving, trying to put a bait on a fish's nose, and frequently the take is instantaneous.

My baits when legering generally tend to be meat-based paste, with the addition of flavours to suit the conditions or time of year. During the daylight hours when roving, I will use baits no larger than a table-tennis ball; when I settle down into a swim for the evening, I will often use baits up to the size of a small apple. When using these larger baits, instead of holding the rod and touch legering, I will often put the rod in a rest and sit with arms folded to stop myself striking small twitch bites. Very often a fish will inspect and nudge a bait for a few minutes before taking, and you will find the tip moving quite sharply while this is happening. The take when it does come will leave you in no doubt, as it is often a case of catching the rod butt as the tip pulls round three feet. One of the benefits of this style of fishing in the dark is the ability to tell the difference between false bites from bats hitting the line, and something actually moving your bait. If you are watching the tip of the rod, or isotope, it is very noticeable that when a bat flies into the line it will cause the tip to describe a small circle rather than a straight movement down the direction of the line.

My biggest fish from the Teme came at night to a large, static bait. I had spent the day roving around and had taken a couple of fish up to 7½lb, so was quite prepared to sit it out in a swim for the chance of a better fish. Conditions were perfect in that the river was at normal level and warm. It had been a very warm day even though it was late October, and the sky was now overcast with no breeze to chill the water. The swim was actually a tunnel under overhanging trees; in fact the only way you were sure the bait was in the water was to listen for the splash. You then had to feel the line to make sure that it went straight down, and not up over a branch! The bottom was clean gravel at around four feet deep, and there was a steady flow of about walking pace. The banks had roots growing out into the water, so the lead was a lump of plasticine moulded around a single shot; this was so that I could pull free if the lead tangled in the roots (or the leaves!).

After just over an hour I was getting the usual twitches experienced when using a large bait, when to order the tip pulled round three feet. But a firm strike produced nothing. 'Oh well, it sometimes happens.' Re-baiting, I cast out to the same spot again; at least there was something present, and it is always worth casting again as long as you haven't pricked the fish and spooked it. Five minutes later a couple of taps, a minute later and the tip pulls around again – and this time the fish is on. To be honest, the fight wasn't that spectacular; the fish was obviously quite heavy, but after a couple of brief runs towards the snags it was quite controllable. Bill, my fishing partner, came down the bank to help with the net, and after netting the fish he took the rod while I lifted the net out of the water. I remember saying to him that the net was snagged, and could he shine the torch down so I could see what the problem was. There was nothing there, of course, it just seemed to weigh a bit heavy. I laid the net out on the grass to have a look, and was still convinced the fish was around 8lb, although it did appear very big across the shoulders.

In the sling and on the scales the Avons went round to 10lb 6oz. I couldn't believe it, and went through the procedure again to make sure. Yes, there it was, my best Teme barbel, in perfect condition and without a mark. She swam off strongly after just a couple of minutes of support. I only wish I had caught the fish in daylight; I always find it difficult to appreciate the size of a fish by torchlight.

A Memorable Trip to the Teme
by Bob Turner

I suppose my adventures on the Teme began in the mid-nineties. After watching John Wilson's *Go Fishing* television series and reading about Andy Orme's experiences on the river, I decided 'that would do for me'. So it was out with the map and some accommodation brochures, and after some deliberation I decided on Pitlands Bungalow at Clifton-on-Teme. On the way I stopped at Alan's Tackle in Worcester, where it was suggested I try the Knightwick stretch to begin with.

The following day, having dropped the wife off in Tenbury Wells in the morning, I loaded the car and set off down to Knightwick. I arrived at the river and wandered downstream, thinking how lovely it was. There were rapids, deeps, rocks, trees, boulders and huge slabs of bedrock. I had never seen anything like it, and I even spotted a few barbel. This was certainly different from the Kennet or any other river I had fished previously. I eventually arrived at the end of the fishery after about an hour, and tackled up using a couple of shot and a size 2 hook, intending to roll meat into any likely-looking areas on the way back. It was quite a bright day, and the fishing was hard until I came to an area with bedrock stretching across the river, leaving a gully along the far bank. I cast upstream and eased the bait back down towards me. The line tightened, and a firm strike resulted in my first Teme barbel at about 4lb. I think I caught five barbel up to just over 6lb that day, all from the gully swim – not huge fish, I know, but I really enjoyed my first Teme experience.

My next visit was a weekend trip to the campsite at Little Hereford. After getting lost in Worcester I arrived on site after a journey of about three and a half hours, with an hour and a half of daylight remaining. This is another very picturesque stretch of river, although not particularly long at about half a mile. It consists of lots of bedrock, with gullies dropping into pools, and with a large pool right at the bottom end. I decided to fish at the end of one of the gullies where the river opened out into a pool, the rationale behind this decision being that if any fish were to move up- or downstream they would have to pass my bait. Loose feed consisting of hemp, tares and corn was introduced via a bait dropper, and the swim was left to rest for an hour or so. The rod was set up with ½oz weight and a size 10 Super Specialist hook baited with corn. Casting into the flow I let the current carry the bait around until it settled where some of the loose feed had come to rest. I did not have to wait long before the rod appeared to be dancing, indicating the presence of feeding fish competing for the food. Sure enough, the rod twitched three feet, and I grabbed it to find myself attached to a very angry barbel. At just over 4lb it wasn't a huge fish, but was nevertheless a very welcome introduction to this stretch. I finished with five fish that evening, up to 6lb 10oz; not monsters, but a good start. Over the weekend I caught eleven barbel, all relatively small fish but typical Teme fishing.

One particularly memorable day I enjoyed on this lovely river was on the occasion of a BCC southern region 'fish in' held at Lindridge on the Birmingham Anglers Association ticket. Keith Evans and Nick Tigwell picked me up in Reading at about 8am for the trip up to Worcestershire. During the journey there was much discussion about the fishing, and also about the football match between England and Germany, taking place on the same day. After stopping for breakfast, we arrived at the river at about 11am – plenty of time for a wander up and down the venue to choose swims. I chose one where the river came through a gully and opened out into a pool; Nick chose an area where the river came over some shallows before dropping into a deeper pool, and Keith fished further downstream under a bush on the near side.

I decided to fish with a feeder using hemp and small trout pellets for feed, fixing a pellet on the hook using a bait band; Nick decided to use the 'bait and wait' approach, dropping in hemp and fishing meat over the top; and Keith elected to fish using boilies as bait. During the afternoon there were various cheers, either for fish being hooked, or more goals scored by England. Later in the day I heard a cheer from Nick, followed by a huge swirling sound, so I went to have a look. Nick was obviously connected to a good fish which, following steady pressure, was duly landed; it weighed in at 10lb 14oz. Photographs were taken, and the fish was returned to the river. What a good end to an excellent day. During the day I caught two fish, the best going just over 6lb. Keith and Nick also caught two fish; both of Keith's were small, so Nick obviously took the honours. Interestingly, on the day no one particular method stood out. Then it was over to the Nag's Head for a few pints of 'Marston's Pedigree'.

Last, but definitely not least, I would like to tell you about my most memorable trip to the Teme. As I remember it the weather had been quite reasonable for late autumn, with rain and wind but with the daytime temperatures staying around the 10°C, following light overnight frost. I was staying in Shropshire for the week, and on this particular day decided to fish at Eardiston. I selected a swim I had fished before, having enjoyed reasonable success in the past, catching fish up to 8lb 13oz. The river here runs over a shallow gravel area, and then slowly deepens off to about five feet over approximately forty yards; the swim is at the end of this area. There is also quite a long stretch below the swim, which cannot be fished because of the undergrowth and the steep bank. On the day, due to the number of anglers on the venue, I decided on a 'bait and wait' approach, using garlic-flavoured hemp and finely diced meat as loose feed, with large pieces of meat on the hook (by 'large' I mean about matchbox size). I dropped in two pints of loose feed, and went for a wander downstream. Returning a short time later, I dropped in another pint of feed. I then checked my set-up, which was very basic: an SSG shot pinched onto a piece of silicone to protect the line, and a size 2 forged hook tied direct to 10lb line. The idea was that the bait would be flicked out into the flow and allowed to swing round under the nearside undergrowth. Hopefully the loose feed would also have washed into this area.

I mounted a piece of bait onto the hook so that it was side-hooked, with most of the hook protruding. I wanted to give myself every chance of hooking any fish that might pick up the bait. The bait was cast out and allowed to bounce round just off the current, and I sat back touch legering with the rod on a rest. There was no action for about an hour, so I dropped in another pint of loose feed and threw a couple of

Bob Turner with his big Teme specimen.

handfuls downstream. I re-cast, and sat back with another cuppa. After a few minutes there were one or two plucks on the line and then nothing, so I gave the line a little pluck myself to try to induce a bite. No such luck, so I reeled in – only to find the bait had gone. I re-baited and cast back to the same spot. I did not have long to wait this time, as there was a violent pull on the line. I struck, but there was nothing; it must have been a liner. I re-baited yet again and cast back to the same spot. Once more I did not have to wait long before there was another good pull on the line: this time there was no mistake and a good fish was hooked. Initially not much happened, then the fish appeared to wake up and went on a strong run downstream, with me wondering when it was going to stop. Eventually,

however, the clutch did its job, and keeping the rod low, the fish was encouraged to swim back upstream. Following one or two more short runs the barbel was on the surface and in the net before it knew what was going on. Putting the rod out of the way, I lifted the fish onto the bank; it felt really heavy. I placed it carefully into the sling, and lifted: just over 11lb. I settled for 11lb 1oz.

It was a super fish: I could barely believe my good fortune.

To sum up, I don't think the Teme gives up its larger fish easily, but the rewards are there to be had. Basically, it's a lovely river in attractive surroundings, quite different from my local River Kennet, and well worth a visit.

27 The Lower Thames

by Peter Hornfeck

The general consensus of opinion considers the Lower Thames to be the lengthy stretch of river running from just below Oxford down to Teddington Weir. From this point onwards the river is tidal, and of no significance as far as barbel angling is concerned. In purely geographical terms this is an enormous tract of water, and a daunting prospect to the would-be barbel angler.

Much has been written about the gravely runs and narrow, small stream characteristics of the upper river, but sadly now, from Oxford downstream, these conditions are but dreams. Gone are the easily identifiable gravel runs and bubbling glides associated with the juvenile watercourse: in its place a murky soup affording only occasional glimpses of the riverbed. Silt is prevalent, and cow cabbage (more of which later) has replaced the streamer weed and flowering ranunculus. The narrowness is long gone too, and now it would need a muscular effort to cast to tantalizing, far-bank swims.

My introduction to this murky environment came at a tender age. In the summer of 1960, I accompanied my father on evening sessions to the weir pool at Romney Island, just below the then road bridge between Windsor and Eton High Street. In those days most weirs were free fishing, and Romney was no exception. Many a late evening was joyfully spent at this productive venue. My father had been a very keen and successful carp angler, especially in the nearby lakes of Windsor Great Park, which were close to home. He also had a passion for chub and roach, and, as a demon exponent of touch legering, succeeded in many fine captures from the relatively nearby Thames. Being very much a traditionalist by modern standards, bread-and-cheese paste served him magnificently, and it was with these baits that I began my love affair with the river and its more elusive inhabitants.

In those days a pushbike was my only means of transport, so a day at Penton Hook, Marlow or Maidenhead was an exhausting exercise. During 1961 a trip with my father on a punt moored in the run-off from Bell Weir at Staines gave me my first taste of a fighting Thames barbel. This time a large lobworm proved successful, and was met with the classic arm-wrenching snatch of a strong fish barrelling down the current at high speed. Of course, at this time I had never caught a barbel, and naturally assumed that the torpedo I had latched onto was a carp. Even then carp were showing up in ever-increasing numbers, and to suspect such a fish was not fanciful, but a relatively realistic assumption. Line was gradually gained, and after a few heart-stopping moments under the rod top, my first bronze-flanked barbel lay in the folds of the net. The needle on the Salter scales settled, quivering on the 5lb 12oz mark! My delight knew no bounds. With trembling hands I unhooked and returned my prize to the murky, turbulent depths of her watery home. The rest of that day passed in a euphoric haze, and I knew then that my angling life had changed for ever.

Life then took a distinct downward turn with the premature death of my father at an extremely early age. His loss not only as parent, but also as my fishing mentor, proved devastating, and indeed it was almost two seasons before I ventured onto the riverbank once more. Furthermore, by now my school exams were high on my list of priorities. So, loaded down with tackle and textbooks, I would peddle off to Runnymede near Staines for many pleasant hours of swotting and angling. The river here is extremely wide, and during the summer, even all those years ago, it was heavily populated with boat traffic. Generally speaking it is a particularly featureless stretch, though because a road runs nearby, it is a popular place for people to picnic.

This pastime inevitably causes an increase in foodstuffs such as unwanted sandwiches being thrown into the river. The ducks and SSGs of course are wise to this, and make merry; but a fair amount finds its way to the riverbed. One fine afternoon I was taught a salutary lesson when, having retrieved my hook bait, I left what I had assumed to be a bare hook resting on the bottom in the margins.

My studies were interrupted by the sound of breaking twigs and splashes and the sight of my rod butt disappearing through a bush into the water. Rapid action saved the day as the would-be tackle thief made a determined getaway. Stiff resistance eventually subsided, and a muscle-bound barbel of 4lb was lifted from the water. At first I suspected this to be a fluke and a totally isolated capture, but I was wrong: over a period of three months no fewer than eight barbel, ranging in size from 4lb to 7¾lb, came from the very edge of the river, and all to bread-related baits. The winter months proved equally successful, and during high water levels, large worms or the smelliest cheese proved irresistible. This relative barbel bonanza didn't last, though, and by the following season they had vanished – but to where?

As with all rivers, location holds the key to success or failure on the Lower Thames. On rivers such as the Hampshire Avon or Dorset Stour this problem is eased a little by virtue of water clarity, but as already mentioned, this luxury is not available on the Thames, and increases the problem tenfold. Nevertheless, although it makes the job of fish detection much harder, it is infinitely more rewarding when success is achieved. In a river of this size even the largest fish population can be spread very thinly, and this in itself makes location all the more difficult. Even so, the barbel angler must not lose sight of the fact that those watercraft techniques that work admirably on the higher profile rivers should not be forsaken on the Thames.

Before tackling the river, it would be advisable to do some concentrated groundwork. Several books over the years have mentioned various areas of the lower river to be barbel producing, and these should not be overlooked, as swims that have produced fish in the past often turn up trumps years later. Word of mouth is, of course, the easiest method of acquiring information, and it can pay handsome dividends; thus it always pays to talk to, and to listen to and learn from other anglers, even if they are interested in other species of river fish – and many a pleasure angler has been comprehensively overwhelmed by an unknown quarry whilst spending an afternoon in the sunshine! Invariably the 'one that got away' is

usually considered to be a large carp, and although this is a distinct possibility, there is every chance that a large barbel was the culprit. From Hampton Court upstream, carp are relatively common and have proliferated quite dramatically over the years. Stretches such as Sunbury, Penton Hook, Laleham, Windsor and beyond all turn up their share of carp at regular intervals – and they also turn up barbel!

Barbel can be found in most weir pools and weir streams, where they vary in size from smaller males in the region of 4lb in weight, up to larger females in the double-figure bracket. However, it should be stated here that the barbel I have caught have generally been of a higher average weight, in the 5–6lb category, and smaller fish have been relatively uncommon in comparison.

Employing all the usual methods of searching and 'mapping' swims is time well spent, and accurate depth investigation is of paramount importance; even the slightest riverbed depression can reward the angler. One such depression in the vicinity of Staines Town produced in excess of four fish in a single session. The need for absolute accuracy of casting was borne out by the fact that a deviation of less than ten feet either side of the spot resulted in no bites whatsoever; but immediately the bait was placed in the appropriate area, bites came at regular intervals. The question of accuracy is brought firmly into focus after dark, when the best policy is to pick a sight mark and stick rigidly to it, if possible. One such direction marker I used was a light on the back porch of a far-bank house; this was fine until the occupant of the property retired to bed and extinguished the light! The lesson here, of course, is to have a back-up!

As if the size of the task were not already enough, the added problems of motorized water users only complicates matters further. In the summer months the boat traffic is incredibly high, and it is really pointless fishing anything other than a boat-free weir pool at this time. Boats are extremely busy on the main river, and their activity only starts to diminish when the locks shut at 7.30pm; even then the comparative tranquillity can be shattered by the numerous 'booze-cruises' that ply their trade in the evenings. As a rule most boat traffic ceases by about 10pm, at which point angling takes on a far more serious perspective. And it is not only the physical presence of boats: they are also responsible for the high density of silt that covers the riverbed. Propellers churning through the water spread an already dirty riverbed into drifts of silt that impair visibility to such an extent that gravel detection is almost impossible. Even so, I have to say that I have

A big lower Thames barbel.

found barbel feeding quite happily despite the
ceaseless thump of boat engines passing overhead,
and the layers of silt seem to be of no concern
whatsoever to the fish.

One plus point in these areas is the preponderance
of 'cow cabbage', which often acts as an attractant to
many species including barbel. The cabbage can
usually be found in areas of slack water, beyond
bends or other obstructions, and these places are
always worth trying. Structures such as bridge supports, jetties, landing stages and other protrusions
create slacks and are a tailor-made environment
for barbel, and always worthy of thorough investigation. The riverbed surrounding such structures
is often cluttered with rocks and other construction
debris, which can make legering a difficult
business; but the use of plasticine as a weight helps
avoid breakages, as lead weights can often become
lodged in crevices. This is particularly true of a
couple of bridge swims that I fish, and several
decent fish have been lost over the years by line
breaking on the rough edges of stones and
brickwork.

This bridge is actually on a bend in the river, and
the amount of underwater current activity is
tremendous, as can be seen in the illustration. By
casting to the wall of the support, the bait will
trundle downstream to just past the end of the
buttress. At this point the current sweeps the bait in a
circular motion in towards the bank, before moving
it back in the eddy that has been created between
buttress and riverbank. It was very noticeable that if
the bait was able to return to mid-flow without being
gobbled by chub, there was a very real chance of a
barbel. The barbel would lie in between the outcrops
of stones, where they could wait for the bait to roll
round into their path. The bite would usually be a
light pluck, followed moments later by a solid
thump. As the fish was not moving around too much,
there were very few takes where the rod would pull
round into an arc.

Weir pools offer a good variety of possibilities,
but again, flow and current behaviour are particularly important features. Fishing the white water
directly below the outflow can be devastating, as the
bait will oscillate quite dramatically and be pulled
back under the sill by the current. Here the barbel
can be found almost under the rod tip – but other
areas of deepwater channels running into shallows
can also be very productive. Fish will often
congregate where the pool narrows and runs into the
main channel, as foodstuffs gather as it flows
between areas of shallow bed and the bank. It is
advisable when studying such areas to make notes

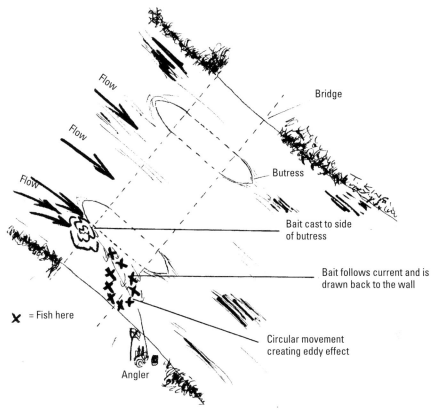

Figure 1 – A typical Thames bridge swim.

and add a few sketches for future use (see the diagram). When dealing with such vast amounts of water, anything in the way of prospective swims, creases, snags and other obstructions should be noted for future reference.

Once an area has been pinpointed for investigation, the question of what baits to use will be next on the agenda. The practice of massive pre-baiting with thousands of lobworms has now been consigned to the history books, even though there is little doubt that these methods succeeded quite spectacularly at the time. Today, of course, such an onslaught would be expensive, and not necessarily productive. There is no doubt the population of Thames barbel in the late nineteenth and early twentieth centuries was far greater than it is today; nevertheless, a campaign of relative saturation tactics could pay handsome dividends if positive location has first been made.

Standard tactics with maggots and hemp that succeed remarkably well on rivers such as the Avon, Stour or Great Ouse do not always come good on the Thames. Vast shoals of bleak and gudgeon patrol the Lower Thames, and are past masters at hoovering up

such delectable particle baits. This is not to say that they should be excluded from the bait box, but it should be remembered that they have this effect. The barbel angler should be prepared to tolerate the incessant twitching of his rod and line as countless bleak and gudgeon make merry. Relief may be forthcoming if one of those legendary Thames bream shoals happens along – although to the purist barbel angler this may prove almost as frustrating as the bleak and gudgeon.

Without question it has been my experience that it is the larger baits that give the greatest chance of success on this river, be it in the weir pools or in the mainstream. Bread-related pastes, and cheese (and the stronger the better) can prove deadly, and highly spiced meats and the famous lobworm also account for a high percentage of Thames barbel captures.

'What about boilies?' I hear you say, and indeed over the past few years the use of boilies on Thames tributaries such as the Kennet, Mole and Wey, along with many other rivers, has proved very effective. Carp anglers moving over to barbel and using carp tactics have captured many specimen barbel from venues countrywide, and it seems the Thames is

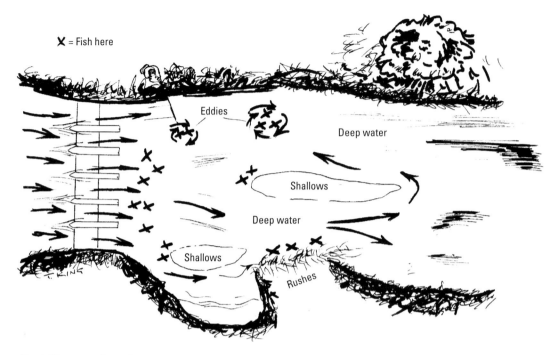

Figure 2 – A Thames weir pool.

holding out against the odds in this area, I'm sure due primarily to its sheer size and scope. Without doubt a determined boilie campaign on areas of the Thames where barbel populations are highest, may well pay high dividends.

One such area that without question has produced barbel more regularly than almost any other single venue is Hampton Court. Barbel and carp have been caught here for many years, and in common with other rivers they are getting bigger and more prolific. The current biggest lower Thames barbel came from this stretch, caught by a member of the Barbel Catchers: Richard Donnelly, whose account of its capture concludes this chapter.

Regarding the future of lower Thames barbel fishing, there are plenty of large areas of river that are relatively unexplored and also offer free fishing. Those stretches that are not free may be fished for a modest fee from a local club, and will afford the angler bent on capturing a Thames barbel every possibility of success. Although some weirs can be fished on a club book/ticket, the acquisition of an Environment Agency Weirpool ticket is highly recommended; this ticket will allow the holder to fish most weirs from Radcot near Oxford, downstream to Teddington. In days past, fishing was usually allowed from the weir structure itself, but increased construction work in recent years has led

to this practice being curtailed. Nevertheless, good areas of the weir and surrounds may be fished, and the permit comes complete with maps showing each fishable weir in detail, and the areas where fishing is permitted. Access and car parking are also shown, and in general the ticket is a must for all would-be lower Thames barbel anglers.

Many barbel anglers shun the lower Thames as being too big, too difficult and not worth the effort; but in doing this they are missing out on a river that without doubt must contain barbel of monstrous dimensions. It was from the lower Thames at Molesey in 1888 that the then record barbel of 14lb 6oz was caught. This record was equalled twice in the 1930s by fish from the Hampshire Avon, and stood for many years until an upsurge in the capture of enormous barbel has left the 14lb 6oz specimen somewhat in the shade. The river is still one of the country's oldest barbel-holding rivers, and many stretches have been recorded over the years as being of major significance to the barbel angler. These stretches, as previously referred to, are still capable of producing fish to this day, and are well worth the effort. Perhaps some day soon the capture of a massive Thames barbel will again make the headlines in the angling press, and the river will become the focus for many who have previously ignored this splendid river!

My First Thames Barbel
by Richard Donnelly

Unlike Peter, I cannot claim a long experience of fishing the lower Thames. I was, however, fortunate enough to land the then BCC record of 10lb 1oz from the Hampton Court stretch in October 2000. It says a great deal about the potential of this river that this was my first Thames barbel, and the fish was caught on only my second cast on my first visit to Hampton Court. I would love to be able to report that it had been followed by regular captures of sizeable fish, but sadly this hasn't been the case. This serves to reinforce Peter's view that location is the key to success, and that certainly a proportion of the barbel are travellers.

My decision to try Hampton Court was made following increasing rumours that the stretch was producing barbel in viable numbers. Chris Dodge, Paul Starkey and I were in the middle of a campaign on the Surrey Mole. Having spoken to several anglers who claimed to have caught barbel of a reasonable size from the Hampton Court stretch, we decided to give it a go as an alternative to the much more intimate River Mole. Coincidentally, Peter had also decided to give it a try at the back end of the season, and had taken four fish in a single evening session.

Although it is generally difficult to obtain reliable information or advice regarding the Thames, we found several references to Hampton Court on the internet, and backed this up with a couple of non-fishing visits to get a feel for the stretch. From our research there appeared to be two consistent messages: first, the fish don't like the boat traffic so it doesn't fish in daylight; and second, the fish are caught in the near margins up to two rod lengths out. We were also told that the stretch didn't fish well for barbel until late autumn/early winter, as the fish were not in the stretch in any numbers throughout the summer months.

For those of you that don't know the area, the Hampton Court stretch runs downstream from Molesey Weir, under Hampton Court Bridge, past Hampton Court Palace on the North Bank and on past Thames Ditton Island. Hampton Court Railway Station is on the south bank immediately downstream of the bridge, and the best known area is situated behind the station in a small public park that provides safe parking and comfortable access. Fishing is free, and understandably this area receives most of the attention. At the downstream end of this park the River Mole joins the main river, having only recently been joined by the River Ember.

Downstream of the confluence and on the same bank there is another public park that extends down as far as the Rowing Club and the 'Fox on the River', a well known riverside pub. Fishing here is still free, but access is not quite so simple, and it appears to receive a little less pressure than the station stretch. We decided to start on this section.

The river here does not have many visible above-surface features. Plumbing and leading around confirmed the presence of gravel and very little weed growth, with the depth being fairly regular in the main channel, following a steady drop-off for about one or two rod lengths out: not much to go on.

The first day that we decided to fish the stretch, we planned to get away from work early and arrive in daylight. In the event Paul wasn't available, so Chris and I agreed to meet at about 3pm on the bank. On arriving, we were pleased to find nobody else fishing, and the river colouring up following heavy rain in the preceding days. The main river takes a while to react to rain, possibly due to the control imposed by the upstream weirs. In contrast, many of the tributaries rise and fall like a fiddler's elbow, and it was apparent that there was a lot of warm, coloured floodwater entering from the Mole and creating a visible slick about a third of the way across the river. This was too good a feature to ignore!

I decided to fish two rods, casting one upstream and across to place a bait on the edge of the coloured water coming from the Mole, and the other downstream about two rod lengths out, as this seemed to be the favoured line. As we weren't expecting too much action before dark, I casually set up the upstream rod and baited it with a glugged fish-meal boilie that I had left over from a recent trip to our usual stretch. I figured that the numerous carp anglers who target this area would have introduced enough boilies to make it worth a go without pre-baiting.

My first cast went a bit further over than I intended and was quickly moved out of position by the flow, so I recast and it landed right on the edge of the crease and held bottom. The rod was put in the rests, and I started to set up the second rod, keeping one eye on the tip that was nodding rhythmically in the flow. I was particularly concerned to spot any boats that might threaten to go through my line before they actually did so!

After a few minutes the inevitable happened, and a narrowboat decided not only to go through my swim, but also to perform a multipoint turn right above where my bait was lying. Its shallow draught meant that it did not foul the line, so I decided to leave the bait out with the intention of re-casting once it had gone and the swim had settled again. I was actually calling across to Chris, who had still to cast out, when out of the corner of my eye I saw my rod tip judder. My immediate thought was that turbulence created by the boat had disturbed the lead, and I was about to reel in when the top hooped over hard and I realized it was a fish.

Not being a regular big river angler, my rod and tackle were more suited to less demanding flows, and the fish went on an initial run towards the far bank, which took me a while to control. I initially thought it must be a carp. Chris had joined me by now, and after a few hair-raising minutes I got the fish in close and we realized it was a barbel, and a good one at that. Fortunately, Chris did a great job with the net and, we were soon admiring the first Thames barbel that either of us had seen, with Chris shouting excitedly – *my* main concern was how I was going to tell Peter that I had achieved in an hour what he had been trying to do for so long: catch a Thames double! I had no need to be concerned, however, as Peter, ever the gentleman, was genuinely delighted at the news, and is still talking to me.

As for the perceived wisdom concerning boat traffic, night fishing and fishing in close, this capture was contrary to all those theories as it came in daylight, under the hull of a moving boat, and with the bait about a third of the way across. This simply confirms why fishing keeps us captivated, and also that whatever rules and theories we seek to apply, we shouldn't stick to them slavishly.

Richard Donnelly displays his Thames double in front of the weekend cottage.

28 The Upper Thames

by Paul Hiom

In spite of bigger captures by others outside the club and from various parts of the river, anyone who fishes the upper Thames will know that catches of double-figure fish are still few and far between. On the upper river at least, a double is still the target weight, and the charm of the river and its resident barbel population remains intact. The Thames does have the potential for very big barbel, and has already produced some remarkable fish to over 14lb. If you include St Patrick's Stream in the equation, fish of over 15lb (probably visitors from the Thames) have been recorded by the club. This makes for incredible future possibilities. I have my eye on a very good fish in the upper reaches that has so far eluded me, but I remain hopeful of a result in time.

The river itself starts its journey at Trewsbury Mead, within the parish of Coates, near Cirencester. The infant river starts to take shape around the village of Ewen, developing on its course through the Cotswold Water Park, gently meandering between the villages of Poole Keynes, Somerford Keynes and Ashton Keynes. It begins to resemble a real river just downstream of Waterhay Bridge where it joins forces with Swill Brook. It then makes its way around Manor Brook Lake and Hailstone Hill, before meeting up with its longest tributary, the River Churn, at North Meadow on the outskirts of Cricklade.

My experience of Thames barbel extends from what I call the boat-free zone between Cricklade and Inglesham, down past Buscot and through to Duxford Loop near Shifford Lock, taking in one or two of the weirs in between. As you could not get a

small riverboat under the three arches in Hannington Wick Road Bridge, you could say that the boat-free zone starts at this point. However, the shallows, gravel and rushes that exist through much of the area downstream of here make it virtually impossible to navigate in earnest much past Inglesham. You may see the occasional canoe or dinghy, but even these are a rarity, much to my delight. In the last fifteen years I have caught barbel from most parts of the upper river, although I only started seriously fishing for Thames barbel in the summer of 2000. For the purposes of sensibly limiting this chapter, I will relate my experience on the area above Inglesham, near Lechlade in Gloucestershire. The majority of my fishing is focused on the stretches between Castle Eaton and just south of Manor Ham Barn. Concentrations of fish become less the closer you get to Manor Ham Barn, but most of the time I have the river to myself, and can relax in my endeavours. The Ordnance Survey Pathfinder Map 1134 is useful in providing information on access roads to the river up to Manor Ham Barn, and is well worth the expenditure.

Unless you are a seasoned small river barbel angler, you may wish to consider first tackling areas where known populations of fish exist, and these areas are not over-fished by any means. If you are a newcomer to barbel, take it one step at a time, and try to get some fish under your belt. This will give you the confidence to tackle more remote areas as your knowledge develops, and will help you cope when trips inevitably get very hard. There are good barbel around Ampney Brook, where it enters the river near the village of Eysey, and double-figure fish have been caught here in recent years. Water Eaton, downstream of the confluence with the River Ray, is another good spot with reasonable numbers of fish.

Barbel are also showing again in the River Ray, which I guess proves that the Environment Agency have made some headway in the water quality of this river. Back on the Thames, the areas up- and downstream of the road bridge at Castle Eaton are worthy of attention. The upstream section can be more difficult to fish due to lapsed management of bank-side reed growth, I suspect a sign of reduced fishing activity on this stretch. Similarly, the downstream stretch can get very overgrown with reeds on the village side of the river past the church, but it is still fishable. On a good day, you will spot one or two fish in the waters around Kempsford, Hannington Wick and down past Manor Ham Barn. These stretches have good tree cover, gravel runs, streamer weed and underwater cabbages. There are some great variations in the depth and contour of the riverbed, and all areas have produced double-figure barbel, with rare fish over 12lb. Water quality is generally very good on the upper river, it is well oxygenated, and supports small populations of the bullhead or miller's thumb, which is always a good yardstick for healthy water.

Pre-season feeding of noted areas can give you a slight advantage when the magical 16 June arrives; however, this is no precursor to success. I have found that the upper Thames and its small head of barbel are very unkind to visitors: they are extremely finicky feeders and biters, and a fish spotted on Monday could be anywhere up- or downstream by Tuesday. Having said that, my observations lead me to believe that these fish do not travel the great distances often associated with fish in some other rivers; nor have I found it necessary to fill the river with bucketfuls of bait. If I can get a small amount of freebies down to where I know some fish are located, and if I can do this without attracting the attentions of the chub, my confidence increases tenfold.

My approach on the river so far has been fairly basic when it comes to tackle, bait and rigs. In most situations I have used a standard small river, roving set-up, namely a 1¼lb test curve 11ft 6in specialist rod, 8lb bs copolymer (usually the light-refractive, excel bass pro) in clear conditions, or 15lb Herculine or Gravitron braid (in floodwater) loaded on to a fixed-spool reel with front drag. You could fish lighter with, say, 6lb mono or copolymer line, but I feel that this restricts you to fishing swims without snags, and Thames barbel do like to be near snags. If I can get away with braid, it is always my first choice as a mainline, as it picks up all sorts of vibrations, plucks and nibbles.

I prefer to use a simple running leger using a John Robert's or Nash weed-green, large bore run ring, with an ounce or so of Korda pear leger. Even in floodwater I prefer to let the bait and lead find its own place to settle; it feels more natural to allow this to happen, rather than just plonking a 2oz or 3oz lead where you think the fish will be. I am a firm believer that there is a lot more going on under water than we

can see with the naked eye or with polarizing sunglasses. I'm not too concerned with resistance, but I do find that the large bore of the run ring helps reduce the amount of weed or rubbish that can get caught up in a standard link leger. I usually tie the lead to the run ring with 3lb mono, or green or clear powergum, lightly knotted just in case the lead gets snagged on roots or heavy weed stems.

My favourite hook-length materials at this time are Fox Barbel Braid in 12lb bs, and the extremely strong Berkley XT in 8lb test. Try as I may I cannot get on with fluorocarbon, and do not trust it as a reliable hook-length material in the lower strengths. Hooks are usually Centurion 2000 for hair-rigged baits, ESP Big T Raptors or Partridge Hooks made for Double T. The Partridge wire meat pattern is excellent when the fish are being finicky. I would say that it is best to fish with whatever you have confidence in. Location is the biggest factor, and the shiniest gear will not catch fish that are not there.

The shallow, winding river is the perfect place for the roving angler, and whilst the summer can be fraught with frustrations in the shape of chub, the barbel are unique and well worth the attention of the patient angler. I find it best to concentrate on one area at a time, getting to know the stretch intimately over a period, and putting in the hours required spotting fish and noting swims. It may sound obvious, but there really is no point fishing these stretches without finding at least one or two fish. A high vantage point can often give you the best opportunity to locate fish, and whilst I do not always condone tree climbing, there will be times when the creative angler will have to make use of his surroundings in order to find the quarry. In my mind, this all adds to the excitement of the hunt.

At spawning times there are places where the fish can be viewed with ease; however, you won't see many. After spawning the fish move off to their usual haunts, and if you can stay in touch with their movements, you can increase your chances significantly. Chub most probably outnumber barbel by fifty to one on the upper river, especially around Hannington, and this presents us with one of the biggest problems in making a deliberate attempt at trying to catch just barbel. Early season will see some barbel following the chub, scoffing their spawn and causing general mayhem, given the aggressive nature of the species. It is lovely to watch this pre-occupation when you are not fishing, but when you are, you can certainly feel as if you are wasting your time.

As June and July pass, there will be times when it will be completely impossible to feed off the chub.

They will keep coming and coming, so that you are more likely to run out of bait than they are to stop arriving; it's almost as if there is a chub larder grapevine, with messengers going off in all directions telling their mates about the free grub back at your swim. This has happened to me on more than one occasion over the years, and at times I have gone home without even placing a baited hook in the water. This can prove very costly, and I remember one occasion on a warm July evening, emptying four pints of hemp, four pints of maggots and two pints of casters into a swim, only to watch about a hundred chub mop up the lot. The barbel will often be there, just off centre of the trickle of bait, sitting under the streamer weed, sometimes picking off the occasional morsel as it drifts by.

You will pick up the odd early season fish using standard maggot, hemp and caster if you don't mind the chub. In fact Thames barbel love maggots and hemp, and by feeding areas with plenty of tree cover, and using a bait dropper, catapult or PVA sensibly, you can occasionally entice a fish on to your hook. However, there really is no such thing as a standard approach on the upper river; it's a case of trial and error, and you need to adapt your tactics frequently to stand a chance of landing a good fish.

As the season progresses, the fishing can become harder, depending upon your point of view and whether you are prepared to fish on through the floods and cold weather. As late autumn approaches, the fishing takes on a new slant and heavy rainfall adds coloration and depth to the water, making it impossible to find fish. This is when all the hard work locating fish in the spring and summer can pay off. With extra colour in the water the barbel are more confident about moving out of hiding. Increased flows, higher water levels and the energy extended to maintain position within the river all add up to hungrier barbel, and as in other rivers and at this time of year, you may stand your best chance of a fish. Fishing into winter is usually determined by keeping an eye on water levels and temperature. The usual rules apply, and it can be worthwhile fishing after a cold spell, or during one when the river is still high with warm rainwater.

The upper Thames is not an easy barbel river, but it doesn't have to be hard, either. I possibly make things hard for myself by fishing away from known areas, but I am after individuals and not shoal fish. The harder I work at it, the bigger the rewards when I catch. When the fishing gets unbearable – and it does! – and when I've forgotten what a barbel looks like, I make the most of my trips to other rivers that offer slightly easier fishing. Please don't let this put you off. If you can master the Thames and its small populations, you should be able to pull fish out of any other water with relative ease.

It is important to point out that most of this part of the river and its barbel do not get much pressure, and for this reason you will still catch on baits long forgotten on other more notable and hence pressurized rivers. Hemp, tares, maggots, luncheon meat, sausage meat, air-injected worms and casters still account for many big fish. Leave the boilies and pellets at home, along with the bivvies and the bedchairs, or save them for another river – and please *do not use peanuts*. Their use by irresponsible anglers has already resulted in the deaths of barbel on the Rushey to Tadpole Bridge stretch near Bampton. The biggest single factors are fish location and the careful presentation of your hook bait.

A Record Ten-Pounder

Being the holder of the Barbel Catchers' river record gives me great pleasure. I worked hard for this fish, and I love the Thames with a passion. However, I do believe that it is only a matter of time before this fish pales into the history books of the club, and that a bigger, perhaps more deserving fish takes pride of place. I hope that it is me who catches it!

My river record was caught in late autumn on a mild overcast evening when the river was only just within its banks. I believe that this fish was the smaller of two that I had spotted on several occasions over the course of two summers. The bigger fish was the target, and one of the reasons why I continue to be drawn to the upper river. I didn't manage to fish until late on in the 2002 season due to an injury to my arm, but by October things were looking up. Rivers levels were high due to hard rain, and I was eager to get to the river. My first session of the year proved fruitless; however, this is what I had become accustomed to, and I was not discouraged. I had baited up several swims with a few small handfuls of curried chopped ham and pork, but couldn't find any fish anywhere in the stretch.

The following week I was back. Water levels were still high, and the atmosphere was damp. Fine rain was almost suspended in the mild, overcast air. I repeated the previous week's pattern of fishing upstream and downstream, dropping a few lumps of meat into various swims. By about 5.30pm it was getting dark, with no signs of any fish. I had decided to fish until around 7pm, and by this time I was in the last swim before home. I cast my baited hook into around six feet of floodwater, allowing the flow

Paul Hiom with a superb upper Thames barbel of 10lb 3oz.

to guide my lead and hookbait along the gravel and attach itself on any obstacles on the riverbed. The terminal tackle settled, and within a minute or so I had a very quick but tentative pull on the bait. In spite of a quick strike I missed that first bite.

I was very disappointed, but decided that if I stood any chance of hitting these bites, I was going to need to resort to the hair rig with the meat fished very tightly to the bend of the hook. I slipped a size 6 partridge-wire meat hook on to my mono hook length, and re-cast to the same spot. Within seconds, the fish was on and I was playing what felt like a good barbel. Thames barbel can sometimes be a bit hit-and-miss when it comes to the fight, but this one was staying deep and fighting well in the floodwater. It tried heading for the tree roots on the opposite bank, but with a little side strain, I managed to steer it away from the snag. Steadily easing it up through

the current and onto the surface I caught my first glimpse of it: it looked like a good fish, though at that stage I wasn't sure how big it was. Thames barbel can be very misleading, as they are generally short fish with big heads.

This one was no exception, and a few minutes later as I pulled the landing net close to the bank, I knew it was a double. I left the fish in the landing net for a few minutes to recover, before lifting it onto my unhooking mat. I gently eased the fish into the weigh sling and the scales were pulled around to 10lb 4oz. I was over the moon with this fish, and called my brother on the mobile to come and take a photograph. Two hours later the fish was photographed and verified at 10lb 3oz, before being carefully held in the current and then released back into its flooded home.

29 The Non-Tidal Trent

by Mick Wood

The River Trent is an extraordinary river in almost every respect. Its sheer size and the amazing power of its swift-flowing waters can intimidate the unprepared angler before a cast has been made. Running down through the countryside just north of Stoke, the river flows east through Staffordshire, touching the northern end of the West Midlands, then traversing the counties of Derbyshire and Nottinghamshire before cutting north through Lincolnshire. The Trent has a variety of tributaries including many small lowland rivers such as the Tame, Soar and Mease. These rivers mix their contents with those of upland rivers such as the Dove and Derwent, which drain the fells of the Peak District. These many and varied feeders make conditions difficult to predict, as influxes of rainwater can arrive quickly, slowly or not at all. This situation adds greatly to the challenge of coming to terms with this river.

The Trent at Sawley, one of the river's more scenic venues.

Winter action for Dave Oakes.

If certain rivers have changed face in recent years, then the Trent has had more faces than a town-hall clock! We have seen it progress from an open sewer to a point during the 1960s when the river became a match angler's paradise. The river, albeit still far from being pollution free, produced roach fishing that in terms of both quality and quantity compared more than favourably with any other river in the country. The water quality gradually improved and chub arrived on the scene, as did large numbers of carp that spawned enthusiastically in the artificially warm water created by power station outflows. Then during the 1970s barbel arrived, and large catches of small fish began to appear regularly in matches – the matchmen even considered small barbel as a nuisance, because they took longer to play and land than chub, wasting valuable weight-building time!

During the 1990s the river changed yet again. First of all the old coal-fired power stations were closed down, thus ending the discharge of artificially warmed water into the river. Spawning now only occurred 'normally' during the late spring, reducing the excessive numbers of small barbel in the river. The Trent water quality then began to improve as the numerous water-treatment works on the river were brought up to acceptable European standards.

Although many anglers thought the now clean running water was disadvantageous for roach and chub angling, there was an explosion of natural food. The murky water and silted gravel that had previously prevented macro-invertebrate recruitment had given way to a clean riverbed, to which the natural light could penetrate. Most noticeable was the spectacular increase in freshwater snails, a rich source of protein for barbel.

Throughout the nineties barbel sizes increased beyond the wildest expectations of those who had fished the river during the previous decade. The first 15lb fish, when it arrived, was nothing more than expected. The majority of the biggest fish were initially being caught in the tidal reaches of the river downstream of Cromwell Weir, but in recent years the non-tidal sections of the Trent have started to catch up.

I first ventured forth onto the Trent in 1999, and succeeded only in making a series of errors that resulted quite frankly in poor catches. I spent too much time listening to what other anglers were saying, rather than adapting my own methods in which I already had a great deal of confidence. I tried to make do with 'standard' barbel tackle, which in most cases was not up to the job. Hopefully most newcomers to the river will be fortunate enough to have good, accurate information on where and how to start. Should this not be the case, then a great deal of perseverance will be the first pre-requisite. There is nothing wrong with this, however, as lessons learned the hard way are lessons learned well.

On a river that has many miles of open access and is up to eighty yards wide, the first consideration just has to be location. The following general observations are good starting points. First of all, early in the season the areas just downstream of the many weirs are as good as anywhere. Barbel will congregate here for spawning, and then spend some time in the well-oxygenated water cleaning up. Some barbel will remain in the weir pools for several weeks, but soon a great many will begin to migrate downstream into steadier flows. Away from the weirs, look for the huge sweeping bends for which the Trent is famous. The current is usually thrown across to the outside of the bend where it increases in pace, scouring the riverbed clean. Often the outside of these bends will be shored up with boulders to prevent bank erosion from boat wash. These same boulders are the primary habitat for those little packets of barbel protein in a shell! Find the natural food on the cleanest part of the riverbed where the flow is strongest, and you will find barbel. The next useful pointer is to keep your eyes open. River Trent barbel, in common with those of the middle Severn, tend to crash out in daylight, and I mean crash! A double-figure barbel clearing the river by two feet is quite a sight. Such surface activity will occur most frequently where the largest concentrations of barbel are to be found.

Keep your eyes on the match results as reported in the weekly angling papers. Match results are a good way of quickly identifying barbel hotspots. Finally, act upon any information passed on from a trusted source. Very often a fellow barbel angler will be happy to pass on a few location tips, particularly if he himself is about to move on to pastures new.

I stated earlier that standard barbel tackle was often inadequate on the Trent. Whilst there are venues where 1¼lb test-curve rods and 1oz leads can be used, such tackle will be severely limiting in other areas, and on occasions almost useless. Rods should be in the 1¾lb to 2lb test-curve range, and 12ft in length. Quivertips are an unnecessary embellishment, as the bites are usually 'three-feet twitches'. Reels should be robust enough to cope with the casting and retrieving of heavy feeders, and should be loaded with line with a minimum bs of 10lb. A 'Baitrunner' facility might just stop a couple of hundred pounds' worth of gear from flying into the river. The line will suffer from abrasion due to the numerous rocks that litter the riverbed in the most productive areas, so my preference is for monofilament line, as any wear and tear can easily be seen or felt. Line damage is a lot more difficult to detect when using braided lines. Check the last few feet of line on every occasion you hook a barbel, and at the very least after every ten casts, just to be on the safe side.

Hooks should be of a strong, forged pattern, and

Dave Oakes leans into a powerful fish.

remembering those rocks, keep checking the point between casts. Finally, the most critical factor in preventing fish losses is to sit with your hand on the rod. The instant the rod goes round you need to exert maximum pressure on your quarry to get your line clear of rocks. If the barbel is still on after three seconds, then it should be yours.

A Bull of a Barbel

So what of my own fishing on this formidable river? To begin with I fished casters and hemp through a feeder, with casters as hook bait. While this did produce the occasional barbel, the attentions of the numerous gudgeon, roach and chub proved to be hugely frustrating. A switch to large lumps of meat on the hook at dusk, so effective on many venues, produced even more of those ravenous chub. I looked at the methods of those who had been fishing the river for several years. In recent times the combination of a boiled HNV hook bait fished in conjunction with a pellet/hemp/broken boily method mix had become all the rage, but I discarded this approach for two reasons: first, with so little angling pressure on my chosen venues, I felt that this method, whilst effective, should not really be necessary. Second, I felt that my sporadic visits to the river would not make this approach worthwhile; so I went 'back to basics'.

The River Severn, like the Trent, produces large catches of barbel in daylight. One of my most effective methods on the Severn was to fish meat as a particle, which involves feeder fishing minute cubes of meat mixed with hemp. Hook bait is a small cube of meat on a size 14 hook tied direct to 6lb line. In 2001, I decided to adapt this method for the Trent, a decision that instantly transformed my results. The rod I bought specifically for the job was a Seer S series 2lb test curve Power Specialist, my reel a Shimano 5000RE loaded with 10lb Fox Soft Steel monofilament. My feeders were Drennan 2.5oz Ovals, reinforced with PVC tape and loaded with extra weight if the river was carrying extra water. Hook bait was a small cube of meat, or a 'Meaty Fishbite' fished on a size 10 Drennan Super Specialist.

I would commence operations by depositing on the riverbed a one-pint mix of hemp, finely diced meat, micro-trout pellets and sweetcorn. For the first two hours I would re-cast every five minutes, often catching the occasional bream or chub. Although I did catch the occasional barbel early into the session, more often than not it would take three hours of feeding before the first barbel would show. I now found myself taking multiple catches on every visit, usually between five and eight barbel with several into double figures, and a best that season of 11lb 2oz.

During 2002 I returned once more, and again the situation had changed. As the individual barbel had become bigger, the groups had become smaller. Catches of two or three fish a session became par for the course, which meant some pretty long waits between bites, and this on a venue with little attractive scenery to admire as the hours pass by. But then that special fish would come along and all the effort seemed worthwhile. For this particular session I had selected a swim where it was possible to fish at

Mick Wood with his first Trent double at 11lb 2oz.

A 'real bull of a fish' at 12lb 1oz.

A fine winter fish of 10lb 14oz.

just two rod lengths out, and had opted to use my old Speedia centrepin. Six hours fishing and feeding produced just one barbel of 8lb 14oz. But then towards the back end of that early October afternoon my rod tip lunged round, the Speedia screeched, and a real bull of a barbel fought doggedly in ten feet of fast-flowing water. The fish weighed 12lb 1oz, the culmination of four years of trials and tribulations, self-doubts and 140-mile round trips from my home in Yorkshire.

Whereas the maximum size for barbel on the tidal Trent seems to have levelled off at the 14lb to 15lb mark, on the non-tidal river, once the poor relation of the downstream venues, barbel sizes are still on the increase. Whether or not they will significantly exceed the 15lb mark remains to be seen, but it is this unknown quantity that is a major draw to the middle Trent. As the wind howls down the Trent valley and the waves break on the boulders at your feet, who knows what this awe-inspiring colossus of a river will turn up on the next occasion the rod tip lunges towards its mysterious depths.

30 The Tidal Trent

by Mark Cleaver

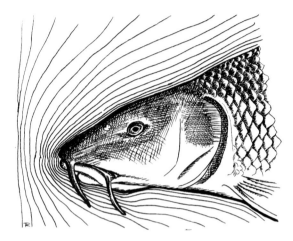

The resurgence of the River Trent as a barbel fishery has created a considerable amount of interest during the past couple of years. My interest in the Trent and its barbel began over twenty-five years ago, when I was fortunate enough to obtain – and still have – an old book entitled *Where to Fish*, edited by H. D. Turing and dated 1932. A chapter of this book was dedicated to the River Trent and its tributaries. Hidden away amongst the old sepia pages and faded text were references to barbel on the River Dove at Uttoxeter; barbel also inhabited the River Derwent at Masson Weir near Matlock Bath in Derbyshire, and were even reported from Car Dyke, a tributary of the River Devon. Last but not least was the River Trent itself, where barbel were present as high up as Swarkstone, down through Shardlow, Sawley, Beeston, Bleasby, Fiskerton and as far down as Newark. For some reason there was no reference to barbel on the tidal reaches when this book was published. That said, another chapter of the book provided a list of notable barbel captures from the British Isles; the biggest of these fish weighed 16lb 10oz, and was caught on 25 October by Frank Sims whilst fishing the tidal Trent. This fish was witnessed by J. W. Martin, also known as the Trent Otter. Its capture was somewhat unsportsmanlike, as it was taken on a nightline, using lamprey as bait. The location of its capture was downstream of the old Carlton Mill.

Over the years pollution led to the decline of the Trent barbel population, and my old book became only of historical value. As a consequence it lay on my bookshelf and collected dust for many years. It was not until the mid- to late 1990s that my interest in Trent barbel was re-awakened with several reports of barbel captures in the angling press, and one of my neighbours took a barbel weighing 8lb during a match. I borrowed a couple of old books from a friend, one of which was entitled *My Fishing Days and Fishing Ways* by none other than J. W. Martin himself. The second book was an old *Angling Times* publication entitled *Coarse Fishing with the Experts*, which also contained two articles by J. W. Martin. Much of his writing related to barbel fishing on the tidal river, from Collingham Weir downstream to Dunham Bridge. My imagination worked overtime, reading fascinating accounts of multiple barbel captures and sightings from a number of renowned locations. Areas of particular note to him were Collingham Weir, Footsitts Meadow at Carlton-on-Trent, the Sentry Box Swim below the Old Mill at Carlton, the stretch at Besthorpe, the famous Putty Nob swim at Girton, Scotchman's Hole at Marnham, and the Shuttle Door swim at Dunham Bridge.

Suffice to say, it wasn't long before I was on the banks of the tidal Trent in pursuit of those elusive Trent barbel. Prior to actually targeting any one specific stretch, I decided to familiarize myself by retracing J. W. Martin's footsteps from Collingham Weir down to Dunham Bridge. To assist me I purchased an Ordnance Survey map covering Lincoln and Newark-on-Trent (Landranger 121), which gave me all the access points to the river. Of more benefit, however, was a booklet that I managed to acquire from the National Rivers Authority Severn Trent Region, entitled the *River Trent Angling Guide*. This booklet was a godsend: it mapped out every stretch of the Trent from Stone in Staffordshire through to Gainsborough, listing riparian owners, fishing clubs and stretches accessible on day ticket.

I spent many hours walking the banks of the tidal Trent locating areas of potential. Upon first observation the river appears to be barren, devoid of

Cromwell weir, the upstream limit of the tidal river.

overhanging bushes and bank-side features, though this is compensated for by the number of gravel beds, ledges, deep bends and holes. Other features such as stream confluences, dykes and bridge parapets were also of interest. Happily the dearth of bank-side features was also accompanied by a dearth of angling pressure, and I walked miles without seeing another angler, or any sign of angling activity – yet the banks of the riverside gravel pits appeared quite heavily fished. I cannot understand why so many anglers prefer stillwater fishing to river fishing. The only stretch of river fished regularly was Collingham Weir, and this was frequented by carp anglers, and more latterly by carp-turned-barbel anglers. I have never been one for fishing amongst crowds, and so decided to steer clear of these places and concentrate elsewhere.

After considering all the options, I decided to target a half-mile stretch around Carlton Mill, just above Besthorpe. This stretch offered the greatest variety of features, including large bends, deep holes, gravel beds, cow drinks, stream inlets, a concrete jetty and the occasional overhanging willow. Prior to actually fishing, it was necessary to do some preparatory work. I pinpointed a number of

interesting locations, and set about plumbing the bottom in order to establish the contours of the riverbed. One consistent feature was the uniformity of depth. At normal level much of the river averaged around ten feet deep at one-rod distance; the depth then dropped off gradually to around thirteen feet at three-rod distance. There was a deep hole at the top end of the stretch, which dropped off to twenty feet. Towards the bottom end of a straight run I discovered a shelf where the riverbed rose up to five feet deep. Having carried out the initial plumbing, I then decided to search the bottom by casting and retrieving a leger. This method is excellent for establishing the nature of the bottom and the presence of any weed or snags, and on this occasion it revealed the riverbed to consist almost entirely of gravel. There was no significant weed growth, and no noticeable snags until one reached the immediate proximity of the bank, where the whole stretch is strewn with large rocks, deposited over the years to combat bank erosion. It was clear from the outset that these rocks could cause potential problems when playing fish.

Given the rock situation and the strong currents typical of a large tidal river, I had to pay serious attention to the choice of appropriate tackle. I considered that two basic principles had to be followed. First, tackle had to be strong and capable of controlling fish in a heavy current in the close proximity of rocks. Second, it had to be abrasion resistant: both line and terminal tackle had to be able to withstand the wear and tear imposed by abrasive and often sharp-cornered rocks. From experience gained fishing the lower Severn, I was confident with my choice of tackle. Thus for normal conditions my rod choice would be my trusty Graham Phillips 'Stepped Up Barbel' rod, and for flooded conditions I would choose my Century Pulse 'T. W. Floodwater Barbel' rod. Reel would be the reliable and sturdy Shimano Baitrunner Aero 4010. Whatever the water conditions my line would be 15lb Berkley Big Game, as this would offer the necessary strength and excellent abrasion resistance. Sensitivity of terminal tackle would be maintained by the use of 15lb Kryston Super-Nova, which is supple, smooth and also has good abrasion-resistant qualities. Hooks would be Drennan Continentals or Drennan Super Specialist. Swivels are often a neglected item of tackle, and can let you down when you least expect it; I use Berkley ones that are tested to 50lb bs. It is also important that the landing net and handle are strong: it is no use ensuring that your rod and line are fit for the purpose, only for your

landing net to collapse when you are about to land a large fish in a strong current. Suffice it to say that mine are strong and durable.

Preparations and preliminaries complete, it was time to actually do some fishing. My first session took place in early August 2000. It was planned as an evening-come-night session, so I arrived in the late afternoon at about 4.30pm. After walking the bank I decided to fish an attractive-looking glide situated just below a deep hole at the top end of the stretch. I baited with a four-pint mix of hemp, corn, and diced luncheon meat. Over the baited area I decided to fish the same cocktail of particles in my modified swimfeeder rig, combined with a large piece of flavoured meat as hook bait.

With everything in place, I then settled down for what turned out to be a long and slow night's fishing. However, at approximately 4am in the morning the rod took on a life of its own, a fish having hooked itself and decided to go on tour downstream. I eventually gained control, and netted a pristine barbel that weighed in at 7lb 7oz. It had been a long night, but the wait had been worthwhile. I was delighted with my first Trent barbel, and went home that morning tired but happy. Subsequent fishing sessions saw me continue to catch barbel on a regular basis from a variety of swims; I would average a couple of fish per session, but nothing of any note.

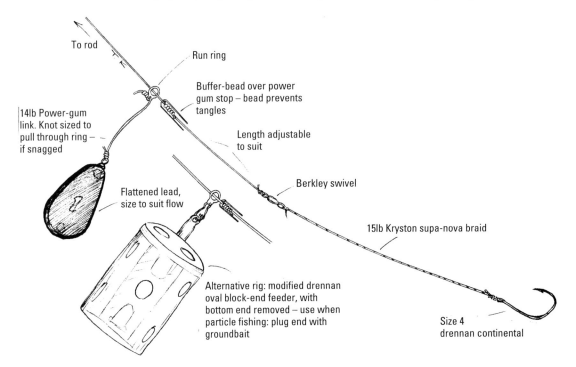

Modified leger/feeder rig.

It was not until late September that I stumbled upon a swim that proved to be a bit of a flier: it provided me with a 9lb 12oz fish, my personal best for the Trent. This was the stamp of fish I had been looking for, and was hopefully a prelude to something bigger, possibly my first double. My next session was in early October, and the same swim produced three fish up to 7lb 3oz. Unfortunately I wasn't able to fish the river again until early December, when I arrived in the late afternoon and fished until midnight. The river was eight feet up and surprisingly clear, the water temperature a warm 9.5°C. Unfortunately my 'flier' swim was almost impossible to fish due to the pace of the current, so I opted to fish a slack area further downstream and adjacent to a shelf that I had discovered during my initial plumbing exploits. This proved to be a wise decision, as I ended the session with three barbel, the biggest going 8lb 8oz.

I caught a couple of small fish during a session in the run-up to Christmas, and then the weather turned cold. January was fruitless due to the freezing weather conditions. I had one session in early February when I had three fish, the biggest going 7lb 8oz. Soon after this session, fishing was unfortunately completely curtailed due to the outbreak of foot and mouth disease. Thankfully this had all subsided by the start of the 2001 season, so with eager anticipation I resumed my quest for that special fish. My first session produced only one fish of 6lb 1oz, followed by a resounding blank. Small fish were the order of the day up to late July – but then everything changed dramatically.

It was 21 July, my son's birthday, and I had succeeded in upsetting the wife, who thought I should be at home for the birthday celebrations rather than fishing. But fate beckoned regardless, and I had that irresistible urge to try my 'flier' swim again; by mid-morning I was driving up the long track towards the small car park adjacent to the river. There was one car parked up, and this belonged to a couple of anglers fishing downstream; so as usual I had the rest of the river to myself. I was feeling confident as I unloaded the tackle and made my way upstream. The weather was overcast and cloudy, with the river approximately five feet up and coloured. These were ideal conditions. I initially decided to give my flier swim a miss, preferring to save it for later in the day. I tackled up and fished a swim on the top bend, where I had caught a couple of fish the previous winter. I gave it three hours, but there was little sign of activity and I decided to make a move downstream. I stopped and contemplated fishing a couple of swims that looked tempting, but no! It had to be my flier swim!

In this swim there is no need to fish any further than two rod lengths out, as the flow races down the near bank. I had recently been using two rods, and this session would be no different. I decided not to bait up with the dropper, but instead to fish the downstream rod with a block end feeder and maggot rig, gradually building the swim up and drawing fish from downriver. I regularly use this tactic during the day, and change at dusk if eels become a problem. The upstream rod was tackled up with my standard

Mark Cleaver's first good barbel from the tidal reaches, at 9lb 12oz.

leger rig (see diagram), which was baited with flavoured meat coupled with PVA stringers to ensure a regular supply of feed in close proximity to my bait. The first fish came out to the downstream rod at approximately 5pm – a tiddler of about 6oz caught on maggot. The next fish followed quite quickly, again on the downstream rod using maggot. But things were looking up, as this one weighed 7lb 8oz. The capture of this second fish was followed by a lull in activity, and it was sunset before any further action was forthcoming. I proceeded to take a string of small fish ranging between 2lb and 5lb in weight. All of these fish came to the upstream rod on flavoured meat. By this time darkness had descended and I was getting a little frustrated with the stamp of fish. My next bite, however, was about to make all my efforts on the Trent worthwhile!

It was about 10.30pm, and I was straining to see the beta lights. My attention was drawn momentarily to a small tremble of the downstream rod. Out of the corner of my eye I also detected a small pull on the upstream rod at virtually the same time. Instinctively I struck. My arm was wrenched forward by something resembling a torpedo heading down river. This was obviously a decent fish. I held the rod high

in order to clear the downstream rod, picked up the landing net and stumbled downstream on the treacherous rocks. After an initial twenty-yard surge, the fight began to subside. The fish just did not seem to offer the dogged resistance one normally associates with barbel. I was beginning to think it was one of the common carp that inhabit this stretch of river, as I had caught one from this swim the previous season, weighing about 9lb. After about five minutes the fish grudgingly came to the net. When it first broke surface I was even more convinced it was a carp because of the depth of its body. A brief moment of disappointment ensued, only to be overtaken by panic when I landed the fish and started to lift the net. It was huge, and not a carp but a really enormous great barbel. I held the net in the water for two or three minutes to allow it to recover, and kept repeating to myself 'It's huge, it's absolutely huge!'.

What a time to be on your own! The other two anglers had long gone, and it was fortunate that all the weighing gear was in position. I carefully carried the fish back to my swim, laid it on the unhooking mat and removed the hook. The scales were zeroed with the weigh sling attached, and I placed the fish

Mark's 13lb barbel, a big fish from a big river.

into the sling and checked the reading. Unbelievable! The scales settled at exactly 13lb. It took a few seconds for me to realize the significance of this, namely that it was 11oz bigger than my previous personal best from the lower Severn. My first double from the Trent, and it was a thirteen! I used one of the large retention sacks that I carry to allow the fish to recover while I decided what to do next. My first instinct was to find a witness who could assist with the camera. I rang my fishing mate, but he was down in the pub; then I tried to contact my friends Howard Maddocks and Brian Ridley, who were both out fishing on the River Dove. Not too far away I thought, but they didn't have mobiles.

With no chance of getting any assistance I took the decision to retain the fish until first light, when I could photograph it and return it safely. The rocks are a real hazard in the dark, and it would be difficult to find a suitable place for a photograph without risking damage to the fish. During the intervening period I caught three more barbel weighing 5lb, 2lb 8oz and 5lb 8oz respectively. I couldn't help wondering why such a huge barbel would turn up out of the blue amongst so many small ones. Never mind, I wasn't complaining, particularly as I finished the session with twelve fish in total. More importantly, I had achieved my ambition of catching a double-figure Trent barbel, and what a double! I have caught a number of doubles since, but none has given me the same feeling of achievement as that first one from the Trent.

As a footnote to this experience, I have listened to varying accounts of how tidal conditions have an impact on the quality of fishing. Some anglers are of the opinion that a falling river is productive, others believe the opposite is true. From my personal experience I haven't noticed any significant difference either way.

My Fourteen-Pounder by Steve Withers

The annual 'national fish-in' is one of the highlights on the Barbel Catchers Club calendar and provides the ideal opportunity to visit pastures new, fish rivers you would probably only read about and of course have a few beers and talk barbel with old friends. When the venue of the 2002 fish-in was decided as Collingham on the tidal Trent, I can't say it filled me with any great enthusiasm. From discussions with those who fished the area, and from a few pictures in the weeklies, I had a mental image that left me feeling it was not going to be my kind of event. Certainly it would be a far cry from the more intimate fishing I was used to on my local waters of

the Hampshire Avon and Dorset Stour. This, together with the long drive from Dorset, would have been reason enough to give the day a miss; but the fishing really is only a small part of why you go to a fish-in, and the general cameraderie is always the highlight of these occasions. I convinced myself it would be a shame to miss out on the opportunity to fish a new river.

As it turned out, due to various commitments only two of us from the Wessex region were able to make the trip: Chris Thomson (aka Thommo) and myself. We decided that if we were going to travel so far, then it made sense to make a long weekend of it and travel up on the Friday with the intention of putting a few hours in on the river; we hoped this would give a realistic chance of one of us catching our first Trent fish. Having no idea what to expect on the tidal stretch of such a big river, I had a chat with a couple of the lads who had fished the area before. On their advice we set off armed with more lead than I've ever carried in my life, powerful rods and a pile of bait. The bones of a strategy were at least agreed, albeit without any idea of what to expect. As we were going to be fishing for two days, the plan of attack was to choose a swim, bait it heavily, and try to fish it for the two days in the hope of pulling in some fish. If we managed to catch any barbel from a new river it would be considered a success.

After a five-hour journey from home on the Friday we were booking into our accommodation just after lunch; following a quick pint, we were on the bank at Collingham by mid-afternoon. This was certainly going to be a culture shock compared to the Stour and Avon – just where do you start? Other than the weir pool, which was about the size of a football pitch and had anglers shoulder to shoulder, much of the water appeared featureless, and it was almost impossible to pinpoint any obvious holding areas. A fair number of other BCC members had the same idea about fishing on the Friday, and after a walk and a chat with some of the lads, we decided to slip into a couple of swims between the car park and weir pool. The choice was based upon nothing more than the possibility of the weir pool being an obvious holding point. At least we were not too far away should the fish move out after dark – and probably more importantly, with the amount of tackle and bait we had brought with us, it wasn't very far to walk!

Our intention was to fish until midnight on the Friday in the hope that this would give us the best chance of catching something over the weekend; besides, everyone who knew the area thought that success was much more likely after dark. A few casts to see if there was anything of interest showed about eight feet of steady water with no obvious features other than a sharp drop-off about twenty feet off the bank. The flow was not as powerful as we had anticipated, as the river was running very low and clear due to lack of rain over several weeks; in fact as the tide peaked the flow was reduced to a virtual standstill. We had taken plenty of loose feed consisting of hemp, groats (which form a lovely milky, sticky binder), trout pellets in a mixture of various sizes, broken boilies and method feeder mix to bind the lot together. Out went a load of bait by hand, and we sat back ready to see if anything would happen.

Rigs were standard nylon hook links to 10lb reel line with hair-rigged boilies. A 2oz watch-type sea lead was used to mould a ball of loose feed around similar to the method feeder style. Hook baits were Mainline NRG boilies, the remains of my summer carping sessions and a bait that had also proved to be consistent for barbel.

That evening's fishing was without doubt one of the most bizarre of my angling career. The weir pool upstream of us resembled the Tardis, and seemed to have an endless capacity to take even more anglers: I have never seen so many anglers on a river crammed into such a short length of bank side, including three bivvies complete with Tilly lamps, and as dusk approached a glow in the sky signified the lighting of a large bonfire! To make matters worse, when we had set up, the nearest angler to us was about a hundred yards downstream; but at dusk two other anglers arrived and proceeded to set up camp below us, so we were now surrounded! With everyone using what appeared to be the standard tactics of two rods pointing to the sky with bite alarms, this was

not going to be a quiet night; and so it proved.

People were walking the bank collecting huge lumps of driftwood to keep the fire raging, and showers of sparks would rise high into the air at regular intervals as they were deposited onto the fire. Anglers were still arriving well after dark, stumbling through the undergrowth with head torches and wheelbarrows full of tackle, and disappearing into the weir pool. There was a constant stream of bleeps from bite alarms in all directions, and head torches flashing across the water like something from the film *Dambusters*. This, combined with large rafts of foam the size of mattresses coming down the river, and barges complete with headlights heading up to the lock in the weir pool, created a quite surreal scene.

Amazingly, despite all of this commotion, just into dark my rod flew round and I leaned into what was obviously a good fish. But disaster struck after only a few seconds, and everything went slack as my line parted either on a snag or the gravel shelf. This was really sickening, as we had known from the start that this wasn't going to be an easy venue; I'd possibly blown my only chance of the weekend to catch a Trent barbel. To make matters worse, over the next couple of hours all I had was two snotty bream to round off the evening!

With no further action for either of us, we packed up around midnight and made our way back to the pub where we were staying. We then had to face the final insult of the day in having to trek through the bar laden with all our tackle, accompanied by much amusement and heckling from a bunch of locals enjoying a late-night lock-in. Surely it couldn't get any worse!

Measuring up.

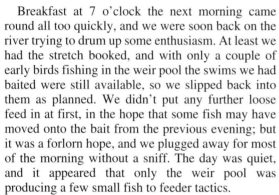

Steve Withers displays his Trent monster of 14lb 11oz.

Back she goes.

Breakfast at 7 o'clock the next morning came round all too quickly, and we were soon back on the river trying to drum up some enthusiasm. At least we had the stretch booked, and with only a couple of early birds fishing in the weir pool the swims we had baited were still available, so we slipped back into them as planned. We didn't put any further loose feed in at first, in the hope that some fish may have moved onto the bait from the previous evening; but it was a forlorn hope, and we plugged away for most of the morning without a sniff. The day was quiet, and it appeared that only the weir pool was producing a few small fish to feeder tactics.

We had agreed to fish until 8.30pm, which would give us an hour into dark and still allow enough time to get back to our rooms for a wash and change, ready to meet up for a beer and a curry. Mid-afternoon came, and the remaining bait was launched into the swim, more with a view to avoiding having to carry it back to the car, rather than with any great expectation of success! As the day wore on I think everyone was beginning to accept that nothing much was going to happen. However, just as dusk was gathering I had the first indication of the day with a sharp pull on the rod, just to prove there *was* life out there. Then about twenty minutes later I had a repeat of the evening before: the rod flew round and I was into a fish that powered off downstream at a great rate of knots. This time I was determined to keep the rod as high as possible in an attempt to avoid any snags and the

gravel shelf. At first I was convinced it was a good fish, then it seemed to wallow around and work its way upstream until eventually I wasn't sure whether it was a game eight-pounder or a real lump. But as it came towards the net it was obviously a decent fish, and looked to be a double. Thommo did the honours with the net, and when we put the torch on it the estimate grew – it was one of those fish that just got bigger every time you looked at it.

Onto the scales, and they bounced around towards the 15lb mark, confirming something very special. Thankfully not everyone had packed up, so those fishing nearby had the opportunity to share the moment and witness a truly magnificent fish. She was 30½in long with a 19½in girth, and a final weight of 14lb 11oz, and was in excellent condition with hardly a scale out of place. An overdose of photos and lots of superlatives from all followed before she was slipped back, let's hope to disappear for a while; a personal best and new BCC river record. And if ever you were going to choreograph the capture of a big fish, then you couldn't write the script better than to catch a BCC river record on such an occasion.

So there you have it, the culmination of hours of meticulous planning, flogging away in all conditions, notching up the blanks, sorting all the problems of location – and finally it all slots into place, and you reap the rewards. Well, not quite – but then again, we all need Lady Luck to shine on us once in a while! Now where's next year's fish-in?

31 The River Wey

by Steve Carden

In retrospect it all seems so very easy now, although it certainly didn't feel that way at the time. 'That time' was mid-November 2002, a mild, wet day with a raging flood about to burst through the banks of the normally sedate River Wey. The water temperature was in the mid-forties, which one might have expected to have been all well and good for the intrepid barbel angler. Sadly, however, this was not quite the case, and a day of intense frustration was drawing to a close. I had been fishing this new stretch of the river since August, and although the fishing had been slow, I was beginning to enjoy some familiarity with it, having winkled out a few fish to 6½lb. Though wait a moment: all good stories have a beginning, so let us start there.

Having spent my early years as a Barbel Catchers Club member travelling to the Hampshire Avon and Dorset Stour with somewhat limited success, I began to seek fishing closer to home. For the previous season this had been provided by Kent's River Medway, and although this had yielded a personal best of 9lb 8oz, the barbel were scarce and very difficult to catch. (This was some three or four years before the Medway shot to the top of the barbel-fishing charts with a succession of record-breaking monsters.) It was a fellow BCC member who, fortunately for me, suggested I try Surrey's intimate River Wey. He pointed me in the direction of a club that controlled various sections on the lower reaches of the river between the town of Woking and its

confluence with 'Old Father Thames' in the stockbroker belt at Weybridge. A couple of the club's stretches were producing bags of fish in the 2–4lb bracket, with fewer but larger examples, including the occasional double, being taken from other areas. At this stage in my nascent barbel-fishing life, this plan of action proved to be ideal, the lower Wey being only an hour's drive from my home on the Sussex coast, with plenty of fish to be caught in reasonably unknown waters.

Interestingly, in 1988 when the first BCC book was published, the venerable Bill Rushmer wrote of the Wey in a chapter about the Thames and its tributaries, and he has kindly allowed me to quote from his piece:

> The Wey is not an easy river to fish, as it suffers from flash floods and is at present experiencing an explosion of mini barbel. On many sections there is a marked increase in the number of barbel being caught, whilst other sections are now producing the odd fish, which in the past were not noted for the species. I believe the long term prospects on the river are excellent as the barbel spread out and mature.

I have quoted Bill's remarks because of their accuracy both then and now – although I do wonder if even the sage-like Bill suspected that some fifteen years later, Titans of over 14lb would be captured. At this time the BCC river record stood at 9lb 1oz, a fish taken by Mick Newland; regrettably I never met Mick, so was never able to learn more of its capture at first hand. My own target was simply to bank as many fish as possible, and this I accordingly did, regularly filling my boots with numerous barbel of medium proportions, mainly in the summer months spanning a couple of years, and culminating in a then very respectable fish of 6lb 15oz.

The most remarkable session during this period occurred on a stiflingly hot afternoon in August 1988. Upon arriving at the river around lunchtime, and discovering that the pitch I coveted had already been claimed, I sulked off to the adjoining stretch; this one ran past a housing estate, and so was free fishing in those days. After passing a few swims I spotted a shoal of chub and a brace of small barbel languidly finning up and down a gravel run. Unfortunately, because it was the school holidays, the river was teeming with human and canine activity some twenty yards downstream on the opposite bank, and further investigation revealed a group of adolescents swinging across the river on a rope. By this time the air temperature was rising towards 80°C and my blood pressure was close to boiling point, so I certainly didn't feel confident of much success.

I hacked my way back through the towering Himalayan balsam to where I'd previously noticed the fish, hope triumphing over experience. I baited the run with hemp and casters, wondering to myself whether the shoal's activity would increase as the bank-side shenanigans decreased, then heaved a bait dropper into the head of the swim around a dozen times (my dropper technique still leaves much to be desired). Finally I cast out my Drennan swimfeeder and size 12 hook, ineptly disguised by a pair of casters. It was by now nearly tea time, I'd been on the venue for two hours, and I was absolutely shattered – but I had barely begun to wipe my sweating brow when the tip of my Terry Eustace Avon rod jerked round. Following a short but furious scrap I netted what I expected would be a bonus barbel of 2lb; I was therefore dumbfounded when ten minutes later one of its brethren glided into my net, quickly followed by fish number three. I took a short breather whilst chatting to a newly arrived friend, and then carried on fishing – and a steady succession of barbel succumbed to my bait; by the time the swim died in early evening I'd landed nine in just two hours. The two largest specimens weighed an identical 3lb 3oz, and incredibly not one of the many chub I'd seen had been tempted to my hook. I fished on until late, hoping to complete a memorable session with a river best, but my stock of good fortune had no doubt been exhausted. Nevertheless it was a delighted angler who drove home, reliving a wonderful catch in the most unlikely of circumstances.

For the start of the 1990 season I elected to fish one of the club's more difficult waters. This was on a section adjacent to one of the Wey's largest weirs, and it was on the banks of that very pool in July that one of the most sensational stories in barbel history unfolded. Older readers will need no reminding of the 'Jason Bailey affair', but for those of more tender years I shall attempt a reprise of those extraordinary events. It began when the *Anglers' Mail* ran a story accompanied by photographs concerning the capture of two fish of around 13lb and 15lb caught by eighteen-year-old Jason, reportedly taken a few days apart.

My own astonishment on reading those reports can only be imagined. There was I, fishing just a couple of hundred yards downstream (and nurturing faint hopes of a nine- or ten-pounder) of where a callow youth was apparently obliterating the British record. If my memory serves me well, a newly constituted committee had just discarded Aylmer Tryon's longstanding record of 14lb 6oz, and Martin Hooper's Avon fish of 13lb 7oz was expected to fill the vacancy. The pictures in the press report were of poor quality, which led to a good deal of scepticism from many experienced observers, most believing the sizes to be nearer to 9lb and 11lb. I was certainly of a similar conviction, and the *Mail* also adopted a decidedly cynical tone in their write-up.

A week later whilst enjoying my usual mid-week sojourn I was accosted by a gangling and somewhat morose teenager whom I immediately recognized as Master Bailey. We exchanged the usual anglers' pleasantries, and when Jason noticed my BCC enamelled badge he quizzed me about joining the club in the belief that membership of such an august body would give his reported captures the credibility they had hitherto been denied. The poor lad was obviously sorely distressed at his perceived treatment by the press and from local anglers. We discussed various details regarding his weighing procedure, during which he informed me that Waymaster agricultural scales (normally used for weighing large sacks of meal and animal feeds) had been the only equipment available to him at that time. Jason lived with his brother and father in a tied cottage on the side of the weir, and his only witness had been his brother, Martin. I'm afraid that I gently suggested to him that he must have misinterpreted the scale reading, and we parted amicably.

A mere seven days after our meeting I was stunned to see Jason's image emblazoned across the front pages, holding a massive-looking barbel of 15lb 12oz. It was reported that two independent witnesses had seen the fish weighed on newly purchased Avon dial scales. For the rest of the year that tiny lock-keeper's cottage became the centre of the barbel-fishing universe, as various angling luminaries descended upon Walsham weir to investigate the legitimacy or otherwise of Jason's claim to fame. Despite lobbying from the highly respected Fred Crouch and Ray Walton, the fish was never accepted as a record by the record fish committee, nor, with almost equal certainty, was it recognized by the majority of barbel specialists or by locals actually fishing the Wey. Strangely, many of the doubters' concerns rested upon the captor, inasmuch as they refused to countenance that such a monster could fall to the rod of an inexperienced youth.

For what it's worth, I believe this to be palpable nonsense. Surely the wonder and magic of fishing lies in the knowledge that *anyone* can better the record, even the proverbial small boy with his bamboo rod and bent pin – and long may it remain so! My difficulty lay not with the angler, but with the river itself. In my view it was quite possible that fish of 11lb or 12lb existed in the system, but – though not wishing to appear arrogant – I also thought it highly unlikely that a barbel way over 15lb would appear out of nowhere, fall a couple of times to the same angler and never be seen again. All of these now largely forgotten events are confined to angling folklore and a few dusty old press cuttings, and unless Jason can provide some new evidence or witnesses, they are likely to remain so.

The impact of all this controversy on my own pursuit was enormous, as my quiet and previously unknown little tributary enjoyed its Warholian fifteen minutes of fame and became unbearably busy, so much so that I transferred my affection to the then-unheard-of River Medway.

As a result of health problems I ventured back to the Wey in 1997; I needed to reduce travelling time, and therefore sought more easily accessible waters. It also helped that my business led to frequent trips into Surrey, which meant I could fish in the evenings after work, rather than enduring the day-long tiring sessions, followed by the long drive home, to which I had become accustomed. I should confess that it also hadn't escaped my attention that double-figure barbel were a far more realistic target than had previously been the case – indeed, the BCC river record had been increased to 10lb 4oz by Alistair Southby in 1993.

As is usual with the Wey, the fishing was never easy, and I duly struggled through the early months of the season before landing a personal river best 8lb 4oz fish in September; a fortnight later I improved on this with a fish of 9lb 11oz. Despite these successes, that first season back was very much a learning process, and I had to wait until the following autumn before I began to enjoy more consistent activity – and even then the ten-pounders that I knew existed in the stretch still eluded me. In fact, I well remember one day in late October bemoaning my luck to another Wey regular with whom I'd become good friends, complaining that everybody and his uncle appeared to have captured a double except me. But within an hour of our

conversation he was photographing a new BCC river best of 10lb 12oz. We were both delighted. And half an hour later I'd returned to his swim asking him to witness a 10lb 2oz fish. By this time I was ecstatic!

With this breakthrough my confidence rose considerably, and throughout the rest of the season I banked barbel between 8lb and 10lb, including another brace of 10lb 12oz and a further BCC best of 11lb 6oz.

Allow me to interrupt my narrative at this point, with some advice regarding BCC river records – and I speak from experience here, as I also hold the record for the Sussex Ouse. The first and most obvious step is to join the Barbel Catchers Club; the second is to then ensure that you are the only member actually fishing your chosen venue. Keep to this useful guideline, and I assure you that greatness can be achieved!

I left my home on the evening of 9 March 1999 with the objective of fishing one of my favourite swims, and hoping for a back-end whopper. My intention was to fish until around 11pm, bait up, settle down as well as I could for a fitful slumber in the car and commence fishing again in the early hours. (I am not a lover of all-night fishing, but will occasionally deploy these means if real life impinges upon my normal bank-side hours.) So it was all the more exasperating that the only other enthusiast on the fishery was ensconced in my desired swim. Cursing at the fate of even the best laid plans, I eventually flopped into a peg in which I had enjoyed some summer sport, but which looked rather unappealing in the wintertime. This swim was selected purely for its proximity to the car park so that with any luck I might hear the other chap depart, allowing me to execute my original plan.

At about 9pm I cast across stream and into a river some twelve inches deeper than usual and still showing a tinge of colour from recent floods. The coated lead bounced a couple of times and settled. I pointed my Northwestern quivertip rod as directly to my bait as possible, and released some braid, causing a small bow to form. Six inches of Fireline was held in the fingers of my rod-holding right hand. Within thirty seconds my hair-rigged sausage was picked up and carried towards the near bank in a very chub-like fashion. I neglected to strike and the bait was dropped.

Undeterred I wound in, checked the bait was still intact, and repeated the process. Exactly the same sequence of events was met with a firm sweep of the rod. A surging run and yards of line taken against the clutch of my Shimano 1000 reel assured me that this was a barbel, and a big one at that. As I clawed back

10lb 12oz, one half of Steve's double-figure brace. . .

. . . and the other half at 10lb 2oz.

some of the line from this initial charge, the fish kited under some near-bank trees twenty feet downstream and snagged itself. It appeared to be either under or over an obstruction, as each time I gained a few inches of line everything went solid. If I eased the pressure the fish won line but was unable to free itself. A spread of alders, sycamores and tangled undergrowth made it impossible for me to get downstream of it. I therefore employed every trick I knew from within the confines of my tight little swim. Following a despairing upward lurch I heard a ghastly splintering sound as the rod parted on the cork butt section – hell! In the words of the late great Spike Milligan, 'So what are we going to do *now*?' I tried without success to force the remaining two sections into the broken butt, but to do so I needed to cut off the butt ring and try again. This I did, leaving me with something resembling a boat rod, and once more I attempted to play the still-tethered fish.

Just as buses always seem to come in pairs, so does trouble, and the rod snapped again, giving a new definition to a three-piece rod. The helpless creature at the end of my braid was now attached only via my reel and two-thirds of butt. Left with only one alternative, I grabbed my landing net and set off in search of my quarry. My torchlight eventually picked it out, wallowing just below the surface in a snarl of tree roots at the bottom of a somewhat steep and inaccessible bank. In the pitch-black night I identified the shape of an obviously good double tethered to a branch barely inches under water. I gingerly felt my way down among brambles and trunks, and forced my spoon net between a knot of branches until it was almost touching the barbel's belly. I heaved mightily, and lifted the net as rapidly as my ebbing strength permitted. A resounding crash and massive swirl resulted in an empty net – I felt mortified – surely I'd blown it. Incredibly, the fish was still bound up in its woody prison.

I somehow managed a precarious foothold a further six inches down the bank, and with my left arm embracing a trunk I again pushed the net in my right hand into the river – and this time I was in luck. Pure adrenalin helped me haul my prize back up the slope, where we both collapsed in an inglorious heap. An hour or so had passed since I'd first hooked the fish, and wishing to avoid distressing it any more than necessary, I proposed to weigh it and return it without photographs.

Having estimated it at approximately 11lb, I was completely awestruck when the scales punched round to register a massive 13lb 8oz. I sincerely could not believe my own eyes, and suspected that my Avons might have been faulty. So I made the fish safe, and set off in search of assistance. Fortunately the aforementioned angler was just packing up, and I recall gabbling to him that either my scales were wildly inaccurate, or I had achieved something very special. I confess that I half expected to be made to look rather foolish (no change there, then!), and tried to compose myself as I lifted the sling onto his Avons. The needle settled in the same spot as my own had done, and confirmed a new personal best and BCC river record, which I fully expected to stand for many years to come. And then came that truly memorable day in November 2002.

My Quality Fourteen-Pounder

When I arrived earlier that day I was brimming with confidence – it would be the first time I'd fished this section in such excellent conditions. Of course, as often happens with a spate river, rubbish was coming down at all levels; nevertheless I felt sure that if I could pin a bait somewhere on the riverbed I could expect a fish or two – they surely had to be active. But by late afternoon I was at my wits' end: however much weight I employed, including back leads, and however close to the bank in slack water I fished, it was impossible to present a bait for more than a few minutes before my line was swamped with detritus.

Eventually my patience gave out and I threw my tackle into the car, my mind turning to thoughts of the long drive home, a glass of red wine and the

This is what a 13lb 8oz barbel can do to a fishing rod!

Steve Garden shows off his BCC river record for the Wey: 14lb 2oz.

Brownie points I would achieve for such an early return (always an important consideration for the family orientated angler). But as I turned into the main road I cursed to myself as I hit a queue of traffic: rush hour! Almost involuntarily I indicated right, and with my brain now in overdrive I set off to the next stretch of river.

This water has a weir where I was 90 per cent sure I could drop a bait into dead water just over its sill; from this vantage point I could also keep an eye on the line of traffic inching its way to the M25. I decided to fish for an hour or so until the traffic thinned. Although this weir pool had rarely produced any fish for me, the stretch itself is one of the most productive on the river, and has yielded a good many quality fish to others in the previous three years.

I gently lowered a hair-rigged HNV bait just to the left of the sill, and as is usual for me, pointed the rod down towards a free-running Arlesey bomb; this was held a foot or so away from a Starpoint hook by an adjuster stop. By holding a loop of my braid mainline between my fingers and thumb, I would be able to feel and interpret most of the goings on down below. As I sat and watched the traffic through the trees for fifteen minutes or so, absolutely nothing occurred: sheer bliss – my line was completely untouched by any of the flotsam that had been plaguing me earlier in the day, and my bait was at last visible to any passing fish; and I mean 'passing',

because nothing appeared to be resident. Undeterred I reeled in, dropped half-a-dozen baits into the foam, and went for a wander. Within ten minutes I returned for a final cast, as the traffic was beginning to dissipate.

Within seconds of my rig settling I felt an almost imperceptible pluck on the line. However, none of the line moved through my fingers, and I therefore suspected that a leaf or twig had brushed against it. A further quarter of an hour passed before I decided enough was enough, and wound in. But as I swung my tackle to hand, I was surprised to see no bait where once a bait had been. Had I missed an opportunity? Of course, another cast was required and duly executed. Within seconds I experienced an identical pluck, followed by a steady pull of line through my fingers. I struck, and an obviously decent fish ploughed off into the main current. After a dogged and largely unspectacular fight (often the case, I find, with larger specimens) I eased a very fat barbel into the net. A friend had mentioned to me that a big twelve had been caught a number of times from this area in the summer months, and I suspected I might have that beast in my landing net. You can therefore imagine my astonishment when the scales revealed a weight of 14lb 2oz, a new personal best and BCC river record.

Really remarkably easy, this fishing thing, isn't it?

32 The River Wharfe

by Mick Wood

In 1987 I made the decision to begin barbel angling in Yorkshire for the first time. Apart from a handful of sessions on the Warwickshire Avon and Warwickshire Stour, all of my attempts for barbel had been on the middle reaches of the River Severn; but now my home county rivers were calling. I had moved back to Yorkshire in 1981, and during the intervening years had spent the summers fishing for tench. I now felt that the time had come for a change – but where would I start? Yorkshire is blessed with six major barbel rivers where the species is indigenous, and with well in excess of 100 miles of fishing to choose from, a little thought was required.

The Yorkshire Derwent I dismissed immediately, as the barbel populations are so low that I thought it prudent to build up my experience elsewhere. The Yorkshire Ouse I also put on hold. The Ouse is an unlikely-looking barbel river, being largely deep and slow with few recognizable barbel swims; so the Ouse could wait, too. The Nidd had a reputation, unfairly in hindsight, for producing large catches of small fish. The Ure offered a wide variety of barbel fishing scenarios, from the breathtakingly beautiful upper reaches of Wensleydale to the more stately depths downstream of Boroughbridge; but it was also the furthest river from my home. The Swale had a lot to offer, apart from one vital ingredient: that of surprise. Virtually every Yorkshire barbel angler was on the river, and I simply did not fancy following in the boot prints of everyone else.

This left the River Wharfe. In common with the Nidd, the Wharfe had a reputation for producing large catches of small barbel – but it had at least produced a fish of exactly 10lb way back in 1959. I surmised, correctly, that this comparative lack of double-figure fish would cause a lot of barbel specialists to avoid the river, and therefore give me the chance, in big fish terms, to do a bit of pioneering. The more I thought about it, the more I liked the idea, and so the Wharfe it would be.

The Wharfe rises from sources over 2,000ft (600m) above sea level, with the upland streams of Wharfedale being joined by those of Langstrothdale and Ammerdale. The fells of the Yorkshire dales are largely peat-covered limestone, and in days gone by this peat layer would soak up the rain like a sponge until saturated, at which point the surplus rainwater would run off into feeder streams. The main river, when compared to the present day, would rise and fall slowly. However, the powers that be decided that Upper Wharfedale would benefit from 'gripping': this is when irrigation channels are cut in a herring-bone pattern in the peat, to reduce the water-holding capacity of the fells and accelerate run off. This immediately caused the present-day situation, where the Wharfe rises and falls faster than any other river I have ever fished, a state of affairs that is exacerbated by the extensive pot-hole systems that exist beneath the dales. It is not uncommon for the Wharfe to rise twelve feet in six hours, level off, and then drop four feet by the time you come to pack up! 'The quicker it comes in, the quicker it goes out' would be an apt saying when applied to the Wharfe. Awareness of how and why the river behaves as it does during heavy rainfall is of obvious importance to the barbel angler.

The Wharfe exits the Yorkshire Dales at Bolton Abbey, its middle reaches flowing through the towns of Ilkley and Otley, but it is not until we reach the weir at Harewood that it becomes of interest to the barbel angler. Barbel are present from this point all the way down to the river's confluence with the Ouse at Cawood. The tidal reaches downstream of Tadcaster do have pockets of barbel, most notably at Ulleskelf, and big fish in excess of 10lb have been caught in recent years. For all this promise the tidal

The River Wharfe.

reaches are uninspiring in appearance, and receive only limited attention from barbel anglers: almost certainly a mistake. It is between Harewood and Tadcaster on the non-tidal reaches where the majority of barbel anglers concentrate their efforts – and with good reason, for this is one of the most prolific stretches of barbel river in the country, with the village of Boston Spa being at the epicentre. Boston Spa was where I would make my start.

The river here is full of character, with long, shallow, willow-lined straights punctuated with deep, mysterious bends. Even when low and clear the Wharfe displays a peaty hue that betrays its origin in the Dales; this amber coloration makes it difficult, though by no means impossible, to employ stalking tactics. Many barbel rivers are difficult to read, in that what appear to be perfect barbel swims often contain nothing more than red herrings. This is not the case, however, on the Wharfe, where if a swim looks good, then it usually *is* good. Virtually any feature will hold barbel: overhanging willows, dense beds of streamer weed, subtle and not-so-subtle changes in depth and angle of flow, the entry of side streams and shallow stretches of broken water are all worth a look.

My first approach was to use the method that had seen many barbel caught on my regular trips to the Severn, namely the basic leger rig that still serves me well to this day. This allows the quick change from swimfeeder to bomb (or a change in size or weight of either) without having to break the tackle down. More often than not I would fish with a swimfeeder filled with a mixture of casters and hemp, with four casters on a size 12 hook. Nothing could be simpler, and nothing needed to be more complicated. This method accounted for some large multiple catches, with my biggest fish during that first season weighing 7lb 12oz.

The following season I did very little in the way of experimentation, and continued to catch numbers of fish. The most significant development came with my first attempts to catch a Yorkshire barbel in winter, something that was generally considered to be a waste of time. In January 1988 I caught three small barbel on a low clear river, and a week later caught my first big winter barbel on the same caster/hemp/feeder tactics. It weighed 9lb 10oz, one of the biggest barbel ever caught from the Wharfe at that time, and a really special fish for January. The capture of that barbel encouraged me to persevere

8lb plus of Wharfe barbel.

Mick with a fine winter fish of 9lb 2oz.

with winter fishing. The process helped me to develop my floodwater techniques, which would become invaluable in the ensuing seasons. I experimented with flavoured meats, using garlic sausage in preference to plain luncheon meat, then developed the idea of using a variety of flavours on meat, and extended this theme by cooking my hemp seed in a variety of spices.

The following season I started to look at new stretches of the Wharfe that were under far less pressure than the Boston Spa stretch, and whilst the caster and hemp approach still worked, the method was far from selective. The Wharfe has huge populations of other species present, particularly chub and, in those days, dace and eels. I started to use sweetcorn on a regular basis, but early results were poor. Barbel can be notoriously slow to wean on to new baits, and it says everything about the lack of barbel-angling activity on my new stretch that it took six weeks and twenty-four large cans of corn to produce my first barbel on the bait. It then outfished casters and meat, and, more importantly, the other species rarely picked it up on the strong tackle required for barbel angling. This situation has not changed in the ensuing years, and corn is still the number one bait for summer barbel fishing on the Wharfe.

During the 1990s I spread my wings further afield, catching barbel from several rivers but always concentrating on the Wharfe. I adopted a variety of methods, catching barbel by feeder fishing, trundling, float fishing, upstreaming and stalking; and slowly but surely it became apparent that the average size of Wharfe barbel was on the increase. During the early years the capture of two or three barbel in excess of 7lb during a season would be a good result; then a year after joining the Catchers I caught a club record for the Wharfe of 8lb 9oz, a record that would very nearly see out the decade.

Throughout the second half of the 1990s, fish of 7lb plus were becoming quite numerous, and we were catching 'eights' every season. Then in the summer of 1998 our fishing was blown apart: we heard that a barbel of over 10lb had been caught several miles upstream of our chosen venues, and the source of this information was very reliable. Myself and my long-standing angling companion Iain Wood had spent several years pioneering a comparatively little-fished stretch of the Wharfe with reasonable success, but a couple of 'scraper

eights' were our best fish, and my BCC river record had not really been threatened. Then early one summer morning Jon Wolfe and myself walked along the banks of the Wharfe to witness and photograph a fish for Iain. It weighed 11lb 4oz! In the context of what had been caught previously, this was, in my opinion, the most extraordinary barbel ever caught in Yorkshire. Iain's fish opened the floodgates, and that same season three of my friends also caught 'doubles', including a new river record at 11lb 12oz to Leeds angler Steve Reed.

My Specimen Barbel

It was about this time that I had started to use stalking tactics whenever conditions allowed. I had returned to a fairly shallow section of the river where observation of barbel and their feeding habits was quite possible, which in turn meant that selectivity was reasonably practical. The large numbers of barbel in the Wharfe meant that fishing blind was like fishing for the proverbial needle in a haystack, but by watching them at close quarters, I was able to observe that they were creatures of habit, and that certain fish would always enter the baited area on the same line. By baiting more than one area of my swim it was at times possible to separate the largest fish. Always baiting with hemp or corn, it would rarely take more than a few minutes for the first

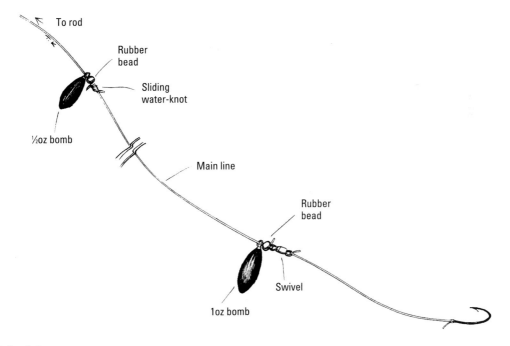

Back-lead rig.

Observing. . .

. . . playing. . .

. . . netting. . .

. . . and displaying. Stalking tactics account for this 8lb 1oz barbel.

barbel to appear and subsequently feed on my free offerings. The number of barbel I caught exceeding 7lb increased dramatically, but still a really big fish eluded me. On one particular occasion I was certain that a fish that looked over 10lb would make a mistake as it avidly munched its way through my swim. But then quite suddenly it turned and departed at speed, my rod tip briefly following it: it had picked up my line on its pectoral fin. A hard lesson had been learned and a chance had gone begging, but it meant that a new weapon would be added to my armoury, namely a back lead.

Where circumstances allow it, the use of a back lead can dramatically increase the chances of fooling a wily old barbel into taking the hook bait. My observations over a number of years have convinced me beyond any doubt that next to bank-side disturbance, the thing most likely to spook a barbel is the line from where it enters the water down to the end rig. There are several ways to avoid this, the simplest of which is to employ a three-foot hook

length. Another method, where the nature of the bank allows, is to push your rod tip down to the riverbed. I like to use a permanently rigged back lead to pin down the line immediately above the end rig.

When rigging up a back lead it is important that it is lighter than the lead or feeder of the end-rig, as in the diagram, so that it flies out in a straight line when casting. The back lead is stopped by a water knot and bead so that it is adjustable and will slide off in the event of a breakage, thus avoiding the possibility of a fish being tethered. Once the rig has been cast into place, tighten up gently so that the back lead is not lifted off the bottom. This rig also comes into play when floating debris is fouling the line.

One early August day I found myself in a quandary. Fishing directly under the rod tip in three feet of water I had perhaps two dozen barbel in front of me. The majority were in the 3lb to 6lb bracket, but two of them looked a decent size. They simply would not be separated, and so I decided to fish and see what happened. I caught a good number of the smaller barbel, which then dispersed, leaving the two biggest fish alone. These I caught on consecutive casts, and both were over 7lb. This was interesting. Many barbel experts believe that barbel do not shoal in the true sense of the word, in the way that roach and bream do. What happens is that two or more groups, which can vary greatly in number, congregate in a specific area due to the favourable conditions of the swim; this is why certain individuals or small groups of barbel (but rarely all the fish) will leave the swim and subsequently rejoin it. This is not the behaviour of a true shoal fish, and observation of this occurrence was soon to prove decisive.

I had been tipped off about a group of barbel in a swim that I had never previously given a second glance. I decided to take a look, and as it was only two feet deep I decided to employ stalker tactics. I threw in a few handfuls of hemp, and tackled up my basic leger rig with 8lb line through to a size 10 hook. After feeding the swim a couple of times I noticed two really big fish amongst their lesser brethren. All were feeding in a single group, and I soon caught a few barbel of moderate size. Within

two hours all the smaller fish had dispersed, and only four remained; two of these looked big, whilst the other two looked really big. The only problem was that they had dropped downstream and were holding position a little further out than before. There was an annoying amount of dead weed fouling the line, so I set up a back lead to counter this problem – and the trap was set.

Soon after casting out, the barbel returned and the two biggest were closest to my sweetcorn hookbait. After what seemed like an eternity the rod flew round, and immediately I was absolutely convinced that I was connected to a rare Wharfe 'double'; and so it proved. The fish was my 1,111th barbel from the Wharfe and weighed 10lb 7oz, the culmination of thirteen years of effort. I punched the air in triumph, and could not begin to describe the elation I felt. All those years and all those fish! By comparing photography I discovered that this fish was one of a pair of double-figure barbel that had resided several miles upstream, its sister weighing over 11lb. I could not help but wonder if we were destined to meet.

During September the autumn rains arrived causing a twelve-feet flood. I managed to catch this flood as it topped and turned, catching seven barbel

Wharfe barbel number 1,111 for Mick, his first double at 10lb 7oz.

This fish of 11lb 6oz set a new BCC Wharfe record at the time of capture.

on flavoured meat, the biggest 9lb 2oz. A week later the conditions were repeated, and Rob Stoker and myself found the Wharfe in perfect condition: eight feet up and dropping, on a pleasantly warm day. After that previous floodwater session I was full of confidence as I placed a pint of hemp and finely chopped meat behind an upstream willow by means of a bait dropper. My hook bait was three 'Meaty Fishbites' on a size 6 hook that I cast just through the crease over my feed. My confidence at first proved unfounded, there being no response as I worked my hook bait down the swim. After a few hours I cast to the downstream willow to a point where, despite countless attempts over the years, I had not tempted a single bite. Ten minutes after casting I found myself in a furious tug of war with an extremely angry adversary. Everything held, and the fish was soon mine. Even as I drew her across the net cord I could see she was the ten pounder's partner because she had only three barbules. Rob did the honours

with the camera and scales: 11lb 6oz and a new Barbel Catchers' river record. Amazingly, four hours after returning her I caught the fish again from the upstream willow. The only other angler I know who has caught the same 'double' twice on the same day is Jill Orme, who achieved the feat on the lower Severn – which is quite coincidental, as Jill built the rod that I was using!

As we go boldly into the new millennium, the River Wharfe continues to progress as a specimen barbel river. At the end of the 2002–03 season my tally of 116 Wharfe barbel included thirty-five fish between 7lb and 9lb 7oz, an undreamed-of proportion of above-average-size specimens when compared to my early days on the river. During that season Steve Reed increased his river record to 11lb 15oz, and without doubt the Wharfe now sits proudly alongside the Swale and the Yorkshire Derwent as a premier barbel river.

33 The River Wye

by Steve Kimpton

The River Wye begins life in mid-Wales some 2000ft up on the slopes of the Plynlimon Mountains, and only a few miles from where the River Severn rises. It travels 150 miles through several towns, including Rhayader, Builth Wells, Hay-on-Wye and Hereford before joining the Severn estuary just south of Chepstow. The Wye is a spate river and can rise and fall quickly. It is a powerful river in times of flood, and each year sees new fish-holding swims created and old ones destroyed.

In places the river is up to sixty yards wide. It can be only a few inches deep and running over gravel in one swim, and then twelve feet deep and rocky in the next. It has deep holes, gravel beds, gullies, smooth glides and snags galore created by fallen trees. Some stretches are fast flowing, and others can be deep and slow. There are areas of streamer weed, sharp bends and rock ledges. It is a river that has everything a barbel angler could wish for, and the natural beauty of the Wye valley and its unspoilt scenery really has to be seen to be believed; the saying, 'God's own country' is not an understatement, and it is a delight to fish for barbel in such beautiful surroundings.

Wye barbel are not indigenous to the river, and are rumoured to have been illegally stocked or to have originated from the nearby River Lugg. Barbel from the Severn were first introduced into the Lugg in the early 1960s, and there were reports in the early 1970s of barbel of up to 8lb being caught from the Lugg. Eventually they made their way down the Lugg to the confluence with the Wye, and it is from

here that the first double of 10lb 6oz was caught in about 1976. The landmark in the history of the Wye barbel fishing was the time from the mid-1970s, when barbel began to appear in the main river. Initially they spread only a short way downstream, but their spread upstream, when it came, was far more prolific. Spawning was observed near Hay-on-Wye in the spring of 1982, and by 1989 they were as far upstream as Builth Wells; the major upstream population seemed to settle around Bredwardine. The greatest number of fish, however, continued to exist within a few miles of Hereford, with large numbers at Fownhope and Belmont. By 1990 barbel were found throughout the Wye from above Builth Wells, downstream to Tinteon on the tidal section. The Wye has a long history of being one of the top game rivers in the country, but with a lot of restricted access to coarse anglers. With the decline of salmon on the Wye and the subsequent loss of revenue, riparian owners are now continually opening their waters for coarse fishing. This is good news for general coarse anglers as well as for barbel anglers.

When I first began fishing the Wye for barbel I used an 11½ ft, 1¼lb TC rod, but I soon realized that I was a bit under-gunned. I was fishing a snag swim when I hooked into a powerful fish that made a run for a sunken tree. I tried to put pressure on and stop the barbel before it got into its refuge, but it gave me no chance: before it even got into the snag the rod was bent to its maximum, and the 8lb line snapped like cotton. There was no problem with the line, as it was brand new, and I inspected it afterwards and found nothing wrong with it. Please don't underestimate the power of Wye barbel: they are in immaculate condition and fight like tigers.

Since then I have stepped up my tackle for Wye barbel, and I now use two different rods. My first choice is a 12ft, 1½lb test curve North Western for normal river conditions, a very forgiving rod that will bend from tip to butt, and a pleasure to hold all day. My other choice is a 12ft 1¾lb test curve Fox rod, that I use for heavy floods or snag fishing. I use fixed spool reels loaded with either 10lb or 12lb 'Pro-gold' mainline, depending upon river

Steve Kimpton with a big Wye barbel of 10lb 6oz.

conditions; I have total faith in this line, as it has never let me down. I have also been experimenting recently with 'Pro Clear' line and have used the 12lb in summer conditions when the water is low and clear, and I am convinced that I get more bites when using this line than I do when using a coloured line. The only problem I have experienced is that it tends to 'pigtail' if you're not careful when tying knots, even when the knot is wet before pulling tight. The knots I use are five-turn grinner knots.

Hooks are T-6 Raptors made by ESP, the size depending on the bait I am using. I also use Drennan Super Specialists in the smaller sizes. Hook links are ESP fluorocarbon Ghost 10lb in clear conditions, or a link of the mainline in more coloured water conditions.

On the stretch of the Wye that I fish most regularly my hook baits have been mostly meat based: bacon grill in all its different guises, using large, ragged chunks as big as golf balls on a size 2 hook, down to tiny pieces on a size 14 hook. I have used different flavoured and coloured meats with some success, but still suffer quite a few blank sessions.

A couple of seasons ago I had an 11lb 8oz personal river best on meatballs, which have been

another good bait for me on the Wye. They have accounted for numerous doubles over the last few years, not only for me but for my angling mates, too. They will still catch barbel now, although I think that the barbel where I fish have definitely become wise to them, as it's not only my catches that have dwindled: other anglers who are using them have also struggled.

Over the last few seasons I have been thinking quite a lot about baits for the Wye, as my catch rate was gradually decreasing, with fewer barbel in a session, and a lot more blanks than in previous seasons. I was sure that the barbel were still there and hadn't moved, as they showed themselves by flashing, and sometimes I saw the odd one rolling. I attributed my increasing lack of success to the baits I was using. I have tried other baits, all the usual ones of maggots, corn, paste and boilies, and have had some success on them all, but have always gone back to meat – a confidence thing, probably, as it doesn't feel quite right without meat on the hook. However, with diminishing returns when using meat I had to do something about it, and make things happen; it was no good just sitting there and going through the same old routines, I had to make changes.

*A pristine Wye fish for
Steve.*

The Wye in flood.

I needed a different bait that was not meat-based, bait that the barbel would take with confidence, and that would not spook them. It needed to be cheap, easy to obtain, and capable of being used as an attractor as well as on the hook. Finally, I wanted bait that was adaptable to different river conditions, and that was not being used by many other anglers on the river. I thought long and hard, and decided that trout pellet was the answer.

I have experimented with pellets for a couple of seasons now, mainly using them to get the barbel feeding in my swim. I have found them to be very flexible for use as an attractor. If you want to use them hard, they can be administered straight out of the bag; if you want them soft, they can be soaked until they become a mush; and they can be used anywhere in between by simply adding more or less water until you achieve the required consistency. They will take on a flavour additive if needed: I have used both hemp oil and CSL with good results. As a hook bait they are available in different sizes, and they can be used as single baits or in multiples, banded to the hook or on a hair. Pellets are also easy to break down and make into a paste by scalding with hot water. They store well, and they last for ages if kept dry.

Anyone who fishes the Wye in summer conditions cannot fail to notice the millions of minnows that abound in the river; you only have to throw a handful of bait into the margins and watch the result. Many anglers bait a swim with particles and fish all day over the top of it, thinking that their bed of bait is still there, when in reality it has been eaten by the minnows. With this in mind, in the swims that I will be fishing regularly I bait very frequently. A bait dropper is not the answer, as the Wye is a big, wide river and in some swims I fish the far bank; it has to be the feeder, and I use the open-ended type with a combination of soaked pellets flavoured with CSL Before commencing fishing I add some pellets straight out of the bag, and mix them in to form a stiff mix. The idea is that the broken down, soaked pellets will be picked up by the current and create a scent trail, drawing fish onto the harder pellets added to the mix just before fishing. Hook bait is a 6mm slicker pellet banded to a size 10 hook. My hook link is fluorocarbon, with 12lb Pro Clear mainline.

My first visit to the Wye using the pellet feeder was in July 2002, and the river looked to be about four inches up, but very clear. I had a friend with me, and we fished adjoining swims only a few yards apart. He fished with meat, and I fished the pellet feeder with pellet on the hook, and during the day I caught seven barbel to 9lb, whilst my friend blanked

on meat. My confidence using the pellet feeder method grew a little, to say the least.

It was mid-August before I could get back to the Wye again; I had a few days off work, and so I booked into the Red Lion at Bredwardine. The river conditions didn't look too good, lower than I had seen them before, and very clear. I decided to try the pellet feeder again, an open-ended feeder with a stiff mix as used in July, with banded pellet on the hook. I was continually casting a baited feeder every ten minutes to ensure some bait was in the swim at all times; in this manner, if barbel arrived in the swim, an attractive bed of bait would always be present in spite of the minnows. At first I was concerned that the feeder going in so often might spook the barbel, but as it happened I needn't have worried, as my results showed: the session produced seven barbel, including three over 8lb. The method had worked again, and I was well pleased.

The next day was a Tuesday and I decided to fish a different swim, again using the pellet feeder. During the day six barbel came to the net, including one of 9lb 1oz, and a fin-perfect 9lb 12oz specimen. I couldn't stop smiling!

I couldn't wait to get back on the river the next day. Wednesday arrived, and again I tried a different swim. In the morning I had a 7lb 4oz and an 8lb 1oz before deciding to move to a swim about fifty yards upstream where it was a little deeper, with a few snags littering the riverbed. I was just settling into the swim when the bailiff arrived. We chatted about the river conditions, and I asked him what fish had been coming out recently. He told me that two thirteen-pounders had been caught recently, one at 13lb 2oz and the other at 13lb 9oz. With the Wye record coming from this same stretch in November 2000 (14lb 9oz, caught by Tim Joyce) it just goes to show the potential the Wye has for big barbel. An hour after the bailiff had gone I had a barbel around 6lb, then nothing for the next three hours. During this quiet period I kept the feeder going in every ten minutes. Around teatime I had a firm pull on my finger (I almost always touch leger), and after two strong runs and a steady plodding fight, a fin-perfect 10lb 9oz barbel came to the net. After weighing, resting and releasing, she swam off strongly.

More mix in the feeder and another banded pellet on the hook, but this time I decided not to re-cast every ten minutes; I left the feeder in, thinking I had put a fair bit of bait in during the quiet period, and if a few fish had moved into my swim I didn't want to disturb them. This decision paid off, as another solid pull on my finger resulted in another double of 10lb 6oz. I rested her, then returned her to the water, and she swam off strongly. Two doubles in two casts; I was elated: fantastic, a superb result. For me, this was barbel fishing at its very best. I fished on, and had an 8lb 2oz just into dark.

On Thursday morning I was back in the doubles swim: I had to have another go. I sat there thinking what else the swim might produce; in fact I could have sat all day without a bite, as I was still on a high from the day before. Nevertheless I caught steadily during the day, taking six barbel to 9lb 6oz. I travelled back for two sessions in September, the river conditions being low and clear on both occasions. I caught nine more barbel, including a very long, empty fish of 10lb 11oz, again on the pellet feeder.

In conclusion, I think that the pellet feeder method evolved over a couple of seasons, as I was trying to overcome the differing problems that I was facing. It has been a success in the low clear conditions of summer, and I am sure it will be just as effective in the higher water conditions of the autumn and winter months. I must admit the outcome has been very satisfying so far. If, like me, you find your usual methods, tactics and bait not working for you, and doubts begin to set in, get your thinking cap on, try something different, and maybe surprise yourself.

Fellow Catchers member Howard Maddocks has an entirely different approach to catching Wye barbel. Here is his account of how he caught the present Barbel Catchers' River Wye record fish.

What a Cracker! By Howard Maddocks

Every year I have a full week's fishing in the company of fifteen other like-minded anglers. Twenty years or so ago we always visited the Royalty Fishery in Christchurch, Dorset, but after thirteen successive years we decided it was time for a change. The fishing on the Royalty was becoming more difficult, with diminishing catches due to increasing angling pressure, and we all thought a change might be as good as a rest. In 1995 a couple of us had been researching for a new spot for our annual fishing week, and we discovered the beautiful Wye valley with its lovely river and barbel fishing aplenty. We decided to make the Wye our new venue.

In 1998 whilst on our now annual trip to the River Wye I caught my personal best barbel from the river. On Wednesday 28 August the weather was hot and sunny as I travelled down the lane through a

Another double for Steve – 10lb 13oz.

The River Wye, full of character.

farmyard towards the fishery. I was met by a low, clear River Wye: not the best conditions for barbel fishing. I unloaded my gear whilst pondering on the best tactic to use for the day's fishing ahead. I decided my best bet would be to rove from swim to swim, covering as many miles as possible.

I selected meatballs as my bait for the day, and I would need to take plenty with me if I was going to travel miles along the riverbank. Needing to travel as light as possible, I took only my 12ft Shimano barbel rod, a large landing net, a Shimano 4000 Spirex reel loaded with 8lb Maxima line, one SSG shot pinched on a piece of silicone tubing and a size 4 star-point hook. I needed this light end rig to allow me to inch the bait along the margins. In faster swims I usually use two SSG shots. My preferred method is free-lining using no shot at all. I like to fish as light as possible, with my finger hooked around the line so I can feel the slightest pick-up; hopefully I will have hooked the barbel before it has time to eject the bait. Touch legering is my elected method of fishing. I have caught lots of barbel using this method; it has saved many a blank day.

I wandered down the river, observing its characteristics, and made my way to a spot that I have named the 'Tree Root Swim'. This swim is eight feet deep at normal summer level, and the river travels through it at a steady walking pace, which is a good indication of a barbel-holding swim. It is a popular spot, and is subject to considerable angling pressure. It has fifteen-feet high banks, and it is very tricky trying to lower oneself down to the water's edge, especially if it has rained all day and the bank is very wet. In such conditions my view is, forget it: no fish is worth losing your life for. I would not even contemplate night fishing in the swim in these conditions, it's much too risky.

When I arrived I was amazed to find no one else in the swim; I often have to return some time later in the day when the swim has been vacated. Stealthily I began to crawl down the steep riverbank whilst gripping the rod in my hand, and at the water's edge lowered a half piece of meatball into the swim. I watched the line until the bait settled on the bottom of the riverbed, then tightened it slightly until it bowed; I watched it lifting up and down, indicating the barbel were actively feeding in the swim. I knew that striking too soon could foul hook a fish (patience is of the utmost importance), and the shoal could also be spooked. I knew I must wait until the rod top pulled round.

At that precise moment that was exactly what happened, and I was into a barbel. I kept a very tight line with a full bend in the rod to stop the fish heading for the tree roots and becoming snagged. It fought energetically for at least five minutes before I could net it: a lovely five-pounder. It was good to know the fish were feeding that day; catching the five-pounder could have spooked the rest of the shoal. Many roving barbel anglers, having caught a fish from that particular swim, would have moved on after the disturbance created by the fish, but I always try another cast, you just never know – and so it proved that day.

I lowered another piece of meatball into the swim and tightened the line as before. The rod pulled round immediately, and I was now playing another barbel, which felt a much bigger fish. It was hugging the bottom and moving doggedly upriver. Following a spirited fight, a very large barbel indeed graced my landing net. As I lifted the net I realized that it was a double-figure fish. I quickly unhooked it in the water, and held it in the landing net, allowing it to recover. I staked the landing net securely to the bank with two bank sticks, then made my way miles upriver, through woods and over stiles, to inform my mates of my big catch. Having eventually located them and recounted my catch to them, we all made the fifteen-minute trek back to the Tree Root Swim, where my fish was still resting safely in the landing net.

Expectantly my mates all crowded at the top of the bank for a glimpse of the fish. First we soaked the weigh sling and zeroed the scales, then I carried the barbel carefully up the steep bank and placed it on the wet sling. We all watched the scales go round and stop at just over 12lb: 'What a cracker!', I thought to myself. We all took some photographs as quickly as possible in the afternoon sunshine; daytime shots make clearer photographs for the album. Then, conscious of the barbel's welfare, I returned the fish to the landing net and carried it down to the water's edge where I placed it gently in the flow. It soon showed signs of recovery and was eager to swim away. We all stood watching whilst it swam back into the depths; then slowly we dispersed to continue our fishing.

I remembered my first impression that morning, which had been that the likelihood of catching any barbel was minimal due to the gin-clear river conditions. But I was proved wrong, and had caught a five- and a twelve-pounder, which goes to show you don't always need textbook conditions to catch good barbel.

34 The Future of Barbel Fishing

by Bob Singleton

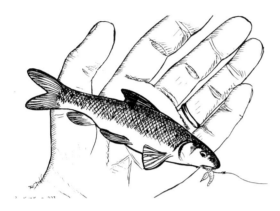

The first Barbel Catchers' book, entitled *Barbel*, benefited from an excellent final chapter written by Pete Tillotson and headed 'The Future of Barbel'. Pete was BCC Chairman at the time, and has since become an honorary life member in recognition of his services to the club.

Upon being invited to contribute a similar chapter for this, our second book, I knew that I had a tough act to follow. In theory the task should have been much easier than it was fifteen years ago. When Pete wrote his chapter, specialist barbel fishing was practised by a relatively small percentage of anglers, and the BCC together with the Association of Barbel Enthusiasts were the only two specialist barbel clubs in existence. However, developments during those intervening years have been quite staggering, and there is no doubt that barbel fishing is currently one of the fastest growing areas of the coarse fishing scene. One thing that I can confidently predict is that this trend will continue into the foreseeable future, and this undoubtedly has implications, potentially good and not so good, for all barbel anglers. Before discussing those implications I feel it would be useful to review a few of Pete's predictions of fifteen years ago; and we will see that in these he was extremely perceptive.

First, regarding barbel growth rates, Pete felt that the River Trent had the potential to once again become a prime barbel river: how true that has proved to be, particularly over the last four or five years. Many people now believe that the Trent holds more double-figure barbel than any other river in the country.

Second, Pete believed that the River Wye, although a rank outsider to produce the next record, would definitely produce some very large barbel in the future. Once again this prediction has proved accurate. (It is interesting to reflect that in the BCC's first book the rivers Wye and Ribble were covered in the chapter entitled 'Minor Rivers'; both have subsequently produced barbel of 14lb plus.)

Third, Pete felt at the time that although those perennial favourites the Hampshire Avon and the Dorset Stour were the prime candidates to produce the next record (both were regularly producing specimen barbel), the Great Ouse was a good outside bet. We could all have benefited from a few quid on that one!

Finally, he believed that the British barbel record was likely to remain an elusive target. The record at that time was either Joe Day's 13lb 12oz Hampshire Avon fish (according to the British Record Fish Committee list) or Aylmer Tryon's 14lb 6oz fish, also from the Hampshire Avon (recognized by the National Association of Specialist Anglers). Most 'thinking' barbel anglers accepted the latter fish as the record, and what a tremendous fish it was. It had remained virtually unchallenged for over fifty years, and most barbel anglers agreed that it was likely to remain the target for many years to come. No one could have foreseen how dramatically barbel growth rates would accelerate as a result of global warming (and hence milder, wetter winters), together with a significant increase in the number of people barbel fishing (and thus the amount of food going into the rivers). Fifteen years ago no one would ever have predicted that by the turn of the century the British record barbel would be a fish approaching 20lb in weight. Who knows, by the time you read this, the first official 20lb British rod-caught barbel may have been recorded. . .

When considering the future for barbel fishing, I feel that we have to accept yet another parallel with carp fishing: it is inevitable that commercialism in its various forms will have a significant affect on the barbel angler. With an ever-increasing demand for

A BCC river record from the Thames for Steve Smith at 12lb 3oz.

Trevor King with his new Holybrook record.

quality barbel fishing the most select waters will undoubtedly become available only to those willing to pay the asking price. This is application of the simple law of supply and demand, and it is already beginning to happen across the length and breadth of the country. Many of the prime stretches of barbel fishing on our prominent barbel rivers are no longer available to the day-ticket angler, and I believe that the process will accelerate rapidly over the next few years. Even on waters where day-ticket fishing continues to be available, prices will increase

significantly. This situation is exacerbated by the fact that over the last ten years there has been a gradual drift of match anglers from the rivers to the artificial carp ponds. This has resulted in a considerable loss in membership (and thus revenue) for the major angling organizations, many of which can no longer afford to retain all their waters. Often when prime stretches of river angling are placed on the market they become syndicate waters, and the sign that proclaims 'PRIVATE FISHING – NO DAY TICKETS' is being seen much more regularly.

Bob Singleton with a good Swale barbel from a day ticket venue.

Whether you consider this development as a good or a bad thing depends entirely upon your point of view. Many people believe that syndicate fishing discourages newcomers to the sport and therefore threatens the very future of angling itself. The opposite view is that syndicate fishing, while undoubtedly restrictive, usually eliminates the problems of the mindless few who spoil things for the majority. Anglers who are prepared to pay syndicate fees are generally speaking environmentally aware, and are much more likely to handle fish correctly and take their litter home. This argument of course applies to any sport (you won't see golfers playing in trainers and jeans on a private golf course) but it is one that we are all going to have to come to terms with sooner or later. One way or another, the cost of 'quality' barbel fishing will increase, and if you want the very best you will have to pay accordingly.

On a more upbeat note we are told that the pattern of milder, wetter winters is set to continue, and that in turn can only mean continued acceleration in barbel growth rates as the fish continue to feed throughout the year. Even in the relatively short period during which this book was being compiled,

. . . and still the club records fall: John Costello with a 12lb 14oz Teme barbel.

BCC members have broken no fewer than six BCC river records (the Wharfe, Ure, Teme, Dove, Thames and Holybrook). These six new river records are included in the appendices. In my own Yorkshire region of the BCC, two of our members have now caught barbel from Yorkshire rivers in every month of the fishing season, a feat that would have been considered impossible at the time our first book was published. At that time the majority of anglers considered winter barbel fishing in Yorkshire to be not worth the effort.

Rivers are generally becoming cleaner, and barbel are continuing to spread into new locations. Here in Yorkshire, rivers such as the Don, the Dearne and the Rother now hold considerable stocks of barbel. Fifteen years ago the Rother was thought to be incapable of supporting life, and its transformation has been little short of miraculous; while the once heavily polluted river Don is now producing barbel into double figures. The major potential cloud on the horizon in terms of the barbel's environment is the continued threat of increased water abstraction. No matter how clean and pollution free the water in our

rivers may become, there still has to be enough of it. Rivers such as the Hampshire Avon and the Wensum are prime examples of the results of large-scale abstraction. Anyone who fished either of these rivers in their heydays will know that they are now only a shadow of their former selves.

Will the barbel record be beaten in the near future? I believe it will. River records in general will continue to increase over the foreseeable future, and that elusive 20lb target could be achieved within the next five years.

When attempting to predict which river will produce the first 20lb-plus barbel, logic points inevitably towards the existing record holder, the Great Ouse. Sightings have been made of fish considered to be significantly larger than the current record of 19lb 6oz, and I believe that it is only a matter of time before such a fish is banked from the river. The stretch of the Great Ouse that produces these monsters continues to receive concerted attention from specialist anglers virtually throughout the whole coarse fishing season. The quantity of HNV offerings being constantly introduced into a

Geoff Dace 'ups' his Dove record to 13lb 3oz.

Mick Wood takes his Wharfe best to 12lb 10oz.

relatively short stretch of this small river, together with the high crayfish population, means that the barbel should continue to grow. How long this situation can continue is, however, the main question. As with many of our rivers, there is concern regarding natural fish recruitment levels in the Great Ouse. Several stockings of barbel have been carried out by the Environment Agency in recent years, using fish from their Calverton fish farm, and the river currently appears to have a thriving barbel population, possibly to the detriment of 'silver' fish species. However, without healthy natural recruitment levels, the future is less certain.

Although the Great Ouse has to be considered the favourite to produce another British record barbel, there are several other rivers with the potential to produce extremely large fish, and these have already been covered in earlier chapters. Personally I believe for several reasons that one of the real 'dark horses' could be the Trent. Most anglers are aware that the principal requirements for fish growth are regular and plentiful supplies of nutritious food items, the space in which to grow and unpolluted water. The Trent has always had the first two in abundance, and over recent years the river has benefited from a huge

improvement in water quality. The river is now producing a constant stream of double-figure fish, many of which are never reported. Specimens of up to 16lb plus have been recorded recently.

The Trent is by UK standards a very big river, being on average fifty metres wide and with a central depth averaging four or five metres; it is therefore much less affected by long periods of dry weather than is the case with most of our prime barbel rivers. Nor does it suffer seriously from abstraction. So, while river levels obviously fall during long dry periods, the river continues to flow at a reasonable rate and the barbel's environment remains virtually unaffected. The river also supports a high population of natural foods, particularly freshwater snails and shrimps. Furthermore, when assessing the Trent's credentials as a potential record producer, another factor must be taken into account: that not only is the Trent wide and deep, but it is also 150 miles (240km) long. Serious barbel fishing could be said to begin at the point where the River Dove joins the Trent above Burton-on-Trent, and to end at Dunham Bridge in the tidal reaches: a total distance of approximately 75 miles (120km), or half the length of the river. Many stretches capable of producing big barbel currently receive little or no attention from specialist barbel anglers, whilst winter barbel fishing on the river is almost non-existent at the time of writing. I expect the Trent to produce quite a few surprises over the next few years, as more and more capable barbel anglers begin to realize its virtually untapped potential.

In summary, the future for the barbel angler looks very rosy indeed, with a wider spread of the species, continued acceleration of growth rates, cleaner rivers and more people entering the sport. A real 'barbel boom': what more could we ask? Just as in any other sport however, those dedicated barbel anglers who want the best may have to dig a bit deeper into their pockets in the not-too-distant future.

Appendix I: BCC River Records

Name	River	Date	lb	oz
Paul Starkey	Blackwater	20 September 2002	7	6
Tony Hart	Bristol Avon	31 May 1995	13	6
Tony Miles	Cherwell	31 May 1989	12	5
Steve Chell	Churnet	02 July 1998	3	14
Andy Harman	Colne	31 May 1991	8	7
Andy Harman	Colnebrook	31 May 1991	8	1
Rob Stoker	Dane	27 February 1999	10	4
Dave Oakes	Dearne	25 July 2001	2	2
Steve Chell	Derby Derwent	31 May 1996	8	11
Steve Jaques	Don	27 October 1999	1	6
Huw James	Dorset Stour	20 October 2000	14	2
Geoff Dace	Dove		13	3
Jim Knight	Drapers Osier Bed Stream	27 August 2000	7	2
Andy Cowley	Frome	31 May 1995	10	15
Warren Day	Great Ouse	03 October 1999	16	14
Dave Williams	Hants Avon	31 May 1992	14	6
Dave Williams	Hants Avon	31 May 1992	14	6
Trevor King	Holy Brook		13	4
Phil Dunn	Ivel	12 January 2002	11	8
Peter Tesch	Kennet	29 September 1999	13	14
Ray Kent	Lea	31 May 1993	12	5
Keith Evans	Loddon	09 October 2001	11	8
Mike Burdon	Lugg	31 May 1994	10	12
Dave Taylor	Medway	31 May 1992	14	11
Paul Starkey	Mole	26 January 2003	13	5
Steve Jaques	Nidd	09 September 1997	7	14
Alan Towers	Ribble	22 July 2000	10	4
Ian Beadle	Roden	31 May 1990	1	15
Howard Maddocks	Severn	30 November 1997	16	3

Name	River	Date	lb	oz
Steve Chell	Soar	10 July 2002	6	8
Keith Evans	St Patricks Stream	27 October 2001	15	8
Steve Carden	Sussex Ouse	31 May 1992	9	6
John Medlow	Sussex Rother	08 March 2000	9	15
Dave Mason	Swale	31 May 1987	11	6
Martin Meechan	Tees		9	4
John Costello	Teme		12	14
Brian Crawford	Tern	31 May 1991	4	2
John Sheldon	Thame	21 August 2001	9	12
Steve Smith	Thames		12	3
Peter Tesch	Thames		12	3
Steve Withers	Trent	28 September 2002	14	11
Martin Meechan	Ure		10	15
Barry Norris	Vyrnwy	31 May 1996	6	1
Mick Wood	Warks Avon	27 October 2000	12	2
Nick Palmer	Warks Stour	31 May 1989	8	6
Andy Dennison	Wear	31 May 1996	9	1
Dave Plummer	Wensum	31 May 1983	13	6
Steve Carden	Wey	12 November 2002	14	2
Mick Wood	Wharfe		12	10
Mike Burdon	Windrush	31 May 1995	9	12
Howard Maddocks	Wye	31 May 1998	12	0
Jon Wolfe	Yorks Derwent	31 May 1989	12	6
John McNulty	Yorks Ouse	25 September 1998	10	10

Appendix II: BCC Top Fifty

Name	River	Date	lb	oz	Season
Warren Day	Great Ouse	03 Oct 99	16	14	1999–00
Howard Maddocks	Severn	30 Nov 97	16	3	1997–98
Keith Evans	St Patricks Stream	27 Oct 01	15	8	2001–02
John Costello	Severn	06 Oct 98	15	7	1998–99
Stan Sear	Great Ouse	15 Sep 01	15	1	2001–02
Stan Sear	Great Ouse	04 Nov 00	15	0	2000–01
Dave Taylor	Medway	31 May 92	14	11	1992–93
Steve Withers	Trent	28 Sep 02	14	11	2002–03
Steve Pope	Severn	31 May 93	14	8	1993–94
Dave Williams	Hants Avon	31 May 92	14	6	1992–93
Roy Bates	Great Ouse	28 Nov 00	14	6	2000–01
Dave Williams	Medway	31 May 92	14	6	1992–93
Dave Williams	Hants Avon	31 May 92	14	6	1992–93
Stephen Henry	Great Ouse	15 Sep 00	14	4	2000–01
Dave Williams	Hants Avon	31 May 91	14	4	1991–92
Huw James	Dorset Stour	20 Oct 00	14	2	2000–01
Steve Carden	Wey	12 Nov 02	14	2	2002–03
Greg Buxton	Dorset Stour	31 May 84	14	1	1984–85
Steve Withers	Hants Avon	14 Mar 03	14	1	2002–03
Chris Thomson	Hants Avon	01 Nov 03	14	1	2003–04
Chris Thomson	Hants Avon	09 Mar 03	14	1	2002–03
Chris Binge	Great Ouse	31 May 96	14	0	1996–97
Steve Withers	Dorset Stour	25 Oct 00	13	14	2000–01
Peter Tesch	Kennet	29 Sep 99	13	14	1999–00
Mike Nicholls	Severn	31 May 90	13	14	1990–01
Warren Day	Great Ouse	18 Jan 00	13	14	1999–00
Steve Withers	Hants Avon	28 Feb 03	13	13	2002–03
Steve Pope	Severn	31 May 92	13	13	1991–92
Martin Cullen	Severn	24 Aug 01	13	13	2001–02

Name	River	Date	lb	oz	Season
Lee Fletcher	Trent	20 Jun 00	13	12	2000–01
Mark Cleaver	Trent	01 Sep 03	13	11	2003–04
Warren Day	Great Ouse	05 Nov 99	13	11	1999–00
Chris Thomson	Hants Avon	01 Nov 02	13	10	2002–03
Chris Thomson	Hants Avon	22 Dec 02	13	10	2002–03
Bob Turner	Kennet	06 Jan 99	13	9	1998–99
Roy Bates	Great Ouse	14 Nov 02	13	9	2002–03
Chris King	Great Ouse	31 May 94	13	9	1993–94
Steve Carden	Wey	09 Mar 99	13	8	1998–99
Andy Orme	Hants Avon	31 May 89	13	7	1989–99
Ray Woods	Medway	31 May 96	13	7	1996–97
Colin Woods	Hants Avon	31 May 89	13	7	1998–99
Dave Plummer	Wensum	31 May 83	13	6	1982–83
Peter Tillotson	Kennet	22 Feb 01	13	6	2000–01
Kevin Hodges	Dorset Stour	31 May 85	13	6	1985–86
Steve Withers	Hants Avon	02 Nov 96	13	6	1996–97
Tony Hart	Bristol Avon	31 May 95	13	6	1995–96
Geoff Dace	Severn	06 Nov 99	13	6	1999–00
Paul Starkey	Mole	26 Jan 03	13	5	2002–03
Stan Sear	Great Ouse	31 May 95	13	5	1994–95
Chris Binge	Great Ouse	31 May 95	13	5	1994–95
Dave Williams	Medway	31 May 90	13	5	1989–90

Index